◆ INFANT DEVELOPMENT ◆

INFANT DEVELOPMENT
Ecological Perspectives

edited by
HIRAM E. FITZGERALD
KATHERINE HILDEBRANDT KARRAKER
& TOM LUSTER

RoutledgeFalmer
New York • London

Published in 2002 by
RoutledgeFalmer
29 West 35th Street
New York, NY 10001

RoutledgeFalmer is an imprint of the Taylor & Francis Group.

10 9 8 7 6 5 4 3 2 1

Library of Congress Cataloging-in-Publication Data
Infant development : ecological perspectives / edited by Hiram E. Fitzgerald, Katherine Karraker, Tom Luster
    p. cm.
Includes bibliographical references and index.
ISBN 0-8153-2839-7
    1. Infants—Development. 2. Infants—Development—Environmental aspects. I. Fitzgerald, Hiram E.   II. Karraker, Katherine H. III. Luster, Tom.

RJ131.I767 2001
305.232—dc21

2001034802

Printed on acid-free, 250-year-life paper.
Manufactured in the United States of America.

Contents

Preface

The 1990s were designated by the American Psychological Association as the decade of the brain and intense research during the decade brought to fruition remarkable discoveries related to synaptogenesis, neural network formation, neurotransmitter action, bioregulation, and linkages between brain structure and function. From our perspective, equally remarkable findings to emerge from the decade of the brain involve the extent to which development of the brain and nervous system was found to be bound to the environments in which development takes place. Indeed, the synergy from such intensive studies spilled over into the public domain and, seemingly for the very first time, the general public began to realize that caregiving and education really were connected to brain development.

In many respects, the twentieth century could bear the title of "the century of the baby." Never before in the history of the human species was there such a span of time in which so much attention was given to the first five years of human life. Early in the century, psychoanalytic theorists (Sigmund Freud, Erik Erikson), cognitive developmentalists (Jean Piaget), behaviorists (John Watson), and maturationists (Arnold Gesell) focused attention on the importance of the first three years of life for setting foundations for subsequent development. During the 1920s and 1930s, investigators began to establish major research laboratories to study the basic sensory, perceptual, motor, and learning abilities of infants and toddlers. Such investigations led to development of formal examinations that could be used to compare infants and toddlers against normative standards. A paradigmatic shift in Western psychology took place during the 1950s and 1960s, with the result that the tabula rasa infant became the competent infant.

Investigators, liberated from restrictive mechanistic models of behavior, enthusiastically embraced organismic theories and challenged infants as never before to reveal the secrets of their early postnatal development. The shift from mechanistic to organismic paradigms paved the way for the emergence of general systems theory, first formally presented in the 1930s by Ludwig von Bertalanffy in lectures at the University of Chicago, and its modern offshoots: Forrester's systems dynamics, Miller's living systems, Sameroff's systems theory, Ford and Lerner's developmental systems theory, and Bronfenbrenner's ecosystems. More similar than different, systems approaches focus attention on the issue of context. All development takes place in a context, regardless of whether that context is at the cellular level or at the level of community.

Context is the focus of the current volume. We invited a number of our colleagues to join us in a venture: rather than preparing traditional review chapters, we asked each writer to focus on the critical issues and questions that needed to be answered in the first decade of the twenty-first century. Within their topical area, what are the critical questions that need to be resolved in order to propel the field further? What contextual boundaries need to be defined that will assist the understanding of system differentiation and organization? What are the major factors that structure developmental pathways and that maintain or change the individual's travel along that pathway? What are the implications of such work for parents or policy makers? Each contributor provides strong responses to these questions, and although they vary in the extent to which they address each question, there is no variation from the basic premise that understanding infancy and early development requires an ecological framework, a focus on context, and on synergistic transactional linkages between the developing child and her or his environments.

We are deeply indebted to Linda Chapel Jackson for her extraordinary editorial skills, shaping widely divergent chapters into something that resembles an organized systemic whole. We also are indebted to Marguerite Barratt, director of the Institute for Children, Youth, and Families for her continued support of the Michigan State University book series. And we would be deeply insensitive if we failed to thank all of our colleagues, graduate students, and community partners, who continually provide us encouragement and support. Finally, a resounding hurrah and thanks to all of the research participants who are represented in these various chapters because, in the final analysis, it is only through the cooperative spirit and engagement of individuals, families, and agencies that we are able to fashion the scientific study of human development.

Hiram E. Fitzgerald
Katherine Hildebrandt Karraker
Tom Luster

February 2001

Pathways to Developmental Outcomes in Preterm Infants

Catherine S. Tamis-LeMonda
& Joanne Roberts

1

◆ ◆ ◆ ◆

Birthweight-specific mortality has decreased tremendously over the past several years due to the use of surfactant and improvements in obstetric and neonatal intensive care. Consequently, there has been an increase in the number of preterm births over this time. As an example, from 1985 to 1995 the rate of preterm births rose 12%, from 10.0% to 11.0% of all births (March of Dimes Birth Defects Foundation, 1997). This increase has led to a growing concern about the consequences of low birthweight and its associated medical complications for infants' developmental outcomes. Even moderately low birthweight infants are sometimes shown to be developmentally delayed and/or to suffer visual-motor impairments. Nonetheless, a great percentage of preterm infants evidence few if any developmental delays, and for many such infants initial delays virtually disappear over the course of the first few years of life. A complex web of biological, social, economic, and cultural factors explains the contrast between the seeming resilience of certain preterm infants and the vulnerability of others.

In the present chapter, a transactional, multifaceted approach is taken to understanding individual differences in the developmental trajectories of premature babies within their broader social contexts. This ecological approach is central to early diagnosis and prevention as well as to the implementation of effective interventions with infants who face the numerous obstacles associated with prematurity. figure 1 graphically depicts the model that will be discussed. A summary of the pathways in the model is in order. Low birthweight and associated medical complications in premature infants may directly influence developmental outcomes (Path 1) as well as indirectly influence outcomes through their effect on babies' regulation of information processing, social-communicative, attentional, and emotional resources (Paths 2 and 3). In turn, infants' perinatal status and associated regulatory difficulties may influence caregivers' psychological functioning, views about, expectations for, and interactions with their young babies (Paths 4, 5, 6 and 7). The quality of parent-infant interactions further affects infants' development of self-regulation (Path 8) and long-term outcomes (Path 9). In addition, the caregivers of preterm infants themselves experience a range of background/contextual factors (e.g., poverty; Path 10) that may be associated with infant perinatal status as well as further influence caregivers' psychological functioning (Path 11) and interactions with their young babies (Path 12).

The model presented in figure 1 not only captures the plight of many premature infants, but can also be applied more generally to the ecological conditions of infants deemed to be "at risk" for other reasons, as for example, babies who are born to poverty. Thus, the focus on prematurity is meant to provide an illustrative example of the embedded contexts in which babies develop, and to further an understanding of the ways endogenous and exogenous risk and protective factors interact and influence infants more generally.

The chapter is structured around the pathways of influence presented in figure 1. We begin by discussing the medical complications or risk factors that often surround preterm birth and may directly affect a baby's long-term prognosis. We then discuss the role of babies' regulatory abilities in buffering or exacerbating the outcomes of prematurity, and address the ways in which these regulatory capacities affect and are affected by caregivers' psychological functioning, views, and behaviors. Finally, we consider the infant-caregiver relationship within its larger context by discussing factors that ameliorate and/or exacerbate the challenges faced by preterm infants and their families, such as social support and socioeconomic status.

Perinatal Factors

Preterm infants are particularly vulnerable to low birthweight. Medical complications present at birth that may directly compromise their developmental outcomes (Path 1), as well as indirectly affecting their development through links to babies' regulatory abilities (Path 2) and parenting expectations (Path 4). Low birthweight infants are forty times more likely to die in the first month of life and twenty times more likely to die before the age of one (Rosenbaum, 1992). Despite these statistics, however, there has been a steady decline in birthweight-specific mortality over the past three decades, leading to a concomitant increase in investigations concerned with the long-term sequalae of prematurity, low birthweight and associated medical complications (Blackman, 1991; Landry, 1995).

Figure 1   FACTORS CONTRIBUTING TO DEVELOPMENTAL OUTCOMES IN PRETERM INFANTS

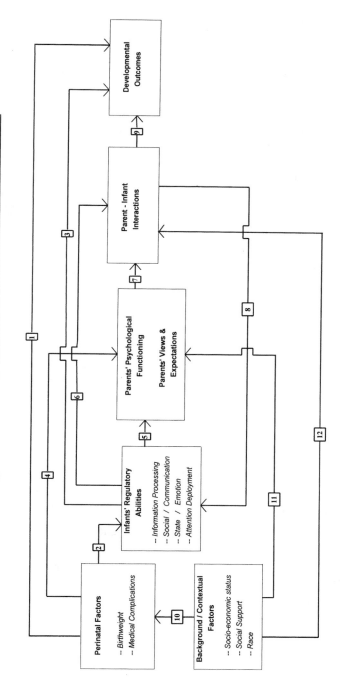

Birthweight

Low birthweight is conventionally defined as less than 2,500 grams and very low birthweight is defined as less than 1,500 grams. In the United States, the major determinant of low birthweight is premature delivery (Paneth, 1995). Research indicates that low birthweight infants' risk for developing cognitive, attentional, and neuromotor problems increases as birthweight decreases (Hack, Klein, & Taylor, 1995); and preterm infants who are symmetrically small for gestational age (i.e., with head circumferences, length, and weight below the tenth percentile) are at increased risk of developmental delay (Vohr, Garcia-Coll, & Oh, 1990).

The rate of neuorological abnormalities for children weighing less than 1,000 grams at birth is approximately 20% (Teplin, Burchinal, Johnson-Martin, Humphry, & Kraybill, 1991; Saigal, Szatmari, Rosenbaum, Campbell, & King, 1991). Children weighing between 1,000 and 1,500 grams at birth have a 14% to 17% rate of neurological conditions, and children with a birthweight between 1,500 and 2,499 grams have a 6% to 8% incident rate (McCormick, Brooks-Gunn, Workman-Daniels, Turner, & Peckman, 1992). Cerebral palsy is the most common neurological affliction in low birthweight children (Hack, et al., 1995). In the general population, the prevalence of cerebral palsy is 1.4 to 2.4 per 1,000 children (Pellegrino, 1997). Preterm infants who weigh less than 1,500 grams at birth are thirty times more likely to develop cerebral palsy than their full-term counterparts (March of Dimes, 1997; Pellegrino, 1997). Moreover, low birthweight children have been found to score significantly lower on intelligence tests in comparison to their normal birthweight peers, and cognitive deficits are particularly pronounced for infants weighing less than 1,000 grams at birth (Hack, et al., 1995).

Medical Complications

The long-term prognosis of preterm babies is largely affected by the medical correlates of low birthweight, including respiratory distress syndrome (RDS), intraventricular hemorrhage (IVH) and bronchopulmonary dysplasia (BPD).

RDS is the most common physiological disorder of prematurity and results in increased levels of carbon dioxide and lowered levels of oxygen in the blood; over 50% of premature infants will have RDS (Sammons & Lewis, 1985). RDS is the fourth-leading cause of infant mortality and a leading cause of death for premature infants (MacDorman & Atkinson, 1998). RDS is the inability of the baby to breathe without support and represents a continuum of breathing problems from short breathing difficulties to a bronchopulmonary dysplasia (BPD). Babies who have BPD are at increased risk for neurodevelopmental abnormalities (Meisels, Plunkett, Roloff, Pasick, & Stiefel, 1986), particularly when placed under assisted ventilation for longer durations (Davidson, Schrayer, Weilunsky, Kricker, Lilos, & Reisner, 1990).

Intraperiventricular hemorrhage (IVH) occurs in approximately 40% of very low birthweight babies (less than 1,500 g) (Sell, Gaines, Gluckman, & Williams, 1985). Hemorrhages are classified on a scale from I to IV, with type IV—intraventricular hemorrhage with parenchymal hemorrhage—considered the most severe (Blackman, 1991). However, the presence of IVH does not necessarily indicate poor developmental outcomes, and its absence does not guarantee normal development. Nonetheless, children who have IVH perform more poorly on later indices of cognitive, motor, and neuromotor functioning (e.g., Lowe & Papile, 1990; Waikato, 1993), and developmental deficits seem to increase with the severity of hemorrhage (Papile, Munsick-Bruno, & Schaefer, 1983; Shankaran, Slovis, Bedard, & Poland, 1982). Because IVH does not typically occur without some form of RDS, it is sometimes difficult to disentangle the independent and relative contribution of IVH or RDS to developmental delays.

Infants' Self-Regulatory Abilities

While medical complications may directly affect the cognitive outcomes of preterm infants, a number of behavioral sequelae to prematurity exist that may mediate the eventual outcomes of these infants, in certain cases buffering and in others exacerbating the potentially deleterious effects of prematurity on babies' long-term functioning. Infants' ability to regulate resources necessary for effective information processing, attention, social/communicative exchanges and states and emotions may be of primary importance for optimizing interactions with individuals and objects in their environment. Limitations to regulatory abilities may directly affect babies' developmental outcomes (Path 3) as well as indirectly affecting outcomes through an effect on caregivers' psychological functioning, views, expectations, and behaviors (Paths 5 and 6). In contrast, infants who demonstrate more effective control of their regulatory capacities may be better able to negotiate and navigate their environments, and thus are somewhat protected against the challenges associated with low birthweight status.

Variation in regulatory abilities often portends long-term cognitive and social adjustment across infants generally (Path 3). Consequently, researchers have increasingly focused on whether and how regulatory mechanisms might underlie stabilities in children's cognitive and social functioning from infancy through the school-aged years (Rose & Tamis-LeMonda, 1999). In addition, developmental theorists have often asked whether and how constitutional factors in infants, including regulatory capacities, might contribute to a child's susceptibility or vulnerability in high-risk conditions (Rutter, 1985; Werner, 1993).

Information Processing

Information processing refers to an infant's ability to effectively and expediently access and retain information from the environment, and is most commonly assessed through paradigms such as habituation and recognition memory. In habituation paradigms the infant is exposed to a repeated stimulus, most typically a static visual display of geometric figures or familiar objects (e.g., faces) to assess patterns of decline in attention such as total looking time. Traditionally, the infant's response decline is thought to reflect the formation of a mental schema by the infant; thus, the time it takes an infant to habituate is thought to index the speed of information encoding. In the recognition memory paradigm, infants are initially presented with either a single visual stimulus or with two identical stimuli for a fixed period. The familiar and a novel stimulus are next presented simultaneously and differential responding is assessed during a test phase. Provided familiarization is sufficient, infants generally spend a greater percentage of the test time looking at the novel stimulus. This "novelty" response is thought to index processes of encoding, memory, retrieval, and discrimination.

Independent investigators using different stimuli, procedures, and populations, have provided converging evidence that visual information processing measures in infancy explain moderate variance in representational abilities and IQ performance in early childhood (e.g., Rose, Feldman, Wallace, & Cohen, 1991; Rose, Feldman, Wallace, & McCarton, 1991; Tamis-LeMonda & Bornstein, 1989, 1993).

Empirically, Rose and colleagues have identified significant differences between the performance of preterm and term infants as well as between preterms who have or have not experienced respiratory distress syndrome on information processing paradigms such as habituation and recognition memory (Rose, Feldman, Wallace, & Cohen, 1991; Rose, Feldman, Wallace, & McCarton, 1991). In an early study by Rose (1980), babies were brought to the laboratory when they were six months of age and were tested for recognition of abstract patterns and faces. Initially, when familiarization times were quite brief (five to twenty seconds, depending on the problem), only full-terms exhibited significant novelty preferences. However, preterms' performance improved dramatically when familiarization times were increased, suggesting that they were not as quick to encode the stimuli as their full-term counterparts. These findings were reinforced and extended in a second study in which the slower processing speed of preterms was found to persist through the first year of life (Rose, 1983). In a more recent longitudinal study in which the sample of preterms was restricted to those of very low birthweight infants (i.e., less than 1,500 g at birth), preterms not only had lower novelty scores than full-terms, but also took longer to accrue the required amounts of looking at the familiarization stimulus and showed less active comparison of the stimuli (Rose, Feldman, McCarton, & Wolfson, 1988).

Similarly, Ross and colleagues (Ross, Auld, Tesman, & Nass, 1992) compared preterm infants with and without IVH to full-term infants on habituation and novelty preference tasks as well as on Bayley Mental Development Index scores at ten months. They found poorer performance by preterm infants on information processing tasks, but differences between full and preterm infants were evident only in the presence of IVH. Babies with IVH took more trials to habituate (and fewer of them habituated at all) than the other two groups. Together, these findings suggest that a limitation to early information processing abilities may in part explain why some preterm infants continue to exhibit delays in cognitive functioning over time.

Social-Communication

Like information processing abilities, the ability to regulate social exchanges with primary caregivers is important for all infants, as social interactions provide meaningful information about the world, foster attachment security, encourage the further involvement of caregivers, and support the development of problem solving skills and language (Baumwell, Tamis-LeMonda, & Bornstein, 1997). For infants facing socioeconomic or biological adversities, social regulatory capacities (e.g., successful achievement of joint attention with caregivers) may be an important "buffer" against such risks (Raver, 1996).

Numerous investigators have found that preterm infants have special difficulty in regulating their engagements with others, as indicated by increased gaze aversion, decreased joint play, and low levels of joint attention (see Landry, 1995, for a review). For example, Garner, Landry and Richardson (1991) examined the development of joint attention skills in both high- and low-risk low birthweight infants in comparison to fullterm infants. High-risk infants were characterized by IVH grade III or IV or progressive dilation or bronchopulmonary dysphasia in the neonatal period. High-risk infants showed more passive levels of looking and functional play. Both preterm groups displayed difficulty in directing maternal attention and coordinating eye gaze behavior, suggesting that low birthweight is also associated with difficulties in maintaining joint attention with social partners.

Others have found preterm infants to be less alert and less responsive than full-term infants (e.g., Field, 1980). Crnic and colleagues (Crnic, Ragozin, Greenberg, Robinson, & Basham, 1983) showed that, during interactions with their mothers, preterm infants vocalized and smiled less, averted their gaze and bodies more often, displayed unclear cues, and were less responsive than were full-term infants. The low levels of responsiveness exhibited by the preterm infant appeared to subsequently elicit increased activity from the mother, which resulted in heightened gaze aversion from the infant, prompting further maternal activity. This cyclical pattern was found to exist over the infants' first twelve months and was less gratifying for both the mother and the child as indicated by the lowered quality and tone of the dyadic interaction. Unfortunately, in many instances preterm babies' difficulties in regulating social interaction endure throughout infancy and childhood when early medical problems, such as severe IVH, are present (Garner, et al., 1991).

States and Emotions

An important component to early social interactions is the infant's ability to regulate states and emotions. Preterm infants are often at risk for poor state organization and difficult temperaments, and difficulty in temperament has been associated with decreased parental involvement and increased parental hostility and criticism (Wachs, 1999).

For example, preterm infants have been shown to demonstrate high irritability and state liability, which in turn predicts lowered exploratory play at eight months (DiPietro & Porges, 1991). In a study by Als and colleagues (Als, Duffy, & McAnulty, 1988), preterm and term infants were clustered into three groups of decreasing regulatory abilities using the APIB (Assessment of Preterm Infants' Behavior; Als, Lester, Tronick, & Brazelton, 1982). Preterm infants were largely represented in the third (least organized) group, showing low levels of alertness and animation, high levels of stimulus overload, low thresholds for tactile and sensory input, and low levels of emotional self-regulation. These limitations may help explain the more frequent gaze aversion of preterm infants as well as their inability to sustain joint attention for extended periods with their caregivers.

Attention Deployment

Finally, an infant's ability to regulate attention and effectively direct efforts toward ongoing tasks or goals is central to learning and cognitive development (Power, Chapieski, & McGrath, 1985; Tamis-LeMonda & Bornstein, 1991, 1993). In some instances, preterm infants may have difficulties regulating their attention to objects and events in their surroundings. For example, preterm infants have been shown to have difficulties sustaining visual attention (Cohen & Parmelee, 1983; Kopp & Vaughn, 1982), show less focused and active attention when examining objects (Landry & Chapieski, 1988; Ruff, McCarton, Kurtzberg, & Vaughan, 1984), take longer to organize their exploratory initiatives (Ruff, 1988), and take longer to inhibit responses to visual stimuli in order to attend to other stimuli (Landry, Leslie, Fletcher, & Francis, 1985). As noted by Landry (1995), these findings suggest that preterm infants find it particularly difficult to shift attention between objects and from one object to another, making the task of exploration and learning particularly challenging for some of these babies.

Summary

To summarize thus far, premature birth status and its accompanying medical complications is sometimes associated with neurodevelopmental delays and lowered performance on standardized intelligence measures over short and long periods. These delays are observed in the context of medical complications associated with prematurity, such as IVH and RDS. In addition, certain preterm infants have been found to experience difficulties in information processing and in regulating their social-communicative exchanges, states and emotions, and attention to objects and events in their environments—difficulties which may in part explain the long-term delays evidenced in some of these infants.

PARENT–INFANT INTERACTIONS

In addition to babies' medical histories and regulatory abilities, a confluence of social-environmental factors affects developmental processes in preterm infants. Empirically, measures obtained from the social contexts in which preterm infants are reared, especially the quality of babies' relationships with their primary caregiver(s), are often better predictors of the outcomes of preterm infants than are perinatal factors. For example, Leonard and colleagues (1990) found that although increased grades of intracranial hemorrhage in preterm infants were associated with increased cognitive abnormalities, the factors associated with the highest incidence of later abnormality were parenting risk factors. Similarly, Cohen and colleagues (Cohen, Parmelee, Beckwith, & Sigman, 1986) found that social factors played a major role in determining the outcomes of preterm infants at eight years, over and above neonatal complications. Others have also demonstrated the critical role of preterm infants' social environment in determining the long-term outcomes of prematurity (Bradley, Whiteside, Mundfrom, Casey, Kelleher, & Pope, 1994; Liaw & Brooks-Gunn,1993).

These findings are both promising as well as daunting. The promising news is that perinatal risks associated with prematurity might be minimized in the context of a nurturant and supportive environment. That is, many preterm infants, including those who have sustained various medical complications, demonstrate normal developmental trajectories, often due to positive relationships with their primary caregivers. As such, secure relationships with primary caregivers may serve as important protective factors against the risks of prematurity. The bleak news is that preterm infants, who already face biological challenges, are especially susceptible to delays when exposed to insensitive social partners and to risks that indirectly affect babies through their effects on the interactions of their primary caregivers.

For all infants, caregiver sensitivity—including emotional attunement and responsiveness to the abilities and needs of the infant—enhance and support a baby's sense of security, self efficacy, language development, behavioral independence, and social and cognitive competencies (Bornstein & Tamis-LeMonda, in press). Specific to premature infants, numerous studies have indicated that the sensitivity of the mother is critical to a baby's long term outcomes. For example, Bradley and colleagues (1994) investigated the relationship between resiliency in low birthweight children born to poverty and caregiver sensitivity. They found that, of 243 participants, only 12% of the children were classified as resilient at the age of three, even when children with perinatal medical problems and chronic medical conditions were excluded from study. Those low birthweight children who did appear to be resilient were those who had more responsive, accepting, stimulating, and organized caregivers and who tended to live in safer and less crowded surroundings. Children who experienced less than three protective caregiving factors showed no signs of resiliency.

Similarly, Liaw and Brooks-Gunn (1993) assessed cognitive outcomes at three years of age in a group of 762 low birthweight, premature children. They found that children's social experiences, as measured by subscales of the HOME (Parental Responsivity, Parental Acceptance, Organization of Environment, Play Materials, Parental Involvement, and Variety of Stimulation) were significantly associated with children's cognitive development and continued to explain variance independent of biological complications and family variables.

In another set of studies, Landry (1995) assessed relations between the sensitivity of mothers' attention-directing behaviors and toy exploration in six-month-old premature infants. They found that appropriately timed attention-directing behaviors in mothers enhanced the toy exploration of their high-risk infants. Mothers who allowed infants to maintain their focus of attention rather than shifting them to a different toy facilitated joint attention by placing fewer demands on these infants' limited attention abilities. The authors noted that this strategy might serve to support babies' developing autonomy and exploratory mastery, thereby compensating to some degree for the otherwise negative effects of biological risk.

Unfortunately however, the sensitivity of mothers of preterm infants is often compromised. Research in the 1970s and 1980s showed that by four months of age mothers of premature infants tend to overstimulate their babies in an apparent effort to elicit responses from their less active infants (Barnard, Bee, & Hammond, 1984; Beckwith & Cohen, 1980; Field, 1979). This overstimulation in turn leads to even more gaze aversion and inattention in these babies. Others have also found that mothers of preterm infants are less sensitive than mothers of term infants, and in turn their infants are less responsive (Zarling, Hirsch & Landry, 1988). Moreover, differences in maternal sensitivity persist even after controlling for differences in infant responsiveness. Thus, there exists a circular interaction pattern in which caregiver insensitivity may cause lowered responsiveness in infants, leading to greater maternal efforts to urge infant response, feeding back into the infant's continued gaze aversion, again provoking inappropriate and heightened maternal activity, and so forth.

PARENTS' PSYCHOLOGICAL FUNCTIONING AND VIEWS

One of the pathways through which prematurity may affect an infant's developmental outcomes is through its influence on the mediating measures of the caregiver's psychological functioning and/or expectations and views (Paths 4, 5, and 6), which may in turn influence parent-infant interactions (Path 7). To the extent that a caregiver is depressed or emotionally affected by his or her own circumstances or those of his or her infant, parenting competence may be compromised. Empirical research indicates that depressed and/or anxious mothers exhibit lowered positive affect, less hugs and praise, less structure and guidance, lowered activity and contingent responsiveness, slower responsiveness, less nurturance, more frequent disengagement and intrusiveness, greater withdrawal, more looking away, problems tracking the baby's activity, and less talking and motherese (e.g., Gelfand & Teti, 1990; McLoyd & Wilson, 1991). Consequently, it is unsurprising that maternal depression adversely affects a range of child outcomes.

In situations in which infant risk (such as prematurity) is coupled with contextual risk (such as poverty), mothers' psychological functioning might be particularly threatened. The rate of depression for mothers who have just given birth is 12% and the rate of depression for women in poverty is approximately 20% (Field, Healy, Goldstein & Guthertz, 1990), a perplexing figure given the high prevalence of preterm infants born to poverty. Empirically, mothers of preterm infants tend to show anxiety and a lack of confidence in their caregiving abilities through the course of their babies' first year of life (e.g., Crnic, et al., 1983); it is likely that these insecurities will further affect their interactions with their infants.

Nonetheless, there are many caregivers who demonstrate psychological strength in the face of risk, and this psychological resiliency may attenuate risks associated with prematurity by enabling them to sensitively interact with their young children. Research on positive dimensions of parents' psychological functioning, although limited, suggests that a mother's sense of self efficacy and competence does help buffer the stressors associated with rearing a child with special needs, including a preterm infant (Teti, O'Connell, & Reiner, 1996).

In addition to affecting caregivers' psychological functioning, prematurity may also affect caregivers' views and/or expectations about their infants' capabilities, thereby influencing the quality of the parent-infant relationship. Recent studies have demonstrated clear links between maternal views and expectations and parenting, and have suggested that internalized schema operate as guides to parenting.

In the case of prematurity, it has been suggested that parents form biased expectations about their infants based on a set of beliefs they hold about preterm infants in general. These beliefs have been labeled a "prematurity stereotype" and serve as a self-fulfilling prophecy as parents behave toward babies in line with their expectations. Over time, biased expectations, behaviors, and interpretations lead adults to elicit the expected behavior from their infants, thereby confirming their original expectations (Stern & Karraker, 1988, 1989). For example, Frodi and colleagues (Frodi, Lamb, Leavitt, & Donavan, 1978) monitored parents' physiological and mood responses to videotapes of infants who were described as normal, difficult, or premature. Parental arousal was highest and sympathy was lowest when viewing a crying infant who was labeled as premature. Similarly, parents of full-term babies and parents of preterm infants rate babies who are labeled as premature as less developed, less cognitively competent, less behaviorally active, more difficult to care for, less enjoyable, less social, less healthy, and less liked than babies labeled as full-term (Miller & Ottinger, 1986; Stern & Karraker, 1988).

Additionally, parenting might suffer due to the high levels of concern, altered goals, and lowered expectations of parents of preterm infants. Parental concern about child behavior is a strong predictor of children's global developmental delay (Glascoe, 1994), and parents of preterms discuss the violation of their parenting expectations more often than parents of term infants (Boukydis, Lester, & Hoffman, 1987). To the extent that parents possess a hierarchy of goals, goals that are threatened become the overriding concern and area of maximal parental effort (Levine, Miller, & West, 1988). As such, parental concerns about the plight of premature infants might alter the quality of interactions that are directed to these infants. In some instances, those concerns may lead to enhanced interactions with infants; in other instances, concern about infant status might adversely affect the parent-infant relationship.

BROADER CONTEXTUAL FACTORS

Broader contextual factors may act as risk or protective factors that increase or decrease the infant's reactions to his/her perinatal circumstances, largely through their effect on the parent-infant relationship. Risk factors are stressors that heighten an individual's vulnerabilities to adverse circumstances; protective factors have been defined as influences that change, diminish or alter the individual's response to risk (Rutter, 1990). Risk and protective factors are thought to interact in specific ways with various vulnerabilities, such as preterm birth, and thus may not always influence individuals in the absence of adversity (Rutter, 1985; Werner, 1993). In this final section, we discuss two factors that may be conceptualized as risk and/or protective factors (depending on their magnitude and direction) in the context of parent-infant interactions: the caregiver's social support network (or lack thereof) and sociodemographic status. Support and/or sociodemographic status may moderate relations between premature birth status and developmental outcomes, again through an influence on the caregiver's psychological functioning and the quality of the parent-infant relationship (Paths 11 and 12). Finally, we discuss findings on the relation between race and the prevalence of preterm births, which is likely explained by the strong associations between race and socioeconomic status.

Support Networks

Social support may be particularly important to caregivers experiencing the challenges associated with caring for a premature infant. Supportive social networks have been found to buffer the deleterious effects of a variety of risk factors and may be especially important in families in which the extended family plays a role in everyday caregiving. Empirically, positive dimensions of social support relate positively to mothers' involvement and/or responsiveness (e.g. Crnic, Greenberg, Robinson, & Ragozin, 1984; Pascoe, Loda, Jeffries, & Earp, 1982), affect toward child, general life satisfaction, and satisfaction with parenting (Crnic, et al., 1983) and relate inversely to mothers' restrictiveness and punitiveness (Hashima & Amato, 1994; Jennings, Stagg & Connors, 1991).

Using data from the National Survey of Families and Households, Hashima and Amato (1994) examined the relationship between social support and punitive parental behavior. Annalyzing data from 1,035 ethnically diverse households, the authors reported that parents of low socioeconomic status who lacked support during times of crisis were more likely to report yelling at or hitting their children. The greater the number of people that poor families identified as supportive, the less likely they were to report problematic parenting practices.

Studies contrasting families with preterm and full-term infants suggest that a complex relation exists between infant birth status and social support. Although parents of full-term and preterm infants receive similar levels of instrumental and emotional support from relatives, parents of preterm infants are found to make more visits to health care professionals and to utilize more services (Boukydis et al., 1987). Moreover, parents of preterm infants place more importance on medical professionals as a source of support and report contacting parents with similar children more than parents of full-term infants. As such, they are able to share the problems associated with their preterm infant with others. In turn, parents of premature infants who have access to other parents with premature infants make fewer visits to health care professionals; and parents of preterm infants who report less instrumental and emotional help from relatives perceive their children as more temperamentally difficult (Boukydis et al., 1987). Others have found that parents' participation in a support peer group increased the amount of time mothers of premature infants spent visiting and playing with their infants while in the hospital and also enhanced their ability to care for their preterm infants (Minde, Shosenberg, Marton, Thompson, Ripley & Burns, 1980). In a three-month follow-up, mothers who participated in the support group continued to display a pattern of increased involvement and confidence.

Fathers are also a central, and perhaps primary, source of support to mothers. Empirically, spousal support has been found to moderate the effect of economic strain on parenting by reducing levels of maternal depression (Lyons-Ruth, Zoll, Connell, & Grunebaum, 1986) as well as the impact of depression on maternal parenting style (Simons, Lorenz, Wu & Conger, 1993). The importance of fathers as a source of support extends to preterm infants as well. In families with preterm infants, father involvement has been found to predict mothers' overall adjustment. Highly involved fathers of preterm infants have been found to be largely responsible for household chores—perhaps freeing mothers to handle the sometimes unpredictable caregiving needs of preterm infants (Boukydis et al., 1987).

Nonetheless, the relations between different forms of social support and parenting are not always straightforward, particularly in parenting a preterm infant. For example, in one study, relations between mother-child interactions and social support networks differed in groups of preterm and full-term infants (Zarling, et al., 1988). Specifically, highly enmeshed social support systems were associated with less maternal sensitivity in mothers of preterm infants but with greater sensitivity in mothers of full-term infants. The authors suggest that boundary density (i.e., highly enmeshed support networks) may actually increase maternal stress for mothers of very low birthweight children by reinforcing concern and confusion about how to parent a preterm infant, thereby adding to the anxiety of mothers.

Similarly, Miller-Loncar, Erwin, Landry, Smith and Swank (1998) found no significant differences in their study of the relationship between infant medical risk and maternal reports of social support in preterm and full-term groups, perhaps due to the low levels of medical complications of the preterm infants in their study. Instead, ethnicity predicted the structure of support networks and SES significantly related to maternal satisfaction with social support networks. Across all ethnic groups, mothers from high socio-economic backgrounds reported greater satisfaction with family and friends than low-income mothers. Thus, social support may act as either a risk or protective factor for parents of preterm infants, depending on a range of factors, including the source of support, the extent of support, and the income status of parents.

Socio-Economic Status

As for all babies, the developmental outcomes of preterm infants are largely influenced by the socio-economic conditions into which they are born. In particular, low birthweight and its associated medical complications especially threaten the healthy functioning of infants who must likewise confront the adverse conditions of poverty.

Poverty and the Prevalence of Premature Births

Empirically, socio-economic status (SES) is one of the principal risk factors associated with low birthweight. Low birthweight is most prevalent in low-income families and is particularly high for African Americans (Institute of Medicine, 1985). Data from the National Longitudinal Survey of Youth indicates that the risk of having a low birthweight infant is 14.1% for white mothers who live in poverty both prior and during pregnancy, a rate that is 3.3 times that of women who do not experience poverty at either time (Starfield, Shapiro, Weiss, Liang, Paige, & Wang, 1991). An income shift for white women from poor to nonpoor status reduces the risk of low birthweight delivery by 8.2%. Conversely, a status change from nonpoor to poor increases the risk from 4.4% to 8.9%. African American women who are poor both prior to and during pregnancy are 1.3 times more likely to have a low birthweight child (Starfield et al., 1991). In one study, women experiencing financial problems in a high-risk county in California were 5.9 times more likely to have a low birthweight infant (Binsacca, Ellis, Martin, & Petitti, 1987). In another investigation, the risk of a white teenage mother giving birth to a low birthweight infant was 2.8 times higher if she resided in an area in which the median income was less than $11,000 versus an area with a median income over $33,000 (Gould & LeRoy, 1988).

In addition to direct measures of SES, other demographic indicators are also associated with preterm birth. In a study conducted with 8,903 women who gave birth over a three-year period at Boston Hospital for Women, the impact of four economic risk factors on the premature birth rate was investigated: maternal age under twenty, single maternal marital status, maternal educational achievement under twelve years, and dependency on welfare. The presence of one risk factor increased the chance of having a preterm infant from 4.6% (no risks present) to 7.0% (one risk). When two or more risk factors were present, the preterm birth rate increased to 11.2% (Lieberman, Ryan, Monson, & Schoenbaum, 1987). Others have shown that Caucasian women with under twelve years of formal education are 54% more likely to give birth to low birthweight babies (less than 1,500 grams) and twice as likely to have babies of moderately low birthweight (between 1,500g and 2,500g) than college educated women (Kleinman & Kessel, 1987).

Clearly, however, the relation between poverty and low birthweight is complex. As Illesley and Mitchell argue, socio-economic status is a social construct which in itself does not cause low birthweight but rather operates on the developing fetus indirectly through a number of mediating mechanisms:

Social class (like 'environment') thus emerges as an indicator of other and more direct influences whose significance varies with the context in which it is employed. In relation to birthweight its significance lies in its ability, in one measurement, to encapsulate all those past experiences in the life of a mother which have affected her biological functioning as a reproductive agent. If no relationship exists in a given society between social class and birthweight it either means that, in that society, women of different social classes do not have differential exposure to health related influences...or, more probably, that the measure of social class employed does not efficiently encapsulate a woman's relevant past experiences. (Illesley & Mitchell, 1984, pp. 9–10)

This indirect affect of SES on low birthweight is demonstrated in Kramer's (1987) meta-analysis of 895 studies in which 43 potential predictors of gestational duration were evaluated. Results indicated that maternal age and socioeconomic status lead to changes in one or more direct determinants of gestational age, including prepregnancy weight, prior premature birth, prior spontaneous abortion, in utero diethylstilbestrol exposure, and smoking. In addition to these factors, socio-economic status limits a mother's access to medical care and proper nutrition; increases her stress; compromises the mother-child relationship; and leads to maladaptive behaviors such as smoking, teenage pregnancy, and drug use (Gould & LeRoy, 1988; Halpern, 1993). Similar paths of indirect influence are evidenced with respect to maternal education: 51% mothers with less than twelve years of education report not receiving prenatal care throughout their first trimester of their pregnancy, compared to 21% of mothers with more than twelve years of education (Chandra, 1995).

Consequences of Poverty for Preterm Infants

Numerous investigators have noted the negative consequences of poverty for families and for infants in general. Poor families routinely experience a lack of heat, plumbing problems, peeling paint, insect and rodent infestation, and overcrowding—living conditions that profoundly impact residents' self-esteem, dignity, and sense of hope (McLoyd & Wilson, 1991). Children from low-income families have higher rates of health problems such as asthma, ear infections, pneumonia, bone fractures, and lead poisonings. They also demonstrate significant delays in their intellectual and academic achievements, are more likely to exhibit behavioral problems and learning disabilities, and show higher levels of school dropout (Peters & Mullis, 1997; Smith, Brooks-Gunn, & Klebanov, 1997).

Preterm infants who face the social risk of poverty are in a condition of double hazard given the fragility of their situation (Escalona, 1982). Consequently, premature infants living in poverty have a very low prognosis of obtaining normal outcomes in all developmental domains (Bradley, et al., 1994; Bradley & Whiteside-Mansell, 1997). Thus, in addition to gestational age and birthweight, socio-economic status has been shown to be a strong predictor of language and intellectual development in preterm infants (Largo, Pfister, Molinari, Kundu, Uipp & Due, 1989). Similarly, low levels of parental education appear to exacerbate the effects of prematurity on intellectual outcome. In a study of 108 low birthweight children, Hunt and colleagues identified a powerful interaction between parent education and neonatal illness in relation to children's neurological functioning at eight years of age (Hunt, Cooper, & Tooley, 1988). Specifically, when high neonatal illness and low parental education were both present, 54.5% of children manifested moderate to severe outcomes and only 18.2% showed an absence of neurological difficulties. When parents were well-educated only 10% of children showed compromised outcomes, regardless of level of neonatal illness. Aylward, Verhurlst, and Bell (1988) examined relations between a composite index of SES and children's performance on the McCarthy Scales at 36 months. The SES-Composite Index was found to strongly predict all five scales of the McCarthy.

Race

An approximately 2:1 ratio in low birthweight infants between African-American and Non-African-American ethnic groups has persisted over the past twenty years (Institute of Medicine, 1985). In 1997, 6.5% of low birthweight infants were born to white mothers, in comparison to 13.0% born to African-American mothers (Ventura, Martin, Curtin, & Mathews, 1999).

The reasons for this gap are unclear but factors such as maternal age, socioeconomic status, and genetics have been proposed. Teenage mothers are at risk for premature birth and African-American mothers have higher rates of teenage births than other ethnic groups. In 1997, approximately 22.2% of all births to African-American mothers were to women nineteen years old and younger in comparison to 11.2% of all births to white mothers (Ventura, Martin, Curtin, & Mathews, 1999). In addition, significantly more African-American mothers live in poverty than white mothers, and poverty among African-American families appears to be more enduring, with almost 90% of all long-term poor children in 1992 being African American (Corcoran & Chaudry, 1997). Interestingly, research has indicated that African-American infants weighing less than 2,500 grams have a better chance of survival than white infants of the same birthweight, further clouding issues surrounding preterm birthweight and race (North & McDonald, 1977).

Clearly, the relationship between race and low birthweight is a complex one. The long-term effects of persistent poverty and social neglect, in combination with genetic and biological factors, have likely all contributed to the racial differences found in the rates of premature and low birthweight babies.

SUMMARY

Development is both a systematic and dynamic process in which factors in both the developing individual and his or her social context function as a complex system, rather than independently, to influence developmental adaptation and change (Bradley & Whiteside-Mansell, 1997). In the present chapter, we examined pathways to developmental outcomes in preterm infants in order to illustrate the complexities of infant development in its many embedded contexts. As indicated in figure 1, various configurations of risk and/or protective factors at the level of the individual, dyad, and broader social context, act in concert to determine the developmental outcomes of preterm infants, as they do for infants more generally.

With respect to factors in the infant, prematurity might adversely affect developmental outcomes when the medical risks of RDS and/or IVH are present, and when an infant demonstrates difficulties in his or her information processing, social-communicative exchanges, state and emotion regulation, and/or attention deployment. In contrast, infants who are able to effectively regulate their intake of information, attention, states, and emotions will be in a better position to engage in optimal interactions with persons and objects in their surroundings, thereby supporting adaptive learning and development. Nonetheless, although variation in infants' regulatory abilities may be partly explained by premature birth status, these abilities undergo rapid and systematic change over the course of the first few years as babies continually construct, shape, and react to their social experiences.

To the extent that development is a bidirectional process, babies' approaches and responses to the world unfold in and are influenced by the context of their primary attachment relationship(s). For some dyads, a cyclical, perpetuating, and unhealthy pattern of non-reciprocal interactions may develop early on, thereby compromising the positive development of the infant. An infant who is initially unresponsive and unable to sustain attention toward objects, activities and social partners might engender lowered feelings of efficacy in parents and make it difficult for a parent to engage in responsive interactions, and vice versa. Over the course of development, the dyad's natural course of reciprocity and intersubjectivity may be seriously impaired if one or both partners is unable to attune to the cues and needs of the other (e.g., Brinker, Baxter, & Butler, 1994).

For other dyads, mutually beneficial interactions will develop and thrive even in the face of infant perinatal risk and limitations. In particular, caregivers who continue to be sensitive to their infant's needs and capabilities, for example by maintaining, rather than redirecting, their infants' attention, will support healthy developmental gains in their babies. Parental sensitivity, therefore, is both an outcome of and contributor to infant development. In the specific case of prematurity, parenting sensitivity has been found to protect or buffer infants from the consequences of their medical conditions, regulatory limitations, and other risks associated with prematurity.

Because the infant-parent relationship exists within its broader context, the long-term prognosis of prematurity will also be affected by risk and protective factors outside the dyad, such as social support and socioeconomic status. Parents may more readily face the challenges of rearing a preterm infant when support is strong, but not overly enmeshed, and when they are not also confronted by the adversities of poverty. Unfortunately, however, low birthweight is often the outcome of poverty, and the stressors associated with poverty often augment those already experienced by the parents of preterm infants, thereby making the task of parenting a new and vulnerable infant an ongoing challenge. According to Wahler and Dumas (1989), the environmental stressors of poverty, coupled with the demands of child care, are likely to impede a caregiver's attention to her child's cues. Consequently, the caregiver will neither surveille the behaviors of her child nor her own responses to those behaviors, leading to interactions that are more intrusive than responsive. Such a situation can pose a particular threat to infants who already demonstrate limited information processing and regulatory capabilities. It is thus unsurprising that preterm infants who live in poverty are especially vulnerable to developmental delay given the multi-faceted and complex array of risks that they face. For these reasons, support to such families may be essential in assuring that the basic needs of the family are met and that the additive experience of stress does not compromise the caregiver's ability to cope (Bromwich, 1997).

CONCLUSIONS AND FUTURE DIRECTIONS

The research presented in this chapter illustrates the complex challenge of modeling the processes that affect the developmental trajectories of preterm infants, as well as infants more generally. An ecological approach to infant development such as that proposed here underscores the numerous co-dependencies that exist among health status, context, psychological functioning, parenting, and child outcomes. Moreover, this essay points to the synergistic relation between research and application—the design of successful preventive interventions with infants, families, and communities facing risk is largely informed by research on the confluence of factors that affect infants' growth. Four research directions are critical to advancing knowledge and practice in this area in the future: (1) program evaluation research, (2) longitudinal studies on the long term outcomes of prematurity on children and families, (3) studies on the larger context of prematurity, and (4) consideration of ethical dilemmas posed by the survival of extremely low birthweight infants.

First, research into the effective components of prenatal services is greatly needed. The strong association that exists between socio-demographic risk, such as poverty, and biological risk in infants (here prematurity) highlights the urgency of directing efficacious primary prevention services toward low-income, pregnant mothers. Indeed, there exists evidence that consistent and early prenatal care reduces the risk of low birthweight. However, the relative effectiveness of different facets of prenatal care is not understood; consequently, the development of practical and preventive prenatal programs has lagged behind knowledge about the causes of premature birth (Shiono & Behrman, 1995). As a first step toward evaluation research, descriptive data on the current state of prenatal care in the United States (as well as in other countries) is needed. For example, the extent to which national guidelines and standards for prenatal care (laid out by the American College of Obstetricians and Gynecologists and the American Academy of Pediatrics) are followed is relatively unknown (Institute of Medicine, 1985). Differences in the implementation and definition of prenatal services may partly account for variation that exists in premature birthrates across expectant mother programs. In the context of national descriptive data, researchers will be in a better position to evaluate the efficacy and safety of various components of prenatal services (e.g., risk assessments, education classes, drug therapies), as well as whether and how combinations of services affect the incidence and outcomes of premature birth. Moreover, program evaluations must also consider whether and how prenatal programs accommodate specific populations of women, depending on their specific needs. In short, program evaluations should aim to isolate effective components of prenatal services, the conditions under which those components work, and how such programs might form successful alliances with other agencies in the community.

Second, longitudinal research investigations (and/or studies based on secondary analyses of large-scale, multi-site national data sets) are needed to address the long-term impact of premature birth on children and families. In a meta-analysis of eighty studies on preterm infants, Aylward, Pfeiffer, Wright and Verhulst (1989) noted that nearly 70% reported follow-ups of five years or less. Given the advancements of medical technologies, more subtle impairments associated with low birthweight, such as learning disabilities, might go undetected in the absence of carefully designed, long-term follow up.

Third and relatedly, longitudinal investigations must include assessments of parents, parental expectations, parent-infant interactions, the home environment, and larger contextual factors that play a role in the long-term prognosis of preterm infants. Insofar as infant development is a context-dependent, transactional process, the pathways of individual infants cannot and should not be separated from the families and circumstances in which they develop. The outcomes of such infants will depend on the relative balance of risks and protective factors they encounter. Certain situations, such as sensitive parenting, serve a protective function by buffering the deleterious effects of prematurity on development, whereas others, such as poverty, increase the risk of adverse outcomes for premature infants. Research must take a more ecological approach to the study of premature infants in order to understand infant development from multiple perspectives and consequently to demonstrate heightened relevance for interventions with families and children.

Finally, the increase in survival rates of premature children raises a number of ethical issues with respect to the administration of intensive treatment to infants born with severe malformations, illness, and extreme immaturity (Shiono & Behrman, 1995; Tyson, 1995). The survival of these very low birthweight children is a relatively new phenomenon, and research on the potential benefits versus costs to children and families has not kept up with medical advances. In 1960, over 90% of infants that weighed less than 1,000g did not survive. Today, the survival rate for infants weighing between 750g and 1,000g is over 70% (Blackman, 1991). Scholarly and moral reflections on how and why different communities make the choices they do with respect to the care of very-low birthweight infants is urgent. In some neonatal centers intensive care is provided to all immature infants, regardless of their health status. Other centers are more selective in their care, basing treatment decisions largely on birthweight or gestational age (Tyson, 1995). The Child Abuse and Treatment Act of 1984 declared the failure to medically treat children a form of child abuse and neglect, except in cases where treatment is futile or inhumane. However, the law is vague as to the administration of intensive care to extremely premature children. Although intensive care treatment may be lifesaving, in some cases it may only serve to prolong the pain and suffering of both infants and families (Shiono & Behrman, 1995). The effectiveness of technologies and medicines for this population of premature children must be considered with respect to short- and long-term effectiveness. As a result, doctors and parents will be able to make more informed decisions regarding the treatment of children who may have limited chances of survival and/or a disturbingly poor prognosis.

The pathways to developmental outcomes in preterm infants discussed in this chapter can be applied to all infants, especially those facing biological or social risks. The term resiliency has been used to describe individuals who either manifest or sustain developmental competency in the presence of environmental hazards, or who exhibit the ability to recover from stressful events (Werner, 1993). In infancy, the extent to which a baby demonstrates resiliency in the face of challenge is determined by a confluence of constitutional and social factors, which continue to affect one another in reciprocally dynamic ways. It is important to note, however, that although seeds of risk and protection are often planted during the infancy period, both non-normative and normative life events continue to exert telling influence on the individual's growth throughout the course of the lifespan. Thus, the effort to ensure appropriate levels and forms of support to families in need, from infancy onward, continues to be a goal of both researchers and practitioners.

REFERENCES

Als, H., Duffy, F. H., & McAnulty, G. B. (1988). The APIB, an assessment of functional competence in preterm and full term newborns regardless of gestational age at birth. *Infant Behavior & Development*, 11, 319–331.

Als, H., Lester, B. M., Tronick, E. Z., & Brazelton, B. (1982). Toward a research instrument for assessment of preterm infants' behavior. In H. E. Fitzgerald, B. M. Lester, & M. W. Yogman, *Theory and research in behavioral pediatrics* (Vol. 1, pp. 35–64). New York: Plenum.

Aylward, G. P., Pfeiffer, S. I., Wright, A., & Verhulst, S. J. (1989). Outcome studies of low birthweight infants published in the last decade: A metaanalysis. *Journal of Pediatrics*, 115, 515–520.

Aylward, G. P., Verhulst, S. J., & Bell, S. (1988). Birthweight, gestational age, and specific dysfunction at 36 months. *Developmental Medicine and Child Neurology*, 30, 10–11.

Barnard, K. E., Bee, H. L., & Hammond, M. A. (1984). Developmental changes in maternal interactions with term and preterm infants. *Infant Behavior & Development*, 7, 101–113.

Baumwell, L., Tamis-LeMonda, C. S., & Bornstein, M. H. (1997). Styles of maternal interaction and toddler language comprehension: The importance of maternal sensitivity. *Infant Behavior & Development*, 20, 247–258.

Beckwith, L., & Cohen, S. E. (1980). Interactions of preterm infants with their caregivers and test performance at age two. In T. M. Field, S. Goldberg, D. Stern, & M. Sostek (Eds.), *High risk infants and children: Adult and peer interactions* (pp. 155–180). New York: Academic Press.

Binsacca, D. B., Ellis, J., Martin, D. G., & Petitti, D. B. (1987). Factors associated with low birthweight in an inner-city population: The role of financial problems. *American Journal of Public Health*, 77, 505–506.

Blackman, J. A. (1991). Neonatal intensive care: Is it worth it?: Developmental sequelae of very low birthweight. *Pediatric Clinic of North America*, 38, 1497–1511.

Bornstein, M. H., & Tamis-LeMonda, C. S. (In press). Mother-infant interaction. To appear in G. Bremner & A. Fogel (Eds.), *Handbook of infancy*. London: Blackwell Publishers, 2000.

Boukydis, C. F. Z., Lester, B. M., & Hoffman, J. (1987). Parenting and social support networks for parents of preterm and fullterm infants. In C. F. Z. Boukydis (Ed.), *Research on support for parents and infants in the postnatal period* (pp. 61–83). Norwood, NJ: Ablex.

Bradley, R. H., & Whiteside-Mansell, L. (1997). Children in poverty. In R. T. Ammerman & M. Hersen (Eds.), *Handbook of prevention and treatment with children and adolescents: Intervention in the real world context* (pp. 13–58). New York: Wiley.

Bradley, R. H., Whiteside, L., Mundfrom, D. J., Casey, P. H., Kelleher, K. J., & Pope, S. K. (1994). Early indications of resilience and their relation to experiences in the home environment of low birthweight, premature children living in poverty. *Child Development*, 65, 346–360.

Brinker, R. P., Baxter, A., & Butler, L. S. (1994). An ordinal pattern of analysis of four hypotheses describing the interactions between drug addicted, chronically disadvantaged and middle-class mother-infant dyads. *Child Development*, 65, 361–372.

Bromwich, R. (1997). *Working with families and their infants at risk*. Austin, Texas: Pro-Ed.

Chandra, A. (1995). *Health aspects of pregnancy and childbirth: United States, 1982–1988* (Vital and Health Statistics, Series 23, No. 18). Washington, DC: National Center for Health Statistics.

Cohen, S., & Parmelee, A. (1983). Prediction of five-year Stanford-Binet scores in preterm infants. *Child Development*, 54, 1242–1253.

Cohen, S. E., Parmelee, A. H., Beckwith, L., & Sigman, M. (1986). Cognitive development in preterm infants: Birth to 8 years. *Journal of Developmental Behavioral Pediatrics*, 7, 102–110.

Corcoran, M. E., & Chaudry, A. (1997). The dynamics of childhood poverty. *The Future of Children*, 7, 40–54.

Crnic, K. A., Greenberg, M. T., Robinson, N. M., & Ragozin, A. S. (1984). Maternal stress and social support: Effects on the mother-infant relationship from birth to eighteen months. *American Journal of Orthopsychiatry*, 54, 224–235.

Crnic, K. A., Ragozin, A. S., Greenberg, M. T., Robinson, N. M., & Basham, R. B. (1983). Social interaction and developmental competence of preterm and full-term infants during the first year of life. *Child Development*, 54, 1199–1210.

Davidson, S., Schrayer, A., Wielunsky, E., Kricker, R., Lilos, P., & Reisner, S. H. (1990). Energy intake, growth, and development in ventilated very low birth-weight infants with and without bronchpulmonary dysplasia. *American Journal of Disease of Children*, 144, 553–559.

DiPietro, J. A., & Porges, S. W. (1991). Relations between neonatal states and 8-month developmental outcomes in preterm infants. *Infant Behavior & Development*, 14, 441–450.

Escalona, S. K. (1982). Babies at double hazard: Early development of infants at biologic and social risk. *Pediatrics*, 70, 670–676.

Field, T., Healy, B. I., Goldstein, S. & Guthertz, M. (1990). Behavior-state matching and synchrony in mother-infant interactions of nondepressed versus depressed dyads. *Developmental Psychology*, 26, 7–14.

Field, T. M. (1979). Interaction patterns of preterm and term infants. In T. M. Field, A. M. Sostek, S. Goldberg, & H. H. Shuman (Eds.), *Infants born at risk* (pp. 333–356). Jamaica, NY: Spectrum.

Field, T. M. (1980). Interactions of high risk infants: Quantitative and qualitative differences. In D. B. Sawin, R. C. Hawkins, L. P. Walker, & J. H. Penticuff (Eds.), *Exceptional infant: Vol. 4. Psychological risks in infant-environmental transactions* (pp. 120–143). New York: Brunner/Mazel.

Frodi, A., Lamb, M., Leavitt, L., & Donavan, W. (1978). Fathers' and mothers' responses to infant smiles and cries. *Infant Behavior & Development*, 1, 187–198.

Garner, P. W., Landry, S. H., & Richardson, M. A. (1991). The development of joint attention skills in very low birthweight infants across the first 2 years. *Infant Behavior & Development, 14,* 489–495.

Gelfand, D. M., & Teti, D. M. (1990). The effects of maternal depression on children. *Clinical Psychology Review, 10,* 329–353.

Glascoe, F. P. (1994). It not what it seems: The relationship between parent's concerns and children with global delays. *Clinical Pediatrics, 33,* 292–296.

Gould, J., & LeRoy, S. (1988). Socioeconomic status and low birthweight: A racial comparison. *Pediatircs, 82,* 896–904.

Hack, M., Klein, N., & Taylor, H. (1995). Long-term developmental outcomes of low birthweight infants. *The Future of Children, 5,* 176–196.

Halpern, R. (1993). Poverty and infant development. In C. H. Zeanah (Ed.), *Handbook of infant mental health* (pp.73–86). New York: Guilford.

Hashima, P. Y., & Amato, P. R. (1994). Poverty, social support and parental behavior. *Child Development, 65,* 394–403.

Hunt, J. V., Cooper, B. A. B., & Tooley, W. H. (1988). Very low birthweight infants at 8 and 11 years of age: Role of neonatal illness and family status. *Pediatrics, 82,* 596–603.

Institute of Medicine (1985). *Preventing low birthweight.* Washington, DC: National Academy Press.

Jennings, K. D., Stagg, V., & Connors, R. E. (1991). Social networks and mothers' interactions with their preschool children. *Child Development, 62,* 966–978.

Kleinman, J. C., & Kessel, S. S. (1987). Racial differences in low birthweight: Trends and risk factors. *New England Journal of Medicine, 317,* 749–753.

Kopp, C. B., & Vaughn, B. E. (1982). Sustained attention during exploratory manipulation as a predictor of cognitive competence in preterm infants. *Child Development, 53,* 174–182.

Kramer, M. S. (1987). Intrauterine growth and gestational duration determinants. *Pediatrics, 80,* 502–511.

Landry, S. H. (1995). The development of joint attention in premature low birthweight infants. Effects of early medial complications and maternal attention-directing behaviors. In C. Moore & P. J. Dunham (Eds.), *Joint attention: Its origins and role in development* (pp. 223–250). Hillsdale, NJ: Erlbaum.

Landry, S. H., & Chapieski, L. (1988). Visual attention directing exploration in preterm infants: Effects of medical risk and maternal interactions. *Infant Behavior & Development, 53,* 174–182.

Landry, S. H., Leslie, N. A., Fletcher, J. M., & Francis, D. J. (1985). Visual attention skills of premature infants with and without intraventricular hemorrhage. *Infant Behavior & Development, 8,* 309–321.

Largo, R. H., Pfister, D., Molinari, C., Kundu, S., Uipp A., & Due, G. (1989). Significance of prenatal, perinatal, and postnatal factors in development of AGA preterm infants at five to seven years. *Developmental Medicine and Child Neurology, 31,* 440–456.

Leonard, C. H., Clyman, R. I., Piecuch, R. E., Juster, R. P., Ballard, R. A., & Behle, M. B. (1990). Effect of medical and social risk factors on outcome of prematurity and very low birthweight. *Journal of Pediatrics, 116,* 620–626.

LeVine, R. A., Miller, P. M., & West, M. M. (Eds.). (1988). *Parental behavior in diverse societies: New direction for child development*. San Francisco: Jossey Bass.

Liaw, F. R., & Brooks-Gunn, J. (1993). Patterns of low-birth-weight children's cognitive development. *Developmental Psychology*, 29, 1024–1035.

Lieberman, R. E., Ryan, K. J., Monson, R. R., & Schoenbaum, S. C. (1987). Risk factors accounting for racial differences in the rate of premature birth. *New England Journal of Medicine*, 317, 743–748.

Lowe, J., & Papile, L. (1990). Neurodevelopmental performance of very low birthweight infants with mild periventricular, intraventricular hemorrhage. *American Journal of Disease of Children*, 144, 1242–1245.

Lyons-Ruth, K., Zoll, D., Connell, D., & Grunebaum, H. (1986). The depressed mother and her one-year old infant: Environmental context, mother-infant interaction and attachment, and infant development. In E. Tronick & T. Field (Eds.), *Maternal depression and infant disturbance* (pp. 61–82). San Francisco: Jossey-Bass.

MacDorman, M. F., & Atkinson, J. O. (1998). *Infant mortality statistics from the 1996 period linked birth/infant death data set* (Monthly Vital Statistics Report. Vol. 46, No. 12). Washington, DC: National Center for Health Statistics.

March of Dimes Birth Defects Foundations (1997). *The March of Dimes StatBook: Statistics for monitoring maternal and infant health*. White Plains, NY: Author.

McCormick, M. C., Brooks-Gunn, J., Workman-Daniels, K., Turner, J., & Peckman, G. J. (1992). The health and developmental status of very low-birthweight children at school age. *Journal of the American Medical Association*, 267, 2204–2208.

McLoyd, V. C., & Wilson, L. (1991). The strain of living poor: Parenting, social support, and child mental health. In A. C. Huston (Ed.), *Children in poverty: Child development and public policy* (pp. 105–135). New York: Cambridge University Press.

Meisels, S. J., Plunkett, J. W., Roloff, D. W., Pasick, P. L., & Stiefel, G. S. (1986). Growth and development of preterm infants with respiratory distress syndrome and bronchopulmonary dysplasia. *Pediatrics*, 77, 345–352.

Miller, M., & Ottinger, D., (1986). Influence of labeling on ratings of infant behavior: A prematurity prejudice. *Journal of Pediatric Psychology*, 11, 561–572.

Miller-Loncar, C., Erwin, L. J., Landry, S. H., Smith, K. E., & Swank, P. R. (1998). Characteristics of social support networks of low socioeconomic status African American, Anglo American, and Mexican American mothers of full term and preterm infants. *Journal of Community Psychology*, 26, 131–143.

Minde, K., Shosenberg, N., Marton, P., Thompson, J., Ripley, J., & Burns, S. (1980). Self-help groups in a premature nursery: A controlled evaluation. *Journal of Pediatrics*, 96, 933–940.

North, A. F., & McDonald, H. M. (1977). Why are neonatal mortality rates lower in small black infants than in white infants of similar birthweight? *Journal of Pediatrics*, 90, 809–810.

Paneth, N. S. (1995). The problem of low birthweight. *The Future of Children, 5,* 1–14.

Papile, L. A., Munsick-Bruno, G., & Schaefer, A. (1983). Relationship of cerebral intraventricular hemorrhage and early childhood neurological handicaps. *Journal of Pediatrics,* 103, 273–277.

Pascoe, J. M., Loda, F. A., Jeffries, V., & Earp, J. A. (1982). Perinatal precursors of home stimulation in families of sick newborns. *Journal of Developmental and Behavioral Pediatrics,* 3, 22–24.

Pellegrino, L. (1997). Cerebral palsy. In M. L. Batshaw (Ed.), *Children with disabilities* (4th ed.). Baltimore: Paul H. Brooks.

Peters, E., & Mullis, N. (1997). The role of the family and source of income in adolescent achievement. In G. Duncan & J. Brooks-Gunn (Eds.), *Consequences of growing up poor* (pp. 340–381). New York: Sage.

Power, T. G., Chapieski, M. L., & McGrath, M. P. (1985). Assessment of individual differences in infant exploration and play. *Developmental Psychology,* 21, 974–981.

Raver, C. (1996). Relations between social contingency in mother-child interaction and 2-year-olds' social competence. *Developmental Psychology,* 32, 850–859.

Rose, S. A. (1980). Enhancing visual recognition memory in preterm infants. *Developmental Psychology,* 16, 85–92.

Rose, S. A. (1983). Differential rates of visual information processing in full-term and preterm infants. *Child Development,* 54, 1189–1198.

Rose, S. A., Feldman, J. F., McCarton, C. M., & Wolfson, J. (1988). Information processing in seven-month-old infants as a function of risk status. *Child Development,* 59, 589–603.

Rose, S. A., Feldman, J. F., Wallace, I. F., & Cohen, P. (1991). Language: A partial link between infant attention and later intelligence. *Developmental Psychology,* 27, 798–805.

Rose, S. A., Feldman, J. F., Wallace, I. F., & McCarton, C. (1991). Information processing at 1 year: Relation to birth status and developmental outcome during the first 5 years. *Developmental Psychology,* 27, 723–737.

Rose, S., & Tamis-LeMonda, C. S. (1999). Visual information processing in infancy: Reflections on underlying mechanisms. In L. Balter & C. S. Tamis-LeMonda, (Eds.), *Child development: A handbook of contemporary issues* (pp. 64–84). Philadelphia: Psychology Press.

Rosenbaum, S. (1992). Child health and poor children. *American Behavioral Scientist,* 35, 275–289.

Ross, G., Auld, A. M., Tesman, J., & Nass, R. (1992). Effects of subependymal and mild intraventricular lesions on visual attention and memory in premature infants. *Developmental Psychology,* 28, 1067–1074.

Ruff, H. A. (1988). The measurement of attention in high-risk infants. In P. Vietre & H. G. Vaughan (Eds.), *Early identification of infants with developmental disabilities* (pp.xx–xx). New York: Grune and Stratton.

Ruff, H. A., McCarton, C., Kurtzberg, D., & Vaughan, H. G. (1984). Preterm infants manipulative explanation of objects. *Child Development,* 55, 1166–1173.

Rutter M. (1985). Resilience in the face of adversity: Protective factors and resistance to psychiatric disorder. *British Journal of Psychiatry*, 147, 598–611.

Rutter, M. (1990). Psychosocial resilience and protective mechanisms. In J. A. Masten, D. Cicchetti, K. Nuechte, & D. J. Weintraub (Eds.), *Risk and protective factors in the development of psychopathology* (pp. 181–214). New York: Cambridge.

Saigal, S., Szatmari, P., Rosenbaum, P., Campbell, D., & King, S. (1991). Cognitive abilities and school performance of extremely low birthweight children and matched term controls at age 8: A regional study. *Journal of Pediatrics*, 118, 751–760.

Sammons, W. A. H., & Lewis, J. M. (1985). *Premature babies: A different beginning*. Princeton, NJ: Mosby.

Sell, E. J., Gaines, J. A., Gluckman, C., & Williams, E. (1985). Early identification of learning problems in neonatal intensive care graduates. *American Journal of Disease of Children,* 139, 460–463.

Shankaran, S., Slovis, S., Bedard, M. P., & Poland, R. L. (1982). Sonographic classification of intracranial hemorrhage: A prognostic indicator of mortality and short term neurologic outcome. *Journal of Pediatrics*, 100, 469–474.

Shiono, P. H., & Behrman, R. E. (1995). Low birthweight: Analysis and recommendations. *The Future of Children*, 5, 4–18.

Simons, R. L., Lorenz, F. O., Wu, C., & Conger, R. D. (1993). Social network and marital support as mediators and moderators of the impact of stress and depression on parental behavior. *Developmental Psychology*, 29, 368–381.

Smith, J. R., Brooks-Gunn, J., & Klebanov, P. (1997). The consequences of living in poverty for young children's cognitive and verbal ability and early school achievement. In G. J. Duncan & J. Brooks-Gunn (Eds.), *Consequences of growing up poor* (pp.132–189). New York: Sage.

Starfield, B., Shapiro, S., Weiss, Liang, K. Y., Ra, K., Paige, D., & Wang, X. (1991). Race, family income and low birthweight. *American Journal of Epidemiology*, 134, 1167–1174.

Stern, M., & Karraker, K. H. (1988). Prematurity stereotyping by mothers of premature infants. *Journal of Pediatric Psychology*, 13, 253–262.

Stern, M., & Karraker, K. H. (1989). Modifying the prematurity stereotype: The effects of information in negative perceptions of infants. *Journal of Social and Clinical Psychology*, 8, 1–13.

Tamis-LeMonda, C. S., & Bornstein, M. H. (1991). Individual variation, correspondence, stability and change in mother and toddler play. *Infant Behavior & Development*, 14, 143–162.

Tamis-LeMonda, C. S., & Bornstein, M. H. (1989). Habituation and maternal encouragement of attention in infancy as predictors of toddler language, play, and representational competence. *Child Development*, 60, 738–751.

Tamis-LeMonda, C. S., & Bornstein, M. H. (1993). Infant antecedents of toddlers exploratory competence. *Infant Behavior & Development*, 16, 423–429.

Teplin, S. W., Burchinal, M., Johnson-Martin, N., Humphry, R. A., & Kraybill, E. N. (1991). Neurodevelopmental, health, and growth status at age 6 years of children with birthweights less than 1001 grams. *Journal of Pediatrics,* 118, 768–777.

Teti, D. M., O'Connell, M. A., & Reiner, C. D. (1996). Parenting sensitivity, parental depression and child health: The mediational role of parental self-efficacy. *Early Development and Parenting, 5,* 237–250.

Tyson, J. (1995). Evidence-based ethics and the care for premature infants. *The Future of Children, 5,* 197–214.

Ventura, S. J., Martin, J. A., Curtin, S. C., & Mathews, M. S. (1999). *Births: Final data for 1997* (National Vital Statistics Report, Vol. 47, No. 18). Washington, DC: National Center for Health Statistics.

Vohr, B. R., Garcia-Coll, C., & Oh, W. (1990). Increased morbidity in very low birthweight and small for gestational age infants with reduced head circumference at birth: A two year follow-up study. *Pediatric Research, 27,* 10A.

Wachs, T. (1999). The what, why, and how of temperament: A piece of the action. In L. Balter & C. S. Tamis-LeMonda (Eds.), *Child psychology: A handbook of contemporary issues* (pp. 23–44). Philadelphia: Psychology Press.

Wahler, R. G., & Dumas, J. F. (1989). Attentional problems and dysfunctional mother-child interactions: An interbehavioral model. *Psychological Bulletin, 105,* 116–130.

Waikato, V. (1993). Developmental outcomes of very low birthweight infants with intraventricular hemorrhage. *Perceptual and Motor Skills, 77,* 894.

Werner, E. E. (1993). Risk, resilience, and recovery: Perspectives from the Kauai longitudinal study. *Development and Psychopathology, 5,* 503–515.

Zarling, C. L., Hirsch, B. J., & Landry, S. (1988). Maternal social networks and mother-infant interactions in full-term and very low birthweight, preterm infants. *Child Development, 59,* 178–1845.

AUTHORS' NOTE

We thank P. Ahuja, B. Dreyer, and A. Mendelsohn for their comments and assistance. Address correspondence to Dr. Catherine S. Tamis-LeMonda, at the Department of Applied Psychology, New York University.

INFANT ATTENTION AND THE DEVELOPMENT OF COGNITION
Does the Environment Moderate Continuity?

John Colombo
& Terrill F. Saxon

2

◆ ◆ ◆ ◆

Our views of the human infant have changed radically over the past thirty years. One of the most salient of these views was the idea that cognitive or intellectual function in childhood was unpredictable from infancy (Fagen, 1995). From the 1930s through the 1970s, it was widely demonstrated that infant sensorimotor performance did not reliably predict to measures of intellectual function in childhood. As a result, it was widely held that cognitive development underwent a reorganization between infancy and school age, and thus was "discontinuous" across this time span (McCall & Mash, 1995). During the early 1980s, however, modest but statistically significant correlations were observed between measures of infant cognitive performance and childhood measures of intelligence and language (e.g., Fagan & McGrath, 1981). Demonstrations of the relationship between early and later intellectual function have since been repeated for a number of variables in numerous reports (e.g., Bornstein & Sigman, 1986; Colombo, 1993, 1997). Given that some aspects of cognitive performance in infancy predicts to intellectual status in childhood, some qualities and/or quantities of cognitive function have come to be regarded as "continuous" from infancy (Bornstein & Sigman, 1986). The ability of measures of infant cognitive performance to predict childhood cognition and intelligence is the focus of this chapter, and we will hereafter refer to this as the *prediction phenomenon.*

Demonstration of the prediction phenomenon has opened up new areas of basic inquiry for developmental research. In addition, it has raised the possibility that individuals at risk for cognitive deficits might be identified early in life, when compensatory or corrective interventions might be applied most effectively and efficiently. Although the empirical consequences of the prediction phenomenon have been wide-ranging, the theoretical approaches it has inspired have been less satisfying. Generally, the prediction phenomenon has been approached from a theoretical point of view that has emphasized product over process. That is, individual differences in infant cognition have been largely regarded as reflections of an intellectual "product" which exists during infancy and which simply perseveres into childhood and adolescence. This viewpoint can readily be recognized as an extension of the psychometric tradition, and this approach biases the consideration of the prediction phenomenon in two ways. First, it places an emphasis on the reliability and stability of the products (Colombo & Fagen, 1990) rather than on how such products might grow or change. Second, and more importantly from the perspective of this volume, it generally carries with it the connotation that the predictable aspects of cognition and intelligence are static and unaffected by exogenous factors. In other words, the presumption has been that the continuity of cognitive function from infancy to adulthood is generally unmediated or unmoderated by environmental influence.

In retrospect, neither of these biases seems intuitively prudent when considering or characterizing early human development. First, minimizing the role of growth and change (a.k.a., "development") in accounting for the relationship between abilities or behaviors from infancy to later childhood seems unrealistic, because we know that infancy and early childhood is a period rife with dynamic behavioral reorganization and complex developmental functions. Second, devaluing the role of the environment also seems unreasonable, because so much of the variance in childhood cognition, language, and intelligence has significant and important environmental correlates.

The purpose of this chapter is to extend the scope of interpretation of the prediction phenomenon, and to provide some alternative conceptualizations for it. To try and accomplish this task, we first review the measures that have been shown to be predictive from infancy. Next, we examine some of the basic models that have been proposed to account for it, beginning with simple models that are wholly consistent with the psychometric approach and working toward more complex models that incorporate change and environmental input. At each turn, we briefly consider the evidence for and against each of the models. A specific purpose of this chapter is to raise the possibility that the prediction phenomenon may be better accounted for with complex models that incorporate change and environmental input rather than with the simple psychometric models that have been prevalent to date. If this possibility is correct, it has important implications for the measurement of infant cognitive development and for our understanding of childhood intelligence. Not the least of these is the possibility that environmental conditions may moderate what appears to be a simple demonstration of continuity and prediction from infancy. We end the chapter by considering some specific hypotheses as to how individual differences in infant cognition might interact with environmental variables and by exploring the implications of the more complex models for how we might think about early cognitive development, as well as for how the design of early identification and early intervention might be affected.

WHAT MEASURES PREDICT INTELLIGENCE FROM INFANCY?

The first step in understanding the models to be discussed in the chapter is to formulate a description of the measures of infant cognition or cognitive performance that have been shown to predict to childhood intelligence. At this writing, measures from a number of different laboratory paradigms have been reported to have predictive validity.

Visual Attention

Habituation is a common, easily used, and noninvasive procedure for measuring visual learning in human infants. In this paradigm, a stimulus is repeatedly presented and the infant's learning of the stimulus is inferred from the resulting decline in looking across these presentations. Depending on the technical procedure that is used to assess habituation, a number of measures are available to quantify the learning that occurs during habituation and how such learning changes across the first year(s) of postnatal life. For more restrictive procedures in which the presentations are determined by the experimenter, the "slope" or amount of decline in attention across the session is usually taken as the primary measure. For those in which the infant is allowed to attend to the stimulus ad libitum, measures of how long the infant looks during the initial portions of the session have been shown to be the best indicators of individual differences of early cognitive processes (see Colombo & Mitchell, 1990). Measures of both habituation magnitude and look duration have been reported to correlate with later measures of cognition and language, as well as with standardized measures of intellectual performance into adolescence (see Bornstein, 1990; Bornstein, Slater, Brown, Roberts, & Barrett, 1997; Colombo, 1993, 1997, for recent reviews).

Recognition/Discrimination Performance

The paired-comparison paradigm is another technique for assessing visual learning. In this procedure, the infant is presented with a stimulus and allowed to study it for some amount of time and then given the choice of looking at the previously-studied ("familiarized") stimulus, or a novel one. Under conditions in which the amount of study time is sufficient for the infant to have learned the stimulus, and where the stimuli are discriminable, the infant typically spends more time looking at the novel stimulus than the familiarized one. This "novelty preference" has been reported to predict to standardized tests of vocabulary and intellectual performance out to early adolescence (e.g., Fagan, 1990).

Ocular Reaction Time and Anticipatory Looking

In a third procedure designed to assess infants' learning and attention, stimuli are presented in predictable patterns at different locations in the visual field. For example, stimuli may appear to the left and right of midline in an alternating pattern (e.g., left-right-left-right). Using frame-by-frame video analysis, it is possible to measure how quickly the infant moves his or her eyes toward the appearance of the stimulus in the visual field (this is a measure of reaction time, or RT). In addition, after repeated exposure to the alternating pattern, the infant begins to "anticipate" the appearance of the stimulus in its next location (Canfield, Wilken, Schmerl, & Smith, 1995). Both the RT and anticipation measures have been reported to correlate with later standardized assessments of intelligence (e.g., Dougherty & Haith, 1997).

Other Measures

When the entire prediction literature was last reviewed (Colombo, 1993), only one other measure was considered: a measure of long-term memory for an operantly conditioned response (Fagen & Ohr, 1990). In reality, many other measures have been used to predict childhood outcomes from infancy, or have been shown to discriminate between groups of infants that will show differential outcomes later in childhood. For example, perinatal or medical risk variables (Molfese, DiLalla, & Lovelace, 1996) can predict developmental outcome to some degree. Beyond these, however, it is worth mentioning behavioral measures such as the A-not-B task performance (Diamond, Prevor, Callender, & Druin, 1997), global measures of temperament and attention span (e.g., Robson & Pederson, 1997), MRI (e.g., Skranes et al., 1998), and simple measures of learning (Farran & Harber, 1989). In addition, there are sizeable literatures showing continuity of electrophysiological measures of cerebral development (e.g., Molfese, Molfese, Gill, & Benshoff, 1997) and autonomic regulation (e.g., Doussard Roosevelt, Porges, Scanlon, Alemi, & Scanlon, 1997) from infancy to childhood. For the purposes of the current chapter, however, we maintain a focus on the variables mentioned above, particularly those derived from selective looking procedures such as habituation and recognition/discrimination.

How Well Do These Measures Predict?

A second issue that is relevant to our evaluation of the different models of cognitive continuity from infancy to childhood is how well these measures predict to childhood cognitive performance (e.g., McCall & Carriger, 1993). The magnitude of the infancy-to-childhood correlations varies from study to study, explaining as little as 4% and as much as 50% of the variance in later intelligence. However, it is accurate to say that, on average, these measures account for somewhere between 10% to 15% of the variance in childhood intelligence (Colombo & Frick, 1999).

Such correlations may be statistically significant, but in general, they are not clinically informative (McCall & Carriger, 1993). The modest magnitude of these correlations has prompted some researchers to denigrate their importance (Lucas, 1997). However, several points are worth noting in defense of low correlations. First, low zero-order correlations do not always necessarily reflect the true importance of an association (e.g., Abelson, 1985). Second, the predictive power of infant measures is constrained by low levels of test-retest reliability (Bornstein & Sigman, 1986). If one recalculates the predictive validity of the infant measures after correcting for this unreliability, the potential effect size in terms of proportion of variance accounted for rises to nearly .60 (Colombo, 1993).

Summary

A number of different measures of cognitive performance and process assessed during infancy predict modest amounts of variance in childhood intelligence. Although the measures do not provide levels of prediction that are clinically or practically useful for indicating specific cognitive outcome for individual infants at this time, the correlations are statistically significant and consistent across many studies. As such, they are theoretically important and thus require explanation. Having described the components and limitations of the prediction phenomenon per se, we now turn to a consideration of how such correlations have been explained.

MODELS OF THE PREDICTION PHENOMENON

The "Single Process" or Domain-General Model

As we have noted, the finding that measures of infant cognition are correlated with an overall measure of cognitive function during childhood and adolescence (i.e., IQ) may be interpreted within the context of a simple psychometric model. As such, the prediction phenomenon may be considered simply as a glorified case of test-retest reliability or convergent validity. Such a model can be depicted schematically as shown in figure 2.1. Here, both the infant and childhood measures are driven by an underlying "latent" construct of cognition or intelligence that transcends any particular cognitive function or skill; that is, the construct is "domain-general."

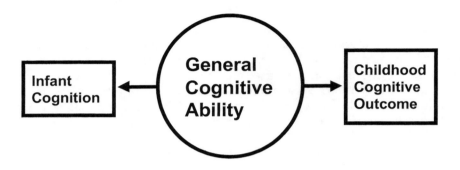

Figure 2.1 Infant and childhood cognition as continuous indicators of the same underlying construct.

It would be nice if this model was correct. It is parsimonious, it is easy enough to understand, and it can be easily tested. However, we think that the model is probably wrong for two reasons. First, several of the measures of infant cognition that correlate with childhood cognition do not load together on the same components when factor-analyzed (Jacobson et al., 1992). Second, it has been reported that the infant measures are differentially sensitive to certain specific postnatal insults. For example, while efficiency in information processing is affected by prenatal alcohol exposure, recognition performance is not (Jacobson, 1998). Alternately, recognition memory performance is affected by prenatal exposure to polychlorinated biphenyls (Jacobson, Fein, Jacobson, Schwartz, & Dowler, 1985), while processing efficiency is not (Jacobson, Jacobson, Sokol, Martier, & Ager, 1993). This suggests that even the earliest measures of cognitive function may reflect a system that can be characterized as being more "modular" in nature.

The "Multiple Process" or Domain-Specific Model

This evidence supporting the existence of a modular cognitive system in infancy has led to the proposal that at least some of the different measures of infant cognition reflect different underlying cognitive constructs (Colombo, 1997). Indeed, it has been proposed that these may reflect the function of different underlying neural substrates (Colombo, 1995; Colombo & Janowsky, 1998). This slightly more complicated model is depicted in figure 2.2. In addition to being consistent with the evidence reviewed above, the second model implies that the continuity is driven by skills or abilities that are specific to a particular cognitive domain, and some level of competence within these domain-specific skills persists into childhood and adolescent intellectual performance.

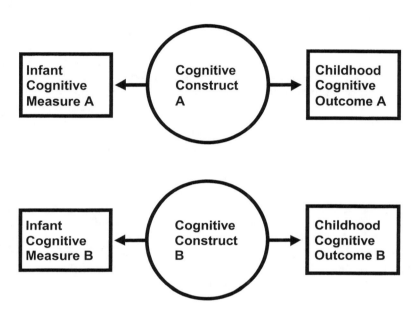

Figure 2.2 A model of the association between infant and childhood cognition that is mediated by two separate and modular underlying cognitive constructs ("A" and "B").

The presumption that cognitive abilities might in fact be modular during infancy is itself something of a novel concept. However, a pressing issue in the context of the prediction phenomenon might be the identification of these multiple factors. At its most baroque and complex extreme, we might simply assume that each variable that shows prediction from infancy to childhood constitutes its own factor. Presumably, each of these variables would account for unique and additive variance to overall measures of childhood intellectual performance. On the other hand, it is possible that several of the measures reduce to a set of two or three factors that share concurrent variance in infancy and share predictive variance from infancy to childhood. This has been the more popular interpretation and is the one that most of the extant evidence supports. For example, classifications of infant measures into indicators of "processing speed" or "memory" have been proposed independently from several analyses (Colombo, 1993; Jacobson, 1995; Jacobson et al., 1992; Rose & Feldman, 1995a,b).

An Additive Model: Infant and Environment

Figures 2.1 and 2.2 reflect somewhat different positions with regard to the development of cognition, but they share the notion that continuity is solely attributable to constitutional factors within the infant. Indeed, some studies have suggested that measures of early attention and cognition are uncorrelated with sociocultural indices (e.g., Mayes & Bornstein, 1995; Jacobson et al., 1992), but an obvious—and quite reasonable—possibility is based on the notion that developmental outcome is a function of both the infant's own cognitive abilities and the environment in which the infant is reared (see, e.g., Colombo & Mitchell, 1990).

The next model in this sequence reflects this possibility by proposing that the rearing environment during infancy combines with infant cognitive measures to predict childhood cognitive outcome in an additive manner (see figure 2.3). For simplicity's sake, the infant's cognitive skills are depicted as a single factor (as shown in figure 2.1) but it is entirely possible that multiple cognitive processes could be involved (as shown in figure 2.2). The fundamental difference between this model and those that have been articulated before is that the paths to childhood cognitive outcome are elaborated by the addition of exogenous or environmental inputs during infancy. As such, the inclusion of some measurement of the environment allows for an overall increase in the amount of variance accounted for in the child's cognitive ability.

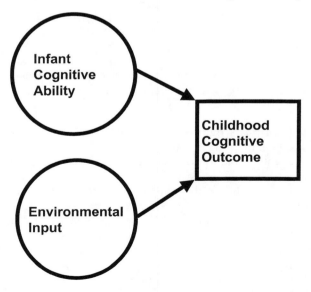

Figure 2.3 Both infant cognitive ability and environment contribute to childhood cognition in this model, although the contribution is parallel and additive.

A critical feature of the additive model, however, is that environmental influence is represented by an *independent path* that runs parallel to the infant's cognitive factor toward childhood outcome. In this model, optimal environmental or constitutional conditions serve to enhance cognitive outcome, and suboptimal environmental or constitutional conditions diminish it. Optimal conditions on both factors yield the best outcome, suboptimal conditions on both yield the worst outcome, and mixed conditions yield outcomes that fall somewhere in between.

In many ways, the additive model represents an improvement over the simple psychometrically-inspired models. Furthermore, a number of longitudinal studies have provided evidence that is consistent with an additive model of cognitive development from infancy (Bornstein, 1985; Mitchell, McCollam, Horowitz, Embretson, & O'Brien, 1991; Ruddy & Bornstein, 1982; Tamis-LeMonda & Bornstein, 1989). That is, measures of the infant's environment contribute unique variance over and above that provided by the infant's own cognitive performance to the prediction of cognitive outcome. At the same time, however, it is worth noting that this additive model fundamentally represents the traditional resolution of the nature/nurture issue: Each of two channels of influence (however characterized—genetic/environmental, maturation/learning, innate/acquired) contribute to the equation that yields developmental outcome. In light of recent theory (Edelman, 1987; Oyama, 1985) and evidence (Gottleib, 1997; Sameroff, 1983) about the nature of developmental systems, this additive resolution may not accurately represent the complex interplay of factors in the determination of individual outcomes.

Furthermore, while some evidence may support the additive model, it is also the case that a more complex model will require a more intensive longitudinal design strategy than has been typically used. In essence, many of the studies that support the additive model were not adequately designed to test for more complex paths. In the next section, we examine models that incorporate such paths.

A Transactional Model: Infant Environment

The most complex of the models we will consider here proposes that infant cognition *interacts* with environmental parameters over time. As such, the infant's or child's cognitive status at any point is derivative of the interactive processes that have occurred previously. Historically, the work of Bell (1968, 1971, 1979) and Sameroff (1975; Sameroff & Chandler, 1975) suggested that a child's development was less a function of the infant and caretaker characteristics in isolation than of the dynamic system properties of the environment. This general concept is applied to a transactional model that is outlined in figure 2.4. In this model, it would be hypothesized that an infant's cognitive status interacts with (for example) some parameter

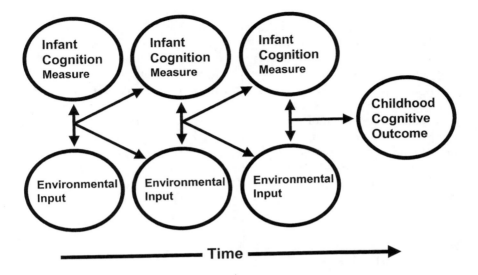

Figure 2.4 A transactional model in which infant cognition and environmental quality interact with one another at each time point. The interaction is denoted by the vertical line between infant and environment at each age, and the intervening outcomes at each successive age is represented as an outcome of that previous interaction. Childhood cognition is ultimately a function of these multiple transactions.

of caregiver stimulation input across multiple time points. Over time, these interactive processes determine mature and stable cognitive outcome[1].

What advantage does this approach offer beyond that provided by the psychometric approach that has generally dominated the prediction literature? The prediction phenomenon has recently been addressed from the point of view of developmental cognitive neuroscience (Colombo & Janowsky, 1998). When one confronts the need to explain the statistical continuity of cognitive development from infancy in terms of the general principles of CNS development and change, the inadequacies of the simple measurement model in dealing with such change become quite obvious:

> A cognitive neuroscience of continuity must satisfactorily address the fact that the neural systems of interest change dramatically over the first months and years of life. The numbers of synapses, efficiency of neural transmission, myelination . . . are all modified during early development. So possibly the biggest quandary for the future of developmental cognitive neuroscience is not *what* cognitive processes show continuity in individual differences or what neural system subserves the cognitive process, but *how* continuity is maintained when the neural hardware mediating

the processes is continuously modified. It may be very difficult to attribute such continuity to the simple survival of individual differences on a single component or parameter of information processing from infancy. (Colombo & Janowsky, 1998, pp. 383–384).

Within the framework of this model, we propose that the different forms of infant cognitive behaviors previously enumerated (length of attention, swiftness of learning, preference for novelty, facility for recognition, rapidity of orienting, ability to remember across nontrivial intervals, etc.), may elicit different forms of response from the infant's environment. This, in turn, may affect the infant's cognitive ability (for better or worse), and extend the chain of transaction on through until childhood. Note that, even in this transactional model of continuity, one would expect that a modest (but perhaps statistically significant) correlation would be observed between measures of cognitive performance in infancy and cognitive outcome in childhood. In other words, the transactional model would be consistent with the extant data on the prediction phenomenon. However, within the model, the causal chain is neither straightforward nor limited to one channel of influence.

Summary

To this point, we have put forth a series of arguments in favor of a transactional or developmental-systems conceptualization of the prediction phenomenon. We have noted that the prediction phenomenon has been predominantly interpreted in terms of simple psychometric models, and have argued that such an interpretation is at odds with recent characterizations of early development. We have further argued that more complex models that incorporate aspects of change and environmental input are not inconsistent with the general findings within the prediction phenomenon, and have raised the possibility that such models may better account for the underlying paths that give rise to the phenomenon per se. At this point, the next logical step is to try to determine whether a transactional model of intellectual continuity has empirical support in the extant literature. That is the task of the next section.

Is the Transactional Model Feasible?

Before reviewing the literature on transactional paths in early cognitive development, it seems worthwhile to determine what kinds of evidence would be consistent with such a transactional model. Essentially, we will be examining studies in which both the infant and the environment have been assessed in an effort to determine whether each contributes to cognitive outcome in childhood. That is, we will be looking for evidence to support the model presented in figure 2.4 from studies designed from the point of view of the additive model shown in figure 2.3. Recall, however, that the additive model assumes that the constitutional and environmental channels of influence should be independent. As such, the additive model would not necessarily predict that assessments of these channels would be correlated. A transactional model, however, would predict that such intercorrelations exist. Thus, we will be looking at the degree to which measures of infant and environment correlate with one another, and whether those correlations vary in assessments conducted across time or across components of infant cognitive performance. The presence of such intercorrelations would be consistent with the existence of transactional paths.

Evidence on Infant Environment Interactions in Early Cognitive Development

A number of studies have sought to determine whether infant and environmental variables jointly determine cognitive development in later life. Perhaps the first of these was Ruddy and Bornstein's (1982) study of the contribution of infant habituation efficiency and maternal didactic interaction/language at four months of age to cognitive outcome at twelve months. The combined influence of these internal and environmental factors at four months accounted for 40% of the variance in Bayley performance at one year, and each of the factors accounted for a significant share of unique variance. Of particular interest to the question at hand, however, is the observation that some of the concurrent correlations between habituation and interaction variables were statistically significant, or approached significance. For example, infants who habituated quickly were found to have mothers who vocalized more frequently. Given the design of the study and the small sample size, the path of influence between these factors cannot be determined, but the general finding is consistent with the interactive hypothesis.

Bornstein (1985) subsequently reported on a longitudinal follow-up with a small sample ($N = 14$) of infants. The sample was tested on efficiency of habituation at four months, measures of maternal didactic interaction at four and thirteen months, and developmental outcome measures (vocabulary at thirteen months and standard intellectual assessments at 48 months). Habituation efficiency was a good predictor of both cognitive outcomes. The didactic measures showed interesting patterns of prediction. First, the measures were not stable from four to thirteen months. Second, the four-month assessment of maternal didactic interaction predicted well to both cognitive measures, but the thirteen-month assessment did not. Finally, habituation efficiency was correlated with the interaction measures at both four and thirteen months. Of particular interest in this regard was the fact that the path coefficient from the four-month habituation measure to the thirteen-month didactic measure was +.62. Thus, early (i.e., four-month) infant cognitive measure "drove" the later didactic interaction. It is tempting to suggest from this pattern of data that mothers may have "adapted" to their infants' attentional patterns, although this cannot be definitively established.

A more extensive follow-up to the Bornstein (1985) study was subsequently published by Tamis-LeMonda and Bornstein (1989). This study featured the assessment of infants' cognitive performance (visual habituation) at five months, and didactic interaction (characterized as "maternal encouraging attention") at two points during the first year (five and thirteen months of age). Cognitive outcome was operationalized in terms of vocabulary and symbolic facility during the second year. The focus of the results emphasized the evidence for parallel and unique contributions of both infant cognition and maternal interaction to cognitive ability in the second year (i.e., the model presented in figure 2.3). However, this study did yield some evidence in support of an interactive framework: Infant cognition at five months significantly influenced maternal behavior at thirteen months (the structural equation path coefficient was .30). As above, one interpretation of this finding might be that mothers "adjusted" their interaction styles based on previous experience with their infants' attentional patterns.

The Tamis-LeMonda and Bornstein (1989) study has been criticized because of its use of structural equation modeling with a relatively small sample size ($N < 40$). However, their findings were essentially repeated by Mitchell et al. (1991). This study featured a large sample ($N > 200$) of preterm and full-term infants assessed on various cognitive indicators (look duration and novelty preference) at three and ten months of age. A global assessment of the quality of mother-infant interaction was collected at each time point, and cognitive-intellectual outcome was measured with standardized tests during the second and third years. The "best fit" model reported did not include interactive causal paths between measures of infant cognition and measures of mother-child interaction. As with the Tamis-LeMonda and Bornstein (1989) report, however, the study yielded evidence for the unique contribution of both infant cognition and maternal interaction variables to performance on the Stanford-Binet at thirty months.

A study mentioned earlier in the discussion of evidence for multiple underlying constructs (Bornstein & Tamis-LeMonda, 1994) also deserves mention here. The primary focus of this study was on the antecedents of three different measures of infant cognition assessed at five months of age. Most relevant to the topic of this discussion, however, was the finding that the efficiency of visual learning (again, from habituation) at five months was correlated with a concurrent measure of maternal didactic interaction. Once again, the results do not lend themselves to a definitive interpretation, but they do lend some support to the possibility of there being transactional paths of influence among these variables, as infant visual attention was concurrently associated with the interaction assessment. Furthermore, the data from this study are in agreement with both the Bornstein (1985) and the Tamis-LeMonda and Bornstein (1989) reports in suggesting that the transactional path may occur earlier in infancy, rather than later.

More evidence for this possibility was offered by a short-term longitudinal study published by Saxon, Frick, and Colombo (1997). Here, a relatively large sample ($N > 60$) of infants was assessed on a visual attention "battery" at six and eight months. At both ages, assessments of maternal didactic "style" and joint attention were also taken. The design of the study therefore yielded a cross-lagged panel design involving both measures of cognition and interactive quality. The direct aim of the study was to assess possible transaction among the variables across time by examining the panel cross-lags. Despite the fact that infant attention was stable from six to eight months, and that many of the interactive variables also showed significant stability across those two time points, none of the cross-lagged correlations between the cognitive and interactive variables attained statistical significance. Thus, the data did not support the notion of a transactional association between infant attention and either didactic or joint-attention interaction measures after six months of age. Of some interest, however, was a concurrent relationship between several aspects of maternal didactic style and infant attention at six months. Here, the mothers of infants whose attentional profiles tended to be characterized by long-duration looks on the laboratory assessment tended to be less active and less engaged in the interaction sessions ($r = .32$). This was not true at eight months, and there was no cross-influence among these variables from six to eight months. However, the evidence is again consistent with the possibility that mothers might have adjusted to their infant's attentional patterns. Again, the results suggest that if such an adjustment did occur, it happened before six months of age.

An intriguing longitudinal study ($N > 90$) carried out by Marian Sigman's research team at UCLA has provided data for the prediction of many aspects of mature cognition from an assessment made in early infancy. Sigman, Cohen, Beckwith, and Parmelee (1986) first reported duration of looking in very early infancy to be negatively correlated with childhood performance on intellectual assessments, and Sigman, Cohen, Beckwith, Asarnow, and Parmelee (1991) subsequently extended the observation of continuity to early adolescence. Most recently, Sigman, Cohen, and Beckwith (1997) have provided evidence that the phenomenon extends to eighteen years of age, but may also be subject to a qualification with respect to the amount of maternal language input experienced by the children. Measures of the frequency of maternal vocalizations were taken at one, eight, and 24 months of age. Both the looking and maternal vocalization measures predicted children's cognitive outcome. However, Sigman et al. (1997) reported that the two variables significantly interacted in their prediction of later cognition: The frequency of maternal vocalizations effectively raised the performance of only those children who looked for shorter durations during early infancy. This parameter of the infant's language environment had no effect for those infants who looked for prolonged periods early on.

The most recent entry on this topic was Miceli, Whitman, Borkowski, Braungart-Rieker, and Mitchell's (1998) study of the association of temperamental and maternal factors with measures of infant visual processing. With a moderately sized sample ($N > 40$), greater maternal involvement (as measured during a free-play observational episode) contributed significant unique variance to infant recognition performance on one of two paired-comparison tasks. However, the pattern of influence was somewhat unexpected, as greater maternal involvement was associated with lower performance. This finding was especially pronounced for infants who were rated as "highly responsive" in temperament on the Bayley Infant Behavior Record. The authors make a provocative interpretation of the finding. Essentially, they suggest that, for infants who are highly responsive to the environment and to testing situations, high levels of maternal involvement may be intrusive and distracting. As such, this suggestion is in accordance with the notion that caregivers' didactic manipulation of infant attention during interaction may actually interact with the infant's basal attentional profile.

Summary

Virtually all of the studies on individual differences in infant attention and the style or manner of caregiver interaction suggest that a transactional model is tenable. In nearly every study, there is evidence for concurrent or time-lagged relationships between infant cognitive measures (usually attentional measures derived from habituation) and some measure of the type, amount, or style of caregiver interaction. If there are any generalities to be drawn from this brief review, we would suggest the following. First, some of the infant-environment relationships are counterintuitive or in unexpected directions (e.g., Miceli et al., 1998). Second, and perhaps more importantly, the infant-environment correlations appear to be stronger during early parts of the first year (e.g., prior to six months of age) than they are later on (e.g., Saxon et al., 1997). These findings suggest to us that an investigation of the prediction phenomenon from a transactional framework infancy is a worthwhile endeavor.

If the transactional model is correct, then it is the case that the continuity observed between early measures of infant cognition and later cognitive developmental status is moderated by the environment. At this point, it might be most helpful to present a concrete example of such a scenario. This is done in the next section.

SOME SPECIFIC INFANT ENVIRONMENT HYPOTHESES

In this section, we take the concept of the infant-environment match a step further. Here, we explore the possibility that different styles of infant attention may transact with particular styles of caregiver interaction in the equation that ultimately leads to individual differences in cognitive-developmental outcome in childhood. If we seriously entertain this possibility, individual differences in infant cognitive measures (particularly those we have worked with, in which attention to events or objects is the primary consideration) must be viewed in a different light. In the past, such infant measures have been interpreted as reflections of underlying cognitive mechanisms or processes, and their importance was gauged solely in terms of how well they tapped these latent constructs or abilities. In the scheme that follows, we emphasize the fact that cognitive mechanisms are reflected in various *behaviors*. For example, based on the measures we discussed at the start of the chapter, these would involve attentional measures that include patterns of prolonged or brief looking, rapid or slow reaction times, and positive or negative reactions to novelty. We do not deny that these attentional patterns are derived from underlying cognitive mechanisms, but here they can be conceptualized as behaviors that may act to elicit particular responses from the environment, or serve as setting variables upon which environmental input may be successfully imposed.

The example that follows involves a consideration of specific styles of parental interaction that have been the focus of recent investigations, and so it may be helpful to the reader to begin with some background on the issue. As part of Tomasello's (1992) "attentional-mapping hypothesis," caregivers and infants are thought to engage in various activities that lead to joint attention. In episodes of joint attention, the caregiver and infant share a joint attentional focus on objects that are used, or events that happen, during one-on-one interaction or play. It has been widely observed that the amount of joint attention observed in caregiver-infant interaction correlates rather strongly with the child's language development. However, joint attention may be achieved in different ways; two particular interactional styles have been identified. One style, *attention following*, occurs when the caregiver uses the infant's attentional focus as a cue to determine which event or object might be an appropriate point for conversation or discussion (i.e., the caregiver "follows" the infant's lead). The other style, which is called *attention switching*, occurs when the caregiver attempts to direct the infant's attention from an object or event on which he or she is focused to another one for purposes of conversation or discussion (i.e., the caregiver actively "switches" the infant's attentional focus).

In keeping with an interactional model, it is plausible to propose that attention following and attention switching might interact with infants' attentional profiles to contribute to cognitive outcome. For example, one might generate a 2 x 2 contingency table, in which infants' attentional profiles are crossed with caregivers' interactional styles.

Using this approach, one finds two sets of hypotheses that are equally tenable (see table 2.1). First is a set of hypotheses based on an optimal

Table 2.1 Different Combinations Generated by the Infant Attention_Caregiver Style Interaction

(a) Predictions of Cognitive Outcome Generated by Environment _ Infant "Match" Hypotheses

	Infant attentional profile	
Caregiver's interactional style	Long-looking	Short-looking
Attention switching	Less optimal	More optimal
Attention following	More optimal	Less optimal

(b) Predictions of Cognitive Outcome Generated by Environment _ Infant "Stimulation" Hypotheses

	Infant attentional profile	
Caregiver's interactional style	Long-looking	Short-looking
Attention switching	More optimal	Less optimal
Attention following	Less optimal	More optimal

"match" between the infant's attentional capacities and the caregiver's interactional styles. Twenty years ago, Thomas and Chess (1977) proposed that the "match" between styles of infant temperament and caregiver interaction served as the primary backdrop for social and cognitive development. Miceli et al. (1998) have recently reiterated this sentiment in their study of the interaction between temperamental and maternal factors as determinants of infant cognitive performance. Here, long-looking infants, who appear to process information more slowly (Colombo & Mitchell, 1990) and who tend to disengage attention from visual stimuli less readily (Frick, Colombo, & Saxon, 1999) than short-looking infants, might profit most from caregivers whose interactive style is adapted to their slower rate of visual exploration and encoding through attention following. Short-lookers, on the other hand, who process information more quickly and who more readily switch attention from one stimulus to another, might be better paired with caregivers whose style is characterized by attention switching, with a more active and varied in presentation of objects during play (see table 2.1a).

A second set of hypotheses is based on the notion that the paramount concern might be the delivery of environmental stimulation to the infant (e.g., Hart & Risley, 1995). These hypotheses make opposite predictions from the "match" hypothesis with regard to the types of interactions that might yield good cognitive outcomes. Here, long-looking infants might be best served by caregivers who actively and continuously provide stimulation through attention switching. Short-lookers might not need the environmental support or "scaffolding" provided by switching, and thus might profit more from "setting their own agenda" with caregivers who engage in attention following (see table 2.1b).

We have actually had an opportunity to examine such interactions based on a longitudinal follow-up of a small subset of infants tested in the Saxon et al. (1997) study. Twenty-one of the more than sixty infants in this study were tested at forty months on the standard Weschler preschool scale. One change to the formats shown in tables 1a and 1b is necessitated by the fact that attention switching and attention following are not mutually exclusive. That is, caregivers who score high on one of the styles do not necessarily score low on the other (Saxon et al., 1997). As a result, it is necessary to generate two 2 X 2 tables, one each to represent high and low values of attention switching and attention following. In each, we split values of look duration at six months at the median to form groups of long- and short-looking infants. These two groups are then crossed with high and low values of attention switching in one table and with high and low values of attention following in the other. As with look duration, both of these latter groups are formed through median splits of caregiver switching and following at six months. The results are presented in table 2.2.

It is important to note that the differences portrayed in table 2.2 do not attain conventional levels of statistical significance largely because of the

Table 2.2 Weschler Preschool IQ (40 Months) as a Function of Individual Differences in Infant Look Duration at 6 Months and High Versus Low Frequencies of Caregiver Attention Shifting (a) and Attention Following

(a) Caregiver Attention Shifting and Look Duration

	Infant attentional profile	
Caregiver attention shifting	Long-looking	Short-looking
High	109.2	98.0
Low	99.7	105.5

(b) Caregiver Attention Following and Look Duration

	Infant attentional profile	
Caregiver attention following	Long-looking	Short-looking
High	104.8	106.3
Low	103.0	98.7

small sample sizes involved (there are no more than six children in any one cell). As a result, we are in no position to make strong claims about these specific findings. However, we do think that the trends displayed here suggest the potential importance of this type of approach and we encourage others to consider such interactions in longitudinal analyses.

The data shown in table 2.2 do indeed suggest that the different caregiving styles may interact with the infant's attentional profile to yield different developmental outcomes. The pattern evident in table 2.2a is consistent with the "stimulation" hypothesis set laid out in table 2.1b. That is, increased attentional switching was beneficial to long-looking infants, but less switching was better for short-looking infants. In addition, table 2.2b suggests that attention following was more beneficial for short-looking infants than for long-looking infants, again in general accord with the "stimulation" hypothesis set.

However, let us propose a step beyond the one we have proposed. The interaction model we have presented is attractive, but it assumes that neither the caregiver nor the infant adjusts to one another or otherwise changes. In fact, developmental hypotheses have been proposed for adaptation and change in attention following and switching. For example, attention following is thought to be appropriate or facilitative during joint attention at later ages, or when the infant is capable of initiating his or her own didactic opportunities (e.g., Bakeman & Adamson, 1984). At younger ages, however (e.g., six months), attention switching has been proposed to be a means by which the mother can support the infant's passive interest in objects (Dunham & Dunham, 1995). Given that look duration also undergoes interesting changes during the first year (Colombo & Mitchell, 1990; see also Colombo, Harlan, & Mitchell, 1999), it is possible that the best model might incorporate changes in each of these factors across ages and cross-correlations between a particular infant's current cognitive ability with the style that a particular caregiver might be predisposed to use. This description more closely approximates a fully-transactional set of relationships in which both infant and caregiver adjust to one another over the course of time, as shown in figure 2.4.

SUMMARY AND CONCLUSION

In this chapter, we have described the prediction phenomenon, in which measures of cognition in infancy show significant prediction to cognitive status in childhood and adolescence. We presented a series of models that seek to explain the prediction phenomenon, beginning with simple psychometrically-inspired systems that rely on underlying cognitive factors within the infant to explain continuity and ending with complex models that incorporate environmental influence that transacts with infant cognitive factors over time. We have shown how these more complex models are still consistent with the fundamental observations reported in the prediction phenomenon. As such, we have tried to make the case that environmental input acts as a *moderator* in producing the continuity observed in the prediction phenomenon. Furthermore, we have presented both theoretical and empirical perspectives that bear on the feasibility of the more complex models. Finally, we have outlined a series of hypotheses involving infant attention and caregiver interactional style that provide a concrete example of the kind of tests that might be used to evaluate these complex models. In this last section, we presented some preliminary longitudinal evidence that we feel bolsters the case for further consideration of such models.

If environmental moderation truly contributes to the continuity of cognitive development several important implications for theory, research, practice, and service to infants and children cannot be overlooked. Some of the theoretical and empirical implications have been delineated elsewhere (e.g., Colombo, 1997; Colombo & Frick, 1999). In this final section, however, we briefly outline some of the more practical considerations that these complex models present.

First, simply speaking, these transactional models quite forcefully reiterate the importance of environmental input in the determination of cognitive and intellectual development in infants and children. Despite the fact that developmental scientists in the behavioral sciences and education often hold this as a fundamental and unspoken assumption, it is an assumption that needs to be repeated and emphasized often. We have tried to show that correlations between early measures in infancy and later status in childhood do not necessarily eliminate consideration of environmental contributions.

Second, these transactional models clearly imply that our ability to predict cognitive development or status in childhood solely from measures of the infant's cognitive performance will always be seriously limited. Although a measure of the infant's cognition may provide a clue to that infant's intellectual status later in childhood, such clues may not, in and of themselves, ever provide a clinically or practically useful means for early identification of infants at risk for later cognitive deficits. If these complex models more accurately represent the developmental paths to cognitive ability in childhood, any attempt to identify individuals at risk for cognitive deficits will necessarily involve the assessment of the environment as well.

Third, the more complex models we have presented here also imply that early identification may not be best addressed by assessments of the child and his or her environment at one or two points during infancy. Rather, they clearly suggest that the best strategy for early identification involves periodic tracking during infancy and the assessment of a developmental course of both infant and environmental factors. Perhaps the best analogy for this implication comes from the common way in which height and weight is assessed by pediatricians during infant development. For example, a single assessment showing that an infant is in the tenth percentile for weight is not necessarily an indication of long-term risk. Rather, that risk is indicated by a failure to grow and change (e.g., failure to maintain that percentile rank) as indicated by intensive and repeated (i.e., longitudinal) assessments across the first several years. As such, the transactional models of cognitive development imply the need for the same longitudinal assessment strategy.

The fourth and final implication of these more complex models is that interventions designed for infants who might be at risk for later cognitive deficits should incorporate a longitudinal and developmental strategy as well. We have noted that different environmental strategies (e.g., caregiver styles) may be differentially effective at different ages. Environmental interventions that might therefore be appropriate for infants at a less mature stage of cognitive function may not be appropriate infants who have attained a more mature status. Thus, effective implementation of such interventions will include training caregivers not only in how to deliver different interventions, but in how to know (based on an assessment of the infant's cognitive status) which of the interventions is appropriate.

It is worth noting in closing, that these complex models of development present the developmentalist with truly imposing challenges. However, it is also quite likely that the accurate early identification of individuals at risk for cognitive deficits and the implementation of appropriately designed interventions early in life will be highly cost-effective relative to remedial programs implemented later in life. In this chapter, we have outlined a potential path to this goal that will be difficult but worthwhile in the long run in terms of both human and societal capital.

REFERENCES

Abelson, R. P. (1985). A variance explanation paradox: When a little means a lot. *Psychological Bulletin*, 97, 129–133.

Bakeman, R., & Adamson, L. B. (1984). Coordinating attention to people and objects in mother-infant and peer-infant interaction. *Child Development*, 55, 1278–1289.

Bell, R. Q. (1968). A reinterpretation of the direction of effects in studies of socialization. *Psychological Review*, 75, 81–95.

Bell, R. Q. (1971). Stimulus control of parent or caretaker behavior of offspring. *Developmental Psychology*, 4, 63–72.

Bell, R. Q. (1979). Parent, child, and reciprocal influences. *American Psychologist*, 34, 821–826.

Bornstein, M. H. (1985). How infant and mother jointly contribute to developing cognitive competence in the child. *Proceedings of the National Academy of Science*, 82, 7470–7473.

Bornstein, M. H. (1990). Attention in infancy and the prediction of cognitive capacities in childhood. In J. T. Enns, et al. (Eds.), *The development of attention: Research and theory* (Advances in psychology, Vol. 69., pp. 3–19). Amsterdam, Netherlands: North Holland.

Bornstein, M. H., & Sigman, M. D. (1986). Continuity in mental development from infancy. *Child Development*, 57, 251–274.

Bornstein, M. H., Slater, A., Brown, E., Roberts, E. & Barrett, J. (1997). Stability of mental development from infancy to later childhood: Three "waves" of research. In G. Bremner, A. Slater et al. (Eds.), *Infant development: Recent advances* (pp. 191–215). Hove, UK: Psychology Press/Taylor & Francis.

Bornstein, M. H., & Tamis-LeMonda, C. S. (1994). Antecedents of information-processing skills in infants: Habituation, novelty responsiveness, and cross-modal transfer. *Infant Behavior and Development*, 17, 371–380.

Canfield, R., Wilken, J., Schmerl, L., & Smith, E. G. (1995). Age related change and stability of individual differences in infant saccade reaction time. *Infant Behavior and Development*, 18, 351–358.

Colombo, J. (1993). *Infant cognition: Predicting childhood intelligence*. Newbury Park, CA: Sage.

Colombo, J. (1995). On the neural mechanisms underlying individual differences in infant fixation duration: Two hypotheses. *Developmental Review*, 15, 97–135.

Colombo, J. (1997). Individual differences in infant cognition: Methods, measures and models. In J. Dobbing (Ed.), *Developing brain and behavior: The role of lipids in infant formulas* (Chapter text: pp. 339–372; Commentary and Author's replies: pp. 372–385). London: Academic Press.

Colombo, J., & Fagen, J. W. (Eds.). (1990). *Individual differences in infancy: Reliability, stability, and prediction*. Hillsdale, NJ: Erlbaum.

Colombo, J., & Frick, J. E. (1999). Recent advances and issues in the study of preverbal intelligence. In M. Anderson (Ed.), *Development of intelligence*. London: University College of London Press.

Colombo, J., Harlan, J. E., & Mitchell, D. W. (1999, April). *The development of look duration in infancy: Evidence for a triphasic course.* Poster presented at the meeting of the Society for Research in Child Development, Albuquerque, NM.

Colombo, J., & Janowsky, J. S. (1998). A cognitive neuroscience approach to individual differences in infant cognition. In J. E. Richards (Ed.), *The cognitive neuroscience of attention: A developmental perspective* (pp. 363–392). Hillsdale, NJ: Erlbaum.

Colombo, J., & Mitchell, D. W. (1990). Individual and developmental differences in infant visual attention. In J. Colombo & J. W. Fagen (Eds.), *Individual differences in infancy* (pp. 193–227). Hillsdale, NJ: Erlbaum.

Diamond, A., Prevor, M. B., Callender, G., & Druin, D. P. (1997). Prefrontal cortex cognitive deficits in children treated early and continuously for PKU. *Monographs of the Society for Research in Child Development*, 62, 1–205.

Dougherty, T. M., & Haith, M. M. (1997). Infant expectations and reaction time as predictors of childhood speed of processing and IQ. *Developmental Psychology*, 33, 146–155.

Doussard Roosevelt, J. A., Porges, S. W., Scanlon, J. W., Alemi, B., & Scanlon, K. B. (1997). Vagal regulation of heart rate in the prediction of developmental outcome for very low birth weight preterm infants. *Child Development.* 68, 173–186.

Dunham, P., & Dunham, F. (1995). Optimal social structures and adaptive infant development. In C. Moore & P. Dunham (Eds.), *Joint attention: Its origin and role in development* (pp. 159–188). Hillsdale, NJ: Lawrence Erlbaum Associates.

Edelman, G. (1987). *Neural Darwinism.* New York: Basic Books.

Fagan, J. F. (1990). The paired-comparison paradigm and infant intelligence. *Annals of the New York Academy of Sciences*, 608, 337–364.

Fagan, J. F., & McGrath, S. K. (1981). Infant recognition memory and later intelligence. *Intelligence*, 5, 121–130.

Fagen, J. W. (1995). Predicting IQ from infancy: We're getting closer. *Contemporary Psychology*, 40, 19–20.

Fagen, J. W., & Ohr, P. S. (1990). Individual differences in infant conditioning and memory. In J. Colombo & J. W. Fagen (Eds.), *Individual differences in infancy* (pp. 155–192). Hillsdale, NJ: Lawrence Erlbaum Associates.

Farran, D. C., & Harber, L. A. (1989). Responses to a learning task at 6 months and I.Q. test performance during the preschool years. *International Journal of Behavioral Development*, 12, 101–114.

Frick, J.E., Colombo, J., & Saxon, T. F. (1999). Individual and developmental differences in disengagement of fixation in early infancy. *Child Development*, 70, 537–548.

Gottlieb, G. (1997). *Synthesizing nature/nurture.* Mahwah, NJ: Erlbaum.

Hart, B., & Risley, T. (1995). *Meaningful differences.* Baltimore: Brookes.

Jacobson S.W. Evidence for speed of processing and recognition memory components of infant information processing. Paper presented at the biennial meeting of the Society for Research in Child Development, Indianapolis, IN. (1995).

Jacobson, S. W. (1998). Specificity of neurobehavioral outcomes associated with prenatal alcohol exposure. *Alcoholism: Clinical and Experimental Research,* 22, 313–320.

Jacobson, S. W., Fein, G. G., Jacobson, J. L., Schwartz, P. M., & Dowler, J. K. (1985). The effects of intrauterine PCB exposure on visual recognition memory. *Child Development,* 56, 853–860.

Jacobson, S. W., Jacobson, J. L., O'Neill, J. M., Padgett, R. J., Frankowski, J. J., & Bihun, J. T. (1992). Visual expectation and dimensions of infant information processing. *Child Development,* 63, 711–724.

Jacobson, S. W., Jacobson, J. L., Sokol, R. J., Martier, S. S., & Ager, J. W. (1993). Prenatal alcohol exposure and infant information processing ability. *Child Development,* 64, 1706–1721.

Lucas, A. (1997). Commentary on Colombo. In J. Dobbing (Ed.), *Developing brain and behavior: The role of lipids in infant formulas* (pp. 378–380). London: Academic Press.

Mayes, L. C., & Bornstein, M. H. (1995). Infant information-processing performance and maternal education. *Early Human Development,* 4, 891–896.

McCall, R. B., & Carriger, M. (1993). A meta-analysis of infant habituation and recognition memory performance as predictors of later IQ. *Child Development,* 64, 57–79.

McCall, R. B., & Mash, C. (1995). Infant cognition and its relation to mature intelligence. In G. Whitehurst (Ed.), *Annals of child development* (Vol. 11, pp. 27–56). Greenwich, CT: JAI.

Miceli, P. J., Whitman, T. L., Borkowski, J. G., Braungart-Rieker, J., & Mitchell, D. W. (1998). Individual differences in infant information processing: The role of temperamental and maternal factors. *Infant Behavior and Development,* 21, 119–136.

Mitchell, D. W., McCollam, K., Horowitz, F. D., Embretson, S. E., & O'Brien, M. (1991, April). *The interacting contribution of constitutional, environmental, and information processing factors to early developmental outcome.* Society for Research in Child Development, Seattle, WA.

Molfese, D. L., Molfese, V. J., Gill, L. A., & Benshoff, S. (1997). Correlates of language development: Electrophysiological and behavioral measures. In H. W. Reese, M. D. Franzen et al. (Eds.), *Biological and neuropsychological mechanisms: Life-span developmental psychology* (pp. 71–94). Mahwah, NJ: Lawrence Erlbaum Associates.

Molfese, V. J., DiLalla, L. F., & Lovelace, L. (1996). Perinatal, home environment, and infant measures as successful predictors of preschool cognitive and verbal abilities. *International Journal of Behavioral Development,* 19, 101–119.

Oyama, S. (1985). *The ontogeny of information.* Cambridge, UK: Cambridge University Press.

Robson, A. L., & Pederson, D. R. (1997). Predictors of individual differences in attention among low birth weight children. *Journal of Developmental and Behavioral Pediatrics,* 18, 13–21.

Rose, S. A., & Feldman, J. F. (1995a). Prediction of IQ and specific cognitive abilities at 11 years from infancy measures. *Developmental Psychology, 31,* 685–696.

Rose, S. A., & Feldman, J. F. (1995b, March). *Cognitive continuity from infancy: A single thread or a twisted skein?* Presented at the meeting of the Society for Research in Child Development, Indianapolis, IN.

Ruddy, M., & Bornstein, M. H. (1982). Cognitive correlates of infant attention and maternal stimulation over the first year of life. *Child Development, 53,* 183–188.

Sameroff, A. (1975). Transactional models in early social relations. *Human Development,* 18, 65–79.

Sameroff, A. J. (1983). Developmental systems: Contexts and evolution. In P. Mussen (Series Ed.) & W. Kessen (Volume Ed.), *Handbook of child psychology. Vol. 1: History, theory, and methods* (pp. 237–294). New York: Wiley.

Sameroff, A. J., & Chandler, M. J. (1975). Reproductive risk and the continuum of caretaking casualty. In F. D. Horowitz (Ed.), *Review of child development research* (Vol. 4). Chicago: University of Chicago Press.

Saxon, T. F., Frick, J. E., & Colombo, J. (1997). Individual differences in infant visual fixation and maternal interactional styles. *Merrill-Palmer Quarterly,* 43, 48–66.

Sigman, M. D., Cohen, S. E., & Beckwith, L. (1997). Why does infant attention predict adolescent intelligence? *Infant Behavior and Development,* 20, 33–140.

Sigman, M. D., Cohen, S. E., Beckwith, L., Asarnow, R., & Parmelee, A. H. (1991). Continuity in cognitive abilities from infancy to 12 years of age. *Cognitive Development,* 6, 47–57.

Sigman, M. D., Cohen, S. E., Beckwith, L., & Parmelee, A. H. (1986). Infant attention in relation to intellectual abilities in childhood. *Developmental Psychology,* 22, 788–792.

Skranes, J., Vik, T. Nilsen, G. Smevik, O., Andersson, H. W., & Brubakk, A. M. (1998). Can cerebral MRI at age 1 year predict motor and intellectual outcomes in very-low-birthweight children? *Developmental Medicine and Child Neurology.* 40, 256–262.

Tamis-LeMonda, C. S., & Bornstein, M. H. (1989). Habituation and maternal encouragement of attention in infancy as predictors of toddler language, play, and representational competence. *Child Development,* 60, 738–751.

Thomas, A., & Chess, S. (1977). *Temperament and development.* New York: Brunner-Mazel.

Tomasello, M. (1992). The social bases of language acquisition. *Social Development,* 1, 68–87.

AUTHORS' NOTES

John Colombo is Professor and Graduate Director of the Department of Human Development at University of Kansas.

Preparation of this chapter was supported by NIH Grants HD29960 and HD35903 to the senior author. The authors thank Julie Harlan, Julie Maikranz, Allen Richman, Jill Shaddy, Dale Walker, and the editors of this volume for constructive comments on earlier drafts.

NOTE

1. The form of figure 2.4 is by no means an original idea, as the general form of transactional models can be found in many developmental sources dating back over twenty years. A model very much like the one depicted in figure 2.4, however, guided the Kansas Infant Development Project, a longitudinal study run from 1985 to 1990. Dr. Frances D. Horowitz, Dr. Marion O'Brien and Dr. Wayne Mitchell all contributed to the development of this model, and thus deserve acknowledgement here.

NUTRITION
How Does It Affect Cognitive and Behavioral Development in Young Children?

Mark Swanson

3

◆◆◆◆

The answers to the question in the title of this chapter start well before birth. Indeed, the influence of nutrition begins even before conception. This chapter will discuss the ways nutrition definitively—and possibly—affects brain development. We must also be sure to acknowledge other biologic and environmental factors that interact with nutrition to influence brain development. Finally, this chapter will also discuss the role of prevention and intervention in countering the adverse effects of poor nutrition.

PRENATAL ISSUES

Preconceptual Issues

It has often been noted that teenagers are more likely to have adverse pregnancy outcomes than older women: smaller babies, a higher number of premature babies, more stillbirths, and more neonatal deaths. While factors such as lack of prenatal care, indifferent compliance with diet, and the use of drugs and alcohol have been offered as explanations, there has been recent interest in the nutritional status of teens before they become pregnant. Women who are underweight before pregnancy are likely to gain less than the optimal 9.1 kg during pregnancy (Brown et al., 1992) and to have lower birthweight babies. Additionally, women who have recently delivered babies may not have replenished their nutrient stores of trace minerals, vitamins, and essential fatty acids when they become pregnant again and thus may not be able to provide the optimal nutrition environment for the new fetus.

Prenatal Nutrition

Normal growth parameters are considered to be those between the 5th and 95th percentiles for age. For birth length, this range is 18¹/₂ inches to

21¹/₂ inches for boys, and 18 inches to 21 inches for girls. For birth weight, the range is 2.6 kilograms to 4.2 kilograms (5.7 pounds to 9.2 pounds) for boys and 2.5 kilograms to 3.8 kilograms (5.5. pounds to 8.4 pounds) for girls. For head circumference, the range is 32.5 cm to 37.2 cm for boys and 32.2 to 35.7 cm for girls. The first parameter in the fetus affected by malnutrition is weight. The next is length. The last one is head size. Accordingly, one can judge the degree of malnourishment by looking at the baby's proportions. If the baby's head is small, that is evidence of the most lasting and severe malnutrition in fetal life.

Many studies have looked at the effects of malnutrition during pregnancy on prenatal brain development. Most have found no impact for mild malnutrition on brain development, as nutrients (calories, lipids, micronutrients) are directed to the brain under conditions of mild malnutrition. There is still some risk involved with the malnutrition associated with low birthweight. Women who do not have adequate caloric intake to sustain optimal weight gain must catabolize their maternal tissue, leading to excess production of acetone (a by-product of starvation). Excess acetone in pregnant mothers has been associated with lower IQs in their offspring (Berendez, 1975).

Body mass index (BMI), and the ponderal index are measures of nutrition status. A Brazilian study found that undernourished children who are more proportional at birth, as measured by the ponderal index, are more likely to have developmental delays: four points on the Bayley MDI and seven points on the Bayley PDI (Grantham-McGregor, Lira, Ashworth, Morris & Assuncao, 1998). This is so because symmetrical growth retardation indicates brain injury (compared to asymmetrical growth retardation, which involves only height or weight).

A prenatal diet resulting in maternal weight gain of 25 to 30 pounds will almost always ensure an adequate nutrient environment for the growing fetus and avoid any nutrition-associated risk to the brain. Most pregnant mothers' diets should concentrate on the provision of adequate protein, calories, and lipids. The growing fetus receives nutrition via the placenta. The fetus synthesizes fat from the glucose. Lipids and essential fatty acids are the building blocks of the central nervous system and these also come to the fetus through the maternal circulation. Lipid content increases from 1% at twenty weeks to 15% at term (Widdowson, 1987), a reflection of the need of the growing brain for this vital substrate.

Experiments with rats have shown that selective reduction in essential fatty acids (EFAs) in the diet of the pregnant mother leads to decreased size in midline brain structures, so there is some suggestion that fetal brain malformation may occur when there is extreme deprivation of EFAs in the diets of pregnant mothers. The human fetus exercises effective sparing of the brain from EFA deficiencies, so structural changes in the human brain tend to be microscopic and difficult to detect using conventional in vivo techniques.

There has been interest in the effects of prenatal vitamins on the development of the child. It seems possible that vitamin deficiencies could predispose a child to suboptimal brain development. Recent discovery of the importance of folic acid in preventing neural tube defects has been the most dramatic development in this area. Population-based studies have conclusively demonstrated a decreased incidence of spina bifida and other neural tube defects (situations where the developing fetus incompletely covers the brain or spinal cord with tissue) when prenatal diets are supplemented with folic acid, a common vitamin present in most foods. The addition of folic acid to regular prenatal vitamins has the potential to greatly reduce this severe, chronic disorder.

Zinc deficiency in rats has been associated with malformations in rat babies. This finding has led to increased interest in establishing a causative relationship between deficiencies in trace elements (zinc, copper, manganese, magnesium) and vitamins (folic acid, Vitamin A and Vitamin B12) and birth defects. However, researchers have found no evidence that trace element and vitamin deficiency is the mechanism of other birth defects (Stoll et al., 1999). In a Hungarian study, providing prenatal multivitamins did not result in any changes in cognitive ability at six years (Dobo & Czeizel, 1998). An international study did find decreased incidence of childhood brain tumors in women who used multivitamins during pregnancy, especially those who used supplements all three trimesters (Preston-Martin et al., 1998).

Prenatal Exposures

There is a greater nutritional hazard to pregnant mothers than diet variations, even those practiced by adolescents: the exposure to toxic substances that occur in high concentrations in natural diets in certain areas. The human brain is especially sensitive to methylmercury, a human neurotoxin, which is present in oceanic fish. Studies in Iraq have suggested adverse developmental outcomes associated with high levels of methylmercury in mothers. A recent study in the Republic of Seychelles tested the hypothesis that fetal methylmercury exposure results in adverse neurodevelopmental outcomes. Testing of the children at 66 months age, using standard cognitive and language measures, found mercury effects only in the area of auditory comprehension (Myers et al., 1995).

Another fish-borne contaminant that has received extensive study is polychlorinated biphenyls (PCBs). PCBs bioconcentrate from water into aquatic animals and accumulate in the food chain. Human exposure is mainly from meat, dairy products, and fish. Prenatal PCB exposure had a small negative effect on psychomotor scores at three months of age (Koopman-Esseboom et al., 1996) which had disappeared by eighteen months of age.

Another potentially dangerous substance is pesticides. These include organophosphates, fungicides, and arsenic, all of which are found in the soil of agricultural areas of the U.S. Greater-than-expected urine levels of pesticide residues are found in children of agricultural workers, but the danger of these levels is unknown. Pesticides may prevent or slow cell proliferation and cause unprogrammed cell death. Current research is focusing on in utero midbrain development and postnatal development of the cerebellum and hippocampus. The midbrain provides connections between the cortex and spinal cord, the hippocampus is important in spatial learning and memory, and the cerebellum influences motor activity (Wick, 1999).

Summary of Prenatal Issues

There is a wide range of maternal nutrition that will allow for normal fetal brain growth. Inadequate energy intake, as reflected in low maternal weight gain, is a risk factor, although the fetus does its best to spare the brain of any deleterious effects of malnutrition. Vitamins and trace minerals are usually not a problem, because of the remarkable ability of the human fetus to conserve them. A bigger risk is the nutritional state of the mother. Mothers who have had recent pregnancies may be nutritionally depleted and the children of pregnant teenagers are at risk because the teenager's need for nutrition to complete her own growth competes with her fetus' special need for nutrition. Exposures to environmental contaminants also pose a risk for certain populations whose diet contains contaminated food.

SPECIAL PROBLEMS OF PREMATURE INFANTS

Babies born prematurely have special risks for brain development that are related to nutrition. These include complications of parenteral nutrition, composition of milk, and oral motor issues associated with tube feedings.

Parenteral Nutrition

Babies born very prematurely (< 1500 gms) often have difficulty getting adequate nutrition through their gastrointestinal system. The g-i system simply cannot absorb enough calories to meet the needs of the child. So parenteral alimentation has to be used. This consists of fat (lipids), protein, and calories administered intravenously. The issue regarding brain development is the ideal composition of lipids in the alimentation. Lipids and essential fatty acids are the building blocks of brain development. The challenge is to duplicate as closely as possible the nutrition that the baby would get if he or she were still in utero. Lipids supply most of the calories in intravenous feeding. The type of fat most easily absorbed may not be what the baby needs for optimal brain development, so special attention must be paid to ensure that at least 3% of the calories are provided by linoleic acid to prevent essential fatty acid deficiency.

Docosahexenoic acid (DHA) and arachidonic acid (AA) are two essential fatty acids that appear to play a large role in brain development. Most intravenous lipids supplied to premature babies do not contain DHA or AA. Tissue levels of DHA and AA in vital organs, including the brain, fall during intravenous lipid infusion, so there is concern about potential effects on brain development (Friedman & Frohlich, 1979).

Another challenge of intravenous feeding is aluminum toxicity. Bishop et al. (1997) reported that premature infants with prolonged standard intravenous feeding had Bayley scores ten points lower than those receiving aluminum-depleted intravenous feeding of the same duration.

Composition of Milk

Neonatologists and nutritionists try to supply basic nutrition through the intravenous alimentation while steadily advancing enteral feeding (tube feeding into the intestines). The composition of enteral feedings has also changed over the years as more has been learned about brain development. Breast milk, preferably the mother's own, is the feeding substance of choice. Preterm breast milk contains higher concentrations of fat, protein, and minerals than term breast milk, so it is preferred. Commercial formula does not supply the lipids and essential fatty acids needed for optimal brain growth but is superior to breast milk in supplying protein and calories for optimal weight gain. In all, there remains a great challenge in supplying premature babies with the right combination of nutrients provided in enteral feeding for health, growth, and development.

Oral Motor Development

Another developmental issue facing premature babies is oral motor development. Babies who are fed through nasogastric tubes (thin tubes passed from the nose to the stomach) need oral stimulation to imitate the stimulation they would normally receive through sucking. Oral stimulation should be a part of every premature baby's intervention. Complicating this effort is the fact that premature babies often are on ventilators because of immature lungs. The presence of an endotracheal tube (a tube passed through the mouth into the child's trachea) in the child's oral cavity interferes with normal oral motor function and requires intervention after the child is extubated. The intervention for delayed oral motor development and hypersensitivity should be an oral feeding program, usually directed by a speech or occupational therapist. The program is necessary to promote normal sucking and swallowing as well as overcome sensitivity.

Another issue is the oral hypersensitivity that develops when babies have tubes (either nasogastric or endotracheal) in their mouths for long periods of time. These babies are at risk for delayed oral motor (including oral language) skills. This hypersensitivity makes oral feeding difficult and can interfere with the normally positive parent-child interaction that occurs around feeding.

Finally, some premature babies have such severe lung immaturity that they need long-term breathing support through a tracheostomy. This is an opening in the neck through which a tube passes directly into the trachea. After tracheostomies are removed, these children are likely to have an expressive language disability (Hill & Singer, 1990).

Summary of Issues for Premature Babies

Babies born prematurely are deprived of the finely-tuned nutritional environment they would normally receive through the placenta. Efforts to supply adequate nutrition to premature babies originally focused on promoting weight gain. More and more attention is now being paid to the optimal nutrition for brain development, as the long-term developmental problems of premature babies have become apparent. Continued research is needed to determine which, how much and by what method (intravenous vs. enteral) essential fatty acids should be supplied to the premature baby.

POSTNATAL NUTRITION

The vast majority of babies are born with adequate nutritional status. Their brains have received optimal nutrition through their mothers' placentae. Because the brain is in the midst of rapid growth at the time of birth, it must continue to receive ideal nutrition to finalize its growth. This is especially important in the first three years of life. Issues in postnatal life will be discussed next.

Normal Growth

In the first three months of life, normal weight gain is about one ounce per day (slightly less for girls), so that babies double their birthweight by around four months of age (slightly more than four months for girls, slightly less for boys). Babies triple birth weight by twelve months for girls and $10^{1/2}$ months for boys. On average, babies increase length about 50% in the first year of life. Head circumference increases by just over one-third over the same period.

Failure-to-thrive (FTT) is one term used to describe abnormal growth. Definitions vary, but the most common one includes two growth patterns: 1) children who do not grow normally in length (as determined by falling height percentiles); and 2) children whose weight is less than the fifth percentile for height (as plotted on a standard growth chart). The diagnosis of FTT does not speak to its cause, which can be biological, environmental, or a combination of the two. Chronic malnutrition can certainly lead to FTT.

Mechanisms and Specific Effects of Malnutrition on the Brain

Conventional thinking in the 1960s and 1970s held that the mammalian brain was most susceptible to malnutrition during its time of most rapid growth. Consequently, it was believed that structures such as the hippocampus, cerebrum, and cerebellum would be most susceptible to structural damage if malnutrition occurred during the times of maximum growth. Actual findings in rat studies indicated that the total number of brain cells was not reduced by malnutrition, but that cortical structures were dramatically altered by malnutrition. Predictions for irreversible alteration in cognitive function based on these anatomical effects have proven to be overstated. The mammalian brain has proven to have a great capacity for rehabilitation after proper nutrition is restored.

While these studies have made anatomical recovery from early malnutrition seem more likely, attention has turned to the long-term effects on the response characteristics of the brain in children. The effects of early malnutrition may be mediated through an alteration in neurotransmitter metabolism. There are strong suggestions from animal research that the neurotransmitter system is permanently altered by early malnutrition.

A specific area of interest is a decreased ability in downregulation of adrenergic receptors. A functional consequence of this impaired regulation may be a diminished ability to adapt to stressful situations (Levitsky & Strupp, 1995). Response to endogenous and exogenous neurotransmitter chemicals may be permanently decreased due to early malnutrition.

The hippocampus, a midline brain structure important in modulating activity between the two hemispheres, is irreversibly changed by early malnutrition. The number of cells and their function are decreased by early malnutrition. Additionally, the cerebellum, important in balance and motor function, can be severely affected by early malnutrition. Delays in psychomotor development have been consistently observed in malnourished children. More of the changes in the cerebellum appear to be reversible with nutritional rehabilitation than previously suspected.

So one focus of current research is measurement of brain neural receptor function as the permanent legacy of early malnutrition, rather than structural changes per se. These are likely to be manifested clinically as impaired emotional responses to stress rather than direct effects on intelligence. Two broad headings have emerged as leading possibilities for permanent effects. The first is an alteration in motivation and/or emotional reactivity. The second is decreased cognitive flexibility.

Alteration in Motivation and Reactivity

The motivational/emotional factors would be expected to have a substantial effect on problem-solving ability (Strupp & Levitsky, 1995). This has led to interest in two experimental approaches: selective attention and analysis of response style. A narrowed focus of attention is a likely cognitive outcome of malnutrition. Animal studies have found impaired incidental learning but no effect on intentional learning in malnourished subjects. Response style study is likely to find increased frustration in response to failure.

Decreased Cognitive Flexibility

The issue of cognitive flexibility raises the question of whether the impacts of malnutrition on the brain are a motivational/emotional alteration or a different cognitive impairment. The following discussion summarizes the new thinking about the nature and etiology of long-lasting effects of early malnutrition on the human brain. The clinical manifestations have been studied by a number of researchers, especially in developing countries in Latin America and the Caribbean. While studies vary in specific outcomes, it seems clear that better nutrition is associated with better cognitive and behavioral outcomes, independent of social and environmental factors. One of the most consistent findings has been the positive impact of good nutrition on infant motor skills. Less consistent results have been reported on mental development during the same age range (Gorman, 1995). In Jamaica, malnourished infants were assigned to one of four groups: control, nutritional supplementation, psychosocial stimulation or both interventions. Both interventions were found to have independent beneficial effects on motor development, with the combined interventions more effective than either one alone (Grantham et al., 1991). Husaini and colleagues (1991) found that supplemental feedings in Indonesian infants improved motor but not mental skills. In Guatemala, Pollitt and colleagues (1995) found that infants and young children, given a protein supplement, had improved scores in knowledge, numeracy, reading and vocabulary at school age. Limitations of the studies to date include a lack of specific information about the diets provided. Diets have varied in quality and quantity and often have not been measured very precisely. So the mechanism of the positive response to "good" nutrition remains to be understood. Is it simply the number of calories or is protein important? What about the role of elements such as iron and zinc? Cognitive behavior may be a final outcome, heavily mediated by motor maturation, activity level, and exploratory behavior, as Pollitt and his colleagues have suggested (Pollitt, Gorman, Engle, Rivera, & Martorell, 1995). Studies need to have more process variables collected, consider interaction effects, and last longer than the ages where brain development is typically considered to be sensitive to nutrition in order to better answer these questions.

The provision of nutrition does not occur in a vacuum. It is supplied in the context of family and community. Changes in diet invariably involve dynamic changes in the family unit and often in the community. These variables and their interactions need to be considered in future research.

Effects of Severe Malnutrition on Development

Severe malnutrition is a general description of a variety of clinical pictures that have different etiologies. The International Classification of Disease (ICD) system defines three states of primary malnutrition:

Kwashiorkor-like syndrome. Child appears to be well-nourished but lacks adequate protein. Measurements may be normal but resistance to disease is compromised.

Marasmus-like syndrome. Child is visibly underweight with depleted muscle and fat stores. Serum protein is maintained until late in the course.

Acute state combining kwashiorkor and marasmus. Mildly malnourished child develops this condition as a result of severe trauma and stress.

The studies of severe malnutrition have used growth parameters to define severe malnutrition without regard to etiology. Severe malnutrition occurs most prominently in areas like Sub-Saharan Africa, where drought and armed conflict have led to severe famine.

In acute stages, severe malnutrition causes children to become more apathetic, to be less active, and to explore their environments less as demonstrated most vividly in studies of Jamaican children (Grantham-McGregor, 1995). Developmental levels are extremely low in multiple areas during this acute stage. There is some suggestion that children under six months of age have a poorer prognosis than those who experience severe malnutrition at an older age. It must be remembered that these same children live in unhealthy homes (poor sanitation, overcrowding, household illnesses) and with families who provide little stimulation in the form of toys and books or even parent-child interaction. Some of the decreased parent-child interaction may be cultural.

A review of the literature on severe malnutrition, as performed by Grantham-McGregor (1995), points out the challenges that researchers have faced. Most researchers have tried to match children with severe malnutrition with case controls or siblings. Differences in IQ, cognitive function or school achievement favoring the case controls have generally been found. The differences have been present but less dramatic with sibling controls.

The mechanism by which severe malnutrition affects brain function acutely and chronically is still under investigation. Kwashiorkor and marasmus seem to have similar negative effects on mental development (Galler et al., 1987). Most studies have looked at global IQ measures. Specific effects on reasoning and perceptual-spatial function have been consistently found (Champakan et al, 1968: Hoorweg and Stanfield, 1976; Nwuga, 1977), but effects on other cognitive skills remain to be determined. Motor skills seem to be affected, as clumsiness, motor delay, and sensory integration problems have been noted in different studies (Cravioto and Arrieta, 1986; Galler et al, 1987; Hoorwag and Stanfield, 1976). Behavior problems seem to be characterized by poor attention, more distractibility, and less emotional control (Galler et al, 1983; Richardson et al, 1972; Richardson et al, 1975). Since studies were conducted in such varied areas as Latin America, the Caribbean, Sub-Saharan Africa and Southeast Asia, cultural norms of the study populations limit generalization of these findings.

Since most children treated for severe malnutrition return to the same undernourished, unstimulated environment from which they came, it is difficult to ascribe the consistently-found deficits in cognitive skills, motor skills, and behavior to either acute malnutrition or chronic deprivation of food and stimulation operating alone. The risk is in the combination. There has been virtually no research done on the effects of severe malnutrition in an adequate social environment, because that combination does not often occur. Certainly there is agreement that the co-existence of other environmental and biologic deficits with severe malnutrition can only intensify and exacerbate the effects of malnutrition alone.

The mechanism by which permanent cognitive and behavioral changes occur is partially understood. The quality of the young child's exploration during episodes of severe malnutrition is probably poor. Children seem to explore with less enthusiasm and happiness, which predicts future negative effects on development (Meeks Gardner et al., 1993). Part of this qualitative difference in exploration can be attributed to an unstimulating home environment. A small amount of human research and a larger amount of animal research supports the notion that irreversible brain changes do occur with severe malnutrition, leading to permanent behavioral changes. Marked improvement can occur when normal nutrition is accompanied by good environmental stimulation.

Breastfeeding

Many studies have been done all over the world to examine the beneficial effects of breastfeeding. After all, breastfeeding was the original nutrition for humanity, so there is good reason to think that human milk has benefits for children in all aspects of health, growth, and development. A comprehensive meta-analysis was done by Anderson, Johnstone and Remley (1999), looking at twenty studies that met the inclusion criteria of comparing breastfeeding and formula-feeding while controlling for covariates. After adjustment for covariates (such as maternal education and socioeconomic status), there remained a cognitive benefit of 3.16 DQ points for breastfed children, beginning at six months of age and persisting across older ages. The benefit was higher for low birthweight infants. Benefits increased with duration of breastfeeding. While the difference for an individual child is not clinically significant, the benefit to a whole population of children is substantial.

The mechanism of this benefit has also been studied in recent years. Of primary interest is the role of docosahexenoic acid (DHA) in brain development. DHA has been shown to be necessary for retinal and brain development in primates. DHA levels are related to alpha-linoleic acid intake. Breastfed term infants have higher levels of DHA than do formula-fed infants, suggesting that formula provides insufficient alpha-linoleic acid or that enzymes are not active enough to help attain adequate levels of DHA. A recent trial of DHA supplementation in babies in Australia (Makrides et al., 2000) did not find differences in Bayley scores at twelve or 24 months, but the study was limited by small sample size.

Micronutrients

Iron-deficiency anemia has been clearly shown to have negative effects on cognitive development in children. Most of the studies on anemia have been done in developing countries such as Indonesia and Costa Rica. Specifically, the effects of iron-deficiency anemia on three- to six-year-old children were in the areas of visual attention and concept acquisition. Younger children (ages twelve to eighteen months) had developmental delays (Soewondo, 1995). One study found dramatic (twenty points on the Bayley MDI) improvement in mental development for twelve-to-eighteen month olds treated for iron-deficiency anemia compared to those in a placebo group (Pollitt, 1995). Changes in motor development were even more dramatic. Reversibility of the developmental delays with iron treatment has been inconsistently reported, and this remains a major concern for infants who experience iron-deficiency anemia. A recent study showed a correlation between early anemia and later diagnosis of mild and moderate mental retardation, independent of maternal education, sex, ethnicity, and other variable ages (Hurtado et al, 1999).

Another related issue is that of pica. Iron-deficient, anemic children are more likely to engage in this behavior of eating non-food substances. When there is lead in the environment, these children can experience the additional burden of heavy metal intoxication, which has an independent negative effect on development. Additionally, an intriguing argument has been offered by Pollitt (1995) that the development delays that have been associated with mild-to-moderate protein-energy malnutrition may be attributable to co-existing iron-deficiency anemia. In most cases, published studies of mild-to-moderate malnutrition did not measure to anemia. The likelihood of lasting effects of iron-deficiency anemia, especially in young children, and the ready availability of treatment of this anemia has led to a strong plea from health professionals to more aggressively diagnose and treat iron-deficiency anemia.

Zinc is another element that has been studied extensively only for the last ten years. Most of the single-nutrient deficiency studies on zinc have been done in rats and rhesus monkeys. They have found effects such as lethargy, decreased visual attention, and decreased memory. Studies in humans are understandably harder to conduct, since most zinc deficiency occurs with other nutrient deficiencies. School-aged children in Egypt showed effects of low zinc intake on behavior. Girls showed more attention-seeking behavior, while boys showed higher activity levels (Wachs et al., 1995). In humans, considerable brain sparing takes place, so that dietary zinc deprivation has not been shown to have direct effects on the brain. Rather, the effects may be mediated through non-CNS systems that secondarily affect the brain (Golub, Keen, Gershwin, & Hendrickx, 1995).

Finally, hypothyroidism results from defects in thyroid gland function. Most of these defects are picked up in newborn screening in the U.S. Early treatment with thyroid hormone prevents cretinism, the syndrome of mental retardation and growth failure. Iodine is the vital substrate needed for thyroid function. In countries where iodine intake is limited, persons experience brain deficits on the continuum between normality and full-blown cretinism. In China, persons living in iodine-deficient areas lost between ten and fifteen IQ points (Tai, 1997).

Interactions

Recent studies of the brain increasingly show the positive effects of stimulation and other positive interactions between caretakers and infants on the child's brain development. Most of the nutritional studies in humans at least mention this issue. Children who are nutritionally deprived often are also deprived of normal nurturing and stimulation from their parents and other caretakers. The caretakers may be emotionally or cognitively limited by their own past or by their own current nutritional deprivation. The interaction between child and parent and the interaction between nutritional and emotional environment must be considered in discussions and research about the impact of nutrition on brain development.

Summary of Postnatal Issues

Children born healthy and at term may experience nutritional deficits that threaten normal brain development. Breast feeding almost guarantees optimal lipids, vitamins, and micronutrients. The human brain protects itself from lipid, vitamin, and micronutrient deficiencies while other organs may be deprived, but there are still situations of severe nutritional deprivation where brain development is affected. The role of multiple nutritional deficiencies needs more investigation. Studies of single-nutrient deficiency in humans are not practical, so animal research needs to continue. Human feeding does not take place in an environmental vacuum, future research must consider the parent-child interaction as part of the problem and/or solution in nutritional studies of young children.

ISSUES FOR CONSIDERATION BY RESEARCHERS AND POLICY MAKERS

The previous sections have given an overview of current issues that have been raised in research and clinical practice. Clearly, much work remains to be done to understand the effects of nutrition and malnutrition on the young, developing brain. Some areas for further investigation are identified below with an emphasis on those with policy implications for children in the U.S. and the rest of the world.

While naturally-occurring and man-made famine are horrific disasters, they do represent opportunities to learn more about the effects of severe malnutrition on pregnant mothers and young children. Concentrated effort should be made to collect data on the long-term effects of prenatal and early postnatal malnutrition on children. When entire populations have been malnourished and then experience normal nutrition with a relatively normal social environment, the social/environmental and chronic malnutrition factors are minimized, so that the long-term effects of acute malnutrition can be studied.

Prevention of low birthweight in infants needs more attention from a nutrition standpoint. Most low birthweight results from premature birth. Since premature birth occurs more frequently in certain populations (teenagers, African Americans), the role of nutrition in premature births should be more extensively studied. Pre-pregnancy nutritional status may be a key factor in birth outcome.

Toxic exposures also need more attention from researchers. With more and more contamination in the world's environment, there is an opportunity for better monitoring of prenatal exposures in identified geographical areas and correlating data that with long-term followup of children. The teratogenic effect of contaminants (e.g., PCBs, heavy metals) on the brain and cognitive function must be studied. The search for other easily-treatable conditions such as folate deficiency must continue as long as there are brain malformations of unknown etiology.

While the number of children born prematurely is not large, the investment in each child and the risk of adverse developmental outcome is substantial. Application of technology now saves premature infants at an increasing rate. Attention should now be paid to preserving brain development in the midst of intense efforts to preserve life. Babies need calories to grow and survive. Lipids supply many of these calories, but the optimal amount of essential fatty acids (EFAs) for brain development still needs to be determined. For example, the risks of EFAs to immune and lung function in premature infants need to be quantified and balanced against the benefits to the brain. Premature babies who experience trauma to the mouth, nose, and neck through tube placement need intense intervention in order to maximize their chances of normal oral motor and language development.

Many questions remain about postnatal malnutrition. The duration of the effects of malnutrition needs to be studied through long-term follow-up. The relationship between the timing of the malnutrition (e.g., first few months of life, later in infancy, that occurring in later childhood) and its effects still needs to be established. The precise mechanism of brain injury related to malnutrition still needs to be established. There needs to be more specificity about which cognitive functions are affected. New imaging studies (such as PET scanning) hold promise for further investigation. The contribution of specific nutrient deficiencies (iron, lipids) and the interaction between multiple deficiencies need more elaboration.

Animal research can isolate nutrition effects, but it must be remembered that in humans nutritional insults do not occur in isolation. They most often occur in combination with other biologic risk (e.g., lead intoxication) and variable psychosocial risk (poverty, lack of health care, child neglect). Extensive studies are needed to determine how combinations of factors pose increased risk to the child. The child's external and internal protective factors also need to be determined, so that intervention strategies can be formulated for those at most risk. Gender differences need more attention, since many studies do not even note gender. In cases of mild malnutrition, gender may be an important factor. Mild malnutrition may be associated with mild attentional, behavioral, and cognitive problems, so boys who already are more likely to have problems with attention, learning, and behavior at school may show more of the effects of mild malnutrition than girls.

With the increasing popularity of vitamin and mineral supplementation in adults, it is inevitable that more children will be given these supplements by their parents in hopes of inducing positive health outcomes. Some may hope for better cognitive and behavioral outcomes as well. This area needs great scrutiny. It needs to be determined if there are any adverse (or positive) outcomes associated with supplementation. Research done in the U.S. could complement research in developing countries where vitamin and mineral deficiencies are more likely to occur.

Iron-deficiency anemia is associated with completely preventable cognitive and behavioral deficits in children. While public health programs such as Women, Infants and Children (WIC) intervene with children with established nutritional deficiencies (including iron deficiency anemia), prevention activities are inadequate for many at-risk children. A renewed professional and public awareness campaign for early detection of and intervention for iron-deficiency in the high risk population between six and eighteen months is warranted.

Because of its positive effects on brain development, breast feeding could substantially improve developmental outcomes for the world's children. The nutritional component of this benefit (especially lipid composition) needs more detailed elaboration. Human milk is usually optimal for infant nutrition but may come up short under adverse conditions (stress, under-nutrition) in the mother. Supplementation of essential fatty acids may need to occur under these circumstances. Even more critical is the lipid composition of formula. The optimal combination of lipids to supply adequate calories for growth and to promote maximum brain development still needs to be determined. More understanding of the mechanism by which lipids affect development of the young brain is needed.

International adoption is another area that needs attention. As this form of adoption is used more and more, it has become clear that many of these children experienced malnutrition in their home countries. Only 50% of one group were developmentally normal (Miller, Kiernan, Mathers, & Klein-Gitelman, 1995). Severity of delays was related to growth parameters. Many of these children needed vigorous health and developmental intervention. They all need long-term follow-up, to learn about the reversibility of growth and developmental delays. These findings would apply to other environmentally deprived children.

REFERENCES

Anderson, J., Johnstone, B., & Remley, D. (1999). Breast-feeding and cognitive development: A meta-analysis. *American Journal of Clinical Nutrition, 70,* 525–535.

Berendez, H. (1975). Effect of maternal acetonuria on IQ of offspring. In H. Cole (Ed.), *Early diabetes in early life* (pp. xx–xx). New York: Academic.

Bishop, N., Morley, R., Day, J., & Lucas, A. (1997). Aluminum neurotoxicity in preterm infants receiving intravenous-feeding solutions. *New England Journal of Medicine, 336,* 1557–1561.

Brown, J., Tharp, T., Mckay, C., Richardson, S., Hall, N., Finnegan, J., & Splett, P. (1992). Development of prenatal weight gain intervention program using social marketing methods. *Journal of Nutrition Education, 24,* 21.

Champakam, S., Srikantia, S., Gapalan, C. (1968). Kwashiorkor and mental development. In O. Ghai (ed). Perspectives in pediatrics. New Delhi, India. Interprint.

Cravioto, J. (1977). Not be break alone: effect of early malnutrition and stimulus deprivation on mental development. In O. Ghai (Ed.). Perspectives in pediatrics. New Delhi, India, Interprint.

Dobo, M., & Czieizel, A. (1998). Long-term somatic and mental development of children after periconceptual mutivitamin supplementation. *European Journal of Pediatrics, 157,* 719–723.

Friedman, Z., & Frolich, J. (1979). Essential fatty acids and the major urinary metabolites of the E prostaglandins in thriving neonates and in infants receiving parenteral fat emulsions. *Pediatric Research, 13,* 932–936.

Galler, J., Ramsey, F., Solimano, G., Lowell, W. (1983). The influence of early malnutrition on subsequent behavioral development. II. Classroom behavior. *Journal of the American Academy of Child Psychiatry. 22,* 16–22.

Galler, J., Ramsey, F., Forde, V., Salt, P., & Archer, E. (1987). Long-term effects of early kwashiorkor compared with marasmus. II. Intellectual performance. *Journal of Pediatric Gastroenterology and Nutrition, 6,* 847–854.

Galler, J., Ramsey, Salt P., Archer, E. (1987). Long term effects of early kwashiorkor compared with marasmus. III. Fine motor skills. *Journal of Pediatric Gastroenterology and Nutrition. 6,* 855–859.

Golub, M., Keen, C., Gershwin, M., & Hendrickx, A. (1995). Developmental zinc deficiency and behavior. *Journal of Nutrition, 125,* 2263S–2271S.

Gorman, K. (1995). Malnutrition and cognitive development: Evidence from experimental/quasi-experimental studies among the mild-to-moderately malnourished. *Journal of Nutrition, 125,* 2239S–2244S.

Grantham-McGregor, S., Powell, C., Walker, S., & Himes, J (1991). Nutritional supplementation, psychological stimulation and mental development of stunted children: the Jamaican study. *Lancet, 338,* 1–5.

Grantham-McGregor, S. (1995). A review of studies of the effect of severe malnutrition on mental development. *Journal of Nutrition, 125,* 2233S–2238S.

Grantham-McGregor, S., Lira, P., Ashworth, A., Morris, S., & Assuncao, A. (1998). The development of low birth weight term infants and the effects of the environment in northeast Brazil. *Journal of Pediatrics*, 132, 661–664.

Hill, B., & Singer, L. (1990). Speech and language development after infant tracheostomy. *Journal of Speech and Hearing Disorders*, 55, 15–20.

Hoorweg, J., & Stanfield, J. (1976). The effects of protein energy malnutritian in early childhood on intellectual and motor abilities in later childhood and adolescence. *Developmental Medicine and Child Neurology*, 18, 130–150.

Hurtado, E., Claussen, A., & Scott, K. (1999). Early childhood anemia and mild or moderate regardation. *American Journal of Clinical Nutrition.* 19, 115–119.

Husaini, M., Karyadi, L., Husiani, Y., Sandjaja, K., & Pollitt, E. (1991). Developmental effects of short-term supplementary feeding in nutritionally-at-risk Indonesian infants. *American Journal of Clinical Nutrition*, 54, 79–804.

Koopman-Esseboom, C., Weisglas-Kuperus, N., de Ridder, M., Van der Paauw, C., Tuinstra, L., & Sauer, P. (1996). Effects of polychlorinated biphenyl/dioxin exposure and feeding type on infants' mental and psychomotor development. *Pediatrics*, 97, 700–706.

Levitsky, D., & Strupp, B. (1995). Malnutrition and the brain: Changing concepts, changing concerns. *Journal of Nutrition*, 125, 2212S–2220S.

Makrides, M., Neumann, M., Simmer, K., & Gibson, R. (2000). A critical appraisal of the role of dietary long-chain polyunsaturated fatty acids on neural indices of term infants: A randomized, controlled trial. *Pediatrics*, 105, 32–38.

Meeks Gardner, J., Grantham-McGregor, S., & Chang, S. (1993). Behaviour of stunted children and the relationship to development. *Proceedings of the Nutrition Society*, 52, 36A.

Miller, L., Kernan, M., Mathers, M., & Klein-Gitelman, M. (1995). Developmental and nutritional status of internationally adopted children. *Archives of Pediatric and Adolescent Medicine*, 149, 40–44.

Myers, G., Davidson, P., Shamlaye, C., Axtell, C., Cernichiari, E., Choisy, O, Choi, A., Cox, C., & Clarkson, T. (1997). Effects of prenatal methylmercury exposure from a high fish diet on developmental milestones in the Seychelles Child Development Study. *Neurotoxicology*, 18, 19–29.

Nwuga, B. (1977). Effect of severe Kwashiokor on intellectual development among Nigerian children. *American Journal of Clinical Nutrition*, 30, 1423–1430.

Pollitt, E. (1995). Functional significance of the covariance between protein energy malnutrition and iron deficiency anemia. *Journal of Nutrition*, 125, 2272S–2277S.

Pollitt, E., Gorman, K., Engle, P., Rivera, J., & Martorell, R. (1995). Nutrition in early life and the fulfillment of intellectual potential. *Journal of Nutrition*, 125, 1111S–1118S.

Preston-Martin, S., Pogoda, J., Mueller, B., Lubin, F., Holly, E., Filippini, G., Cordier, S., Peris-Bonet R., Choi, W., Little, J., & Arslan, A. (1998). Prenatal vitamin supplementation and risk of childhood brain tumors. *International Journal of Cancer Supplement*, 11, 17–22.

Richardson, S., Birch, H., Grabie, E., & Yoder, K. (1972). *Journal of Health and Social Behavior.* 13, 276–283.

Richardson, S., Birch, H., & Ragbeer, C. (1975). The behavior of children at home who were severely malnourished in the first two years of life. *Journal of Biosocial Sciences,* 7:155–156.

Soewondo, S. (1995). The effect of iron deficiency and mental stimulation on Indonesian children's cognitive performance and development. *Kobe Journal of Medical Science,* 41, 1–17.

Stoll, C., Dott, B., Alembik, Y., & Koehl, C. (1999). Maternal trace elements, vitamin B12, Vitamin A, folic acid, and fetal malformations. *Reproductive Toxicology,* 13, 53–57.

Strupp, B., & Levitsky, D. (1995), Enduring cognitive effects of early malnutrition: A theoretical reappraisal. *Journal of Nutrition,* 125, 2221S–2232S.

Tai, M. (1997). The devastating consequence of iodine deficiency. Southeast Asian *Journal of Tropical Medicine and Public Health,* 28, Supp. 2: 75–77.

Wachs, T. (1995). Relation of mild-to-moderate malnutrition to human development: Correlational studies. *Journal of Nutrition,* 125, 2245S–2254S.

Wick, S. (1999). Pesticide exposure and the developing brain: Combining molecular, behavioral, field studies for more complete picture. *CHDD* (Center on Human Development and Disability at the University of Washington Health Sciences Center) *Outlook,* 12, 2–6.

Widdowson, E. (1987). Fetal and neonatal nutrition. *Nutrition Today,* 22, 16.

ECOLOGICAL INFLUENCES ON MOTHER–INFANT RELATIONSHIPS

Amy R. Susman-Stillman
& Martha Farrell Erickson

4

◆ ◆ ◆ ◆

We begin this chapter with the premise that a high-quality mother-infant relationship is central to a child's healthy development. It is within this first intimate relationship that a child begins to develop a foundation of security, learns to regulate emotion, masters basic language and cognitive concepts, and establishes relational patterns that are carried forward into later stages of development (Erickson, Egeland, & Sroufe, 1985; Erickson, Korfmacher, & Egeland, 1992; Sroufe & Fleeson, 1986). For this reason, understanding the forces that support or hinder the formation of high-quality mother-infant relationships is key to our ability to promote healthy child development.

The quality of the mother-infant relationship is largely a function of the mother's behavior, particularly her sensitivity to the baby's cues and signals and her ability to attune her response to the baby's needs and characteristics (DeWolff & van IJzendoorn, 1997; Egeland & Farber, 1984). Research also points to various factors that underlie a mother's sensitivity and responsiveness; knowledge and understanding of child development (Newberger & Cook, 1983), realistic attitudes and expectations about child rearing (Brunnquell, Crichton, & Egeland, 1981), and healthy resolution of the mother's issues about how she was cared for in her own childhood (Egeland, Jacobvitz & Sroufe, 1988), among others.

But the mother-infant relationship does not develop in a vacuum; it is subject to the influence of factors beyond the simple dyad. For example, mothers who have a positive relationship with their infants are supported, both emotionally and instrumentally, by others in their network of family or friends (Crockenberg, 1988; Dunst & Trivette, 1990). Also, numerous studies point to the deleterious effects of stressful life events on the mother-infant relationship (Bradley, Whiteside-Mansell, Brisby, & Caldwell, 1997; Pianta & Egeland, 1990).

Broadly speaking, the mother-infant relationship develops within a family (both immediate and extended), a neighborhood, and larger social systems with beliefs and mores relevant to infant development and parenting (for example, social-cultural values). The mother-infant relationship also takes shape within a developmental course that is influenced not only by current ecology, but by ecological forces that operated in earlier stages of the mother's life. It seems reasonable to expect that there are, within all levels of ecology past and present, factors that either support or hinder a mother's ability to sustain the sensitive care an infant needs and therefore affect the quality of the mother-infant relationship.

The what, why, and wherefore of those ecological influences are the focus of this chapter. Under what circumstances are some parents better able than others to nurture their infants? What is known about the ecological forces that shape the quality of the mother-infant relationship? In other words, how does the context in which the mother and baby live support or hinder the ability of a mother to build emotionally supportive relationships with her baby? In this chapter we discuss the significance of an ecological perspective for understanding individual differences among mother-infant relationships; summarize what currently is known about some especially salient ecological, or contextual, influences on mother-infant relationships; and suggest directions for future research, practice and policy.

ECOLOGICAL PERSPECTIVES ON DEVELOPMENT

Unlike earlier times when "much of developmental psychology...is [was] the science of the strange behavior of children in strange situations with strange adults for the briefest possible periods of time" (Bronfenbrenner, 1979, p. 19), an essential question in the field today is: how can we use ecological perspectives to facilitate our understanding of development? There now is a clear theoretical and practical recognition that the broader ecology, along with individual and family-level factors, plays a pivotal role in shaping development (McLoyd, 1998; Parke & Buriel, 1998). Two major theoretical perspectives, formulated over time, have been proposed to guide current and future research: Bronfenbrenner & Ceci's bioecological model (Bronfenbrenner & Ceci, 1994; Bronfenbrenner & Morris, 1998), which is a revision of Bronfenbrenner's theory of the ecology of human development (1979); and Elder's life course theory (Elder, 1998a,b).

Bronfenbrenner's original groundbreaking ecological theory emphasized that human development is a product of a person, process, and context, and that development varies as a function of variations in each of these as parts of development. Building on that earlier work, Bronfenbrenner & Ceci (1994) made two significant improvements in the theory. First, they incorporated the concept of time in each level of the ecological system to emphasize the role of stability/instability in the developmental process and the significance of social change. Second, they expanded their thinking about the role of the person in shaping the developmental process. These two new concepts were integrated into the original theory that ecological environments are a set of "nested structures, each inside the other like Russian dolls" (Bronfenbrenner, 1979, p. 3). For the most part, the original definitions and hypotheses about the systems remain. Briefly, Bronfenbrenner (1979) described four "systems" that exert influence on the child directly or indirectly. The microsystem is a context that contains the developing child, such as the family or the school. The mesosystem represents the overlap between two microsystems, such as the connections between mother-infant and extended family relationships. The exosystem represents the intersection between a context that does not contain the child and one that does, such as a parent's workplace and the home environment. The macrosystem represents societal and cultural influences.

What the updated bioecological theory emphasizes more strongly than Bronfenbrenner's earlier work is a formulation about the ways person, process, context and time together produce development. In the updated formulation, proximal processes are the most powerful influences on development (more powerful than distal, or contextual effects), but the impact of those processes depends upon the context.

Life course theory, a sociological theory now blended with developmental theory (Elder, 1998a,b), provides a useful counterpart to bioecological theory. Four key principles form the core of the theory: historical time and place shape developmental trajectories; timing of life events impacts an individual's developmental course; relationships are a vehicle by which social and historical influences are expressed; and individuals shape their own development as permitted by social and historical constraints. In life course theory, emphasis is placed on understanding how lives are organized and grow and change over time within a constantly changing society. Emphasis is also placed on gauging the processes and mechanisms that link societal and developmental change. In addition, the theory recognizes that understanding the psychological experiences of adults is fundamental to understanding the development of children.

These two complementary ecological perspectives allow researchers to generate testable questions about how development changes as a function of the changing social world. For example: how do broader ecological factors serve to support continuity and/or behavioral change in the mother-infant relationship?

With these two theories as a framework, two broad questions drive the discussion in this chapter: How do "contexts of developmental relevance" (Elder, 1998a, p. 5) influence the mother-child relationship? And how can these ecological perspectives be applied to guide practice, policy and future research on mother-infant relationships?

To ground this discussion in the real life experiences of mothers and infants, let's think for a moment about a young mother named Lisa. And, placing her in two different scenarios, let's consider how ecology and her life course trajectory might come together around her and her baby:

Scenario One: Lisa, a 17-year-old, sees the birth of her baby as an opportunity to become emancipated from her family, which is troubled by alcoholism and conflict. Setting out on her own, she moves into the only apartment she can afford—a tiny efficiency in an old house with thin walls, peeling paint, and rickety stairs. Lisa's high school friends are initially intrigued with her cute new baby and newfound independence, but that wears off quickly and they rarely stop by. The father of Lisa's baby is involved with a new girlfriend. Although he drops off diapers once in a while or brings a friend over to see his baby, the visits always end up in an argument. As part of welfare reform, Lisa enrolled in a job training program to prepare her to be a health aide. But she has to take three separate busses to get from her apartment to her cousin's house, where she leaves her baby, to her job training site. She worries that her $7-an-hour pay is insufficient to allow her to care for herself and her baby. Lisa is acutely aware of society's message to her: You chose to have this baby, so deal with it!

Scenario Two: Lisa is still the same teen mom with the same troubled family history and the same difficult relationship with the father of her baby. But the ecological context in which she cares for her baby is dramatically different. Lisa is enrolled in a school-district program for teen parents, allowing her to complete requirements for her high school diploma while also beginning on-the-job training at a corporation in the neighborhood. Lisa is building new friendships with other moms in similar circumstances. In parenting classes and support groups, she is learning new ways to deal with stressful relationships with her family and former boyfriend. And she is learning that she does not need to pass her childhood pain to her own baby. On-site childcare at Lisa's workplace makes her mornings manageable and allows her to breastfeed her baby during the lunch hour and talk informally with caregivers and other parents. This corporation knowing that employees are more satisfied, loyal, and productive when they are well-paid, respected, and supported in balancing work and family, offers Lisa a future. Lisa's nearby apartment is tiny and sparsely furnished, but the building is clean, secure, and well-maintained. Thanks to a neighborhood revitalization initiative, the streets in the area are well-lighted, and community police are a supportive presence. Neighborhood volunteers and city officials have worked cooperatively to turn a vacant lot into a small playground where parents and children gather to talk and play. Lisa hears a strong message from the society around her: You have a chance to build a better life for yourself and your baby and we will support you as you do that.

It is not hard to imagine that Lisa's relationship with her baby might unfold very differently within these two different scenarios. But what does research really tell us about this? What evidence attests to the influence of family (past and present), social networks, neighborhood, workplace, and larger societal forces on the relationship between mother and infant? And to what extent do personal qualities and life stage mediate or exacerbate those influences? It is those questions to which we turn in the next section of this chapter.

ECOLOGICAL INFLUENCES ON PARENTING AND THE MOTHER–CHILD RELATIONSHIP

Parenting has traditionally been viewed as a one-way flow of influence from parent to child. Intervention typically consisted of giving information to parents or modifying parental practices (McLoyd, 1998). The advent of an ecological perspective in the late 1970s and 1980s led to a conscious reworking of parent education and the emergence of the family support movement. An ecological perspective, which recognizes the multitude of influences on parenting, characterizes parenting as influenced by and responsive to factors at different levels of ecology (Belsky, 1984, 1993). Parents are viewed as mediators, or buffers, of environmental stress (Garbarino & Kostelny, 1993), and parenting styles are recognized as "an adaptation to conditions outside the household, specifically to the social organization of the surrounding community" (Furstenberg, 1993, p. 233). Parenting and family management styles likely result from the interaction between ecological factors and parental competence.

The ecological perspective is evident in research in the 1980s and 1990s, though many analyses were fairly broad. At the broadest level, studies examined the relation of social class to parenting and parent-child relationships. Generally, researchers observed harsher parenting styles in parent-child relationships among families of lower socioeconomic status (Hoff-Ginsburg & Tardif, 1995). These findings were more pronounced for toddlers and preschoolers than for infants, although there is some suggestion that the infant findings were limited by the methodologies used in those studies. It is beyond the scope of this chapter to explore fully the research on class differences, but we refer you to Hoff-Ginsburg & Tardif (1995) for an extended discussion.

Beyond an analysis of simple class differences, researchers addressed the broad constructs of stress (or stressful life events) and social support, examining their impact on mother-infant relationships. Factors that can trigger maternal stress, including conflict and changes in maternal partner relationships (Belsky & Isabella, 1988) and other life events (Pianta & Egeland, 1990), were shown to predict lower quality mother-infant interaction. For example, Pianta and Egeland (1990) found that higher levels of mothers' personal stress were negatively related to mothers' sensitivity and cooperation in feeding and play situations with their 6-month-old babies. Although the mechanisms are not fully clear, the authors hypothesize that the quality of maternal parenting is particularly sensitive to stress and conflict in interpersonal relationships, and that the child experiences this stress through the quality of mother-child interaction. This explanation is complemented by additional research showing that mothers' socioemotional investment in their 15-month old children (maternal acceptance of the parenting role, delight in child, knowledge/sensitivity, and separation anxiety) is significantly related to the quality of the marital relationship, parenting stress, and perceived social support (Bradley, et al., 1997).

A second critical variable in understanding ecological influences is the concept of social support. Social support is generally defined as resources or help provided to individuals or families in response to the need for assistance, including, but not restricted to, emotional, informational, and instrumental support (see Crockenberg, 1988; Dunst, Trivette, & Deal, 1988). Although distinctions are often drawn between systems of formal and informal support, research findings show that both formal and informal social support can benefit families and children by enhancing their well-being, promoting positive parenting behaviors and decreasing negative ones, and encouraging positive child behaviors (Dunst & Trivette, 1990).

Social support helps buffer the impact of stressful events and improve mothers' ability to actively cope with them. Support may even enable mothers to make choices that reduce the incidence of stressful events in their lives. And there is some suggestion that social support helps mothers transfer their positive relationship experiences to interactions with their children (Egeland, et al., 1988). These findings, which emphasize the importance of the provision of social support for families with young children, especially those living under stressful conditions, point to a new set of more complicated research questions with important implications for theory, practice, and policy. For example, is the impact of social support equally powerful whether it comes from a partner, extended family member, caring friend, or professional home visitor? Is there a linear (additive) or non-linear (interactive) effect of support when it is supplied via multiple levels of the ecology? To what extent are different or multiple sources of social support necessary to buffer negative ecological effects, such as dangerous neighborhoods?

These concepts of stress and support remain central (and are either explicit or implicit) in most studies examining the various specific levels of ecology in which the mother-infant relationship unfolds. Keeping these two important concepts at the forefront of our discussion, our next sections highlight major findings on how mothers and babies are influenced by family, social networks, neighborhood, workplace and societal forces.

FAMILY

One of the proximal ecological forces affecting maternal-infant interactions is the family. Within this level of the ecology are multiple interacting components: family of origin (including both past and current interactions), marital (or co-parenting) relationships, and extended family relationships. During the major developmental transition of becoming a parent, the force of family influence, both positive and negative, is keenly felt. A guiding question here is the extent to which family relationships serve as a source of support or stress—or both—for the mother-infant relationship. And to what extent is the mother-infant relationship vulnerable to, or resilient in the face of, those influences?

Family of Origin

Research and theory suggest that a mother's early childhood experience is a powerful influence on her parenting behavior and the quality of the relationship between herself and her infant (Fraiberg, Adelson, & Shapiro, 1980; Sroufe & Fleeson, 1986). A mother's expectations about relationships, self, and others are learned primarily from early relationships with caregivers and are carried forth from childhood to serve as a model for her future interactions with others.

Although there is an established relationship between the quality of care a mother received during her childhood and the quality of her interactions with her infant, studies using the Adult Attachment Interview suggest that the way in which one's developmental history is perceived is an even more powerful factor than the quality of care received. That is, a mother's "state of mind" about her early relationships is a better predictor of her parenting behavior than the actual quality of those early relationships (Fonagy, Steele, & Steele, 1991; Main & Goldwyn, 1984). Specifically, mothers who deny painful childhood experiences, who dismiss the importance of those experiences, or, at the other end of the continuum, are preoccupied with their own painful history, are at risk of passing on their own relationship difficulties to their children. Mothers do best with their children when they have come to grips with their own history, understanding its impact on themselves and also recognizing that they do not have to repeat it with their own children. A mother's perception and understanding of her developmental history, then, becomes one of the "lessons" that she passes on to her infant via the quality of their interactions.

These findings raise important questions about what enables some parents to achieve this "secure/autonomous" state of mind about their own early relationships. At the broadest level of analysis, mothers who have successfully broken the cycle of abuse provide evidence for the role of both formal and informal ecological supports (therapy, supportive partner) in coping with the powerful proximal force of one's developmental history

(Egeland, et al., 1988). Many family support professionals and intervention researchers are using educational and therapeutic strategies to help parents face the past so they can move beyond it (Erickson, et al., 1992; Erickson & Kurz-Riemer, 1999). But to date there is little clear evidence about the specific processes, natural or intentional, by which parents achieve the psychological resolution that enables them to buffer the intergenerational effect of their own childhood hurt. Within a life course perspective, we might ask whether there are certain life experiences and/or periods in development where one would be particularly responsive to support or intervention based on these issues.

One example is the transition to parenthood, which is often a decisive marker of change for a new mother and her family. It is at this time that the intergenerational transmission of positive and/or negative messages becomes salient as expectations change and relationships adapt to new family roles and the increasing maturity of the mother. This is especially true of the relationship between the new mother and her own mother. For adolescent mothers, becoming a mother often is a major step towards emancipation/adulthood. The change may engender stress and conflict in the family, a search for common ground where mutual respect and shared understanding characterize their interactions, or some combination of both.

There is suggestion in the literature that broader ecological forces also may influence the extent to which maternal perceptions of their own mother-child attachment relationships are transmitted to children. One study (Sagi, et al., 1997) that investigated the context of kibbutz sleeping arrangements for infants as a crucial factor in the transmission of attachment found significantly lower correspondence between adult attachment classifications and infant attachment classifications for infants in communal sleeping arrangements as compared to infants in traditional sleeping arrangements. The authors suggest that certain ecological contexts may actually "override" the influence of maternal attachment representation. Although this hypothesis requires further examination, it is likely that certain ecological factors help to shape the perceptions of individuals. A key question here is how the confluence of individual- and broader systems-level factors shapes the psyche of mothers in relation to caring for and nurturing their infants.

Marital Relationships

Parents of infants, especially first-time parents, are confronted with the challenge of balancing their own relationship while building a relationship with their new baby. To what extent does the quality of the marital relationship influence the quality of the mother-infant relationship? Both research and practical experience reveal linkages between the two relationships. The primary paths of influence, however, are somewhat unclear. The spillover hypothesis suggests a positive correlation between marital quality and parent-child relationships, such that high- or low-quality marital relationships correspond to high- or low-quality parent-child relationships. The compensatory hypothesis posits a negative relationship between marital quality and parent-child relationships. For example, a low-quality marital relationship would correlate with a high-quality parent-child relationship. A meta-analytic review of 68 studies of marital quality and parent-child relations (Erel & Burman, 1995) offers support for the spillover hypothesis.

Others who have more closely investigated the literature on couples with very young children offer a conclusion similar to the spillover hypothesis. "Couples characterized by positive mutuality, partner autonomy, and the ability to confront problems and regulate negative affect are responsive to the needs of their infants, promote their autonomy and have more secure and autonomous children, as seen throughout the first 4 years of life" (Heinecke, 1995, p. 295). Clearly documented in the literature are the findings that declines in marital functioning during the first year of the baby's life, or low-quality prebirth marital relationships, are linked to lower quality mother-child relationships (Heinecke, 1995).

But that link may be mediated by how the marital problems are addressed. For example, one investigation of pre- and postnatal patterns of marital relationships (consistently low satisfaction and declining satisfaction) revealed that the way parents handled their marital dissatisfaction (divorce or no divorce) predicted parental responsiveness and child expectation of care (a feature of securely attached children). Parents who experienced consistently unsatisfactory marital relationships, as opposed to those who experienced declining satisfaction with their marital relationships, were more likely to provide quality care for their infants when divorce was part of their conflict resolution plan (Heinecke, Guthrie, & Ruth, 1997).

Under what conditions do marital relationships serve as sources of support or stress to the mother-child relationship? Happy, positive couple relationships provide the support for mothers to build high-quality relationships with their infants, but the converse may not be true for all unhappy couples. For certain couples, the extent and consistency of dissatisfaction in their relationship and their strategies for resolution may also positively predict, at least in infancy, the ability of mothers to appropriately and sensitively nurture their infants. There is also some suggestion in the literature that mothers' ability to parent, as compared to fathers' ability to parent, is less affected by external conditions and stresses (Doherty, Kouneski, & Erickson, 1998). It would be helpful to understand better what enables mothers to parent well even in the face of high-conflict marital relations, especially since parent educators and family support professionals typically have little opportunity to influence the marriage relationship directly.

PERSONAL SOCIAL NETWORKS

The dramatically different ecological contexts of Lisa and her baby discussed earlier illustrate that the contacts and relationships mothers have outside their immediate family can be important sources of support as well as strain. Cochran and colleagues (Cochran & Brassard, 1979; Cochran, Larner, Riley, Gunnarsson, & Henderson, 1990) offer the concept of personal social networks, defined as "those people outside the household who engage in activities and exchanges of an affective and/or material nature with the members of the immediate family" (Cochran & Brassard, 1979, p. 601). In general, personal social networks include extended family, friends, neighbors, and informal service providers such as babysitters or caregivers. Research studying the influence of personal social networks on mothers with young children shows that the information, support and assistance provided by personal social networks helps mothers be more emotionally supportive of their children. In one study, positive parental perceptions of neighbors distinguished between securely and insecurely attached infants (Belsky & Isabella, 1988). In another study, drug-abusing mothers whose infants remained in their care named more people in a social network who could provide adequate social support as compared to drug-abusing mothers whose infants did not remain in their care (Nair, Black, Schuler, Keane, Snow, & Rigney, 1997).

Within a mother's personal social networks, the quality of a mother's extended family relationships likely affect her success in nurturing a relationship with her infant. How does the mother perceive her relationships with her extended family as she works to build a relationship with her infant? Does she feel that the power of the love and caring from her extended family "frees" her to have the confidence to love and nurture her baby as her instinct tells her? Is her family's hope and excitement over the baby reassuring to her as she negotiates the uncertainties of being a new mother? Does she feel drained by the heaps of unsolicited advice she's been receiving, especially because it conflicts with her own understanding and current knowledge? Or is she finding that she is being pulled in too many directions, as a family member and mother?

Within personal social networks, the role of grandmothers has probably received the greatest attention as a critical source of support for mothers (Wilson 1989). In general, as discussed by Apfel & Seitz (1991), grandmothers fulfill a number of roles: to replace, supplement or share, support, and/or mentor the parent. As noted by Spieker & Bensley (1994), the few studies conducted on the influence of social support on quality of attachment of infants born to teenage mothers find proportions of securely and insecurely attached infants similar to those of older parents, mainly because grandmothers provided a great deal of care to their grandchildren. However, there were no positive differences in adolescent maternal behavior as a function of degree of grandmother involvement. Despite the benefits conferred to the babies, the authors hypothesize that in some circumstances, grandmother support may actually constrain the development of adolescent mothers' parenting skills (Spieker & Bensley, 1994).

Particularly in poor, urban, African-American communities, the shared task of childrearing by extended family members and kin is not only common, but also part of an essential survival network where resources are scarce. This is documented through many years of ethnographic research. Jarrett (1995) cites examples of how a supportive adult network, generally comprised of grandparents, aunts, siblings, other relatives, and close friends, often steps in to provide financial, instrumental, and emotional support and guidance for young mothers.

Mothers often value the support they receive from members of their personal social networks beyond their families. One mother participating in a parent education program described her feelings of relief when she had the opportunity to talk with other parents about a tense situation she was encountering with her in-laws, who wanted to babysit for her infant but had dramatically different beliefs than she about how to provide infant care. Another mother was grateful for the care co-op in her neighborhood, which allowed her a break on days when she really needed one. Another group of women described how their early morning walks together had sustained them through their years of balancing work and family.

At the same time that personal social networks provide support to mothers, they also can serve as a source of stress. Jarrett (1995) recognizes that in some circumstances it is advantageous for a mother to cut off or limit her interactions with extended family members if they inhibit her ability to nurture her baby and survive. In other cases, well-intentioned offerings of advice or support can backfire; the seemingly innocent comments of a close friend or neighbor can undermine the confidence of a young mother. And members of personal social networks may have their own issues or problems that cause them to serve as a drain on the interpersonal resources of the network.

Ironically, it can be more difficult to work with mothers who have a large personal social network than with mothers who are socially isolated in their communities if the large network is not supportive of good parenting. In an example drawn from our experience, family support professionals working with first-time mothers who were substance abusers reported their frustration with the personal social networks of the mothers. Because the mothers had a relatively large network of so-called friends with whom they had very frequent contact, they did not perceive a need for social connection and support. Yet these "friends" were largely unsupportive of (and, in fact, overtly destructive to) the well-being of the mother, the child, and the mother-child relationship. Standing in the way of healthy behavior and good parenting, this social network became a liability rather than an asset.

Ecological factors such as social class, parental education, race and ethnicity, and marital status shape the size and scope of personal social networks (Cochran & Niego, 1995), as well as their success. Extended family networks are increasingly stressed by challenging social and economic circumstances (e.g., poverty, dangerous neighborhoods). The effectiveness of grandmother support on mother-infant relationships may be affected by economic conditions and family living arrangements. In fact, studies of co-residence (Chase-Lansdale, Brooks-Gunn & Zamsky, 1994; Oyserman, Radin, & Benn, 1993; Spieker & Bensley, 1994) show that mother and infant living with grandmother did not necessarily confer the assumed benefits on adolescent mothers and their children. When the success rates of different living arrangements were compared (living with grandmother or living with partner), adolescent mothers living with partner and receiving high support from grandmother was most advantageous for security of attachment, while living with partner and receiving low grandmother support was least advantageous for security of attachment (Spieker & Bensley, 1994). And under trying economic conditions, co-residence places additional strain on families.

Although we have some indication of ecological factors that may affect the success of personal social networks, we know little about how participation in parent education programs, neighborhood activities, or early intervention services influences social networks and how the effects of social networks may vary based on characteristics of the mother-infant pairs and the neighborhoods in which they live. For example, mothers feeling confident in their parenting role may create for themselves larger and more supportive social networks, while mothers living in dangerous neighborhoods may not feel safe participating in neighborhood activities and thus cultivate limited personal social networks.

Beyond general questions about ecological influences on personal social networks, the dynamic nature of personal social networks allows one to generate interesting questions about how social networks fluctuate and change with developmental transitions. Particularly for mothers of infants, how does the birth of a baby alter personal social networks? How do mothers perceive these changes? Do they influence mothers' interactions with their babies? Continued study is needed to examine ways in which we can help mothers meet this basic need for human interactive support and connection (Cochran, et al., 1990).

NEIGHBORHOODS AND MOTHER–INFANT RELATIONSHIPS

A new baby coming home from the hospital joins not only a family, but also a neighborhood. Neighbors may come knocking on the door, happy to greet the newest member of their community and rejoice with the family. Or they may stay inside their homes, unaware of their new neighbor's existence. Although the degrees of neighborly connections vary dramatically across neighborhoods, neighborhoods have been viewed as a primary social context for families with young children (Garbarino & Gilliam, 1980). Some impact of the neighborhood on mother-infant relationships, then, may be expected. How might these effects occur? It is unlikely that neighborhoods exert direct effects on infants themselves. Most likely, the effects of neighborhoods on mother-infant relationships are experienced indirectly, through the effects neighborhoods have on mothers. Potentially, mothers can play a powerful role in either buffering or exacerbating the negative effects of neighborhoods on their infant's developmental outcomes. To what extent do neighborhood conditions support or hinder maternal well-being or positive parenting practices?

Neighborhoods experiencing extreme deprivation pose serious challenges to competent parenting and healthy child development. They tend to have high rates of problematic social conditions, such as infant mortality and child abuse (Coulton & Pandey, 1992). With fewer high quality social, economic and institutional resources, coping with the stresses of everyday life becomes more difficult and the mental strain of parents generally increases. When parents are overly stressed, they may experience mental health difficulties (e.g., depression or anxiety), adopt dysfunctional coping strategies (e.g., social withdrawal), or employ parenting strategies not conducive to healthy social and emotional child development in the long term (e.g., harsh parenting; Garbarino & Kostelny, 1993).

A rich qualitative literature from sociology, which examines contextual effects on parenting (Furstenberg, 1993; Jarrett, 1995), illustrates that family management practices such as monitoring of children, parental discipline, and use of community resources in childrearing vary as a function of neighborhood context. However, much of this work has been conducted with families whose children are of school age and older. It is not clear if the neighborhood conditions that lead parents to adopt particular family management and monitoring practices with older children also lead them to alter their interactions with their infants. This area requires further study.

The quantitative work available (Duncan & Aber, 1997; Klebanov, Brooks-Gunn, Chase-Lansdale, & Gordon, 1997; Klebanov, Brooks-Gunn, & Duncan, 1994) gives us some indication that neighborhood forces may be at work, but the large sample sizes and the nature of the study designs and assessments prevent a more in-depth analysis of crucial dimensions of mother-infant interaction. We know of no studies that have examined neighborhood effects on children under the age of one, and only one study that has included children ages one to three—and the outcome variable of interest was developmental test scores, not socioemotional or relational variables (Klebanov, Brooks-Gunn, McCarton & McCormick, 1998). Nonetheless, although the available studies were conducted on samples of preschool children and without specific focus on the parent-child relationship, they are useful for the purposes of our discussion because they have examined the direct and indirect effects of neighborhood characteristics on maternal well-being and parenting.

In the set of studies cited above, five neighborhood factors (low SES, high SES, male joblessness, family concentration, and ethnic diversity), generated from factor analyses of selected variables from the U.S. Census, were used to predict maternal and parenting outcomes. Using these factors, the researchers found that, for mothers of preschool-age children, the presence of poor neighbors was linked to lower levels of maternal warmth and responsiveness, to a more negative physical home environment, and to a less cognitively stimulating home learning environment. The presence of affluent neighbors was related to lower levels of social support. Neighborhood ethnic diversity was negatively related to maternal warmth, a less cognitively stimulating home environment, and lower levels of social support. These findings held even after family-level variables, including family income, female headship, maternal age, and maternal education were controlled.

What these findings indicate is that maternal well-being, parenting competence, and social support vary as a function of neighborhood economic resources and ethnic diversity. Why ethnic heterogeneity is related to negative outcomes is unclear. Before concluding that ethnic heterogeneity is disadvantageous in poor neighborhoods, researchers need to examine other confounding variables, including relative deprivation, housing policies and segregation, and racism (Klebanov, et al., 1997). In general, the neighborhood effects are small, and, in keeping with predictions from bioecological theory, still pale in comparison to the effects of the more proximal family-level variables. Thus, it is essential to think about neighborhood level influences in context with family characteristics (Brooks-Gunn, Duncan, & Aber, 1997).

One useful way to think about how neighborhood context may influence maternal parenting and well-being is in terms of the responsibilities women have as caregivers in a neighborhood. A community social organization framework (Sampson, 1992) suggests that neighborhood structural conditions such as age, gender structure, and economic resources influence neighborhood cohesion, social control and social networks, and as a result, the neighborhood's ability to care for children. Using that framework, Coulton, Korbin, Su, & Chow (1995) constructed a variable called child care burden, an indication of the human resources available for childrearing in a neighborhood. In their tract-level analyses, they found significant positive relations between neighborhoods where the child care burden on females was heavy (neighborhoods with many children per adult, few elderly residents and a low proportion of adult males) and rates of child maltreatment, juvenile delinquency, drug trafficking, adolescent pregnancy, and low birthweight. It stands to reason, then, that in neighborhoods with poor social capital, the childrearing demands placed on women are often overwhelming and likely challenge their parenting competencies. However, in a study using a similar variable indexing the adult composition of the neighborhood (the percentage of elderly in the neighborhood and ratio of caregiving-age males to females in the neighborhood), there was no relation with maternal well-being or parenting, although adult composition of the neighborhood was linked to lower scores on a test of preschool readiness (Susman-Stillman, 1997). More research is needed to understand the maternal caregiving role in the context of the neighborhood and how that translates into the quality of care mothers are able to provide their infants and older children.

Additional attention needs to be paid to studying the external forces that shape the neighborhood context. Garbarino's concept of social toxicity (Garbarino, Kostelny, & Barry, 1995)—that the social contexts in which children develop are poisonous—is relevant here. Certain social conditions that characterize impoverished neighborhoods in particular—namely substance abuse, crime, and violence—significantly challenge the ability of families to provide adequately for their babies (for an extended discussion of the influence of substance abuse and violence on infant development, see Fitzgerald, Zucker, Mun, Puttler, & Wong, this volume; Osofsky, this volume). The culture of substance abuse indicates an availability of drugs, an underground economy, a likely lack of a thriving legitimate economy, and a disproportionate number of poor role models in relation to functional ones in the community. Often a sense of hopelessness and defeat pervades such a neighborhood and its residents. And it is widely recognized that the kinds of behaviors necessary for substance abusers to meet their own needs often clash with those valued by community residents and with those necessary for appropriate and sufficient parenting (Sanders-Phillips, 1998).

Concerns about crime and violence in neighborhoods also contribute a sense of fear and mistrust. One study found mothers' perceptions of neighborhood crime and deterioration were positively associated with psychological distress (Taylor & Roberts, 1997). Although kinship support was found to moderate the degree of psychological distress, it did not completely eliminate the relations between neighborhood crime and psychological distress. This suggests that the moderating power of kinship support is limited in the face of substantial neighborhood problems.

Another factor that characterizes the lifestyle of a significant number of families in urban settings is mobility. A recent study conducted in Minneapolis (Buerkle, 1997) to investigate the effects of changing residence on student achievement and adjustment in elementary school children found that approximately 20% of the children in the sample experienced residential mobility. The mobile families tended to be low-income families of color and headed by a single parent. Interviews with these mobile families revealed that they moved to cope with difficult life circumstances or because they were forced to move, and that they had significant difficulty finding adequate, safe, affordable housing, especially if they had large families. A small percentage of the mobile families experienced upward mobility, moving to a better home, to a safer neighborhood, or closer to employment. Regardless of the reasons for mobility, however, families still viewed moving as temporarily stressful, challenging, and disturbing to family stability.

These findings also may characterize families of infants as well. For example, among families participating in the STEEP program, a preventive intervention for high risk parents and infants, 90% moved at least once during the first year of the baby's life. And approximately 25% of the mothers and their infants moved across county lines during the first year of their baby's life. High rates of mobility for mothers with very young children are indicative of significant interpersonal and ecological stress, often exacerbating the expected stress that accompanies the adjustment to parenthood and life with an infant. Unfortunately, along with the difficulty in maintaining supportive interpersonal ties, high mobility often results in bureaucratic difficulties that make the provision of supportive services a major challenge. Future research should examine the extent to which neighborhood features and services support or hinder mobility and neighborhood stability. Are high rates of mobility linked to housing policies that discourage the development of affordable housing? Or are mobility rates attributable to young mothers escaping high-conflict relationships, or to personal behaviors such as fighting or drug use that lead to eviction?

WORK–LIFE ISSUES AND MOTHER–INFANT RELATIONSHIPS

Perhaps the most potent and ongoing challenge facing mothers of infants today is achieving a balance between the competing demands of work and family. In 1995, the majority of families with young children were working families, with 63% of children under age 6 living with working parents (Annie E. Casey Foundation, 1998). The greatest increase in labor force participation between 1970 and 1990 is among mothers with children under the age of 1, with divorced women largely accounting for this increase, followed by mothers with a spouse (Smith, Brooks-Gunn, & Jackson, 1997; for an extended discussion of maternal employment, see Lerner & Castellino, this volume).

Although data describing labor force participation suggest that "working families" is a way of life for many Americans, the implications may be somewhat misleading, as the definition of labor force participation includes both part and full-time employment. The hours parents spend working, rather than their labor force participation, may be a more salient indicator of parental availability for children. Mayer (1997) notes that despite the increase in number of hours parents spend working, there was little change from 1970 to 1992 in the number of hours per week (approximately 85) parents were technically available for caring for children under age three.

This stability in hours available is most likely due to smaller family sizes. In her calculations, however, she notes that single mothers theoretically have half the time that two-parent families with one parent working have available for child rearing (72 hours versus 184 hours). With increases in single-parent-headed families, the balancing of work and family demands are ever-present in the lives of mothers with young children. The questions of how much time working mothers actually have available to spend time with their infants, and how they spend that time, remain ones worthy of future empirical study.

These demographics underlie the strong demand for quality child care, a particularly vexing problem for mothers of infants. A quote from a research report issued by the Annie E. Casey Foundation illustrates the problem: "The situation for infants and toddlers was particularly distressing. One multi-state study found that only one out of twelve infant and toddler rooms at child care centers provided developmentally appropriate care, and 40% were deemed a potential threat to children's health and safety." The report links low quality child care to low wages and inadequate training for child-care workers, problems that make it difficult to attract and retain skilled staff (Annie E. Casey Foundation, 1998).

How infants fare in day care settings is of great concern. One of the most contentious arguments in developmental psychology is about the effect of day care on the quality of mother-infant attachment. In the 1980s, Belsky (1988) concluded that spending more than twenty hours a week in child care had negative consequences for the mother-infant relationship and child socioemotional development. Some research conducted in the mid-1990s, however, failed to find a link between experience in child care and attachment security (Roggman, Langlois, Hubbs-Tait, & Rieser-Danner, 1994). To settle this ongoing debate, a multi-site comprehensive national study investigating the effect of child care on attachment security was conducted. In this study, maternal sensitivity and responsiveness, not participation in child care, predicted attachment security. However, the quality of child care made a difference for children whose mothers were low on sensitivity and responsiveness. If both mothers and caregivers were low in sensitivity, children were at greatest risk for attachment insecurity. Although the combination of poor mothering and low quality child care is a risk to children's development, participation in child care "constitutes neither a risk nor a benefit for the development of the infant-mother attachment relationship as measured in the Strange Situation" (NICHD Early Child Care Research Network, 1997, p. 877).

As child care is a reality for the majority of today's families, attention should focus on the extent to which child care can be helpful to parents and supportive of the parent-infant relationship. Is there an exosystemic effect related to the intersection of relationships between the adult caregivers and the parent and the infant? For example, does the relationship between the child care provider and mother manifest itself in the relationship between mother and infant? The infant caregiver is a potential source of influence by providing support and education to the mother, and by partnering with the mother to nurture and socialize the infant. In addition, by providing high-quality care to the infant, the caregiver may help shape the infant's behavior, which in a transactional model can also influence the quality of the mother-infant relationship.

Elicker, Noppe, Noppe, and Fortner-Wood (1997) note that adult-adult relationships in early childhood programs have received scant attention from researchers and practitioners. They conducted exploratory work to study the quality of the caregiver-parent relationship by developing the Parent-Caregiver Relationship Scale (PCRS). Based on a review of the literature and discussions with center-based and family day-care providers and with parents, the researchers outlined eight dimensions of the parent-caregiver relationship: trust/confidence; open communication; respect/acceptance; caring; competence/knowledge; partnership/collaboration; shared values; and affection/liking. Initial factor analyses suggest similarities and differences in the ways parents and caregivers view their relationships with each other and with children. Future research should address the significance of these similarities and differences for the adult-adult and adult-child relationships on child outcomes. There is much to be learned by applying a relationship-based approach to the study of adult-adult influences on adult-child relationships. Recent public policy changes regarding welfare provision have revitalized social discourse around the work-family balance. A hotly-debated aspect of recent welfare policy concerns the requirement of mothers with very young children to participate in employment. Some view the requirement as an opportunity to teach mothers to take their parenting responsibilities, namely their financial responsibilities, seriously (Moon, 1994). Others are concerned about the possible ramifications for very young children who live in challenging circumstances (Ozawa, 1994).

For a number of reasons, it is difficult to anticipate the consequences of recent welfare reform policy on families with infants. First, there is little applicable research on which to base predictions. Recent welfare changes differ dramatically from previous changes, so research conducted on the previous changes is of limited value. Notably, past studies are methodologically limited by the samples of mothers, who chose to participate in welfare reform activities, and by their designs, which generally did not employ random assignment to condition (Zaslow & Emig, 1997). Note, however, that the latter flaw has been remedied in current research designs (Zaslow, Tout, Smith, & Moore, 1998). Second, the majority of research on the effects of maternal employment on children has been conducted with middle-class populations, so the degree of generalizability to welfare populations is questionable (Zaslow & Emig, 1997). Third, most of the studies have not focused on outcomes for infants and toddlers, but on outcomes for preschool and elementary-age children.

What do we know about how the welfare reform requirements might influence a mother's ability to parent her baby? One question is whether the timing of a mother's participation in employment-related activities exerts a significant effect. Does "early employment" make a difference? The few studies investigating this question on non-welfare samples yield mixed findings on the socioemotional and cognitive outcomes of preschoolers. Zaslow, et al. (1998) state, "Evidence thus far suggests that maternal employment which improves family income and enhances maternal psychological well-being will have neutral to positive implications for children's development, *perhaps particularly when it occurs beyond the infancy period*" (p. 19, emphasis added). This is a particularly important area requiring further research, as we need to understand factors that can potentially interfere with the development of the mother-infant relationship, especially for infants living under stressful conditions. The issue of mandates and requirements is also of interest. Under what conditions do the standards imposed by welfare reform support or hinder the mother's ability to take care of her baby? Do the effects of the timing of welfare requirements on the mother-infant relationship or children's developmental outcomes differ by age (e.g., more negative effects for infants versus preschoolers)? Do mothers' perceptions of, and responses to, the welfare-to-work policy requirements influence their interactions with their babies?

Recent research findings document limited effects of welfare-to-work participation on maternal well-being and parenting skills. There have been fewer significant findings from observational studies of parenting and child development embedded in evaluations of three welfare reform interventions than had been hoped, and those that emerged are mixed (Zaslow, et al., 1998). Some mothers had higher levels of depression and parenting stress and lower levels of satisfaction with their standard of living, but also showed more positive parenting behaviors and emotional warmth and support towards their preschoolers (Morrison, Zaslow, & Dion, 1998; Weinfield, Egeland, & Ogawa, 1998), although those positive findings persisted only for those mothers who initially had low levels of depression. Other mothers were observed to have lower scores on positive parenting behaviors and emotional warmth and support after their first three months of participation, but most of those differences disappeared by the fifth month of participation (Zaslow, Oldham, Moore, & Magenheim, 1997). In a third study, only the mother's harsh control and negative emotion were affected, with scores showing a small but beneficial effect of heavier participation (Aber, Brooks-Gunn, & Maynard, 1995).

Notwithstanding the incredible challenges welfare reform programs and participants face, these preliminary findings raise questions about whether participation in the programs really can help mothers with childrearing, as assumed by some welfare reformers and child advocates. What factors might interfere with the success of these programs in educating parents and supporting positive parenting? Currently, in the search for program impacts as well as processes that might affect program impact, the intermediate variables used tend to be individual-level variables such as depression. Although individual-level factors may be important, participation in welfare reform programs may very well be affected by the broader ecological context, such as the neighborhood. For example, certain characteristics of neighborhoods, such as the degrees of crime, violence and drug abuse, may limit the ability of mothers to participate in a program (see Garbarino & Kostelny, 1993).

As bioecological theory might suggest, a mother's participation in employment activities may have a significant impact on the quality of the home environment. One hypothesis that has been tested with children ages three through six is that the quality of the mother's working conditions is reflected in the quality of the home environment. Using the Home Observation for Measurement of the Environment (HOME), Parcel & Menaghan (1997) found that mothers who remained unmarried but began employment described as "high in complexity and wages" had home environments whose quality improved somewhat, while mothers who remained unmarried and began employment described as "low in complexity and wages" had home environments whose quality declined significantly. Analyses were only conducted using a global measure of home environment, so it is unclear if the quality of the mother-child relationship was affected. However, as this is a relevant question for understanding the effects of welfare reform on infants, future research should explore the extent to which this finding also applies to the home environment and parent-child interaction among welfare mothers with infants.

Also, because paternity establishment and child support enforcement are key provisions of welfare reform, the role of fathers should be included in studies of welfare reform's impact on mother-infant relationships. However, the recency of these paternal child support provisions precludes any systematic study of how they might influence the quality of the mother-infant relationship and the informal support nonresidential fathers in low-income situations often provide (Zaslow, et al., 1998). There is suggestion in the literature that maternal employment is positively associated with paternal involvement with children (Doherty, et al., 1998), but whether paternal support of working mothers manifests itself in the mother-infant relationship is unknown.

Overall, very little data enriches our knowledge of the effects of welfare reform on the mother-infant relationship, mainly because the requirement that mothers of infants on welfare participate in employment-related activities is new (although states may exempt parents of infants under twelve months of age). The paucity of data is a concern, as the needs of infants are hardly primary in the eyes of welfare reform architects. Although it is encouraging to note that some of the studies in the current wave of research will include infants, it is not clear that the search for processes will include attention to how broader ecological factors might limit or increase the ability of mothers to appropriately care for their infants.

SOCIETAL INFLUENCES ON PARENTING INFANTS

Beyond their own families, personal networks, neighborhoods, and work circumstances, mothers and infants also operate within the larger society and are touched by the cultural and economic forces that define that society. It is beyond the scope of this chapter to engage in a comprehensive analysis of societal influences on parenting, but some aspects would seem to have particular salience with respect to mother-infant relationships. Specifically, we think it is important to consider how culture and the sociohistorical context shape parental beliefs about infants and parenting. What are the societal and cultural messages about how we care for infants? How are those messages transmitted to parents and to what extent do those messages actually influence the way mothers care for their infants?

Across ethnic societies, proverbs represent the traditional cultural beliefs that have been transmitted, largely unchanged, through generations. In essence, they help to provide social cohesion and transmit cultural values. Hillary Rodham Clinton recognized the power of the proverb, selecting an African proverb as the title of her 1996 book *It Takes a Village: And Other Lessons Children Teach Us.* Palacios (1996) offers a range of ethnic proverbs that reflect similar cultural perspectives toward many of the continuing themes underlying developmental psychology: nature versus nurture, individual differences, childrearing, and discipline. In addition, many of these traditional proverbs illustrate the benefits as well as the trials and tribulations of having children, with which current-day parents can also identify. Examples include: "Children are treasures more precious than a thousand granaries" (Japanese) and "Children are a perpetual millstone around the neck" (Japanese) (Palacios, 1996, pp. 81–82). In traditional societies, and to some extent in modern society, proverbs provide parents with a set of expectations and norms from which they rear their children. We don't know how influential proverbs are in directly shaping parental practices, but the advent of science and the dissemination of scientific knowledge have provided perspectives on childrearing that sometimes challenge cultural beliefs (e.g., "Spare the rod and spoil the child" versus research findings on the negative developmental outcomes for children who are punished harshly).

How is the relation between culture and science played out in the "real world"? One empirical example comes from Young (1990), who conducted a content analysis of public information disseminated to parents of infants from 1955–1984, the Infant Care Manual and Parents magazine. In the face of great increases in research-based knowledge about all aspects of infant development during that period, Young was interested in the extent to which information on infant and child development was communicated accurately to parents. She discovered that the information parents received from experts in the areas of perception, cognition and temperament best reflected the scientific knowledge of the time, but the information parents received about the mother-infant relationship, working mothers and child care, feeding, and fathers was more likely to be shaped by a combination of research findings, the sociohistorical context, and cultural values. Advice offered to parents clearly changed over time and, to a certain extent, presented mixed messages about critical issues in caring for infants. For example, according to this study, the message about mother-infant relationships from the 1950s to the early 1970s was that mothers are of primary importance to their infant's development, while from the mid-1970s until the mid 1980s (where the analysis ended), the message was that the quality of interactions between mothers and babies was important but less central to healthy infant development. The message about working mothers and child care in the 1950s and 1960s reflected the maternal role as full-time caregiver for the infants, and if maternal work outside the home was necessary, in-home infant care was considered the only option. By the 1980s, the messages were both about reassuring mothers about "quality not quantity" and that staying home was also a viable role for mothers.

A common example of how culture and parental beliefs and research intersect around infant care is the popular "spoiling myth" (Erickson & Kurz-Riemer, 1999). New parents often report being bombarded with messages from friends, relatives, and sometimes even health care professionals, warning them about the danger of spoiling their baby if they respond to his or her crying. "Just let him cry it out so he'll learn who's in charge," or "she's only crying to get your attention" are common admonishments. And yet research refutes the spoiling myth, certainly as it applies to young infants, pointing instead to consistent, sensitive response to a baby's cries as the pathway to a secure parent-infant relationship—and to less crying by the end of the first year of life and greater autonomy and compliance during the toddler period (Ainsworth & Bell, 1974; Erickson, et al., 1985).

With this backdrop of the different kinds of messages parents have received from child development experts comes a survey recently conducted to ascertain what parents know about early childhood development and their role in it (Zero to Three, 1997). Based on focus groups and a phone survey of a national sample of parents, the researchers found great variability in parents' knowledge of child development. While many parents grasped basic but important messages about child development, such as the idea that babies are learning from the moment they're born and that parents' emotional closeness with their baby can influence intellectual development, they were less aware of the importance of the continuity of caregivers for very young children and of the role of stimulation/overstimulation in development. These findings, in fact, mirror current societal messages, which do not press government or corporations for high-quality child care and overemphasize early stimulation at the expense of parent-infant relationships.

What's a parent to do? What's a researcher, or a practitioner, or a policymaker, to do? How does the confluence of research and sociohistorical context shape the way we think about infants and mother-infant relationships, study them, and make decisions about creating the best opportunities to support them? How do those views shape mothers' individual practices and our public policies around caring for infants? How do we decide which information is critical for parents, and how do we best work with parents to find the appropriate and respectful balance between cultural tradition and sometimes contradictory research-based information?

We know very little about how parents believe the social context shapes their thinking, their parenting, and their understandings, and assumptions about children. To guide future research examining how the sociohistorical context exerts influence on parenting, Youniss (1994) offers the perspective of microsociology, which conceptualizes society and societal influences as interpersonal interactive processes. Societal influences are experienced through the day-to-day interactions between parent and infant. Future research should investigate how these interactions represent societal views and how social realities become part of the relationships between mothers and infants and thus the minds and expectations of very young children.

CONCLUSION

How do "contexts of relevance" influence the mother-infant relationship? And how can ecological perspectives be applied to guide practice, policy, and future research on infant-mother relationships? As the two stories of Lisa suggested, the support and stress experienced at different levels of the ecology can be pivotal influences on the mother-infant relationship.

Bioecological theory and the life course perspective offer theoretical frameworks from which to study the ecological factors that are part of the everyday lives of mothers and infants (Cowan, 1998; De Wolff and van IJzendoorn, 1997). These perspectives force consideration of the multiple ecological influences on parents and children, such as extended family, or personal social networks, as well as the mutual influence mothers and infants exert on each other, as suggested by the transactional model (Sameroff & Chandler, 1975). Luster and Okagaki (1993) point out that studies examining multiple influences on parenting are better able to make predictions about risk and outcome and the cumulative nature of risk. Thus, they are better able to delineate the circumstances under which parenting is most affected both positively and negatively.

As researchers struggle to understand the complexities of interventions that meet with limited success, a contextual perspective seems critical. Mediator and moderator variables tend to be individual-level variables (e.g., maternal depression, self-esteem, maternal education), and although those variables may explain some portion of the variance, ecological factors that may also have explanatory value are often excluded from the research designs. For example, studies of welfare reform interventions often focus on characteristics of the mother to help explain program success. However, external forces such as dangerous neighborhoods or extended family attitudes towards work and child care may shape the ability of a mother to fully and successfully participate in a welfare-to-work intervention. Program success may be limited by ecological factors seemingly unrelated to the program itself. Program evaluators could consider the ecology of the program as well as the ecology of the participants. They might then ask the following question: Would a child abuse prevention program find more limited success in a violent as compared to a non-violent neighborhood?

A contextual approach also can be used to guide research designs, specifically the targeting and timing of interventions. In relation to targeting, at what level or levels of the ecology are certain interventions more efficacious? For example, how effective is parent support group intervention, which aims to build or expand the personal social network for first-time parents as compared to an intervention focused on the individual mother-infant dyad? Under what conditions is one more effective than the other? How can interventions engage the extended family or even the friendship network in supporting positive mother-infant relationships? Using a life course perspective in relation to timing, one might ask how ecological factors influence the times at which the best "windows of opportunity" occur when parents tend to be most amenable to intervention and education. Can we modify features of the ecology to maximize those opportunities?

Information generated from studies that address these issues will enrich practice, as there will be a greater understanding of which features of a mother's ecology are more amenable to change. And programs that target different critical parts of a mother and infant's ecology can be designed. For the most part, prevention and intervention program designs fail to include extended family (or even immediate family beyond mother and infant), personal social networks, and neighborhoods, and instead focus largely on the mother-infant dyad. What results is a heavy emphasis on bringing about personal change, generally in a short period of time and under trying circumstances, and little focus on helping mothers build the natural supports in their families and communities that will help sustain them over longer periods of time. Might services be more effective if service providers were trained to understand how ecological forces either constrain or enable mothers' effective use of services?

Growing evidence of ecological influences on mother-infant relationships should help policymakers recognize the complexity of the lives of mothers with very young children. Our public policies need to reflect the reality that ecological forces, at all levels, have potent effects in the lives of young families. Unfortunately, there is no simple answer to the question of how best to support young families in our current society. One necessary strategy is to strengthen the connections between research, practice and policy. For example, data on the effect of social policy changes (e.g., welfare reform) on mothers with infants and mother-infant relationships can be gathered and used to enrich our operating theories and shape our expectations for how we bring about social change and support citizens in their lives (Etzioni, 1994).

An ecological lens also offers a framework for rethinking the breadth of policy and how funds are subsequently targeted to aid families with infants. Creative, broad-based policies that build on the natural supports in families' lives are needed. A comprehensive policy to support mothers and infants should not focus solely on the level of the mother-infant dyad, but should also be ecologically-based, targeted at the levels of the extended family and the community. A comprehensive policy might include: family-friendly workplace policies; quality, affordable childcare conveniently located for working mothers and involved fathers; safe, affordable housing for young families that would allow them to remain close to extended family if they chose; and accessible transportation to and from work.

A strong, positive mother-infant relationship is an important foundation for healthy development and lifelong learning. Even under the best of circumstances, the needs and demands of an infant stretch the resources of a mother. But too often mothers must "swim upstream" in the context of family, neighborhood, and society to make their job harder rather than easier. It is in the interest of these mothers and children—and ultimately our society—that we develop practices and policies that are well-grounded in knowledge of the most salient factors that support or hinder high-quality mother-infant relationships.

REFERENCES

Aber, J. L., Brooks-Gunn, J., & Maynard, R. A. (1995). Effects of welfare reform on teenage parents and their children. *The Future of Children*, 5(2), 53–71.

Ainsworth, M.D.S., & Bell, S.M. (1974). Mother-infant interaction and the development of competence. In K. Connolly & J. Bruner (Eds.), *The growth of competence* (pp. 97–118). New York: Academic Press.

Annie E. Casey Foundation. (1998). KIDS COUNT report. Available: www.kidscount.org/kidscount/kc1998/overview.htm

Apfel, N.H., & Seitz, V. (1991). Four models of adolescent-mother grandmother relationships in black inner-city families, *Family Relations*, 40, 421–429.

Belsky, J. (1984). The determinants of parenting: A process model. *Child Development*, 55, 83–96.

Belsky, J. (1988). The "effects" of infant day care reconsidered. *Early Childhood Research Quarterly*, 3, 235–272.

Belsky, J. (1993). Etiology of child maltreatment: A developmental/ecological analysis. *Psychological Bulletin*, 114, 413–434.

Belsky, J., & Isabella, I. (1988). Maternal, infant, and social-contextual determinants of attachment security. In J. Belsky & T. Nezworski (Eds.), *Clinical implications of attachment* (pp. 41–94). Hillsdale, NJ: Lawrence Erlbaum Associates.

Bradley, R. H., Whiteside-Mansell, L., Brisby, J. A., & Caldwell, B. (1997). Parents' socioemotional investment in children. *Journal of Marriage and the Family*, 59, 77–90.

Bronfenbrenner, U. (1979). *The ecology of human development: Experiments by nature and design.* Cambridge, MA: Harvard University Press.

Bronfenbrenner, U., & Ceci, S. (1994). Nature-nurture reconceptualized: A bioecological model. *Psychological Review*, 101, 568–586.

Bronfenbrenner, U., & Morris, P. A. (1998). The ecology of developmental processes. In W. Damon & R. M. Lerner (Eds.), *Handbook of child psychology* (5th ed., Vol. 1, pp. 993–1028). New York: John Wiley & Sons.

Brooks-Gunn, J., Duncan, G. J., & Aber, J. L. (1997). *Neighborhood poverty: Context and consequences for children* (Vol. 1). New York: Russell Sage Foundation.

Brunnquell, D., Crichton, L., & Egeland, B. (1981). Maternal personality and attitudes in disturbances of child-rearing. *American Journal of Orthopsychiatry*, 51, 680–691.

Buerkle, K. (1997). *Mobile children and families: Qualitative and quantitative explorations of the meaning and impact of residential mobility and school changes.* Unpublished doctoral dissertation.

Chase-Lansdale, P. L., Brooks-Gunn, J., & Zamsky, E. S. (1994). Young African-American multigenerational families in poverty: Quality of mothering and grandmothering. *Child Development*, 65, 373–393.

Clinton, H. R. (1996). *It takes a village: And other lessons children teach us.* New York: Simon and Schuster.

Cochran, M., & Brassard, J. (1979). Child development and personal social networks. *Child Development, 50,* 609–616.

Cochran, M., & Niego, S. (1995). Parenting and social networks. In M. H. Bornstein (Ed.), *Handbook of parenting* (pp. 393–418). Hillsdale, NJ: Lawrence Erlbaum.

Cochran, M., Larner, M., Riley, D., Gunnarsson, L., & Henderson, Jr., C. R. (1990). *Extending families: The social networks of parents and their children.* New York: Cambridge University Press.

Coulton, C. J., & Pandey, S. (1992). Geographic concentration of poverty and risk to children in urban neighborhoods. *American Behavioral Scientist, 35,* 238–257.

Coulton, C. J., Korbin, J., Su, M., & Chow, J. (1995). Community-level factors and child maltreatment rates. *Child Development, 66,* 1262–1276.

Cowan, P. (1998). Beyond meta-analysis: A plea for a family systems view of attachment. *Child Development, 68,* 601–603.

Crockenberg, S. (1988). Social support and parenting. In H. E. Fitzgerald & B. M. Lester (Eds.), *Theory and research in behavioral pediatrics* (Vol. 4, pp. 141–174). New York: Plenum Press.

DeWolff, M. S., & van IJzendoorn, M. H. (1997). Sensitivity and attachment: A meta-analysis on parental antecedents of infant attachment. *Child Development, 68,* 571–591.

Doherty, W. J., Kouneski, E. F., & Erickson, M. F. (1998). Responsible fathering: An overview and conceptual framework. *Journal of Marriage and the Family, 60,* 277–292.

Duncan, G. J., & Aber, J. L. (1997). Neighborhood models and measures. In J. Brooks-Gunn, G. J. Duncan, & J. L. Aber (Eds.), *Neighborhood poverty: Context and consequences for children* (Vol. 1, pp. 62–78). New York: Russell Sage Foundation.

Dunst, C., & Trivette, C. M. (1990). Assessment of social support in early intervention programs. In S. J. Meisels & J. P. Shonkoff (Eds.), *Handbook of early childhood intervention* (pp. 326–349). New York: Cambridge University Press.

Dunst, C. J., Trivette, C. M., & Deal, A. G. (1988). *Enabling and empowering families: Principles and guidelines for practice.* Cambridge, MA: Brookline Books.

Egeland, B., & Farber, E. A. (1984). Infant-mother attachment: Factors related to its development and changes over time. *Child Development, 55,* 753–771.

Egeland, B., Jacobvitz, D., & Sroufe, L. A. (1988). Breaking the cycle of abuse. *Child Development, 59,* 1080–1088.

Elder, Jr., G. H. (1998a). The life course as developmental theory. *Child Development, 1,* 1–12.

Elder, Jr., G. H. (1998b). The life course and human development. In W. Damon & R. M. Lerner (Eds.), *Handbook of child psychology: Vol. 1* (5th ed., pp. 939–992). New York: John Wiley & Sons.

Elicker, J., Noppe, I. C., Noppe, L. D., & Fortner-Wood, C. (1997). The parent-caregiver relationship scale: Rounding out the relationship system in infant child care. *Early Education and Development, 8,* 83–100.

Erel, O, & Burman, B. (1995). Interrrelatedness of marital relations and parent-child relations: A met-analytic review. *Psychological Bulletin*, 118, 108–132.

Erickson, M. F., & Kurz-Riemer, K. (1999). *Infants, toddlers, and families: A framework for intervention.* New York: Guilford Press.

Erickson, M. F., Egeland, B., & Sroufe, L. A. (1985). The relationships between quality of attachment and behavior problems in preschool in a high-risk sample. In I. Bretherton & E. Waters (Eds.), *Monographs of the Society for Research in Child Development*, 50 (1–2 Serial No. 209), 147–166.

Erickson, M. F., Korfmacher, J., & Egeland, B. R. (1992). Attachments past and present: Implications for therapeutic intervention with mother-infant dyads. *Development and Psychopathology*, 4, 495–507.

Etzioni, A. (1994). Incorrigible: Bringing social hope and political rhetoric into instructive contact with what it means to be human. *Atlantic Monthly,* July, pp. 14–16.

Fonagy, P., Steele, H., & Steele, M. (1991). Maternal representations of attachment during pregnancy predict the organization of infant-mother attachment at 1 year of age. *Child Development*, 62, 891–905.

Fraiberg, S., Adelson, E., & Shapiro, Y. (1980). Ghosts in the nursery: A psycho-analytic approach to the problems of impaired infant-mother relationships. In S. Fraiberg (Ed.), *Clinical studies in infant mental health* (pp. 164–196). New York: Basic Books.

Furstenberg, F. (1993). How families manage risk and opportunity in dangerous neighborhoods. In W. J. Wilson (Ed.), *Sociology and the public agenda* (pp. 231–258). Newbury Park, CA: Sage.

Garbarino, J., & Giliam, G. (1980). *Understanding abusive families.* Lexington, MA: Lexington Books.

Garbarino, J., & Kostelny, K. (1993). Neighborhood and community influences on parenting. In T. Luster & L. Okagaki (Eds.), *Parenting: An ecological perspective* (pp. 203–226). Hillsdale, NJ: Lawrence Erlbaum.

Garbarino, J., Kostelny, K., & Barry, F. (1995). Value transmission in an ecological context: The high-risk neighborhood. In J. E. Grusec & L. Kuczynski (Eds.), *Parenting and children's internalization of values: A handbook of contemporary theory* (pp. 307–332). New York: John Wiley & Sons.

Heinecke, C. M. (1995). Determinants of the transition to parenting. In M. Bornstein (Ed.), *Handbook of parenting: Status and social conditions of parenting* (pp. 277–304). Mahwah, NJ: Lawrence Erlbaum.

Heinecke, C. M., Guthrie, D., & Ruth, G. (1997). Marital adaptation, divorce, and parent-infant development: A prospective study. *Infant Mental Health Journal*, 18, 282–299.

Hoff-Ginsburg, E., & Tardif, T. (1995). Socioeconomic status and parenting. In M. H. Bornstein (Ed.), *Handbook of parenting. Vol. 2: Biology and ecology of parenting* (pp. 161–188). Mahwah, NJ: Lawrence Erlbaum Associates.

Jarrett, R. (1995). Growing up poor: The family experiences of socially mobile youth in low-income, African-American families. *Journal of Adolescent Research*, 10, 111–135.

Klebanov, P. K., Brooks-Gunn, J., & Duncan, G. J. (1994). Does neighborhood and family poverty affects mothers' parenting, mental health, and social support? *Journal of Marriage and the Family*, 56, 441–455.

Klebanov, P. K., Brooks-Gunn, J., Chase-Lansdale, P. K., & Gordon, R. (1997). Neighborhood and family influences on the intellectual and behavioral competence of preschool and early school-age children. In J. Brooks-Gunn, G. J. Duncan, & J. L. Aber (Eds.), *Neighborhood poverty: Context and consequences for children* (Vol. 1, pp. 79–118). New York: Russell Sage Foundation.

Klebanov, P. K., Brooks-Gunn, J., McCarton, C., & McCormick, M. C. (1998). The contribution of neighborhood and family income to developmental test scores over the first three years of life. *Child Development*, 69, 1420–1436.

Luster, T., & Okagaki, L. (1993). Multiple influences on parenting: Ecological and life course perspectives. In T. Luster & L. Okagaki (Eds.), *Parenting: An ecological perspective* (pp. 227–250). Hillsdale, NJ: Erlbaum.

Main, M., & Goldwyn, R. (1984). Predicting rejection of her infant from mother's representation of her own experience: Implications for the abused-abusing intergenerational cycle. *Child Abuse and Neglect*, 8, 203–217.

Main, M., & Goldwyn, R. (1991). Interview-based adult attachment classifications: related to infant-mother and infant-father attachment. Developmental Psychology.

Mayer, S. E. (1997). Indicators of children's economic well-being and parental employment. In R. M. Hauser, B. V. Brown, & W. R. Prosser (Eds.), *Indicators of children's well-being* (pp. 237–257). New York: Russell Sage Foundation.

McLoyd, V. (1998). Children in poverty: Development, public policy and practice. In W. Damon & N. Eisenberg (Eds.), *Handbook of child psychology: Vol. 1* (5th ed., pp. 135–210). New York: John Wiley & Sons.

Moon, A. (1994). Should AFDC mothers be required to work in order to receive benefits? Yes. In M.A. Mason & E. Gambrill (Eds.), *Debating children's lives: Current controversies on children and adolescents* (pp. 319–324). Thousand Oaks, CA: Sage Publications.

Morrison, D. R., Zaslow, M. J., & Dion, M. R. (1998). Completing the portrayal of parenting behavior with interview-based measures. In M. J. Zaslow & C. Eldred (Eds.), *Parenting behavior in a sample of young mothers in poverty: Results of the New Chance Observational Study* (pp. 170–212). New York: Manpower Demonstration Research Corporation.

Nair, P., Black, M. M., Schuler, M., Keane, V., Snow, L., & Rigney, B. A. (1997). Risk factors for disruption in primary caregiving among infants of substance abusing women. *Child Abuse and Neglect*, 21, 1039–1051.

Newberger, C. M., & Cook, S. J. (1983). Parental awareness and child abuse: A cognitive-developmental analysis of urban and rural samples. *American Journal of Orthopsychiatry*, 53, 512–524.

NICHD Early Child Care Research Network. (1997). The effects of infant child care on infant-mother attachment security: Results of the NICHD study of early child care. *Child Development*, 68, 860–879.

Oyserman, D., Radin, N., & Benn, R. (1993). Dynamics in a three-generational family: Teens, grandparents, and babies. *Developmental Psychology, 29,* 564–572.

Ozawa, M. (1994). Should AFDC mothers be required to work in order to receive benefits? No. In M. A. Mason & E. Gambrill (Eds.), *Debating children's lives: Current controversies on children and adolescents* (pp. 325–333). Thousand Oaks, CA: Sage Publications.

Palacios, J. (1996). Proverbs as images of children and childrearing. In C. P. Hwang, M. E. Lamb, & I. Sigel (Eds.), *Images of childhood* (pp. 75–98). New Jersey: Lawrence Erlbaum.

Parcel, T. L., & Menaghan, E. G. (1997). Effects of low-wage employment on family well-being. *Future of Children, 7,* 116–121.

Parke, R. D., & Buriel, R. (1998). Socialization in the family: Ethnic and ecological perspectives. In W. Damon & N. Eisenberg (Eds.), *Handbook of child psychology: Vol. 3* (5th ed., pp. 463–552). New York: John Wiley & Sons.

Pianta, R. C., & Egeland, B. (1990). Life stress and parenting outcomes in a disadvantaged sample: Results of the mother-child interaction project. *Journal of Clinical Child Psychology, 19,* 329–336.

Roggman, L. A., Langlois, J. H., Hubbs-Tait, L., & Rieser-Danner, L.A. (1994). Infant day-care, attachment, and the "file drawer problem." *Child Development, 65,* 1429–1443.

Sagi, A., van IJzendoorn, M. H., Scharf, M., Joels, T., Koren-Karie, N., Mayseless, O., & Aviezer, O. (1997). Ecological contraints for intergenerational transmission of attachment. *International Journal of Behavioral Development, 20,* 287–299.

Sameroff, A. J., & Chandler, M. (1975). Reproductive risk and the continuum of caretaking casualty. In F. D. Horowitz (Ed.), *Child development research* (Vol. 4, pp. 187–244). Chicago: University of Chicago Press.

Sampson, R. J. (1992). Family management and child development: Insights from social disorganization theory. In J. McCord (Ed.), *Facts, frameworks, and forecasts: Advances in criminological theory* (Vol. 3, pp. 63–93). New Brunswick, NJ: Transaction Publishers.

Sanders-Phillips, K. (1998). Infant feeding behavior and caretaker-infant relationships in black families. *Journal of Comparative Family Studies, 29,* 161–171.

Smith, J., Brooks-Gunn, J., & Jackson, A. (1997). Parental employment and children. In R. M. Hauser, B. V. Brown, & W. R. Prosser (Eds.), *Indicators of children's well-being* (pp. 279–308). New York: Russell Sage Foundation.

Spieker, S. J., & Bensley, L. (1994). Roles of living arrangements and grandmother social support in adolescent mothering and infant attachment. *Developmental Psychology, 30,* 102–111.

Sroufe, L. A., & Fleeson, J. (1986). Attachment and the construction of relationships. In W. Hartup & Z. Rubin (Eds.), *Relationships and development* (pp. 51–72). Hillsdale, NJ: Lawrence Erlbaum.

Susman-Stillman, A. (1997). *Neighborhood influences on welfare mothers and their children: What are the effects on maternal, parenting and child outcomes?* Unpublished doctoral dissertation.

Taylor, R. D., & Roberts, D. D. (1997). *Moderating effects of kinship support on the impact of neighborhood stressors on African-American mothers.* Poster presented at the Society for Research in Child Development Biennial Meeting, Washington, DC.

Weinfield, N., Egeland, B., & Ogawa, J. R. (1998). The affective quality of mother-child interaction. In M. J. Zaslow & C. Eldred (Eds.), *Parenting behavior in a sample of young mothers in poverty: Results of the New Chance Observational Study* (pp. 71–113). New York: Manpower Demonstration Research Corporation.

Wilson, M. N (1989). Child development in the context of the Black extended family. *American Psychologist*, 44, 380–385.

Young, K. T. (1990). American conceptions of infant development from 1955–1984: What experts are telling parents. *Child Development*, 61, 17–28.

Youniss, J. (1994). Rearing children for society. In J. G. Smetana (Ed.), *Beliefs about parenting: Origins and developmental implications* (New Directions for Child Development, 66, pp. 37–50). San Francisco: Jossey-Bass.

Zaslow, M. J., & Emig, C. (1997). When low-income mothers go to work: Implications for children. *Future of Children*, 7, 110–115.

Zaslow, M. J., Oldham, E., Moore, K. A., & Magenheim, E. (1997). *The implications of participation in community-based child care for the cognitive and social development of children from welfare families.* Paper presented at the Society for Child Development Biennial Meeting, Washington, DC.

Zaslow, M. J., Tout, K., Smith, S., & Moore, K. (1998). *Implications of the 1996 welfare legislation for children: A research perspective* (Social Policy Report, Society for Research in Child Development, Vol. XII, No. 3).

Zero to Three (1997). *Key findings from a nationwide survey among parents of zero to three year-olds.* Available: www.zerotothree.org

UNDERSTANDING THE CAREGIVING PRACTICES OF ADOLESCENT MOTHERS

Tom Luster
& Laura Bates

5

••••

Many studies have compared the childrearing practices of adolescent mothers and older mothers and have found that more mature mothers, on average, provide more favorable environments for their children (Luster & Brophy-Herb, 2000). These findings do not come as a surprise. For many of us who read this work, our first inclination is to think back to our teenage years and to imagine what it would have been like to be a parent at that time. Being a teenager was difficult enough without having children. Being a parent was challenging enough for those of us who started in our thirties. It must be very difficult to be both a teenager and a parent. "There is no way that I would have been ready to be a parent then," we tell ourselves. Our images of ourselves as immature, "geeky," and self-absorbed teenagers seem to provide a ready explanation for why adolescent mothers receive less favorable scores on measures of caregiving than do older mothers.

Although age and maturity probably are important factors in how we care for our children, the story of adolescent parenthood is more complicated. Why is it that one 16-year-old provides a loving and supportive home for her infant while another meets her baby's physical needs but provides little else that would promote optimal development? Moreover, how do the 16-year-olds who are parents differ from their peers who delay having their first children for many years? In this chapter, we will try to understand the numerous factors that can influence how teenage mothers care for their infants. The chapter is divided into four sections. Three of the sections focus on what we have learned from research concerning three key research questions.

First, how do the characteristics and circumstances of adolescents who become parents differ from the characteristics and circumstances of their peers who delay having children until their 20s or later? To some extent, differences in the caregiving practices of younger and older mothers may be explained by selection factors (e.g., poverty, problems in the family of origin, characteristics of the teens such as depressive symptoms or limited knowledge of child development). It is important to understand the characteristics and circumstances of teens who become mothers in order to understand what happens to them after the infants are born, as well as the environment in which they are raising their infants.

Second, how do the circumstances in which adolescent mothers rear their infants differ, on average, from the circumstances in which older mothers are rearing their infants? If adolescent mothers are more likely than older mothers to raise their infants in poverty or as single parents, this may explain why they differ from older mothers in their approaches to childrearing.

Third, what factors, other than age, contribute to individual differences in the quality of care that adolescent mothers provide for their infants? It is particularly important to understand why many adolescent mothers manage to provide high quality care for their infants.

Before we address these questions, however, we will present three case studies. These case studies focus on three families that were involved in a family support program for low income adolescent mothers in Flint, Michigan. The program was called Family TIES (Trust, Information, Encouragement, Support) and was provided by the Mott Children's Health Center. The case studies are based on interviews with family support workers, called family advocates, who described the families they worked with over a five-year period. The interviews were conducted at two points in time, when the children were age 2 1/2 and six. We present the case studies for two reasons. First, we hope to show why we believe the age of the mother may be a less important influence on her caregiving behavior than other factors. Second, we want to highlight the diversity found in samples of adolescent mothers and in the experiences of their children. The experience of each child born to an adolescent mother is unique, but this reality is often lost in statistics based on aggregated data.

The first case we present focuses on a mother and her family who live in very challenging circumstances. The second case describes a young mother who had to overcome considerable adversity, but provides a supportive home environment for her child. The third case presents a young mother who was an honor student in high school but who has also been a victim of domestic violence. Pseudonyms have been used to protect the identity of the participants.

THREE CASE STUDIES

Dawn and Her Son, Ricky

Dawn was enrolled in the Family TIES family support program while sitting in a car in her driveway. The enrollment interview was conducted in the car because, when the staff arrived, someone in the grandmother's house was threatening another person during a heated argument. At the time of the advocate interview, Dawn lived in her grandmother's house along with twelve other people including her 30-month-old son, Ricky, her mother, and some of her uncles and aunts. The presence of this many people under the same roof created an atmosphere of chaos. The family advocate described the house as a war zone because of the cluttered conditions and the constant fighting that occurred there. In general, people in the household seemed to take advantage of the grandmother, who was weary from the cramped quarters and family conflict but could not bring herself to put people out.

Dawn's father had a reputation for drinking excessively and had recently been released from prison, having served a sentence for robbery and murder. Dawn and her father did not have a close relationship. Dawn's mother abused drugs and alcohol, as did other members of the household. The grandmother let them use drugs in the basement of her home so that they would not use them in the street where it was dangerous.

Dawn's mother was generally inattentive and uninvolved when Dawn was growing up. Her mother was involved in drugs, partying, and dating a lot of men. Children were not a high priority in her life. She did not invest much of her time or energy in childrearing. Dawn seemed to be following a similar pattern. She sat on the couch wrapped in a blanket watching television for much of the day. She was with her children all day but spent little time interacting with them. She showed little interest in teaching her children. Dawn seldom initiated conversations with anyone, including her children. If her child asked a question, she said "no," "I don't know," or "go sit down." She seldom explained things to her children in terms they could understand.

At night, she left her children with her mother or grandmother and didn't say where she was going. She sometimes stayed out all night and was greeted by an angry mother and grandmother when she returned. Harsh words were exchanged and sometimes the words led to an exchange of blows. Dawn called her mother a "bitch" and told the family advocate that her mother did not deserve her respect.

The family advocate believed that nobody gave Dawn the nurturing she needed as a child. Dawn talked about all of the bad things her mother did, but she could not visualize for the family advocate what she wanted to be as a mother. She did not see that her behavior toward her children was much like the care that she had received. The family advocate talked to Dawn about the possibility of counseling but her family did not believe in counseling, and she declined the offer.

Dawn tended to buy big and expensive toys for the children. She seemed to think that if the toys were big and they cost a lot, they were good for the children. Often, however, they were not developmentally appropriate. The family advocate believed that Dawn loved her children and nurtured them as well as she could, but that she did not have a lot to give.

Dawn had completed ninth grade but was no longer attending school at the time of the interview, nor did she plan to return to school. She lived close to the adult high school, which had a day care center, but she refused to attend. When the state of Michigan threatened her with sanctions for not attending school, Dawn became pregnant with her second child.

The family advocate worried about her oldest child, Ricky, the focal child in the intervention. She expected him to have problems when he reached school because of the multiple risks of parental uninvolvement, drug use, and violence that he faced. At 30 months, he walked around with a toy beeper, a toy gun, a cigarette lighter, and an empty pack of cigarettes. The adult roles he imitated in his pretend play were the roles that he had seen others play in Grandmother's house.

Kim and Her Daughter, Emily

Kim's mother died when she was twelve years old, and she lived with her father until she ran away from home at the age of fourteen. Her father had been physically abusive to Kim's mother before she died and had physically abused Kim as well. Even as a child, Kim stood up to her father when he was abusive to her mother, trying to get him to leave her mother alone. Kim thought this was the reason her father seemed to treat her sister (who did not confront him) more favorably in the years after her mother's death.

When Kim ran away from home, she lived with her aunt in Arizona. Kim described the aunt as a free-spirited hippie who liked nature and motorcycles. The aunt was good to Kim and filled a void in her life. However, the aunt associated with drug users and eventually Kim became a daily drug user. In time, she recognized the toll that the drugs were taking on her and returned to the Flint area. She moved into her own apartment, which she paid for with the Social Security money she had been receiving since her mother's death.

While living on her own, she became pregnant and entered the Family TIES program at age eighteen. Six months after Emily was born, Kim married Emily's father, Bill. At the end of the program, when Emily was 54 months old, Bill and Kim were still married, and they had one another child three years younger than Emily. They lived in a trailer home in a rural setting that the advocate rated as a relatively safe area.

The family advocate described Kim as intelligent, empathic, responsible, and mature. The family advocate also viewed her as very child-centered and skillful in her dealings with her children. She wanted to be a better parent for her children than her father had been for her. Kim read books on child development and used the information when she interacted with the baby. She was also open to suggestions from the family advocate. She read to Emily so often that the child could "read" to her, having memorized some of her books.

Bill and Kim limited the amount of time Emily watched television. They structured her time so that she had a regular time for meals, naps, and bedtime. They set up the home environment so that it was safe for the child to explore, and they made sure that Emily had interesting and age appropriate playthings. Both parents enjoyed playing with Emily, and were excited to share news of developmental advances with the family advocate.

The relationship between Bill and Kim had its ups and downs. Many of the down times were related to financial stress. Bill was committed to supporting his family financially but he had a seasonal job and was laid off for several months during the winter. These were lean months for the family and the tension was sometimes evident. Whatever difficulties they had as a couple did not seem to undermine the way either parent dealt with the children.

The family advocate attributed Kim's positive parenting practices to three things: 1) Kim's strength and resiliency; 2) the social support that Kim and Bill received from others, particularly Bill's close-knit family; and 3) the close relationship Kim had with her mother before her mother died. Even though her mother had died ten years earlier, Kim selected her mother as a positive influence on her life when she was interviewed at the end of the program. Kim also reconciled with her father and their relationship improved over the five years that Kim was in the program. Although Kim was still angry with her father for the way he treated her and her mother, she started to understand some of the things that her father did from an adult perspective; she attributed the abusive behavior to the stresses he faced at the time.

Mary and Her Son, Josh

Mary, an attractive teen with beautiful long hair, lived with her mother, a widow. Mary's father died when she was about two years old. Mary had trouble getting along with her mother and they were often in conflict. Mary started dating a much older boyfriend when she was twelve and she became pregnant at age fifteen. Her boyfriend, Ron, had experienced abuse at the hands of his father when he was growing up, and his father also beat his mother.

Ron moved in with Mary and her mother after Josh was born. Mary's mother let Ron move in because she thought he wanted to be a good father to the baby. Shortly after he moved in, domestic violence began. Ron tried to control Mary, and, when angry, he became physically and verbally abusive to her. At times, he threw her around by her long hair. They fought often and never seemed to agree on anything. Even so, she clung to him rather desperately. Mary alternated between kicking him out of the house and begging him to come back.

Mary's mother had no control over Mary or Ron. She wanted Ron out of the house and she fought with Mary over that issue. Mary had thrown Ron out of the house from time to time after he beat her, but each time they reconciled and tried again to live together.

Given the emotional climate in the home, it was somewhat surprising that Josh was doing well intellectually at age four. His Peabody Picture Vocabulary Test (PPVT) score, a measure of receptive vocabulary, was a little above the national average. At the 30-month interview the family advocate had predicted that Josh would do well in school in the cognitive area, but she had serious concerns about how he would do in the social-emotional area. The advocate noted that both Mary and her mother supported Josh's intellectual development. They read to him often. Both Josh and Mary loved books. Mary was described as a good mother, at least in terms of meeting Josh's intellectual needs; this was especially true in the periods when Mary and Ron got along with each other. However, when they did not get along, the home was not conducive to healthy social-emotional development.

Mary was an honor student in high school. The family advocate described her as articulate, self-motivated, and enthusiastic. Being a good student was important to her and she wanted her son to be a good student also. Her son had many age-appropriate playthings in the home, and Mary and her mother interacted with Josh frequently while playing with the toys.

The attention of Mary and her mother was focused on Josh. By the end of the program, Mary had no additional children. She had no plans to have a second child in the near future. She was no longer involved with Ron. Mary received a scholarship to a local college and was attending college at the time the program ended. While she attended college during the day, her mother took care of Josh. Despite his exposure to domestic violence and conflict, Josh's first grade teacher viewed him as well adjusted and gifted in the area of math.

In the three case studies, we have seen that one has to focus on more than the age of the mother to understand the experiences of children born to teenage mothers. The maturity of the mother is one of many factors that is likely to influence how she parents her child and the kinds of experiences that the child has while growing up. Clearly, in the decade ahead, researchers must do more than compare adolescent and older mothers on measures of caregiving. Efforts must be made to understand factors that contribute to individual differences in the caregiving behaviors of younger and older mothers.

The case studies also illustrate that teenage parents differ markedly in the kinds of experiences they provide for their children. Later in the chapter we will focus on the research that examines factors related to individual differences in parenting practices among adolescent mothers, and we will highlight important questions that require further study. We will make reference to these three case studies at various points in the chapter. In the next section, we examine factors related to who becomes a teenage parent.

FACTORS ASSOCIATED WITH BECOMING A TEENAGE PARENT

Studies of adolescent parenthood usually begin shortly after the first child is born, but the story of adolescent parenthood typically begins much earlier. To understand teenage motherhood, we need to consider what happens to the teens in the years before the first child is born. Experiences the teens have during their formative years are likely to influence their personalities, educational progress, employment skills, social networks, and ideas about caring for children. The histories of the young mothers are also likely to influence what kind of future they envision for themselves and their children (Musick, 1993).

Teenage mothers are diverse. They come from all socioeconomic status (SES) levels and ethnic groups, and they differ markedly in terms of personality, educational aptitude, and experiences in the family of origin. Although they are diverse, those who become teenage mothers tend to differ in important ways, on average, from the general population of adolescent females (Luker, 1991). Adolescents who become mothers are more likely than their peers to be low achievers in school and to have low educational aspirations (Moore, Miller, Glei, & Morrison, 1995; Rauch-Elnekave, 1994). Some are like Dawn, who was a poor student and was discouraged by her experiences in school. Unlike her more gifted peers, early childbearing did not threaten to disrupt her educational progress, since she had no desire to return to school. In fact, some teens who have been frustrated by their school experience may hope to have a sense of success and accomplishment in the area of family life (Ludtke, 1997). More traditional avenues to success, in school and in the workplace, do not seem like viable options to some adolescent mothers.

Those who become adolescent parents are more likely than their peers to have a history of sexual abuse, to abuse alcohol and other drugs, and to engage in other problematic behaviors (Boyer & Fine, 1992; Butler & Burton, 1990; Elster, Lamb, Peters, Kahn, & Tavare, 1987; Gershenson, et al., 1989; Moore, et al., 1995; Musick, 1993). Conduct disorders in childhood are also predictive of teenage pregnancy (Kovacs, Krol, & Voti, 1994; Zoccolillo, Meyers, & Assiter, 1997; Zoccolillo & Rogers, 1991).

A disproportionate number of teenage mothers are raised in single-parent households, in families living below the poverty line, by parents who obtained relatively low levels of education, and by mothers who were teenage parents themselves (Hotz, McElroy, & Sanders, 1997; Kahn & Anderson, 1992; Luker, 1991). They are also more likely than other teens to live in neighborhoods with high rates of poverty and to experience the risks associated with high concentrations of poverty (e.g., violence, drug dealing; see Brewster, 1994, and Musick, 1993).

In our own research, we have been sobered by the developmental histories of our young mothers, many of whom were raised in multi-problem families. Some, like Kim, lost their mothers to death. Others, like Dawn, "lost" their mothers to drugs and alcohol. Still others, like Mary, had been abused or exploited by men and had relationship histories that were not conducive to healthy physical or psychological development.

The developmental histories of young mothers are likely to affect both their current circumstances and their parenting practices. If a young mother has "lost" her mother to death or substance abuse, she is likely to be disadvantaged relative to other mothers in terms of the social support she receives once her child is born. If she has had little contact with her father, she may be relatively disadvantaged in terms of financial and emotional support. Her relationship history with significant others and how she interprets and internalizes those experiences are likely to influence her outlook on relationships, her beliefs about caring for children, and ultimately her caregiving practices (Bowlby, 1988; Main & Goldwyn, 1984; Sroufe & Fleeson, 1986).

The contexts in which adolescent parents have been raised also have implications for the contexts in which they will raise their children. Many adolescent mothers who were raised by low income parents in impoverished neighborhoods rear their children in the same neighborhoods. These neighborhood contexts may also influence the young mothers' outlook on how their children should be raised. Many of the young mothers we worked with were concerned about whether their children, especially their sons, would be tough enough to survive in a tough neighborhood. Mothers who sometimes seemed to react harshly to their sons' behavior (e.g., spanking a preschooler for crying) were determined that their sons would not grow up to be "wimps." Some of the young mothers chided our home visitors for "buying into" parenting education ideas (e.g., alternatives to corporal punishment), which they viewed as likely to be ineffective. In other cases, the young mothers were open to new parenting ideas but their partners or parents were worried that these approaches would "spoil" their babies.

We ventured into the Family TIES family support program somewhat naively with the idea that early childbearing was the primary challenge that these young women faced. We were not prepared for the number of young mothers who had experienced a great deal of adversity in their formative years or who were currently coping with challenging circumstances not directly related to early childbearing, such as domestic violence.

As researchers, we know far too little about how the developmental history of the teen, the members of her social network, and the social niche in which she lives combine to influence her beliefs about parenting, her ideas about the characteristics and competencies her child needs to be successful, her vision of the future for herself and her children, and her parenting practices. In particular, researchers have paid too little attention to the developmental histories of teenage mothers. Understandably, researchers may be reluctant to rely on the adolescent's or her parent's retrospective account of her formative years. Nevertheless, ignoring the linkages between what happened prior to the birth of the child and what happens after the birth is likely to lead to an incomplete or distorted picture of adolescent parenthood.

To inform research on the parenting behavior of adolescent mothers, there is also a need for research on who becomes an adolescent mother. It appears to us that the two areas of research have developed independently; some researchers focus on the antecedents of teenage parenthood while other researchers focus on what happens after the baby is born. Researchers trying to understand the parenting behavior of adolescent mothers could gain important insights from research that focuses on who becomes a teenage parent.

DIFFERENCES IN CURRENT CIRCUMSTANCES OF ADOLESCENT AND OLDER MOTHERS

Given selection factors that influence who becomes a teenage mother and the challenges associated with early childbearing, it should come as no surprise that adolescent mothers tend to fare less well than their peers in a number of life-course outcomes. Adolescent mothers are less likely than their peers to finish high school and enter into postsecondary education (Klepinger, Lundberg, & Plotnick, 1995). Many school-aged females drop out of school before they become pregnant, and many others drop out after the pregnancy (Moore, 1996). Those who drop out prior to becoming pregnant are much less likely to receive a high school diploma than those who are still in school when the pregnancy occurs (Upchurch & McCarthy, 1990). Because of their low educational attainment, adolescent mothers tend to have poorer employment prospects than their peers (Hayes, 1987).

Recent studies have attempted to determine the extent to which selection factors (e.g., family background characteristics, low educational aptitude) account for the low average educational attainment of teenage mothers and the extent to which early childbearing attenuates the educational careers of adolescent mothers (Hotz et al., 1997; Klepinger et al., 1995). Findings from several studies (Geronimus & Korenman, 1992; Hotz et al., 1997; Luker, 1991) indicate that simple comparisons—ones that do not control for selection factors—between teenage mothers and females who delay childbearing until their twenties tend to greatly overestimate the effects of early childbearing per se on outcomes such as educational attainment, income, and welfare use. Early childbearing may be as much a consequence of school failure (i.e., starting a family once you consider your educational career finished) as a cause of dropping out of school. However, research indicates that teenage mothers are less likely than comparable peers to receive a standard high school diploma, being more likely to receive a GED instead (Hotz et al., 1997), and are less likely to go on for post secondary education (Furstenberg, 1992). Whatever the cause of the disadvantage, the fact remains that children of teenage mothers are more likely than other children to be raised by parents with low educational levels.

Adolescents also are more likely than older mothers to raise their children as single parents. The proportion of births to adolescent mothers that occurred outside of marriage increased from 15% in 1960 to 79% in 1999 (Moore, 1999). Because of their own limited employment prospects and lack of financial support from the fathers of their children, a disproportionate number of teenage mothers raise their children in poverty and rely on public assistance to meet the basic needs of their families, especially when their children are young. Although many teenage mothers live in poverty when their children are young, their income levels do not differ markedly over time from those of their peers who became pregnant as teens but had miscarriages and thus "delayed" their childbearing until later (Hotz et al., 1997). Thus, the high rates of poverty among teenage parents are due, at least in part, to the disadvantaged backgrounds and characteristics (e.g., low academic aptitude) of many young mothers.

On average, teenage mothers have more children and more closely spaced births than older mothers when family background characteristics and other factors are controlled (Hayes, 1987; Hotz et al., 1997; Maynard, 1996). Having several closely spaced children reduces the likelihood that teens will complete high school or obtain postsecondary education and increases the likelihood that the young mothers will live in poverty (Furstenberg, Brooks-Gunn, & Morgan, 1987). Of course, all of these outcomes for the young mothers have important implications for their children, as they help to define the context in which their children are raised. Children of teenage mothers are more likely than their peers to live in poverty, to grow up in single-parent households, and to share the limited resources that are available in the family with closely-spaced siblings.

The minimal financial resources of many of these families are also likely to affect the children's experiences outside of the family, such as access to health care, day care arrangements, the quality of schools they attend, and the characteristics of the neighborhood in which they live. If adolescent mothers have low incomes and do not have family members available to provide child care, the young mothers may have to patch together child care arrangements in order to return to school. Their infants may be cared for by numerous caregivers, and in some cases the care their infants receive is substandard. Inadequate income is also associated with frequent changes of residence. Many low income adolescent mothers move frequently, seeking more affordable or better quality housing, or as a result of evictions when rent payments are not made. They may move in and out of the homes of their mothers, other relatives, and boyfriends as circumstances in their lives change. Such frequent moves are likely to be stressful for both the young mothers and their children.

Adolescent mothers may also differ from older mothers in terms of their psychological adjustment. Although differences are not found in every study, several recent studies have reported higher rates of depression among adolescent mothers (see Osofsky, Hann, & Peebles, 1993 for a review). Given the troubled histories of some adolescent mothers (e.g., sexual abuse, poor relationships with parents) and the stressful contexts in which many of them care for their children, it is understandable that a substantial number of adolescent mothers score low on indicators of psychological well-being.

Although many adolescent mothers experience a familiar litany of risk factors—poverty, low parental education, neighborhoods with high rates of violence—others experience much more favorable circumstances. Some adolescent mothers are well-adjusted, have done well in school, have well-functioning support systems, and live in safe neighborhoods. In the next section, we will see that individual differences in the characteristics and the circumstances of the teens are predictive of individual differences in their parenting practices.

FACTORS RELATED TO INDIVIDUAL DIFFERENCES IN THE PARENTING BEHAVIOR OF ADOLESCENT MOTHERS

Individual differences in caregiving practices among adolescent mothers are striking. Some mothers provide excellent care for their children, some are abusive or neglectful, and most fall somewhere between these two extremes (Musick, 1993). Moreover, like most of us, adolescent parents may handle some aspects of parenting (e.g., meeting the physical needs of the baby) better than other aspects (e.g., fostering intellectual development).

Why do some adolescent mothers provide more supportive environments for their children than others? Theories regarding the determinants of parenting (Belsky, 1984; Schellenbach, Whitman, & Borkowski, 1992) have emphasized influences in three domains: 1) characteristics of the parent; 2) characteristics of the child; and 3) contextual sources of stress and support. The developmental history of the parent (e.g., the parenting she experienced when growing up) also has been viewed as an important factor. The parent's developmental history is likely to influence such characteristics as her personality and child-rearing beliefs. In this part of the chapter, we will review research regarding each of these areas, starting with the developmental history of the teen.

Developmental History

Of the four areas of influence, the developmental history of adolescent mothers has received the least study. The limited research that is available suggests that experiences in the family of origin affect the caregiving behavior of adolescent mothers. Ward and Carlson (1995) examined the relation between adolescent mothers' relationship histories and how they related to their own infants. Young mothers who were rated as having more secure relationships in their families tended to have infants who were rated as securely attached in Ainsworth's strange situation at fifteen months. They were also rated as being more sensitive in their interactions with their infants.

Studies of developmental history distinguished between adolescent mothers who maltreated their children and those who did not (Zuravin & DiBlasio, 1996). Mothers who neglected their children were more likely than their peers to have experienced frequent changes in the caregivers they lived with while growing up, and also were more likely to have been in trouble with the law during their teen years. Adolescent mothers whose children were physically abused were more likely to have been raised by mothers with emotional problems.

Research on the antecedents of early childbearing has established that a disproportionate number of teenage mothers have been sexually abused. Surprisingly, there has been very little in the teenage parenthood literature on the relation between sexual abuse and parenting. One exception is a study by Spieker and her colleagues of 104 adolescent mother and their children (Spieker, Bensley, McMahon, Fung, & Ossiander, 1996). They found that rates of Child Protective Services (CPS) involvement among preschool children (based on maternal report) were higher if the adolescent mother had been sexually abused. Fifteen percent of the mothers without a history of sexual abuse reported CPS contacts involving the study child; while 39% of the mothers who had a brief history of sexual abuse and 83% of mothers with a history of chronic sexual abuse had children who had been involved with CPS.

In our study, the family advocates worked with the young mothers over a five-year period, and during that time, they learned much about the developmental history of their clients. The impression of the family advocates was that the adolescents who had the most difficulty in the area of parenting, as defined by scoring in the bottom quartile on a measure of caregiving, often lived in the most adverse circumstances while growing up. They are young mothers, like Dawn, who experienced a host of risk factors, including poverty, parental substance abuse, inadequate parental involvement and supervision, lack of positive role models, exploitation by men, and violence in the home and neighborhood. One of the family advocates used the term "misery pots" to describe some of the homes in which her clients were raised.

The advocates believed that many of the young mothers who grew up in these multi-problem households loved their children but were not prepared for providing them with the kind of nurturing that has been linked to optimal development in children. Some of these mothers seemed preoccupied with their own needs, which were often substantial, and therefore did not seem to be as child-centered in their actions as some of the more competent young mothers.

Although the developmental history of the teen is probably an important influence, she is not fated to make the same mistakes as her parents. Some young mothers who experience considerable adversity in their formative years appear to be remarkably resilient and are able to provide high quality care for their children. Kim was one of our young mothers who fit this description. Her mother died when she was twelve, her father was physically abusive to her, she ran away from home, and she had a substance abuse problem for a period of time. Why did Kim seem to be functioning much more effectively in the parenting role than Dawn? Was it the positive relationship she had with her mother before her mother died, the support she received from her spouse and his family, or her personal strength and determination to make a better life for her children than she had experienced? It is not unreasonable to assume that all of these things were important. Clearly, however, more research is needed to understand why many teenage mothers provide high quality care for their children despite the adversity that they have experienced.

Positive relationships with adults other than parents may help to offset negative early experiences in the teens' families. Some studies of women who experienced adversity in childhood but turned out to be good parents showed that having a very supportive relationship with a well-adjusted male partner may have been a turning point in some cases (Quinton & Rutter, 1988). Crockenberg (1987) reported that adolescent mothers who experienced rejection in the family of origin tended to be more angry and punitive with their toddlers than did young mothers with more favorable experiences if they were not in a supportive relationship with a male partner. Among adolescent mothers who had supportive male partners, there was no relation between memories of rejection and current parenting practices. Positive experiences in school may also help to offset the effects of troubled relationships at home (Quinton & Rutter, 1988).

Characteristics of the Young Mothers

Circumstances and experiences during the adolescent mother's formative years help to shape her personal characteristics. Like older mothers, adolescent mothers differ markedly in their personalities, child-rearing beliefs, and intellectual ability. To what extent do individual differences in these characteristics predict individual differences in parenting? One of the most extensively studied maternal characteristics is level of depression. Adolescent mothers who are relatively depressed have been found to be less involved with their infants (Reis & Herz, 1987), to respond contingently less frequently to their toddlers during free-play interactions (Leadbeater,

Bishop, & Raver, 1996), to be more controlling and less sensitive in interactions with their infants (Cassidy, Zoccolillo, & Hughes, 1996), and to
have more negative feeding interactions with their infants (Panzarine,
Slater, & Sharps, 1995). Depression is also predictive of child neglect by
adolescent mothers (Zuravin & DiBlasio, 1996).

One question that requires more study is: what factors contribute to
depression in adolescent mothers? Can depression be traced to a history of
abuse, relationship problems in the family of origin, school failure, or a
family history of mental illness? To what extent do relationships with their
male partners influence the psychological well-being of the young mothers?
We suspect that adolescent mothers, like other adolescents, tend to be in
much better spirits when they perceive that their relationships with their
male partners are going well than when these relationships are strained.
However when their male partners are studied (which is rarely), the focus
tends to be on the partner's involvement in child care and the financial support he provides for the child rather than the quality of the relationship he
has with the mother. Anecdotal evidence from our study showed that some
adolescent mothers were used (e.g., taking their public assistance money),
exploited (e.g., trading shelter for sex), or abused by their male partners.
Some had had a succession of negative experiences with males starting with
sexual abuse in childhood and continuing with domestic violence in adulthood. The adolescent's relationship history with men is another relatively
neglected area that merits attention in future studies.

Other adolescents who may be at risk for depression are young mothers
who look to their infants to fill an emotional need. This may be the need
for love, for a sense of accomplishment, for respect and attention from significant others, or to solidify a relationship with a male partner. If having
a baby does not meet that need, the disappointment of the young mother
may contribute to feelings of depression. However, it is difficult to study
adolescents' motivation for having children or their often complex feelings
about the babies once they arrive (Musick, 1993; Ludtke, 1997); thus,
much of the evidence in this area is anecdotal.

Beliefs about childrearing and knowledge of child development are other
characteristics of adolescent mothers that are likely to influence their caregiving practices. Although parents do not always act on their knowledge or
beliefs, some evidence exists in the literature that the adolescent mothers'
cognitive readiness for parenting and childrearing beliefs are related to
their parenting behavior (Karraker & Evans, 1996; Luster, 1998; Luster &
Rhoades, 1989; Reis & Herz, 1987; Sommer, et al., 1993). Adolescent
mothers, like older mothers, are sometimes hesitant to respond to their
infants' distress for fear of spoiling their babies. Dawn chastised the family advocate for holding the baby on her home visits, fearing that she would
spoil Ricky. Many of the clients we worked with shared the same fear, and
this view was often reinforced by other members of their families.

Some investigators have examined the relation between parenting practices and the educational attainment or educational aptitude of the adolescent mothers. Several of these studies have shown that mothers who are more successful in school tend to receive better scores on measures of home environment or parenting (Luster, 1998). For example, low educational attainment has been linked to child neglect (Zuravin & DiBlasio, 1996). What is not understood is the process by which the mother's school success influences parenting practices, if indeed there is a causal relation. Some mothers, like Mary, who achieve high levels of education may value education more than other mothers and create home environments that are conducive to educational success (Laosa, 1982). Other mothers in our sample had such difficulty reading that it was not surprising that they seldom read to their children. High levels of maternal education may contribute to higher levels of family income, and children in these families may be less likely to live in poverty, or to live in neighborhoods with high concentrations of poverty. It may also be the case that maternal education is a proxy for other characteristics of the mother, such as how organized, motivated, or intelligent she is. Some of the young mothers in our study who grew up in the most adverse circumstances, like Dawn, did not seem to be very motivated in either the area of education or parenting. Both low educational attainment and poor parenting may have their roots in the developmental history of the young mother.

Contextual Sources of Stress and Support

How young mothers cope with the transition to parenthood is likely to depend on the other stressors with which they must contend, and the support they receive from others, especially their families and male partners. Potential stressors that have been examined in studies of adolescent parenting include poverty, large family size, and residing in neighborhoods that have high rates of violence and other problems.

Poverty

Certainly one of the most significant stressors for adolescent mothers is poverty. A high proportion of adolescent mothers live in poverty, particularly while their children are young (Hotz et al., 1997; Maynard, 1996), and poverty is associated with poor developmental outcomes in children born to adolescent mothers (Dubow & Luster, 1990; Furstenberg et al., 1987). Poverty has such a pervasive effect on the experiences of children that it is difficult to know precisely how poverty affects development, but parenting is likely to be one factor that mediates the relation between poverty and poor developmental outcomes in children (McLoyd, 1990). Adolescent mothers are at risk for providing relatively unsupportive home environments for their children if they live in poverty (Luster & Dubow, 1990), even though many poor adolescent mothers provide high quality care for their children. Poverty has also been linked to neglect among adolescent mothers (Zuravin & DiBlasio, 1996).

Number of Children

Having many siblings is also associated with poor developmental outcomes in children born to adolescent mothers (Dubow & Luster, 1990; Furstenberg et al., 1987), and this relation may also be mediated, at least in part, by parenting practices. Having several children is associated with lower Home Observation of the Maternal Environment inventory scores (Luster & Dubow, 1990) and a higher likelihood of neglect (Zuravin & DiBlasio, 1996). In fact, having many children distinguished between neglectful and non-neglectful adolescent mothers better than any other variable in the discriminant analysis conducted by Zuravin and DiBlasio. However, selection factors must also be considered when interpreting the effects of family size. Adolescent mothers who have several closely spaced children are more likely than other adolescent mothers to be low achieving students and to come from disadvantaged circumstances (Kalmuss & Namerow, 1994; Mott, 1986; Polit & Kahn, 1986).

Although we know something about the correlates of rapid second pregnancies, our understanding of the reasons why some adolescents delay having a second child for several years while others have their children closely spaced is quite limited (Rigsby, Macones, & Driscoll, 1998). Further research is also needed to determine the extent to which selection factors account for the poor outcomes for adolescent mothers and their children when mothers have closely-spaced children during their teen years. It is generally assumed that having closely-spaced children explains outcomes like low educational attainment for the mothers and school failure for the children. While it seems likely that closely-spaced children may contribute to these poor outcomes, other interpretations of the data must also be tested in future studies.

Neighborhood Context

A third potential stressor that we have examined in our longitudinal study is the neighborhood context in which adolescents are raising their children. Adolescents who lived in neighborhoods that were rated by family advocates as being unsafe and low in quality of life consistently received low scores on various measures of parenting quality (Luster, 1998). Neighborhood characteristics were also predictive of child outcomes in our study (Luster, Bates, Fitzgerald, Vandenbelt, & Key, 2000), a finding that is consistent with other research (Duncan, Brooks-Gunn, & Klebanov, 1994). One question that requires further study is whether there is an effect of neighborhood characteristics on parenting when other factors are controlled (e.g., characteristics of the mother, family background characteristics, family income). Although selection factors may come into play, we suspect that the social niche in which parents live helps to shape the outcomes they value for their children, their child-rearing beliefs, and other important ideas about how the world works. The threat of violence is likely to be a particularly powerful stressor that is bound to affect parenting strategies (e.g., how restrictive parents are). On the other hand, living in a neighborhood where there is a strong sense of community and where neighbors look out for one another's children may be an important source of support for parents (Garbarino & Kostelny, 1993).

We were struck by the fact that a few adolescent mothers in our study seemed to know little about life outside their neighborhoods. The family advocate who worked with Dawn mentioned that she had spent nearly her entire life within three miles of her home. When the family advocate took her on outings, she was surprised to learn that Dawn was not familiar with some of the best-known landmarks of her city. One has to wonder what kind of world view Dawn has constructed having grown up in a tough neighborhood and having little experience outside that neighborhood.

Other Stressors

There are several other stressors that have not been studied extensively. For example, there has been little written about the problem of domestic violence among adolescent mothers, but for mothers like Mary, it is the most salient feature of their homes. Other teen mothers in our sample also experienced domestic violence but no studies to date have determined how many teenage mothers are victims of domestic violence. There is also little research on the effects of neighborhood violence on teenage mothers and their children. Many teenage mothers must cope with a daily threat of gang-related violence in their neighborhoods.

Other major stressors that occur infrequently in samples of adolescent mothers are seldom studied, but they may exert a powerful influence on the few families that are affected. Social scientists may overlook these variables because they do not explain much of the variance in an outcome like parenting for the overall sample, but, for the families affected, the stressor may affect every facet of their lives. For example, few adolescent mothers have children with chronic illnesses (e.g., asthma) but obviously, such a major stressor would have a pervasive influence on the life of the adolescent mother and other family members.

Social Support

It stands to reason that an adolescent mother's ability to function effectively in the parenting role is influenced by significant members of her social network, particularly members of her family of origin, the father of her baby, or her current partner. Young mothers benefit from having parents and other extended family members who support them financially and emotionally. The child care that family members provide can also be invaluable. The young mothers in our sample who fared the best on a host of outcomes, including parenting measures, seemed to have well functioning support systems.

Systematic studies of the relationship between perceived social support and parenting have often found that mothers with higher levels of support provide relatively high quality care for their children. However, some studies have also reported no relation between perceived social support and measures of parenting (Lamb & Elster, 1985; Luster, Perlstadt, McKinney, Sims, & Juang, 1996; Reis & Herz, 1987). It is not clear why the results are inconsistent from study to study. In some cases, the lack of relationship between social support and parenting may be due to the fact that mothers who have the greatest difficulty adjusting to the parenting role receive the most support from their families; the support is offered by family members in response to a perceived need on the part of the young mothers (Barratt, Roach, Morgan, & Colbert, 1996). In these instances, social support may be helpful to the mothers receiving it, but they would not necessarily receive high marks on measures of parenting when compared to other adolescent mothers.

Those who provide support may also be viewed as sources of stress by the teen. An objective observer may view Mary's mother as having provided high levels of support for her daughter because of the time that she spent caring for her son while Mary attended college. Mary may have viewed her mother differently because of the ongoing struggles they had over Mary's relationship with her abusive boyfriend. Having several network members who are sources of both support and conflict has been linked to poorer parenting and adjustment among adolescent mothers (Barrera, 1981; Voight, Hans, & Bernstein, 1996).

Characteristics of the Child

Parenting is likely to be influenced by the characteristics of the child as well as characteristics of the parent and the context in which the relationship occurs. One hypothesis that has been tested in some studies proposes that adolescents who care for challenging infants may provide less supportive care, on average, than adolescents with easier babies. Babies considered to be difficult to care for are preterm or low birthweight infants, and babies who are temperamentally difficult. There is some evidence to support the hypothesis that preterm and low birthweight infants are at greater risk for poor parenting in the newborn period (Field, 1980; Wise & Grossman, 1980). A question that requires further study is whether or not the effects of having a low birthweight baby persist beyond the newborn period if the infant is generally healthy.

Research on the relation between infant temperament and adolescent parenting has not yielded consistent results. Some studies have found the expected relationship between difficult temperament and less supportive parenting; other studies have found no relation between temperament and parenting. Inconsistent results have also been found in samples of mature mothers with infants (Crockenberg, 1986). As Crockenberg noted, the effect of temperament on parenting may depend on other factors such as characteristics of the mother (e.g., her patience, or her interpretation of the behavior) or contextual factors (e.g., level of social support, or other stressors with which the mother is contending). The importance of the fit between characteristics of the infant and characteristics of the caregiver is often evident to a clinician on a case by case basis. It is challenging to study "goodness of fit" using aggregated data, however, because the characteristics of the infants and caregivers that have the greatest bearing on their relationships can vary from family to family.

The research on individual differences in parenting demonstrates that adolescent mothers differ markedly in their approaches to childrearing. Thus, if we use a social address label like "home of a teenage mother" to describe the environment of an infant, we must accept the fact that this is a very crude indicator of that infant's experiences (Bronfenbrenner, 1989). As we saw earlier, the experiences of Kim's, Dawn's, and Mary's children were very different. Although children born to teenage mothers experience different contexts than do the children born to older mothers, on average, there are also marked differences within samples of adolescent mothers. Therefore, the age of the mother is not likely to explain much of the variance in children's outcomes, especially when other confounding factors (e.g., family background characteristics, current SES) are controlled.

KEY QUESTIONS FOR FUTURE RESEARCH

Throughout this chapter, we have noted research questions that have not been addressed or that require further study. In closing, we would like to note additional questions that should be considered in the years ahead. One question is: Based on what is known about the many challenges faced by some adolescent mothers, what types of interventions can be developed to assist young families that are at particularly high risk because of the mothers' developmental history and current circumstances? As we have seen, more than the age of the mother must be considered in planning family support programs. How does one begin to address the many issues faced by young families like Dawn and Ricky?

A related question that is likely to be helpful to those who plan intervention programs is: When high-risk adolescent mothers are successful and their children are on a positive developmental trajectory, what are the reasons for their success? What can we learn from their success stories that will help us to design more effective family support programs or other services? Too often, research on teenage mothers has been problem-focused. Not enough attention has been paid to those who succeed and the reasons why they succeed.

Another important question that is receiving increasing attention is: To what extent can the outcomes of adolescent mothers (e.g., educational attainment) be explained by early childbearing and to what extent are the outcomes due to selection factors (i.e., who becomes a teenage parent)? Important steps have been taken to address this question by comparing adolescent mothers to other females who became pregnant as teenagers but who did not have a child until several years later because of a miscarriage (Hotz et al., 1997). Others have compared adolescent mothers with their sisters who had their first child after their teen years (Geronimus & Korenman, 1992, 1993). Both approaches compare adolescent mothers to others who should be similar in terms of background characteristics but who differ in terms of the timing of their first birth.

As most mothers of young children now work or go to school, a timely question is: What effect do caregivers other than the teenage mother have on the developing child? Children born to adolescent mothers are often cared for by several people. Although there are some notable exceptions, relatively few studies have focused on the relation between caregiving practices of other caregivers and the developmental outcomes of children born to adolescent mothers. Quite often we focus on the support that other family members provide for the young mothers but do not focus enough on the support they provide directly to the child. We have observed some families in our studies in which the success of the child appears to be due more to the care the child receives from extended family members than from the young mothers. In other cases, the good care that the young mother provides is supplemented by the relationship the child has with a father or father figure and other relatives. Studying the caregiving of other family members can be challenging because in some households the relationships can be quite complex; for example, the child's father and the mother's current partner may both have important relationships with the child.

Finally, we reiterate an earlier point. Studies of adolescent parenthood have not paid sufficient attention to the developmental histories of young mothers. Implicitly, researchers seem to be assuming that what happened in the sixteen years before the child was born is of little concern for understanding the outcomes of the young mother or her child. Our involvement with adolescent mothers over the last several years has convinced us that we should try to understand the linkages between the young mother's developmental history and her current circumstances and behavior. The challenge is determining the best approach to studying the developmental history of the teen. Our understanding of the importance of developmental history emerged over time as our home visitors uncovered more and more information about the teens' past during the five years that they worked with the young mothers. Most studies of adolescent mothers are not long-term studies in which a home visitor has an opportunity to gain the trust of the young mother. Other methods for understanding the mother's relationship history must also be explored.

REFERENCES

Barratt, M. S., Roach, M. A., Morgan, K. M., & Colbert, K. K. (1996). Adjustment to motherhood by single adolescents. *Family Relations, 45,* 209–215.

Barrera, M. (1981). Social support in the adjustment of pregnant adolescents: Assessment issues. In B. H. Gottlieb (Ed.), *Social networks and social support* (pp. 69–96). Beverly Hills: Sage.

Belsky, J. (1984). The determinants of parenting: A process model. *Child Development, 55,* 83–96.

Bowlby, J. (1988). *A secure base: Parent-child attachment and healthy human development.* New York: Basic Books.

Boyer, D., & Fine, D. (1992). Sexual abuse as a factor in adolescent pregnancy and child maltreatment. *Family Planning Perspectives, 24,* 4–11.

Brewster, K. (1994). Race differences in sexual activity among adolescent women: The role of neighborhood characteristics. *American Sociological Review, 59,* 408–424.

Bronfenbrenner, U. (1989). Ecological systems theory. In R. Vasta (Ed.). *Annals of Child Development* (Vol. 6, pp. 187–249). Greenwich, CT: JAI press.

Brooks-Gunn, J., & Chase-Lansdale, P. L. (1995). Adolescent parenthood. In M. Bornstein (Ed.), *Handbook on parenting* (Vol. 3, pp. 113–149). Mahwah, NJ: Erlbaum.

Butler, J., & Burton, L. (1990). Rethinking teenage childbearing: Is sexual abuse a missing link? *Family Relations, 39,* 73–80.

Cassidy, B., Zoccolillo, M., & Hughes, S. (1996). Psychopathology in adolescent mothers and its effects on mother-infant interactions: A pilot study. *Canadian Journal of Psychiatry, 41,* 379–384.

Crockenberg, S. (1986). Are temperamental differences in babies associated with predictable differences in caregiving. In J. V. Lerner & R. M. Lerner (Eds.), *Temperament and child development: New directions for child development* (pp. 53–73). San Francisco: Jossey-Bass.

Crockenberg, S. (1987). Predictors and correlates of anger toward and punitive control of toddlers by adolescent mothers. *Child Development, 58,* 964–975.

Dubow, E. F., & Luster, T. (1990). Adjustment of children born to teenage mothers: The contribution of risk and protective factors. *Journal of Marriage and the Family, 52,* 393–404.

Duncan, G. J., Brooks-Gunn, J., & Klebanov, P. K. (1994). Economic deprivation and early childhood development. *Child Development, 65,* 296–318.

Elster, A. B., Lamb, M. E., Peters, L., Kahn, J., & Tavare, J. (1987). Judicial involvement and conduct problems of fathers of infants born to adolescent mothers. *Pediatrics, 79,* 230–234.

Field, T. M. (1980). Interaction of preterm and term infants with their lower and middle-income teenage and adult mothers. In T. M. Field, S. Goldberg, D. Stern, & E. Sostek (Eds.), *High-risk infants and children: Adult and peer interaction* (pp. 113–132). New York: Academic Press.

Furstenberg, F. F. (1992). Teenage childbearing and cultural rationality: A thesis in search of evidence. *Family Relations*, 41, 239–243.

Furstenberg, F. F., Brooks-Gunn, J., & Morgan, S. P. (1987). Adolescent mothers in later life. New York: Cambridge University Press.

Furstenberg, F. F., Levine, J. A., & Brooks-Gunn, J. (1990). The children of teenage mothers: Patterns of early childbearing in two generations. *Family Planning Perspectives*, 22, 54–61.

Garbarino, J., & Kostelny, K. (1993). Neighborhood and community influences on parenting. In T. Luster & L. Okagaki (Eds.), *Parenting: An ecological perspective* (pp. 203–226). Hillsdale, NJ: Erlbaum.

Geronimus, A., & Korenman, S. (1992). The socioeconomic consequences of teenage childbearing reconsidered. *Quarterly Journal of Economics*, 107, 1187–1214.

Geronimus, A., & Korenman, S. (1993). Maternal youth or family background? On the health disadvantages of infants with teenage mothers. *American Journal of Epidemiology*, 137, 213–225.

Gershenson, H. P., Musick, J. S., Ruch-Ross, H. S., Magee, V., Rubino, K. K., & Rosenberg, D. (1989). The prevalence of coercive sexual experience among teenage mothers. *Journal of Interpersonal Violence*, 4, 204–219.

Hayes, C. (1987). *Risking the future: Adolescent sexuality, pregnancy and childbearing* (Vol. 1). Washington, DC: National Academy Press.

Hotz, V. J., McElroy, S. W., & Sanders, S. G. (1997). The impacts of teenage childbearing on the mothers and the consequences of those impacts for government. In R. A. Maynard (Ed.), *Kids having kids: Economic costs and social consequences of teen pregnancy* (pp. 55–94). Washington, DC: The Urban Institute Press.

Kahn, J. R., & Anderson, K. E. (1992). Intergenerational patterns of teenage fertility. *Demography*, 29, 39–57.

Kalmuss, D. S., & Namerow, P. B. (1994). Subsequent childbearing among teenage mothers: The determinants of a closely spaced second birth. *Family Planning Perspectives*, 26, 149–159.

Karraker, K. H., & Evans, S. L. (1996). Adolescent mother's knowledge of child development and expectations for their own infants. *Journal of Youth and Adolescence*, 25, 651–666.

Klepinger, D. H., Lundberg, S., & Plotnick, R. D. (1995). Adolescent fertility and educational attainment of young women. *Family Planning Perspectives*, 27, 23–28.

Kovacs, M., Krol, R. M., & Voti, L. (1994). Early onset psychopathology and the risk for teenage pregnancy among clinically referred girls. *Journal of the American Academy of Child and Adolescent Psychiatry*, 33, 106–113.

Lamb, M., & Elster, A. (1985). Adolescent mother-infant-father relationships. *Developmental Psychology*, 21, 768–773.

Laosa, L. M. (1982). School, occupation, culture, and family: The impact of parent schooling on the parent-child relationship. *Journal of Educational Psychology*, 74, 791–827.

Leadbeater, B. J., Bishop, S. J., & Raver, C. C. (1996). Quality of mother-toddler interactions, maternal depressive symptoms, and behavior problems in preschoolers of adolescent mothers. *Developmental Psychology, 32,* 280–288.

Ludtke, M. (1997). *On our own: Unmarried motherhood in America.* New York: Random House.

Luker, K. (1991, Spring). Dubious conceptions: The controversy over teen pregnancy. *The American Prospect,* 73–83.

Luster, T. (1998). Individual differences in the caregiving behavior of teenage mothers: An ecological perspective. *Clinical Child Psychology and Psychiatry, 3,* 341–360.

Luster, T., Bates, L., Fitzgerald, H. E., Vandenbelt, M., & Key, J. P. (2000). Factors related to successful outcomes in preschool children born to low-income, adolescent mothers. *Journal of Marriage and the Family, 62,* 133–146.

Luster, T., & Brophy-Herb, H. (2000). Adolescent mothers and their children. In J. D. Osofsky & H. E. Fitzgerald (Eds.), *WAIMH Handbook of Infant Mental Health* (Vol. 4, pp. 369–413). New York: John Wiley & Sons.

Luster, T., & Dubow, E. (1990). Predictors of the quality of the home environment that adolescent mothers provide for their school-aged children. *Journal of Youth and Adolescence, 19,* 475–494.

Luster, T., Perlstadt, H., McKinney, M., Sims, K., & Juang, L. (1996). The effects of a family support program and other factors on the home environment provided by adolescent mothers. *Family Relations, 45,* 255–264.

Luster, T., & Rhoades, K. (1989). The relation between childrearing beliefs and the home environment in a sample of adolescent mothers. *Family Relations, 38,* 317–322.

Main, M., & Goldwyn, R. (1984). Predicting rejection of her infant from mother's representation of her own experience: Implications for the abused-abusing intergenerational cycle. *Child Abuse and Neglect, 8,* 203–217.

Maynard, R. A. (1996). *Kids having kids: A Robin Hood Foundation special report on the costs of adolescent childbearing.* New York: The Robin Hood Foundation.

Maynard, R. A. (Ed.) (1997). *Kids having kids: Economic costs and social consequences of teen pregnancy.* Washington, D.C.: Urban Institute Press.

McLoyd, V. (1990). The impact of economic hardship on Black families and children: Psychological distress, parenting, and socioemotional development. *Child Development, 61,* 311–346.

Moore, K. (1996). *Facts at a glance.* Washington, DC: Child Trends, Inc.

Moore, K. (1999). *Facts at a glance.* Washington, DC: Child Trends, Inc.

Moore, K. A., Miller, B. C., Glei, D., & Morrison, D. R. (1995). *Adolescent sex, contraception, and childbearing: A review of recent research.* Washington, DC: Child Trends, Inc.

Mott, F. (1986). The pace of repeated childbearing among young American mothers. *Family Planning Perspectives, 18,* 118–124.

Musick, J. S. (1993). *Young, poor, and pregnant: The psychology of teenage motherhood.* New Haven: Yale University Press.

Osofsky, J. D., Hann, D. A., & Peebles, C. (1993). Adolescent parenthood: Risks and opportunities for mothers and infants. In C. H. Zeanah (Ed.), *Handbook of infant mental health* (pp. 106–119). New York: Guilford Press.

Panzarine, S., Slater, E., & Sharps, P. (1995). Coping, social support, and depressive symptoms in adolescent mothers. *Journal of Adolescent Health*, 17, 113–119.

Polit, D. F., & Kahn, J. R. (1986). Early subsequent pregnancy among economically disadvantaged teenage mothers. *Family Planning Perspectives*, 76, 167–171.

Quinton, D. & Rutter, M. (1988). *Parenting breakdown: The making and breaking of intergenerational bonds*. Aldershot, UK: Avebury.

Rauch-Elnekave, H. (1994). Teenage motherhood: Its relationship to undetected learning problems. *Adolescence*, 29, 91–103.

Reis, J. S., & Herz, E. J. (1987). Correlates of adolescent parenting. *Adolescence*, 22, 599–609.

Richardson, R. A., Barbour, N. B., & Bubenzer, D. L. (1996). Bittersweet connections: Informal social networks as sources of support and interference for adolescent mothers. *Family Relations*, 40, 430–434.

Rigsby, D. C., Macones, G. A., & Driscoll, D. A. (1998). Risk factors for rapid repeat pregnancy among adolescent mothers: A review of the literature. *Journal of Pediatric Adolescent Gynecology*, 11, 115–126.

Schellenbach, C. J., Whitman, T. L., & Borkowski, J. G. (1992). Toward an integrative model of adolescent parenting. *Human Development*, 35, 81–99.

Sommer, K., Whitman, T. L., Borkowski, J. G., Schellenbach, C., Maxwell, S., & Keogh, D. (1993). Cognitive readiness and adolescent parenting. *Developmental Psychology*, 29, 389–398.

Spieker, S. J., Bensley, L., McMahon, R., Fung, H., & Ossiander, E. (1996). Sexual abuse as a factor in child maltreatment by adolescent mothers of preschool aged children. *Development and Psychopathology*, 8, 497–509.

Sroufe, L. A., & Fleeson, J. (1986). Attachment and the construction of relationships. In W. Hartup & Z. Rubin (Eds.), *Relationships and development* (pp. 51–71). Hillsdale, NJ: Erlbaum.

Upchurch, D. M., & McCarthy, J. (1990). The timing of the first birth and high school completion. *American Sociological Review*, 55, 224–234.

Voight, J. D., Hans, S. L., & Bernstein, V. J. (1996). Support networks of adolescent mothers: Effects on parenting experiences and behavior. *Infant Mental Health Journal*, 17, 58–73.

Ward, M. J., & Carlson, E. A. (1995). Associations among adult attachment representations, maternal sensitivity, and infant-mother attachment in a sample of adolescent mothers. *Child Development*, 66, 69–79.

Wise, S., & Grossman, F. K. (1980). Adolescent mothers and their infants: Psychological factors in attachment and interaction. *American Journal of Othopsychiatry*, 50, 454–468.

Zoccolillo, M., Meyers, J., & Assiter, S. (1997). Conduct disorder, substance dependence, and adolescent motherhood. *American Journal of Orthopsychiatry*, 67, 152–157.

Zoccolillo, M., & Rogers, K. (1991). Characteristics and outcomes of hospitalized adolescent girls with conduct disorders. *Journal of the American Academy of Child and Adolescent Psychiatry, 30,* 973–981.

Zuravin, S. J., & DiBlasio, F. A. (1996). The correlates of child physical abuse and neglect by adolescent mothers. *Journal of Family Violence, 11,* 149–166.

ACKNOWLEDGMENTS

Our research described in this chapter was supported by grants from the Spencer Foundation and the Mott Children's Health Center of Flint, Michigan. The data presented, the statements made, and the views expressed are solely the responsibility of the authors.

DAYCARE AND MATERNAL EMPLOYMENT IN THE 21ST CENTURY

Conflicts and Consequences for Infant Development

Jacqueline V. Lerner
& Domini R. Castellino

6

◆◆◆◆

A mother of an eight-month-old infant pulls up beside a daycare center, family-care home, or babysitter's house. The infant is distressed; she has not had a good night's sleep. She cries at her mother's attempts to soothe her before they enter, and her mother's attempts fail. Her mother, already agitated and late for work, takes the child in and hands her over to a caregiver, quickly mumbles the difficulties of the morning, and hurries off to work. The mother feels guilty for the better part of the day and stresses at work compound her anxiety. Meanwhile, her daughter settles into the morning's activities, takes a short nap, and has a peaceful and playful afternoon.

This scene most likely takes place in thousands of cities across the country every day. It conveys to some people the picture of a selfish mother who is putting her own desires and the benefits of work ahead of the well-being of her child. It summons up a picture, to some, of an unhappy infant, deprived of a good night's sleep, forced to spend the day without her mother. What is to become of this child? Is the care she receives from her caregivers as good as the care her mother would provide?

These are just some of the questions that may arise when this scene is brought to mind. The pressures on mothers today are compounded by a political atmosphere that has prompted discussion of "family values" and what they mean for today's children. On the one hand, some mothers—women receiving welfare benefits, for example—are being pushed into the work force and encouraged to financially support their families. On the other hand, mothers who choose to work—either for financial or personal reasons— are often seen as selfish or as prioritizing their needs and well-being over those of their children. Consequently, mothers are often conflicted about their decisions to work or not to work.

American mothers find themselves in the middle of a debate that seems to be searching for agreement on the roles of mothers and on what's best

145

for America's children. However, as Silverstein (1991) summarizes, it was not until the late nineteenth century that the notion of parenting became focused on the mother as the sole, primary caregiver. Historically and cross-culturally, infants were cared for in a variety of contexts and with persons other than the child's mother as the primary caregiver. For example, Draper (1975) discusses the roles of women in hunting-gathering societies, in which the mother returned to her main role of gathering food after weaning her infant, and the infant was cared for by children in the community. In other societies, infants were cared for by extended family members, often grandmothers or aunts, while mothers worked to contribute to the family income (see Lancaster & Lancaster, 1987). The care of infants in France before the late eighteenth century was relegated to wet nurses who often lived in the country, away from the infant's family, where the infants may have remained for as long as three to five years.

From a historical perspective, then, the idea of mothers being the sole, primary caregivers for their children is a relatively new phenomenon. Most people today don't take such an extended historical perspective, but rather choose to look back in history only as far as the early to mid 1900s when defining the "traditional" family and what the roles of mothers should be. Thus, many mothers today are compelled to compare themselves to their own mothers and to the memories of growing up in the world of a traditional family where Mom was home to see to the proper upbringing of the children and to provide a stable base for the family, and dad was the sole provider of the family's financial resources. Now in the year 2001, some women are torn between outside pressures—or between their own desires to conform to idealized images of the mothers of yesterday and the realities of today's world—including both the increasing opportunities of employment for women and the need for increased income to support families in our society. Still other mothers do not want to duplicate the behaviors of their own mothers. As the definition of motherhood has been transformed over the last generation, mothers are struggling to keep pace with changing roles and increasing demands. Overall, the struggle between choosing to work or not work, the available alternatives for child care, the impact of maternal employment and day care on children's development, and the political atmosphere surrounding this topic paint a complex picture for families in the twenty-first century.

In this chapter we present an overview of current research and what we believe are the key issues regarding the relations between maternal employment, day care, and infant development. We discuss the key concerns of social scientists, policy makers and families and highlight new and continuing issues as we move into the twenty-first century. We first focus on the demographics of mothers in the labor force, on issues related to day care, and on the status of the national response to these issues. We then conclude with a discussion of future directions and recommendations.

MATERNAL EMPLOYMENT AND FAMILY LIFE IN 2000

In the past two decades the United States has witnessed considerable change in the roles of mothers. A staggeringly high divorce rate, escalating rates of both single-parent and blended family homes, and dramatic increases in women—and especially mothers—entering the work force have all contributed to a changing picture of family life in America. With approximately a 50% divorce rate, it is estimated that the majority of children born in the 1990s will spend some time in a single-parent family before the age of sixteen (Furstenberg & Cherlin, 1991; Garfinkel, Hochschild & McLanahan, 1996). Moreover, the preponderant majority—approximately 90%—of all single-parent homes are homes without a father (Schmittroth, 1994). Consequently, most children in single-parent families live in homes where the mother is primarily, if not solely, responsible for the financial well-being of the household.

Partly as a consequence of single mothers taking on the breadwinner role, there has been a considerable increase in women's labor force participation. For example, fewer than 12% of women with children under the age of six were employed in 1950, compared to almost 60% in 1991 (National Center for Educational Statistics, 1993). This figure indicates that more than half of mothers with children younger than school age were employed at the beginning of the 1990s. Moreover, the majority of mothers who were employed had children less than *three years* of age. The most recent statistics indicate that 60.4% of all employed mothers have children two years of age or less, 59.7% have children one year or less, and 53.6% have children under one year of age (Bureau of Labor Statistics, 1999). When maternal employment began to increase over the last three decades, many mothers of infants were still at home. As the above-noted statistics indicate, this is no longer the case today and maternal employment is expected to continue increasing well into this century.

The decision to be an employed mother is prompted by personal, financial, family, and situational factors. Some women are employed because they are the sole providers for their families, some are employed in order to supplement their family income, some to stay out of poverty, and some are employed for personal satisfaction and fulfillment (Lerner, 1994; Scarr, 1998). Many families need the financial resources that working women can provide. In single-earner families, working wives raise the income of their family by approximately 54 percent and, in dual-earner households, wives contribute more than 35 percent of the family income (Kamerman, 1994). In addition, many women who are pushed into the labor force for purely financial reasons have come to enjoy the fulfillment, interpersonal contacts, and pride that employment brings. Some mothers still have a choice—they may not need (or may sacrifice) the amenities that employment can bring because they feel strongly that they need to be home with their children. Others, especially those women who have no choice, may find it difficult to balance the roles of employee and mother.

As we move into the twenty-first century, the demographic changes that have occurred and continue to occur will compel us to take a closer look at family life. For example, the above-noted statistics raise questions about the context of infant development. Since the majority of mothers are employed, most infants today will spend part of their day in the care of someone other than their mother or father. This fact urges child development specialists to look closely at some important questions: Is exclusive maternal care necessary for optimal infant development? What is the best type of alternative care for infants? What is good parenting? How can working women best balance their roles as both employee and mother?

To make the picture even more complex, there are few national supports for working mothers in the form of maternity leave or daycare, leaving each mother virtually alone to solve the complex issues that surround the decision to be employed. Risking job status, negotiating time off, and finding quality daycare are some of the issues that women have to begin to deal with even before the birth of their first child. Our nation has always been ambivalent, and even pessimistic, about maternal employment. However, the U.S. economy cannot function without women as employees and entrepreneurs (Scarr, 1998). Even so, some people continue to maintain negative perceptions about working mothers. Perhaps as a consequence of these perceptions, there remains an assumption in the United States that individual families, unless they are poor, should bear the burden of the cost for child care, whether the child care is used for child enrichment alone or because the mother is employed.

The questions about whether mothers of infants should be employed and the effects of employment on those infants are complex. The infant described at the beginning of this chapter will probably not be adversely affected by her mother's employment if the care she is receiving is of high quality, if her mother's mood and interactions with her are usually positive when they are together, and if there is stability in her home situation. However, there are many individual and contextual factors to be considered examining the effects of maternal employment on infants.

APPROACHES TO THE STUDY OF THE EFFECTS OF MATERNAL EMPLOYMENT AND DAY CARE ON CHILDREN

Although the amount of research on the influences of maternal employment on infants has been increasing rapidly, most of this research has not examined the interrelationships between the developing infant and the changing sociocultural context. Maternal employment is embedded in complex networks of contextual factors such as culture, neighborhood, and family. For example, is the working mother also a single parent? What supports, both in the family and in the community, are available for her and for her children? In addition, many studies fail to assess maternal variables that may relate to actual employment status—for instance, health status. Moreover, variables other than maternal employment status, such as maternal attitudes and role satisfaction, may covary with characteristics of the context such as the father's involvement with the child. All of these characteristics may interact with the characteristics of the child such as age, sex, or temperament to produce developmental outcomes for the child. Furthermore, the investigations designed to address developmental issues have been predominantly cross-sectional, making it difficult to draw conclusions about the process by which maternal employment influences the developing child.

What we have learned from decades of research and writing on this topic is that maternal employment is a distal variable in the context or ecology of the child (Bronfenbrenner & Morris, 1998). Thus, researchers have called for an evaluation of the "indirect" effects of maternal employment on children, asserting that there are really no "direct" effects (Gottfried & Gottfried, 1988; Hoffman, 1989; Lerner, 1994). That is, it is likely that maternal employment effects work "through" other variables to affect the child. Some variables that have been found to be important are maternal role satisfaction and mother-child interaction (Lerner, 1994; Scarr, 1998). Maternal employment may affect a mother's role strain, her mood, and her interactions with her children. These factors may have a stronger influence on child outcomes than solely whether or not the mother is employed. In fact, research has documented such a link (e.g., Lerner & Galambos, 1985). Gottfried (1991) goes so far as to say that previous research that has only compared mothers who were employed and mothers who were not employed (a direct effects approach) is inadequate. This is because differences found between these groups may not be due to maternal employment per se (Gottfried & Gottfried, 1988; Hoffman, 1984; Lerner, 1994). For example, differences in family socioeconomic status, in parental attitudes toward employment, in mothers' work and home stress, in fathers' involvement in child care and household tasks, and in the number of children in the home may all influence child outcomes. Thus, researchers must move beyond employment status as a direct indicator of outcomes for children and give attention to the variables surrounding mothers' employment that may potentially affect their infants.

In addition, research on maternal employment should be sensitive to the issue of bi-directional effects and the reciprocal relations that exist between the active child and the active context; that is, research must take into account the possibility that the child is both a product and a producer of his/her own development (Lerner & Spanier, 1978). As mentioned previously, characteristics of the child such as temperament and gender can contribute to the type and quality of interactions between mothers and children that further influence the child's development. Thus, recent research efforts have focused on an "indirect" or "process" approach, and this research will be briefly summarized in a later section. First, because so many working mothers with infants must use alternative child care arrangements, a brief discussion of child care in the United States is presented next.

CHILD CARE IN AMERICA

When mothers are employed, societal concerns are raised about the environment the child experiences and what effect that environment will have on the infant's intellectual, social, and emotional development. Discussions regarding maternal employment and infant development are inherently tied to discussions related to alternative childcare, since so many children attend care. For example, the use of center daycare for infants and toddlers has increased from 3% in 1965 to 23% in 1993 (Scarr, 1998). Thus, it is difficult to neatly separate the influences of maternal employment from the influence of the alternative care that the infant receives. For this reason, we will discuss these findings together, keeping in mind the intricate relationship between variables related to maternal employment and the quality of the childcare context. Certainly, daycare quality is a proximal variable that will directly influence the child.

Children of employed mothers are cared for in many different childcare arrangements. They may be cared for in their own homes by a relative or non-relative, in a family daycare home, in a daycare home, in a daycare center, or in a babysitter's home. Of the almost 21 million children under age five not enrolled in school in 1995, approximately 40% were cared for by parents, 31% in child care centers, 21% by other relatives, 14% in family care settings, and 4% by sitters (Scarr, 1998). Nine percent of families have multiple childcare arrangements. Thus, the majority of children under age five are cared for by individuals other than their parents for some part of the day. Moreover, child care quality ranges from excellent to terrible in the United States with the average care being mediocre (Scarr, 1998). Variations in quality exist in European countries as well, but not to the same extent as in the U.S. (Lamb, Sternberg, Hwang, & Broberg, 1992). Factors associated with the *number of hours* an infant spends in child care include the mother's work schedule, her earning power, family total income, family size, ethnicity, mother's education and mother's beliefs and attitudes about child rearing. *Type of care* is associated with maternal education, family size, household composition, economics, and beliefs about potential risks that may be associated with maternal employment (NICHD Early Child Care Research Network, 1997). The research that documents the effects of daycare on children has been published extensively (see Cost, Quality, and Child Outcomes Study Team, 1995; NICHD Early Child Care Research Network, 1996a,b; Rubenstein & Howes, 1979). Rather than reviewing this extensive research here, we will highlight the findings relevant to our discussion on maternal employment, daycare, and infant development.

INFANT COGNITIVE AND INTELLECTUAL DEVELOPMENT

Research focused specifically on the influences of maternal employment on infant cognitive and intellectual development is not plentiful. More attention has been paid to the influences on infant social and emotional development and parent/infant attachment. Early studies that assessed infant intellectual and language development had mixed results. For example, some have found no differences in language development between infants of employed and non-employed mothers, but found that infants of employed mothers had higher scores on intelligence measures (Hock, 1980; Schacter, 1981).

It is difficult to evaluate these findings because of the lack of attention to the overall context of the infants' development. That is, in these early studies we have no knowledge about the quality of parenting or of the characteristics of the home that the infant experienced. In fact, any "direct effects" studies—studies that simply compare the infants of employed or non-employed mothers—add little to our understanding of the context or of the "ecology" of maternal employment for infant development and the processes by which maternal employment influences children. We do know, however, that infants' intellectual development is not compromised when they are cared for in high-quality daycare settings (Peisner-Feinberg & Burchinal, 1997).

More sophisticated and extensive studies that evaluate the effects of employment on the home situation, and thus on the child, have found relationships between the mother's employment and the child's cognitive development during infancy or toddlerhood. For example, in one study, variables such as mother's education, attitudes, and the level of stimulation in the home were stronger influences on child outcomes than whether or not the mother was employed (Gottfried & Gottfried, 1984). More recent research has supported the Gottfrieds' findings. For example, Caruso (1996) reported a significant, positive association between maternal occupational prestige and mother-infant interaction quality. Specifically, mothers with higher occupational prestige scored higher on interaction measures with their infants. However, employed groups were not found to differ from non-employed groups in mother-infant interaction. These findings underscore the idea that maternal employment status may not be a very robust variable in assessing outcomes for children.

Interestingly—and consistent with an ecological framework—variables in the child's context prove to be the most meaningful of the variables reported by the Gottfrieds and others. They include variables related to the mother, the quality of parenting and alternative care, and the stability of the family. For example, both early and current research has pointed to the mother's role satisfaction, rather than her employment status, as being related to the infant's development. Happy and satisfied mothers interact more positively with their children, and development is therefore optimally influenced.

Other research that does not focus on the effects of employment per se, has shed some light on the link between maternal separation and infant cognitive development with disadvantaged groups. For example, some research examines the influences of maternal separation when disadvantaged babies are placed in enrichment programs and investigates how these programs affect the infant's cognitive development. Although this research does not specifically examine the influences of maternal employment on these infants, these studies have shown that high-quality early enrichment programs can, and do, improve children's intellectual development (Brooks-Gunn, 1995; Campbell & Ramey, 1987). In fact, there may even be long-lasting effects from such programs. For instance, additional studies have reported that high quality infant and preschool care for poor children is associated with better school achievement and social behavior in later years as compared to similar children without any child care experience or experience in low quality care (ex., Field, 1991; Ramey & Ramey, 1992). This research legitimates the need for quality programs for disadvantaged children. Much more research on the relations between infant cognitive development and maternal employment-related variables is needed, particularly among various racial, ethnic, and socioeconomically diverse populations. A greater amount of research has focused on infants' social and emotional development. We will briefly highlight that literature next.

INFANT SOCIOEMOTIONAL DEVELOPMENT

The most significant research on the influences of maternal employment on the socioemotional development of infants is derived from research on daycare. The use of child care is becoming the norm for children in the United States, and past research has produced somewhat conflicting results regarding the effects of child care on children's developmental outcomes (e.g., Belsky, 1988; Clarke-Stewart & Fein, 1983). Many factors have contributed to the discrepancies in findings. For example, center-based care is usually the focus of research, although it represents only a small proportion of infant and toddler care. As mentioned above, family daycare, babysitters, and relatives are other child care arrangements that add to the diversity of care situations.

As detailed in earlier sections, in order to truly understand the effects of child care one has to evaluate such care within the "ecology" or "system" (Bronfenbrenner & Morris, 1998) in which development occurs. When we evaluate the effects of care within the system in which the child is embedded, variables of interest are broadened to include aspects of the child care center, the quality of care, the number of hours the child spends in care, as well as family actors such as economic resources, attitudes, and values.

Concerns about poor quality care have led to a more systematic study of the influences of nonmaternal care, especially center care, on infants and children. In 1996 the National Institute of Child Health and Human

Development (NICHD) developed the Early Child Care Research Network and launched an extensive longitudinal study of the effects of child care. Results of this initiative show that the stability of early child care arrangements is associated with child outcomes. For example, when there are high levels of stability, infants and children are reported to be more securely attached to their mothers, are more competent with peers as toddlers, and show less aggression than when there are low levels of stability (NICHD Early Child Care Research Network, 1997).

Other findings indicate that the characteristics of the daycare center and of the family are important influences on the infant's development. For example, high quality mothering is the strongest and most consistent predictor of child outcomes. Insensitive mothering, on the other hand, especially when it is combined with low-quality infant care, is related to insecure attachment in the infant. Among child care variables, quality of care is the most important for positive infant developmental outcomes. These results support previous findings that early, intensive, and continuous high quality care is not related to problematic child behavior among two- and three-year-olds (NICHD Early Child Care Research Network, 1997). On the contrary, as noted previously, high quality care for disadvantaged infants has been shown to be better than having no child care experience at all (e.g., Field, 1991; Ramey & Ramey, 1992).

Given the escalating number of mothers entering the work force and the parallel increase in the number of children in out-of-home care, it is clear that our country will face increasing pressures to provide high quality care for all children who need it. Other industrialized countries have made child care a national priority and have successfully dealt with providing high quality care to all children. Certainly, such an effort needs to be subsidized so that all families have access to quality care.

MATERNAL EMPLOYMENT AND PUBLIC POLICY

Perhaps the most obvious influence of maternal employment as we begin the new century is the way that it will continue to shape family life. The impact of maternal employment on child development is an issue that illustrates the potential for collaboration between scholars and decision makers. Indeed, this collaboration is becoming essential given the current and growing trends in our society today. As the percentage of working women with children has increased by double digits each decade since the 1960s, this phenomenon has increasingly gained the attention of policy makers. As a consequence, elected leaders have been presented with an ever-growing number of funding and policy requests (Lerner & Abrams, 1994). For example, mothers who need to work are concerned about the availability of competitive jobs with health care benefits, child care providers are concerned about the appropriateness and affordability of licensing standards, private employers question the prudence of parental leave proposals, social services administrators point to the need for legislation to help low-income women work their way off public assistance, education administrators caution against asking public schools to absorb the cost of self-care programs, and so on (Lerner & Abrams, 1994).

More than 80% of women in the work force are in their prime child-bearing years; 93% of these women will become pregnant at some point in their working lives (Schroeder, 1988). Moreover, almost 62% of mothers with children six years old or younger are currently in the labor force (Dorgan, 1995). Therefore, United States policymakers must address the fact that, following the birth of a child, the majority of mothers remain in the work force. Consequently, after more than ten years of neglect by the federal policymaking community, children and families are again becoming a national priority. In February of 1993, for example, President Clinton signed the Family and Medical Leave Act (FMLA), which allows parental leave for selected employees for a maximum of twelve weeks, guaranteeing job security should they need to leave their job due to the birth or adoption of a child, or for a family medical emergency. However, this leave is entirely unpaid. Thus, it is difficult for many parents who have the option of parental leave to financially afford the time away from work.

In addition to financial concerns, many mothers suffer from feelings of separation anxiety and guilt from leaving their infant and returning to work, as well as facing societal pressures conveying that a mother "belongs" at home with her baby. As indicated previously, mothers work for a variety of reasons, such as financial necessity, or for personal self-worth and fulfillment. Thus, opinion leaders and policymakers must be encouraged to endorse a variety of personal choices for mothers or to support flexible policies that allow mothers to reconcile conflicting attitudes by choosing part-time work, flexible work hours, job sharing, or seasonal work (Lerner & Abrams, 1994). As research has demonstrated, satisfied mothers, whether homemakers or employed mothers, interact most positively with their children (Lerner & Galambos, 1985).

WELFARE TO WORK FOR LOW-INCOME MOTHERS

Our discussion of maternal employment and infant development must also include a discussion of federal policies that impact mothers of infants. Welfare reform is one such policy. Aspects of the current welfare reform initiatives will most certainly affect the infants and children of welfare-dependent mothers.

Welfare reform in the United States has been an issue of growing interest and controversy for more than a decade. Political leaders, policy makers, and private citizens alike are concerned with the current welfare system at both the state and national levels and with the implications that recent welfare reform policies will have on the country and its citizens. After many years of debate, President Clinton signed the Personal

Responsibility and Work Opportunity Reconciliation Act in 1996, a bill that drastically overhauled the welfare system as we had known it. Specifically, the bill calls for a mandatory work requirement after two years of receiving aid, a five-year lifetime limit to benefits for families, a sizable decrease in the Food Stamp program, and other reductions focused on legal immigrants, the disabled, and the elderly poor.

Overall, with this bill in place, welfare funding was reduced by $54 billion over a six-year period. However, while this massive decrease in federal spending sounds appealing for the country as a whole, many scholars, policy makers, and citizens agree that for the current welfare reform program to be effective (i.e., mandatory work and time limits) health insurance must be drastically reformed, earnings must be raised, and job training, child care, and child support need to be addressed (McCrate & Smith, 1998).

The Urban Institute reported that with the current welfare reform bill in place, over one million more children would likely be forced into lives of poverty (Zedlewski, Clark, Meier, & Watson, 1996). This is just one of the problems associated with the current system. Lack of employment opportunities, low-wage jobs that offer little room for advancement, jobs with no or minimal benefits, transportation difficulties, and child care issues are all significant and prevalent barriers to participation in the work force for low-income women. Preparation for the labor market and job training are minimal, even non-existent, for many women.

Since the majority of welfare recipients are low-income single mothers, the issue of who will care for their young children is particularly salient. Obtaining high quality child care may be a problem for many employed mothers, but is particularly challenging for families that lack financial resources. Once child care has been paid for, the remaining money brought home from a low-wage job may not be enough to justify employment. In addition, the loss of Medicaid benefits is another deterrent to getting out of the welfare system and entering a low-paying job. In order to stay off welfare, women need to be employed, but working for minimal wages makes it difficult to afford the quality of child care that is optimal for their children. Consequently, women may experience guilt and higher levels of role strain, and may ultimately have a negative impact on both their children and their work (Kossek, Huber-Yoder, Castellino & Lerner, 1997).

Moreover, many people in our society hold the view that welfare-receiving women have low self-regard and just do not want to work. In fact, the stigma associated with persons receiving welfare benefits in the United States is so prevalent that many who are entitled to benefits often do not pursue them (Goodban, 1985). Recent studies show that the pervasive stereotype regarding welfare recipients may be far from reality. For instance, one study of low-income mothers receiving aid in Michigan reported that they possessed positive feelings of self-worth, positive attitudes toward working, and some job skills and experience (Kossek, et al., 1997).

In addition, nationally based studies demonstrate that welfare recipients continue to work outside the home or to seek work while on welfare. The Institute for Women's Policy research found that over a 24-month period, 42.9% of welfare recipients combined wage labor and welfare, and another 30.8% looked for jobs but could not find them (Spalter-Roth, Burr, Shaw, & Hartmann, 1995). However, because of the types of jobs available, work does not result in economic security for a large number of mothers. Consequently, remaining on welfare seems to be the only alternative for many mothers.

Many programs on the state level have tried to combine welfare with paid employment. These programs have been referred to as workfare. Workfare programs across the country, however, have not proven to be particularly successful. None have been successful in effectively raising significant numbers of families out of poverty. Part of this may be due to the 1981 revision of the AFDC program proposed by President Reagan and subsequently passed by Congress, which increased the nominal implicit tax rate on earnings from 67% to 100%. From 1967 until the 1981 revision, a welfare mother could take a job, and for every dollar in wages she received, she only lost 67 cents in welfare. Mothers could package welfare and work, putting their families into a better economic situation. Since the 1981 revision, women can lose about one dollar in AFDC benefits for every dollar in earnings (McCrate & Smith, 1998).

What is obvious in the dozens of welfare reform initiatives is that little attention has been paid to children. Some programs have required single mothers on welfare to work (e.g., Michigan's Social Contract initiative). This runs counter to the belief that it is desirable for mothers of young children to remain at home with their children. Many middle-class women can make a choice that is consistent with their values—either to stay at home or to be employed. This choice will no longer exist for women in these programs who are welfare dependent because they are forced to accept employment regardless of their child care situation. Moreover, adequate assistance is not given to these mothers to aid in finding appropriate care for their infants, or to assist with paying for child care.

Efforts should be aimed at addressing family issues that may either help or hinder the adjustment from welfare to work. A serious consideration should be how it affects children. Wilson, Ellwood, and Brooks-Gunn (1995) have outlined a number of issues that result when a mother is encouraged or forced to move into the labor market. For example, the nature or quality of parent-child interactions will be affected (Aber, Brooks-Gunn & Maynard, 1995). Direct effects will involve the changes in supports that the child has received through social services (Maynard, 1995), and other more indirect influences will be a result of the changes in the home environment including parental stress, household income, and family relationships. To summarize, as Aber et al. (1995) have pointed out in reference to welfare to work programs, "In the rush to increase the independence of mothers we have ignored some crucial questions about children and family" (p. 64).

CRITICAL ISSUES AND FUTURE DIRECTIONS

With several decades of maternal employment and daycare research behind us, we now turn to what we believe are the most pressing issues to address in the coming years.

National Policy

Until the Family and Medical Leave Act was passed in 1993, the United States was the only country out of seventy-five industrialized nations without a government-sponsored family policy that specified some form of paid maternity benefits, parental leave for parents, and subsidized child care. Given the lack of national supports for working women in our country, mothers have been forced to negotiate leave and time off from work by themselves, as well as find and afford quality child care for their children. As the numbers of women participating in the workforce continue to increase, thereby escalating the numbers of children who require out-of-home care, the United States will be faced with increasing pressures to provide flexible work policies, and high quality child care for the numerous families who need it.

It is clear that in the twenty-first century, maternal employment is the norm for the majority of families in America. Given the statistics that underscore the prevalence of not only women in the workforce, but the increasing numbers of working mothers, it is more evident than ever that the issues that surround working mothers and their children are a national concern. This is true given the number of women in the labor market, the fact that working women contribute substantially to the economy, the number of women with children forced to enter the labor market due to welfare reform initiatives, and the pressing need that remains for *high-quality*, affordable child care.

How the nation addresses these issues will be at the forefront of many debates. Should employers provide flexible work schedules for working parents? Who should pay for child care? Should parents receive paid parental leave and if so, who should pay for the cost of such a policy? How governments, employers, and parents reach agreement on these questions will likely be one of the greatest challenges related to American families in the twenty-first century.

Day Care Quality

The child care system that has emerged in the United States is one in which high quality care is accessible to affluent families and to some poor families who receive support for child care, while middle-income and low income working families are likely to afford only lower quality care (Maynard & McGinnis, 1992). Moreover, poor families are likely to pay a greater portion of their income for child care than non-poor families. The National Child Care Survey (Hofferth, Brayfield, Deich, & Holcomb, 1991) found that mothers whose family income was less than $15,000 paid 23% of their income for child care, whereas mothers with higher incomes paid far less of their income for child care. It seems logical that higher quality care costs more, so the dilemma for many families is the trade-off between quality and cost of care for their children. It is important to remember, though, that high quality care is not only beneficial for children, but also impacts the well-being of parents (Mason & Duberstein, 1992). Therefore, it is in the best interest of all concerned to make high quality care affordable for all children. The question remains how to make this a reality in the United States.

Another unresolved issue concerns the availability of care for mothers who don't work standard business hours. Most daycare centers and family care settings offer child care during daytime hours, Monday through Friday. What are the alternatives for mothers who are required to work nights or weekends? The access to child care for these mothers is even more challenging. As we look ahead, it is clear that many child care issues remain unresolved, but these issues must certainly be addressed as we move into the twenty-first century.

Gender Equity

Most of the above discussion has focused on mothers, their employment and the care of their children. As maternal employment has increased by double digits over the last few decades, the pervasive attitude in the United States has been to leave the problems of child care to the mother (Scarr, 1996). This attitude is not surprising; the traditional view of the family leaves paid work to the father and the care of children to the mother. Thus, mothers have continued to take on most of the responsibility for child care even though they may spend as many hours as fathers do in paid employment. This contributes to role strain and to other stresses that may affect the mother and the functioning of the family (Lerner, 1994). However, with employed women a necessity for the economic integrity of our country, issues now arise that lead to a clear debate over economic, social, and political gender equity. Many women find it difficult to pursue career opportunities because of family commitments, and women have always been faced with issues of unequal compensation. This issue has been addressed in the public domain, and most agree that there cannot be gender equity in the workforce until men take more responsibility for child care.

Some countries have made commitments to gender equity, and while the solutions may not be entirely appropriate for the United States, many of their ideas should be at the center of our efforts. Sweden, for example, is unique in its effort to promote gender equity through social programs. Over a century ago, political forces in Sweden made equality a major goal to avoid exploitation due to gender or social class. The Swedish have adopted an "equal roles family model" which maintains that both mother and father have the right to pursue a career, and both should take equal part in the care of children. Of course, enormous national supports had to be put into place to realize this goal. For example, national day care centers are available to all families, and are of high quality. They are publicly funded and are widely accepted on a national level. In addition, parental leaves are available to mothers and fathers and shorter workdays are encouraged for both parents with no loss of job benefits or job security. Of course, citizens are highly taxed so that these programs can be made available to all families, but the result has been an excellent day care and school system, and less stress for families. It is true that the United States is quite different from Sweden economically and politically, but steps to gender equity within the constraints of our system can still be initiated.

Training

This chapter has identified several issues pertinent to the employment of mothers and to the care of infants. These issues need to be considered in discussions by decision-makers at the federal, state, and local levels whose work affects the employability, work environments, and parenting strengths of working mothers. In addition, the research findings we have discussed have implications for the educational and training institutions that prepare future workers, professionals, and paraprofessionals.

Numerous studies report that high-quality enrichment programs improve children's intellectual development and school achievement. Infant child care and early childhood education are labor-intensive activities whose quality is determined by the expertise of teachers and caregivers. Therefore, academic and practical training of administrators is essential if children are to realize their potential in these settings. Training should be delivered in a range of settings, including two and four year colleges, workshops and conferences, and through competency-oriented practicum experiences. At a minimum, training should encompass information on child development, health, and safety, and advice on how to communicate with parents. At its best, training should present a holistic view of children's cognitive, emotional, social, physical, and nutritional needs.

Child caregivers in the twenty-first century, given the data on working mothers and parents, will also need enhanced skills in family lifestyle assessment, appreciation of the new roles played by fathers, and an ability to involve extended family members in the child's learning process. They will also need an appreciation for the developmental needs of children whose mothers have experienced complicated work histories. It is crucial to recognize that the child is embedded within two interdependently related systems, the child care system and the family system (Bronfenbrenner & Morris, 1998). As such, insights can be gained from exploring the links between these two systems and by asking how one system affects the other.

Research

Many research initiatives have already begun to address the complexities of infant daycare and maternal employment. We have presented findings from studies that have considered that the infant develops in an interdependent system of relationships. If we are going to get closer to a true understanding of the impact of maternal employment and daycare on infant development, researchers need to continue to explore the impact that maternal employment has on the mother and the family. Throughout this chapter, we have pointed to the factors that have been found to be important influences on infant development when mothers are employed, such as maternal role satisfaction, maternal and family stress, and social support. For mothers in general—and especially those in the welfare system—the quality, affordability and availability of child care, flexible work hours, and federal and state support for childcare have been critical factors that impact maternal, family, and infant functioning.

Researchers in the policy domain need to continually evaluate the programs that have been initiated in order to determine if they are meeting their goals. For example, welfare reform initiatives need to be assessed with an effort to determine how various programs affect infants and families, not simply how many women are able to get out of the welfare system. Policy researchers and child development researchers need to combine forces to develop policies that are good for families.

Several ideas have been outlined in this chapter for social scientists and policy makers. Given the employment trends pertaining to women and particularly mothers, we cannot turn away from the notion that the issues pertinent to influences of maternal employment and day care on infants will continue to be important in the decades to come.

REFERENCES

Aber, J. L., Brooks-Gunn, J., & Maynard, R. A. (1995, Summer/Fall). The effects of welfare reform on teenage parents and their children. *The Future of Children*, 5(2), pp. 53–71.

Belsky, J. (1984). Two waves of day care research: Developmental effects and conditions of quality. In R.C. Ainslie (Ed.), *The child and the day care setting* (pp. 24–42). New York: Praeger.

Bronfenbrenner, U., & Morris, P. (1998). The ecology of developmental processes. In W. Damon (Series Ed.) & R. M. Lerner (Volume Ed.), *Handbook of child psychology: Vol. 5. Theoretical models of human development* (5th Ed., pp. 993–1028). New York: Wiley.

Brooks-Gunn, J. (1995). Strategies for altering the outcomes of poor children and their families. In P. Lindsay Chase-Landsale & J. Brooks-Gunn (Eds). *Escape from poverty: What makes a difference for children?* (pp. 87–117). New York: Cambridge.

Bureau of Labor Statistics. (1999). Employment status of mothers with own children under 3 years old by single year of age of youngest child, and marital status, 1997–98 averages.

Campbell, F. A., & Ramey, C. T. (1987). High risk infants: Environmental risk factors. In J. M. Berg (Ed.), *Science and service in mental retardation* (pp. 22–33). London: Methuen.

Caruso, D. A. (1996). Maternal employment status, mother-infant interaction, and infant development in day care and non-day care groups. *Child & Youth Care Forum*, 25, 125–134.

Clark-Stewart, K. A., & Fein, G. (1983). Early childhood programs. In H. Haith & J. J. Campos (Eds.), *Infancy and developmental psychobiology* (Vol. 2, pp. 917–1000). New York: John Wiley.

Cost, Quality, and Child Outcomes Study Team. (1995). Cost, quality, and child outcomes in child care centers. Denver: University of Colorado.

Dorgan, C. A. (Ed.). (1995). *Statistical handbook of working America*. Detroit, MI: Gale Research, Inc.

Draper, P. (1975). !Kung women: Contrasts in egalitarianism in foraging and sedentary contexts. In R. Reiter (Ed.), *Toward and anthropology of women* (pp. 77–109). London: Monthly Review Press.

Elliott, M. (1966). Impact of work, family, and welfare receipt on women's self-esteem in young adulthood. *Social Psychology Quarterly*, 59, 80–95

Field, T. (1991). Quality infant day-care and grade school behavior and performance. *Child Development*, 62, 863–870.

Furstenberg, F. F., & Cherlin, A. J. (1991). *Divided families: What happens to children when parents part*. Cambridge, MA: Harvard University Press.

Garfinkel, I., Hochschild, J. L., & McLanahan, S. S. (1996). *Social policies for children*. Washington, DC: The Brookings Institution.

Goodban, N. (1985). The psychological impact of being on welfare. *Social Service Review*, 59, 403–422.

Gottfried, A. E. (1991). Maternal employment in the family setting: Developmental and environmental issues. In J. V. Lerner & N. L. Galambos (Eds.), *Employed mothers and their children* (pp. 63–84). New York: Garland.

Gottfried, A. E., & Gottfried, A. W. (1988). Maternal employment and children's development: An integration of longitudinal findings with implications for social policy. In A. E. Gottfried & A. W. Gottfried (Eds.), *Maternal employment and children's development: Longitudinal research* (pp. 269–287). New York: Plenum.

Hock, E. (1980). Working and nonworking mothers and their infants: A comparative study of maternal caregiving characteristics and infant social behavior. *Merrill-Palmer Quarterly, 26,* 79–101.

Hofferth, S. L., Brayfield, A., Deich, S., & Holcomb, P. (1991). *National child care survey, 1990* (Urban Institute Report 91–5). Washington DC: Urban Institute Press.

Hoffman, L. W. (1984). Maternal employment and the young child. In M. Perlmutter (Ed.), *Minnesota symposium in child psychology* (Vol. 17, pp. 101–127). Hillsdale, NJ: Erlbaum.

Hoffman, L. W. (1989). Effects of maternal employment in the two-parent family. *American Psychologist, 44,* 283–292.

Kamerman, S. B. (1994). Parental leave policy. In M. A. Mason & E. D. Gambrill (Eds.), *Debating children's lives: Current controversies on children and adolescents* (pp. 340–353). Thousand Oaks, CA: Sage Publications.

Kossek, E. E., Huber-Yoder, M., Castellino, D., & Lerner, J. (1997). The working poor: Locked out of careers and the origanizational mainstream? *Academy of Management Executive, 11,* 75–91.

Lamb, M., Sternberg, K. J., Hwang, P., & Broberg, A. (Eds.). (1992). *Child care in context.* Hillsdale, NJ: Erlbaum.

Lancaster, J. B., & Lancaster, C. S. (1987). The watershed: Change in parental-investment and family formation strategies in the course of human evolution. In J. B. Lancaster, J. Altman, A. Rossi, & L. R. Sherrod (Eds.), *Parenting across the life span* (pp. 187–205). New York: Plenum Press.

Lerner, J. V. (1994). *Working women and their families.* Thousand Oaks, CA: Sage Publications.

Lerner, J. V., & Abrams, L. A. (1994). Developmental correlates of maternal employment influences on children. In C. B. Fisher & R. M. Lerner (Eds.), *Applied Developmental Psychology* (pp. 174–206). New York: McGraw-Hill.

Lerner, J. & Galambos, N. A. (1985). Maternal role satisfaction, mother–child interaction, and child temperament. *Developmental Psychology, 21,* 1157–1164.

Lerner, R. M., & Spanier, G. B. (1978). A dynamic interactional view of child and family development. In R. M. Lerner & G. B. Spanier (Eds.), *Child influences on marital and family interaction: A life-span perspective* (pp. 1–22). New York: Academic Press.

Mason, K., & Duberstein, L. (1992). Consequences of child care for parents' well-being. In A. Booth (Ed.), *Child care in the 1990s: Trends and consequences* (pp. 127–158). Hillsdale, NJ: Erlbaum.

Maynard, R. (1995). Teenage childbearing and welfare reform: Lessons from a decade of demonstration and evaluation research. *Children and Youth Services Review* [special issue: Child poverty, public policies, and welfare reform], 17, 309–332.

Maynard, R., & McGinnis, E. (1992). Policies to enhance access to high-quality child care. In A. Booth (Ed.), *Child care in the 1990s: Trends and consequences* (pp. 189–208). Hillsdale, NJ: Erlbaum.

McCrate, E. & Smith, J. (1988). When work doesn't work: The failure of current welfare reform. *Gender & Society*, 12, 61–80.

National Center for Educational Statistics. (1993). *Youth indicators 1993: Trends in the well-being of American youth.* Washington, DC: U.S. Department of Education.

NICHD Early Child Care Research Network. (1996a). Characteristics of infant child care: Factors contributing to positive caregiving. *Early Childhood Research Quarterly*, 11, 269–306.

NICHD Early Child Care Research Network. (1996b, April). *Infant child care and attachment security: Results of the NICHD Study of early child care.* Symposium presented at the International Conference on Infant Studies, Providence, RI.

NICHD Early Child Care Research Network. (1997). Familial factors associated with the characteristics of nonmaternal care for infants. *Journal of Marriage and the Family*, 59, 389–408.

Peisner-Feinberg, E. S., & Burchinal, M. (1997). Relations between preschool children's child care experiences and concurrent development: The cost, quality and outcomes study. *Merrill-Palmer Quarterly*, 43, 451–477.

Ramey, C., & Ramey, S. (1992). Early educational intervention with disadvantaged children—to what effect? *Applied and Preventive Psychology, 1,* 131–140.

Rubenstein, J., & Howes, C. (1979). Caregiving and infant behavior in day care and in homes. *Developmental Psychology*, 15, 1–24.

Scarr, S. (1998). American child care today. *American Psychologist*, 53, 95–108.

Schacter, F. F. (1981). Toddlers with employed mothers. *Child Development*, 59, 958–964.

Schmittroth, L. (Ed.). (1994). *Statistical record of children.* Gale Research Incorporated, Detroit, MI.

Schroeder, P. (Office of). (1988). *Family and medical leave, Part 1. The work and family sourcebook.* Greenvale, NY: Panel Publications.

Silverstein, L. B. (1991). Transforming the debate about child care and maternal employment. *American Psychologist*, 46, 1025–1032.

Spalter-Roth, R., Burr, B., Shaw, L., & Hartmann, H. (1995). *Welfare that works* (Research Report). Washington, DC: Institute for Women's Policy Research.

Wilson, J. B., Ellwood, D. T., & Brooks-Gunn, J. (1995). Welfare-to-work through the eyes of children. In P. Lindsay Chase-Lansdale & J. Brooks-Gunn (Eds.), *Escape from poverty: What makes a difference for children?* (pp. 63–86). New York: Cambridge University Press.

Zedlewski, S., Clark, S., Meier, E. & Watson, K. (1996). Potential effects of Congressional welfare reform legislation on family incomes. Washington, DC: Urban Institute.

Infants' Characteristics and Behaviors Help Shape Their Environments

Katherine Hildebrandt Karraker
& Priscilla Coleman

7

♦ ♦ ♦ ♦

Our understanding of the behavioral and psychological repertoires of the human infant has changed dramatically over the course of the twentieth century. In the early 1900s researchers viewed the infant as an essentially vegetative, reflexive organism; whereas today researchers are very aware of the perceptual, intellectual, emotional, and social competencies of the young infant. Much empirically derived information about infants, as well as the general view that infants are competent and active, has been shared with parents and professionals. Acknowledgment of the general competency of infants has been accompanied by recognition that infants are capable of influencing those around them. However, despite this widespread recognition, researchers and parents alike are generally more concerned with how variations in infants' physical and social environments impact infant outcomes than with how infants themselves affect their own environments. Thus, while most of the chapters in this volume reflect the predominant orientation—addressing environmental determinants of development—the present chapter provides a counterpoint, serving to remind us that infants play an integral role in forming their own caregiving environments.

This chapter begins with a review of infant competencies and individual differences, followed by a brief historical overview of literature relevant to the belief that the infant plays an active role in constructing his or her own environment. In the next section, the general mechanisms by which infant characteristics and behaviors produce environmental variations are described. The discussion then proceeds to a more specific consideration of genetic influences on infants' environments. The distinction between shared and nonshared environmental influences on infant outcomes also is discussed. Illustrations of the influence of specific infant characteristics and behaviors on the infant's social environment are then provided, with an emphasis on infant temperament. Next, the importance of considering infants' effects on their environments for theorists, researchers, interventionists, and parents is discussed. The chapter concludes with a plea for the adoption of increasingly comprehensive and dynamic approaches to the study of infant and environmental effects on infant developmental processes.

THE COMPETENT INFANT

In the early 1960s, research undeniably demonstrated that infants could see, process information, and exhibit visual preferences (Franz, 1961; cited in Flavell, Miller, & Miller, 1993). Subsequent studies on auditory, olfactory, and gustatory abilities (Berg, Berg, & Graham, 1971; Engen, Lipsitt, & Kaye, 1963), as well as cognition (Cohen & Gelber, 1975; Lewis, 1969; Rovee-Collier, 1987) and social competencies (Cohn & Tronick, 1987; Feinman & Lewis, 1983; Kuhl & Meltzoff, 1982; Lester, Hoffman, & Brazelton, 1985) have repeatedly illustrated that from the early moments of life, infants are actively processing environmental information, learning, and responding to environmental events. Currently there is virtually universal consensus in the research community that at birth infants are equipped with a set of reflexes (e.g., sucking, rooting, gagging, crying), possess fairly well-developed perceptual abilities, and exhibit an amazing ability to learn. All of these competencies facilitate interaction with the environment and encourage growth across multiple domains of functioning. Within a relatively brief timeframe infants learn how to engage in active sensory exploration of the material world, begin to decipher immediate experiences, become capable of locomotion, engage in purposeful behavior, learn to communicate, form socioemotional ties, and develop their own unique personalities. Investigative efforts over the past few decades have clearly demonstrated the diverse and interrelated competencies of infants across all domains of development (Horowitz & Colombo, 1990).

Infants not only come into the world well equipped to become actively engaged in their environments, but individual infants differ substantially in their characteristic styles of approaching and reacting to people and situations. Interestingly, when describing their children's behavior to others, most parents of more than one child are quick to point out dispositional differences rather than similarities. Despite being reared by parents striving to use similar parenting techniques with each child and attempting to provide comparable developmental and educational opportunities, children within the same family frequently behave very differently and possess distinct general orientations to the world. Most people are able to recount numerous examples of parents expressing fascination with how their two children are so very different (one is outgoing and friendly, while the other is reclusive and shy; one accepts "no" rather easily, while the other persists willfully with his or her own agenda; one enjoys novel experiences, while the other thrives on structure and sameness in daily routines; one loves to spend time alone and engage in solitary activities, while the other needs a constant companion; one is finicky about food and clothing, while the other will eat and wear anything). In addition to these temperamental differences, siblings frequently differ from one another based on characteristics such as gender, age, health status, and cognitive skills. The list of potentially distinct personal qualities that can be observed in children is seemingly endless. Many of the differences observed are largely constitutionally-based and are undoubtedly at least in part the result of genetic variations. Others arise from the varied learning histories experienced by different children, even within the same family. In most cases, genetic endowment and experience combine to produce individual traits and behaviors. Regardless of the sources of such variability, parents are likely to behave differently and arrange the environment differently for children with distinct traits and characteristics.

THE ACTIVE INFLUENCE OF INFANTS ON THE ENVIRONMENT: A BRIEF HISTORY

Research on infant development has historically emphasized the causal effects of discrete aspects of the infant's social and physical environment on infant behavior and development. Considerably less scholarly attention has been devoted to identifying the means through which infants are able to influence their environments. Indeed, identified correlations between environmental variables, particularly parent behaviors, and infant outcomes have traditionally been interpreted as providing support for the effect of the environment on the infant, when the alternate assumption of an effect of the infant on the environment is equally plausible (Bell & Harper, 1977; Harris, 1998).

Very little attention was given to child effects on others until data derived from the New York Longitudinal Study (NYLS; Thomas, Chess, Birch, Hertzig, & Korn, 1963) challenged the idea that parents were solely responsible for their children's development (although see Bell & Harper, 1977, for earlier history). Specifically, child behavioral problems sometimes emerged even when parents engaged in positive parenting practices, while adaptive child behaviors were occasionally observed even when parents were disturbed, stressed, or otherwise unable to parent effectively. Further observation indicated that components of children's temperament and particular aspects of their environments combined to produce outcomes. In some cases, children with differing temperaments elicited qualitatively different behaviors from their parents and others, leading to distinct child outcomes (Chess, Thomas, & Birch, 1965).

The idea of bidirectionality in socialization processes was formally introduced by Sears, Maccoby, and Levin in 1957 and the results of the NYLS were published soon thereafter. However, acceptance of reciprocal determinism, the notion of effects flowing from child to parent as well as from parent to child, did not receive extensive attention until the publication of Bell's (1968) now renowned review of research findings highlighting the limitations of the unidirectional approach. In subsequent publications, Bell (1971, 1979; Bell & Chapman, 1986; Bell & Harper, 1977) provided numerous examples of ways in which infants influence parents, such as by eliciting caregiving (e.g., by crying) and by initiating, maintaining, and terminating social interaction (e.g, by smiling, clinging, and looking away). Lewis and Rosenblum edited a volume of essays in 1974 entitled *The Effect of the Infant on its Caregiver*, leading to even greater acceptance of the bidirectional model of parent-infant interaction. Sameroff and Chandler's seminal paper in 1975 concerning the transactional process whereby organismic and contextual influences combine to determine developmental outcomes substantiated the notion of the environment as dynamic, capable of both influencing and being influenced by the child.

The emergence of theoretical work on perceptual and cognitive development that gained attention in the latter half of the twentieth century also conveyed appreciation for the infant's ability to impact his or her environment. For example, Piaget (1970) conceived of cognition as a dynamic, constructive process between the individual and his or her environment. Piaget's theoretical work undoubtedly operated as a primary vehicle for changing ideas regarding the nature of infants' competencies and was particularly instrumental in the growing appreciation of infants as active participants in their own development. Piaget contended that knowledge was a process involving a relationship between the knower and the external world. The child gains understanding of his or her environment by engagement with it, and the individual willfully selects and interprets environmental stimuli rather than passively absorbing information.

The emergence of dialectical and contextualistic perspectives on development over the past few decades has also lent credence to the conception of the infant as actively involved with the environment. For example, Vygotsky contended that development was driven by a dialectical process involving individual maturation, personal experience, and involvement with cultural tools and activities (Behrend, Rosengren, & Perlmutter, 1992). More specifically, Vygotsky argued that intellectual and linguistic development proceeds through the process of internalization whereby externally-experienced events are translated into personal, mental activity. More recently, the notion of the infant as an active agent in his or her development was exemplified in constructive epigenesis as detailed by Bidell and Fischer (1997), which emphasized the central role of self-organizing activity in the development of new intellectual structures and functions over time. According to adherents of this position, both genetic and environmental events are involved in the epigenesis of the intellect; however, their effects are nonlinear—or multidirectional—in nature and are interwoven into a complex array of component systems influencing cognitive outcomes. Ultimately the entire systemic process facilitating intellectual growth is mediated by a creative, constructive agent; the person-in-context.

Despite contemporary consensus that infants and children are capable of influencing and often do have an impact on those around them, the role of child effects in developmental processes has received only scant attention. Many researchers and parents persist in assuming that the primary causal path in the socialization process flows from parents to children, an assumption based on classic theories of development, tradition, and intuition (Harris, 1998). The possibility that children's environments are associated with their behaviors because parents and children share some of their genetic endowment and/or because children shape and select their own environments is usually rejected in favor of the belief that children are socialized by their parents and other environmental experiences. Recent work by behavioral geneticists, most notably Plomin (e.g., 1990) and Scarr (e.g., 1988), and by environmentalists such as Wachs (1992), has begun to incorporate the child's role into models of environmental influence. This work and its implications will be discussed in more detail later in this chapter.

The recently published book by Judith Rich Harris, *The Nurture Assumption* (1998), challenges the belief that socialization by parents is the primary cause of children's behaviors. One thesis of the book is that children are influenced less by their parents than is assumed by parents and researchers. The book even prompted a *Newsweek* cover asking, "Do Parents Matter?" Harris contends that most research documenting parent socialization effects on children can be explained by other processes, including shared genetic endowments. Responses to the book by parents, children, and researchers were numerous and diverse (see *http://home.att.net/~xchar/tna/*). Although the author was rather extreme in some of her contentions (and certainly the book's marketing emphasized her more controversial arguments), much of the public response to the book supports the contention of the present chapter that researchers and parents are more comfortable with the idea that children's behaviors result from socialization by their parents than with the idea that children influence and select their own environments.

HOW INFANT CHARACTERISTICS AND BEHAVIORS CAN AFFECT THEIR ENVIRONMENTS

The infant's environment is obviously composed of multiple layers of diverse forms of potential influence extending from the immediate family outward to features of daycare centers and schools, family friendship networks, other relatives, neighborhoods, communities, and geographical locations. Moreover, all of these potential sources of influence are embedded in dynamic economic, cultural, and political systems that are operative during particular historical periods (Bronfenbrenner, 1979). Not surprisingly, given the time parents typically spend with their infants, the vast majority of studies designed to examine environmental factors related to infant development have focused on parenting. Although other components of infants' environments also have been considered, it is important to recognize that infants' exposures to other environments also may be controlled or mediated by their parents' actions. For example, parents typically determine whether or not an infant will experience regular daycare as well as what form that care will take. Because parents are so central to infants' environments, our discussion will emphasize the ways by which infants can impact their own environments through influencing their parents.

The direct influence of infants' behaviors on adult, and especially parent, behavior is well-documented. From birth, the infant's cries provide a potent stimulus for parents' soothing interventions (Murray, 1979). As infants mature, other emotional signals influence adult behaviors. Parents often will engage in a variety of behaviors to elicit smiles from their infant (Landau, 1977). Social interaction becomes increasingly mutually regulated, with the infant and parent each adjusting their responses based on the partner's prior behavior (Gianino & Tronick, 1988). Infant locomotor skill acquisition further drives parent behavior, as parents attempt to control and protect their exploring infant. Many studies of individual differences in infant-parent social interaction demonstrate that ongoing infant behavior influences parent behavior, and that parents respond differently to infants who display disparate behavior patterns. Interactions with an individual infant can then influence subsequent interactions with that infant through the establishment of behavior patterns or styles, and through the infant's reinforcement and punishment of particular adult behaviors (Gewirtz, 1991).

Other infant characteristics and behaviors influence parent behaviors more indirectly, by modifying parents' cognitions or emotions about their infant. For example, a male infant who shows vigorous arm waving in early infancy may come to be perceived as strong and active by his parents, who in turn begin encouraging large motor activities and early crawling and walking. A female infant who reacts negatively to new situations may come to be perceived as shy by her mother who then protects her from new and potentially frightening experiences. Parental cognitions may also result from non-behavioral characteristics of the infant. A healthy but prematurely-born infant may be thought of as small and fragile, despite evidence to the contrary, and thus be handled gently and protected from rough and tumble play (Stern & Karraker, 1990). Parents may treat male and female infants differently because of the parents' own stereotypes about what males and females are like, regardless of the actual traits of their infant. Such stereotypes and expectations concerning infants can instigate a self-fulfilling prophecy process whereby adults selectively elicit, reinforce, and interpret infant behaviors that confirm their initial expectations (Darley & Fazio, 1980). For example, a mother who believes that girls are more socially oriented than boys might work harder to elicit smiling, reinforce learning people's names more than labeling objects, and be more inclined to interpret looking as a social overture with a girl than with a boy.

The study of parental cognitions is a relatively broad domain, encompassing parents' beliefs, attitudes, values, expectations, knowledge, and desires. Although the connection between parents' cognitions and their behavior is often complex, substantial research has documented both that these cognitions are related to child characteristics and that these cognitions can impact parental behavior (Coleman & Karraker, 1997; Holden, 1995). For example, Mash and Johnston (1983) found lower levels of parenting self-efficacy beliefs among parents with atypically demanding children (those with difficult temperament or behavior disorders) when compared to parents of nonproblem children. Interestingly, the self-efficacy of parents with difficult children tends to decrease as their children grow older, while the self-efficacy of parents of nonproblem children tends to show increases corresponding to child age. Parents who lack a sense of efficacy in their own ability to parent experience difficulty translating their knowledge of parenting tasks into action, become very self-absorbed, are prone to high levels of emotional arousal, and do not show persistence in parenting (Grusec, Hastings, & Mammone, 1994). Research also has suggested that various parental cognitions can mediate between child variables and the quality of parenting. For example, Teti and Gelfand (1991) found that maternal self-efficacy beliefs mediated between infant temperamental difficulty and parenting competence, with difficult temperament influencing the quality of parenting by undermining mothers' feelings of competence in the role. Likewise, Cutrona and Troutman's research (1986) demonstrated that maternal self-efficacy mediated the effects of infant temperament and social support on postpartum depression.

Infants' characteristics also can influence parenting through their effects on parental emotions. In the context of an extensive review of relevant literature, Dix (1991) provides a model to explain the vital role parental emotions play in effective parenting. He states that parental warmth consistently predicts favorable developmental outcomes, whereas parental hostility is clearly associated with maladaptive ones. Dix further notes that this relationship persists throughout infancy and childhood and is present in both normal and dysfunctional families. According to Dix, characteristics of children (such as temperament), and contextual factors (such as parental employment and marital relationships), influence the quality of parenting because they influence the emotions experienced by parents. Substantial evidence supports the notion that emotions are central to the regulation of human behavior (Frijda, 1986; Izard, 1977; Lazarus & Folkman, 1984; Scherer, 1984).

Characteristics of child individuality also may indirectly influence parenting quality through effects on other relationships involving the parent (with a spouse, other children, relatives, co-workers, etc.) or by impacting the parent's competence at work, energy level, or mental or physical health. For example, parents with a temperamentally difficult infant may become sleep deprived and experience performance decrements at work. Resulting stress incurred at work may be reflected in lowered attentiveness and patience in parenting. Or, constant demands pertaining to the health needs of a chronically ill child may leave less time for fostering spousal relationships and concern over one's marriage may make a parent less available emotionally to his or her child.

A final way in which infants can influence their own environments is through the infants' own active selection of, perception of, and susceptibility to experiences. Scarr and McCartney (1983) label this process "niche picking." Because infants differ in temperament and life experiences, even exposure to similar environments can lead to different experiences of those environments for individual infants. For example, some infants may prefer playing with their fathers and some infants may prefer playing with their mothers. Because of this selectivity, some infants will be more influenced by their fathers and some more by their mothers. Similarly, infants with differing temperaments, cognitive styles, perceptual preferences, or prior experiences may be more interested in some toys than in others, and thus infants exposed to the same room full of toys will effectively experience different environments. As infants grow in cognitive competence, they also become capable of perceiving environmental events in individualized ways. For example, some young children may perceive an active and involved babysitter as overbearing whereas others may perceive her as fun and stimulating.

Thus, infants' characteristics and behaviors can influence their environments through a variety of mechanisms. In addition, small infant influences can in some cases be magnified through positive feedback loops (Harris, 1995). For example, a physically attractive infant may elicit increased smiling from adults, which then elicits smiling from the infant, who is then perceived as even more attractive by the same as well as other adults, who continue to smile and interact positively with the infant, thereby maintaining the infant's smiling.

GENETIC INFLUENCES ON INFANTS' ENVIRONMENTS

Many of the infant characteristics and behaviors that appear to influence their environments are likely to have genetic underpinnings. In particular, some temperamental traits appear to be highly heritable (Caspi, 1998), such as affect-extraversion (how positive and outgoing the infant is), activity, and task-orientation (including persistence, attention, and goal-directed activity). Other influential behavioral tendencies, cognitive abilities, and physical appearance are also likely to be strongly related to an infant's genetic endowment, and to have both direct and indirect effects on adults in the infant's environment. Likewise, parental genetic propensities, such as various personality traits and intelligence, may very well affect parents' tendencies to behave in particular ways toward their infants and to influence how they arrange their infants' physical and social environments.

A central question concerns the extent to which infants' environments, and, in particular, their parents' behaviors, are independent from infants' own genetic endowments. A serious difficulty with much of the socialization research that concludes that certain variations in parent behaviors lead to specific variations in infant outcomes is that infants and their parents share some of their genetic endowments. Thus, for example, an association between parental sensitivity and infant secure attachment (which has, indeed, been demonstrated; De Wolff & van Ijzendoorn, 1997) could result from parents and infants sharing genes that regulate social skill. Alternately, parental sensitivity could cause secure infant attachment, or infant social behaviors associated with secure attachment, such as positive greetings and social approach, could elicit parental sensitivity. Even longitudinal studies cannot completely resolve this dilemma. Although parental sensitivity may be evident prior to infant secure attachment, the genetic propensity for secure attachment or the social behaviors that both precede secure attachment and elicit parental sensitivity may be present in early infancy.

Distinguishing the independent influence of parent behavior from infant and parent shared genes is difficult. Adoption studies are often used to attempt to separate these effects (Plomin, 1990). When a correlation between adoptive parents' behavior and their adopted infant's behavior is observed, one can assume that the relationship is not mediated by shared genes. However, the conclusion that the parents' behavior caused the infant behavior remains problematic. The possibility still exists that the infant's genetically driven behaviors elicited those parent behaviors that appear to be causal.

Correlations between adoptive siblings (biologically unrelated children adopted into the same family) and nonadoptive siblings (biological siblings) on measures of the environment are informative about the influence of genes on infants' environments. Evidence for genetic influence is obtained in cases where the correlations are higher for nonadoptive siblings than for adoptive siblings. Such a pattern was found by Plomin, DeFries, and Fulker (1988) for some items on the Home Observation for the Measurement of the Environment (HOME), administered when children were 12 and 24 months old. Genetic factors produced higher correlations for nonadoptive than for adoptive siblings on measures of provision of toys and parental restriction-punishment. Similarly, Dunn and Plomin (1986) reported higher correlations for nonadoptive than for adoptive siblings on a measure of maternal affection derived from observations of mother-child interaction when each child was one, two, and three years old. Both of these findings support the contention that some environmental measures are determined at least in part by child genetic characteristics.

Adoption studies by Plomin and his colleagues also have shown that genetic factors can influence relationships between environmental measures and infant outcomes. These findings illustrate the effects of shared genes between parents and infants described above. Plomin, Loehlin, & DeFries (1985) reported higher correlations in nonadoptive siblings than in adoptive siblings for relationships between HOME scores and both Bayley mental scores and a measure of language development at two years.

Thus, in some cases, an infant's genetic endowment can influence his or her environment. Scarr goes so far as to argue that, when one also considers the role of genes in influencing individuals' reactions to events, "virtually no experiences are uncorrelated with one's genotype" (1988, p. 240). This argument assumes that even when an individual experiences a genetically unrelated event such as a national economic crisis or a hurricane, the individual's perception of and response to that event will be influenced by his or her genetically determined personality and cognitive skills.

ENVIRONMENTAL INFLUENCES ON INFANTS' OUTCOMES

Although recent behavioral genetic research has demonstrated the extensive influence of genes on some behaviors as well as on some environmental measures, environmental factors that are relatively free of genetic influence also have substantial impact on behavior (Plomin, 1990). In 1970, Jinks and Fulker advocated division of environmental variance into two sources, between and within the family. Rowe and Plomin (1981) later focused the two potential forms of variation in child outcomes on siblings. Today the term "nonshared" variance is generally accepted to reflect environmental variation resulting from distinct experiences of siblings in the same family, regardless of whether they are biologically related or adopted. In contrast, "shared" environmental variance is the result of experiences to which all children in the same family are exposed and which make them different from children in other families. Parent education, income level, and mental health are examples of sources of shared variance. These and other sources of shared variance have been studied extensively (and are the primary focus of this book), but research findings point to the greater importance of nonshared environmental factors in explaining individual development (Caspi, 1998; Plomin & Daniels, 1987). This conclusion is most dramatically illustrated by the finding that biologically unrelated children raised in the same home bear little resemblance to one another, especially once they reach adulthood (Plomin, 1990).

Some nonshared environmental influences are related to genetic differences between siblings, such as temperament, but most are not (Plomin, 1990). They may, however, be related to nongenetically determined differences among children. Such differences can result from chance or from children's experiential histories. For example, a toddler who is bitten by a dog may retain a life-long fear of dogs that is not shared by his or her siblings. The children in such a family may then be impacted very differently by a trip to a playground where several dogs are playing nearby. Likewise, young children who have had more or less pleasant interactions with health care workers, day care providers, parents, siblings, and others may acquire behavior patterns that influence their future interactions with the same and similar people.

Several sources of nonshared environmental influence are possible during infancy and early childhood. Differential treatment by parents is the most obvious. Although mothers seem to treat their infants and young children fairly similarly when the children are the same ages, they obviously treat older and younger children differently (Dunn & Plomin, 1990). Thus, variations in birth order can lead to the experience of being treated differently than an older or younger sibling. Differential treatment by parents can also result from parents preferring one child over another or from one child being more effective at eliciting attention from the parent than another. Even the fit (or lack of fit) between the parent's and a child's personalities, or a child's similarity (or lack of similarity) in appearance or behavior to someone the parent knows can influence parents' responses to a child. Other sources of nonshared environmental influence might include variations in a family's financial status over time (for example, they may be able to afford quality daycare for one child but not another), peer group influences (for example, they may live in a different neighborhood during one child's early years), and changes in cultural practices over time (for example, changes in recommendations concerning whether or not infants should sleep on their stomachs, changes in availability of particular toys such as infant walkers, changes in the nutritional content of infant formula).

Although methodologies for studying nonshared environmental effects are largely in the formative stage, it may eventually behoove researchers to examine interactions between shared and nonshared environmental effects more extensively. For example, a shared factor such as parent education may facilitate cognitive development in a very curious, socially-oriented child who frequently enjoys stimulating interactions initiated by her well-educated parent. Yet, a reserved or more object-oriented infant might be less likely to derive as clear benefits from a parent devoted to teaching.

In summary, individual differences among infants and young children have the potential to affect their environments, and environmental variations influence subsequent development. Determining the causal relations among child characteristics, environmental variations, and child outcomes is challenging, and is likely to be the focus of much future research. Nonetheless, the importance of considering the role of child characteristics in determining children's environments is clear. Some examples of specific infant characteristics that have been found to impact their environments are provided below.

ILLUSTRATIONS OF INFANTS' INFLUENCE ON THEIR ENVIRONMENTS

Temperament

Among the various individual difference factors that have been explored by child development researchers in attempts to explain discrepant child outcomes, temperament has been one of the more thoroughly studied. Temperament is also frequently mentioned as a likely influence on parents' reactions to their children and as a characteristic that modifies children's responses to their environments. Differences in the form and strength of children's behavioral tendencies are apparent soon after birth, and much research has focused on the structure and function of temperament from infancy through childhood.

Researchers have proposed various defining dimensions of temperament (Buss & Plomin, 1984; Goldsmith & Campos, 1982; Thomas & Chess, 1977; and others) Nevertheless, most conceptualizations incorporate individual differences in attentional, motor, self-regulatory, and emotional components, with an emphasis on the latter. Based on recent studies of the structure of infant temperament, Rothbart and Bates (1998) concluded that the following dimensions best characterize temperament in infancy: fearful distress, irritable distress, positive affect, persistence, activity level, and rhythmicity. Numerous studies also refer to "difficult" temperament, which is commonly defined as a combination of socially undesirable scores on several of these dimensions, or, in some cases, simply high irritability or distress.

There is general consensus among temperament researchers that temperament is genetically-based and relatively stable over time, yet can be modified by the environment. Further, differences in outcomes for infants with distinct inborn traits may be a direct outcome of the traits or they may be a result of complex processes involving the effects that these traits have on the infant's environment. These processes include the effects of infant temperament on parents' behavior, the "goodness-of-fit" between infant temperament and parent personality and expectations, and temperament effects on infants' reactions to others' behavior.

Most studies related to temperament have investigated the direct, linear effects of different temperament qualities on children's development and behavioral adjustment (Rothbart & Bates, 1998). For example, results of the Bloomington Longitudinal Study revealed that infant/toddler difficultness predicted later with problems externalizing and internalizing (Bates & Bayles, 1988; Bates, Bayles, Bennett, Ridge, & Brown, 1991; Bates, Maslin, & Frankel, 1985; Lee & Bates, 1985). Although this finding appears to be robust, debate continues concerning the mechanisms through which early temperament affects later adjustment (Rothbart & Bates, 1998). Temperament may affect adjustment directly by means of its influence on others, or through more complex paths involving the effects of temperament on the environment.

Several studies have found that parents behave differently toward infants and toddlers with varying temperamental characteristics. For example, difficult infants are less likely to receive sensitive parenting than their temperamentally-easy peers (Bornstein, 1995; van den Boom & Hoeksma, 1994). Specifically, child irritability, demandingness, and withdrawn behavior have been correlated with parental irritation and depressed levels of parental contact and stimulation. Soothability, sociability, and predictability in infants have been shown to be related to positive parenting behaviors such as warmth and responsiveness. During toddlerhood, parents of difficult children often resort to anger-laden, punitive discipline tactics that have the counterproductive impact of inciting anger, aggression, and further defiance and disobedience in the child. Parents of difficult children also are more likely to behave inconsistently, rewarding the child's negative behavior when they are worn down by giving in to the child's demands (Lee & Bates, 1985). Other studies have found that mothers of difficult infants are less responsive and stimulating (reviewed by Lerner, 1993), less sensitive (Seifer, Schiller, Sameroff, Resnick, & Riordan, 1996), more stressed (Halpern & McLean, 1997; Honjo et al., 1998), and more depressed (Cutrona & Troutman, 1986) than mothers of easier infants.

Thomas and Chess's (1977) goodness-of-fit model was proposed to explain how temperament and features of the environment can work together to produce favorable child outcomes. Implicit in the model is the idea that children with different temperamental qualities require different types of childrearing experiences in order for their development to be optimally promoted by parents. Goodness-of-fit provides an explanation for why children with difficult temperaments are at high risk for problematic development. Difficult child temperament combined with harsh and inconsistent discipline effectively produces a poor fit that can increase the child's problematic behavior. On the positive side, when parents of difficult children are able to establish a happy, stable, and consistent rearing environment, their children's behavior tends to become less intense and negativistic over time (Belsky, Fish, & Isabella, 1991).

Studies of children growing up under multiple environmental risk conditions have provided convincing support for the goodness-of-fit model as well. Many studies have shown that children who are the most resilient in response to potentially damaging situations such as parental mental illness or alcoholism, abuse, neglect, or poverty have clearly-defined temperament and intellectual characteristics. Among the critical qualities are sociability and interpersonal skills, positive affect, cognitive competence, and high self-esteem (e.g., Hetherington, 1989; Masten, 1989; Werner & Smith, 1982). In the realm of resiliency, positive affect and sociability seem to work in concert to positively enhance children's chances to persist on a positive trajectory despite adverse circumstances. Other temperament qualities may interact with other characteristics to produce distinct outcomes as well (Rothbart & Bates, 1998). For example, high activity combined with fearfulness in a young child may reduce the degree of impulsive, risk taking behavior, often associated with the need to engage in frequent physical activity.

Temperament characteristics likewise have the potential to heighten or reduce responses to many different caregiving events (Rothbart & Bates, 1998). For example, Kochanska (1991, 1993, 1995, 1997) has suggested that the effects of discipline are moderated by young children's temperament. Gentle discipline and nonassertive guidance utilized by mothers of toddlers were related to moral internalization for children who were temperamentally fearful but not for relatively fearless toddlers. Moral internalization was apparently fostered by the arousal or distress that occurred while the fearful children were disciplined. Belsky, Hsieh, and Crnic (1998) also found that infant temperament related to differential susceptibility to parenting influences. Externalizing problems and inhibition were related to parenting behaviors only for children who were especially negative as infants.

Additional work indicates that temperament biases the processing of information about the self and others, predisposing children to more positive or negative adjustment (Rothbart & Bates, 1998). For example, older children with difficult temperaments have been found to misread the intentions of others as being hostile when in fact they were not. Such a reaction may lead to further negative or aggressive behavior.

In summary, research has provided a number of examples of the influence on infants' temperament on their environment. However, as pointed out by Wachs (1992), studies that do not find relations between infant temperament and characteristics of their interpersonal environments also are extant. Wachs suggests that relations between temperament and environment may, in many cases, be complicated by moderating and mediating relationships with other variables such as caregiver characteristics, nontemperamental characteristics of the child, environmental context, and the stability of child temperament. Further research will be needed to carefully delineate the precise role of infants' temperament in determining their environments and developmental outcomes.

Gender

An infant's gender is highly salient to adults. Indeed, questions about whether a baby is a boy or a girl are among the first asked of new parents (Intons-Peterson & Reddel, 1984). Infants' gender can influence their environments in a variety of ways. For example, inborn differences in the behavior of male and female infants might influence the behavior and cognitions of parents. However, most reviews (e.g., Beal, 1994; Maccoby,

1998) conclude that there are few and relatively minor gender differences in behavior during infancy. Differences increase in the preschool years, presumably as a function of socialization pressure and children's increased understanding of gender roles, although biological gender differences could also contribute to this differentiation.

The most likely way that infant gender influences the infant's environment is through the process of gender stereotyping. Adults' knowledge of the infant's gender may elicit stereotyped notions about what the infant is like and how the infant should act, and these stereotypes can then impact adults' behavior toward the infant. Studies have shown that parents perceive male and female newborns differently (Karraker, Vogel, & Lake, 1995; Rubin, Provenzano, & Luria, 1974), and that parents decorate infants' rooms differently depending on the infant's gender (Pomerleau, Bolduc, Malcuit, & Cossette, 1990; Rheingold & Cook, 1975). Parents also buy different toys for boys and girls. Stern and Karraker (1989) provide evidence that differences in adults' behavior toward male and female infants is due to the operation of gender stereotypes rather than gender differences in the infants'. They reviewed studies in which adults interacted with unfamiliar infants whose gender was labeled either correctly or incorrectly. In general, infants' labeled gender most strongly influenced adults' choices of toys for the infant. Labeled girls were more frequently given dolls to play with while labeled boys were more frequently given male-stereotyped toys such as a hammer or a football.

These studies, as well as studies showing that parents behave differently with male and female infants and toddlers (reviewed by Beal, 1994) indicate that the environments of boys and girls differ beginning in early infancy. As a result of this differential treatment, inborn gender differences, and children's cognitive processing of gender role information, boys and girls come to behave differently themselves. These differences in behavior then further elicit differences in how others respond to them. Young boys and girls also select and process aspects of their environments, leading to divergent experiences. Thus, gender is a characteristic with strong potential for shaping infants' and young children's environments.

Physical Attractiveness

Another way in which infants differ from one another is in their physical attractiveness. Research indicates that adults perceive and treat more attractive infants more positively than less attractive infants, according to a "what is beautiful is good" stereotype (Hildebrandt, 1982; Karraker & Stern, 1990). For example, Langlois, Ritter, Casey, and Sawin (1995) found that mothers of more attractive newborns were more affectionate and playful with their infants than were mothers of less attractive newborns. Other studies have found that adults look longer at cuter infants (Hildebrandt & Fitzgerald, 1978) and pay more attention to cuter toddlers in a group program (Hildebrandt & Cannan, 1985). Given the importance of physical attractiveness in our society (Hatfield & Sprecher, 1986), the environments of more and less attractive infants and young children may differ in other ways as well.

Prematurity

Infants who are born prematurely both look and act differently from full-term infants, and these differences elicit systematic variations in parents' and other adults' behaviors (Goldberg & DiVitto, 1983). Premature infants are often physically smaller, more irritable, and less responsive to stimulation during early infancy than are full-term infants. Mothers of premature infants have been found to interact more actively with premature than with full-term infants during the first year, apparently in an attempt to stimulate their relatively unresponsive infants. Mothers of older premature infants often are less actively engaged with their infants than are mothers of full-term infants, presumably because of the ineffectiveness of maternal activity in soliciting infant responsiveness. These patterns of maternal behavior can lead to feedback loops whereby young infants withdraw from their overly active mothers and older infants remain passive in response to insufficient stimulation.

Infant prematurity can also influence adults' responses through the operation of a "prematurity stereotype" (Stern & Hildebrandt, 1984). Several studies have shown that adults react to knowledge of an infant's prematurity independent of the infant's actual behavior. Infants who are incorrectly labeled as premature are perceived as less physically developed and less physically potent than infants who are labeled as full-term (Stern & Karraker, 1988). Mothers who played with unfamiliar infants incorrectly labeled as premature touched the infants less and selected more immature toys for the infants to play with than did mothers who played with correctly labeled full-term infants (Stern & Hildebrandt, 1986). In response to this manipulation, the infants who were labeled premature also were less active during the interactions than the infants who were labeled full-term. These studies suggest that mothers of premature infants may continue to perceive and treat their infants differently than mothers of full-term infants perceive and treat their infants even when the premature infants have recovered from the early effects of their prematurity. As a result of their mothers' biased beliefs and behaviors, these infants may develop deficits and undesirable behavior patterns (Stern & Karraker, 1990).

These findings indicate that prematurity can impact an infant's environment both through the effects of the infant's behavior and through the effects of knowledge of the infant's birth status on caregivers. Similar processes are likely to occur with other problems and disorders, such as developmental delay (Vogel & Karraker, 1991).

IMPLICATIONS FOR THEORY, RESEARCH, INTERVENTION, AND PARENTING: FUTURE TRENDS

Essentially, all characteristics that differentiate among children, regardless of their source, have the potential to influence children's environments. Further, the resulting modifications in children's environments can then impact children's subsequent development. Recognition of these influences, and the processes underlying them, has the potential to direct future theory development, research design and interpretation, intervention planning, and parenting practices.

Most theories of development appropriately include roles for both organismic and environmental variation within a systems framework. Wachs (1992) points out, however, that many current theories of environmental action are missing critical features. These features include: 1) a description of bidirectional influences across multiple levels of the environment, 2) specification of how environmental factors influence development across time, 3) recognition that environmental influences on individuals are probabilistic rather than deterministic, and 4) inclusion of a process orientation that can drive future research. Wachs also proposes a framework for such a theory. Bronfenbrenner and Morris (1998) also have recently updated Bronfenbrenner's (1979) ecological theory to more strongly emphasize the role of the individual in determining environmental processes. The future should see increasingly coherent and balanced theoretical work that incorporates the role of individuals in shaping their environments across the life-span.

Acknowledgement of the role children play in shaping their own environments is especially crucial for researchers. Future research will likely be designed to identify and discriminate both children's effects on their environments and environments' effects on children. Although correlational research will no doubt predominate over experimental research due to practical and ethical constraints, identification of causal relations will be aided by designs that incorporate behavioral genetics analyses, modeling techniques, careful longitudinal work, and other creative approaches. Identification of a correlation between a child characteristic and an environmental feature should no longer be automatically interpreted as an effect of the environment on the child without appropriate evidence to rule out the effect of the child on the environment. Increasing sophistication of research designs, analytic techniques, and researchers' thinking will guide us toward a more complex, systems-oriented knowledge of the process of developmental change.

Contemporary and future attempts to intervene to enhance infant development are likely to be increasingly sensitive to individual differences among infants. Simply changing the environment may not always change an infant, both because the infant will continue to impact the environment as well and because an intervention that works well for one type of infant or family may not work as well for another. New techniques for matching infants and families with appropriate interventions will build from careful research on the impact of varied intervention procedures with diverse infants and families. This research is likely to inform us that some interventions are most effective when the intervention takes place in the child's preferred environment (Wachs, 1992), and that intervention is more effective when the intervention produces changes in the child that will subsequently allow the child to select and modify future environments. In this way, intervention strategies will both acknowledge and take advantage of the reciprocal influences between infants and their environments.

Finally, the concept that infants influence their environments can be applied to parenting as well. Parents may need to be reassured that it is both inevitable and acceptable to react differently to individual children within a family. Parents also can be assisted in understanding that some of their children's characteristics and behaviors are genetically determined or are influenced by environments outside the home. Parents are therefore not responsible for all child outcomes. However, this perspective should not be used to allow parents to abdicate responsibility for appropriately guiding their children's behavior. Parents of the future will be increasingly aware of and attentive to the interplay between individual child characteristics and children's environments, and will be able to benefit from our increasing knowledge in this area. Ideally, research will lead to explicit recommendations to help parents adapt their child-rearing techniques and provide appropriate environmental stimulation for children with different characteristics.

CONCLUSION

In recent years, the discipline of developmental psychology has begun to embrace a broader view of developmental processes. According to Kindermann and Valsiner (1995), the person-context interactional (or systems) perspective focuses on individual adaptation to changing contexts, environmental modifications in response to changing individuals, and the ability of individuals to shape the development of the environments in which they live. When this model is applied to parent-child interaction, the researcher assumes that parents and infants experience ongoing mutual change over time and the quality of an individual's environment at a later time is a function of earlier interactions. According to this perspective, individuals and contexts are both considered fluid systems capable of reciprocal influence.

Understanding the conditions that promote optimal development becomes quite challenging when we begin to examine individual differences in infant behavioral styles, the diversity of potential responses to parenting behaviors, the great variability in parents' childcare skills, psychological strengths and weaknesses of parents, the wide range of socio-cultural environments into which children are born and develop, and the historical time period that provides the larger context for parenting practices. Although, from a practical standpoint, it may be impossible to delineate specific conditions that will optimize development for all children, in every culture, throughout time, the potential for greater understanding seems dependent upon research conducted within a systems theoretical orientation. There are universal needs of children, such as for health, safety, affection, and stimulation that can only be understood and ultimately met with attention to how children's individual characteristics relate to qualitative differences in children's abilities to avail themselves of environmental opportunities.

REFERENCES

Bates, J. E., & Bayles, K. (1988). The role of attachment in the development of behavior problems. In J. Belsky & T. Nezworski (Eds.), *Clinical implications of attachment* (pp. 253–299). Hillsdale, NJ: Erlbaum.

Bates, J. E., Bayles, K., Bennett, D. S, Ridge, B., & Brown, M. M. (1991). Origins of externalizing behavior problems at eight years of age. In D. Pepler & K. Rubin (Eds.), *Development and treatment of childhood aggression* (pp. 93–120). Hillsdale, NJ: Erlbaum.

Bates, J. E., Maslin, C. A., & Frankel, K. A. (1985). Attachment security, mother-child interaction, and temperament as predictors of behavior problem ratings at age three years. In I. Bretherton & E. Waters (Eds.), Growing points in attachment theory and research. *Society for Research in Child Development Monographs*, (1/2, Serial No 209), 167–193.

Beal, C. R. (1994). *Boys and girls: The development of gender roles.* New York: McGraw-Hill.

Behrend, D. A., Rosengren, K. S., & Perlmutter, M. (1992). The relation between private speech and parental interactive style. In R. M. Diaz, L. E. Berk, et al. (Eds.), *Private speech: From social interaction to self-regulation* (pp. 85–100). Hillsdale, NJ: Erlbaum.

Bell, R. Q. (1968). A reinterpretation of the direction of effects in studies of socialization. *Psychological Review, 75,* 81–95.

Bell, R. Q. (1971). Stimulus control of parent or caretaker behavior by offspring. *Developmental Psychology, 4,* 63–72.

Bell, R. Q. (1979). Parent, child, and reciprocal influences. *American Psychologist, 34,* 821–826.

Bell, R. Q., & Chapman, M. (1986). Child effects in studies using experimental or brief longitudinal approaches to socialization. *Developmental Psychology, 22,* 595–603.

Bell, R. Q., & Harper, L. V. (1977). *Child effects on adults.* Lincoln, NE: University of Nebraska Press.

Belsky, J., Fish, M., & Isabella, R. A. (1991). Continuity and discontinuity in infant negative and positive emotionality: Family antecedents and attachment consequences. *Developmental Psychology, 27,* 421–431.

Belsky, J., Hsieh, K., & Crnic, K. (1998). Mothering, fathering, and infant negativity as antecedents of boys' externalizing problems and inhibition at age 3 years: Differential susceptibility to rearing experience? *Development and Psychopathology, 10,* 301–319.

Berg, K. M, Berg, W. K., & Graham, F. K. (1971). Infant heart rate response as a function of stimulus and state. *Psychophysiology, 8,* 30–44.

Bidell, T. R., & Fischer, K. W. (1997). Between nature and nurture: The role of human agency in the epigenesis of intelligence. In R. J Sternberg & L. L. Grigorenko (Eds.), *Intelligence, heredity, and environment* (pp. 193–242). New York: Cambridge University Press.

Bornstein, M. H. (1995). Parenting infants. In M. H. Bornstein (Ed.), *Handbook of parenting: Vol. 1. Children and parenting* (pp. 3–39). Mahwah, NJ: Erlbaum.

Bronfenbrenner, U. (1979). *The ecology of human development: Experiments by nature and design.* Cambridge, MA: Harvard University Press.

Bronfenbrenner, U., & Morris, P. A. (1988). The ecology of developmental processes. In W. Damon (Ed.), *Handbook of child psychology* (pp. 993–1028).

Buss, A. H., & Plomin, R. (1984). *Temperament: Early developing personality traits.* Hillsdale, NJ: Erlbaum.

Caspi, A. (1998) Personality development across the life course. In W. Damon (Series Ed.) & N. Eisenberg (Vol. Ed.), *Handbook of child psychology: Vol. 3. Social, emotional and personality development* (pp. 311–388). New York: Wiley.

Chess, S., Thomas, A., & Birch, H. G. (1965). *Your child is a person.* New York: Viking.

Cohen, L. B., & Gelber, E. R. (1975). Infant visual memory. In L. B. Cohen & P. Salapatek (Eds.), *Infant perception: From sensation to cognition* (pp. 347–404). New York: Academic Press.

Cohn, J., & Tronick, E. Z. (1987). Mother-infant face-to-face interaction: The sequence of dyadic states at 3, 6, and 9 months. *Developmental Psychology, 23,* 68–77.

Coleman, P. K., & Karraker, K. H. (1997). Self-efficacy and parenting quality: Findings and future applications. *Developmental Review, 18,* 46–85.

Cutrona, C., & Troutman, B. (1986). Social support, infant temperament, and parenting self-efficacy. *Child Development, 57,* 1507–1518.

Darley, J., & Fazio, R. (1980). Expectancy confirmation processes arising in the social interaction sequence. *American Psychologist, 35,* 867–881.

De Wolff, M., & van IJzendoorn, M. H. (1997). Sensitivity and attachment: A meta-analysis on parental antecedents of infant attachment. *Child Development, 68,* 571–591.

Dix, T. (1991). The affective organization of parenting: Adaptive and maladaptive processes. *Psychological Bulletin, 110,* 3–25.

Dunn, J. F., and Plomin, R. (1986). Determinants of maternal behavior toward three-year-old siblings. *British Journal of Developmental Psychology, 57,* 348–356.

Dunn, J., & Plomin, R. (1990). *Separate lives: Why siblings are so different.* Basic Books.

Engen, T., Lipsitt, L. P., & Kaye, H. (1963). Olfactory responses and adaptation in the human neonate. *Journal of Comparative and Physiological Psychology, 56,* 73–77.

Feinman, S., & Lewis, M. (1983). Social referencing at ten months: A second-order effect on infants' responses to strangers. *Child Development, 54,* 878–887.

Flavell, J. H., Miller, P. H., & Miller, S. A. (1993). *Cognitive development* (3rd ed.). Englewood Cliffs, NJ: Prentice-Hall.

Frijda, N. H. (1986). *The emotions.* Cambridge, England: Cambridge University Press.

Gewirtz, J. L. (1991). Social influence on child and parent via stimulation and operant-learning mechanisms. In M. Lewis & L. Feinman (Eds.), *Social influences and socialization in infancy* (pp. 137–163). New York: Plenum.

Gianino, A., & Tronick, E. Z. (1988). The mutual regulation model: The infant's self and interactive regulation and coping and defensive capacities. In T. M. Field, P. M. McCabe, & Schneiderman (Eds.), *Stress and coping across development* (pp. 47–68). Hillsdale, NJ: Erlbaum.

Goldberg, S., & DiVitto, B. A. (1983). *Born too soon: Preterm birth and early development*. San Francisco: W. H. Freeman.

Goldsmith, H. H., & Campos, J. J. (1982). Toward a theory of infant temperament. In R. N. Emde & R. J. Harmon (Eds.), *The development of attachment and affiliative systems* (pp. 161–193). New York: Plenum Press.

Grusec, J. E., Hastings, P., & Mammone, N. (1994). Parenting cognitions and relationship schemas. In J. G. Smetana (Ed.), *Beliefs about parenting: Origins and developmental implications* (pp. 5–19). San Fransscico: Jossey-Bass.

Halpern, L. F., & McLean, W. E., Jr. (1997). "Hey mom, look at me!" *Infant Behavior and Development*, 20, 515–529.

Harris, J. R. (1995). Where is the child's environment? A group socialization theory of development. *Psychological Review*, 102, 458–489.

Harris, J. R. (1998). *The nurture assumption*. New York: Free Press.

Hatfield, E., & Sprecher, S. (1986). *Mirror, mirror…The importance of looks in everyday life*. Albany, NY: State University of New York Press.

Hetherington, E. M. (1989). Coping with family transitions: Winners, losers, and survivors. *Child Development*, 60, 1–14.

Hildebrandt, K. A. (1982). The role of physical appearance in infant and child development. In H. E. Fitzgerald, B. Lester, & M. Yogman (Eds.), *Theory and research in behavioral pediatrics* (Vol. 1, pp. 181–219). New York: Plenum.

Hildebrandt, K. A., & Cannan, T. (1985). The distribution of caregiver attention in a group program for young children. *Child Study Journal*, 15, 43–55.

Hildebrandt, K. A., & Fitzgerald, H. E. (1978). Adults' responses to infants varying in perceived cuteness. *Behavioral Processes*, 3, 159–172.

Holden, G. W. (1995). Parental attitudes toward childrearing. In M. H. Bornstein (Ed.), *Handbook of parenting* (Vol. 3, pp. 359–392). Mahwah, NJ: Erlbaum.

Honjo, S., Mizuno, R. Ajiki, M., Suzuki, A., Nagata, M., Goto, U., & Nishide, T. (1998). Infant temperament and child rearing stress: Birth order influences. *Early Human Development*, 51, 123–135.

Horowitz, F. D., & Colombo, J. (Eds.). (1990). *Infancy research: A summative evaluation and a look to the future*. Detroit, MI: Wayne State University Press.

Intons-Peterson, M. J., & Reddel, M. (1984). What do people ask about a neonate? *Developmental Psychology*, 20, 358–359.

Izard, C. E. (1977). *Human emotions*. New York: Plenum.

Jinks, J. L., & Fulker, D. W. (1970). Comparison of the biometrical, genetical, MAVA, and classical approaches to the analysis of human behavior. *Journal of Cross-Cultural Psychology*, 26, 314–330.

Karraker, K. H., & Stern, M. (1990). Infants' physical attractiveness and facial expression: Effects on adults' perceptions. *Basic and Applied Social Psychology*, 11, 371–385.

Karraker, K. H., Vogel, D. A., & Lake, M. A. (1995). Parents' gender-stereotyped perceptions of newborns: The eye of the beholder revisited. *Sex Roles*, 33, 687–701.

Kindermann, T. A., & Valsiner, J. (Eds.) (1995). *Development of person-context relations*. Hillsdale, NJ: Erlbaum.

Kochanska, G. (1991). Socialization and temperament in the development of guilt and conscience. *Child Development*, 62, 1379–1392.

Kochanska, G. (1993). Toward a synthesis of parental socialization and child temperament in early development of conscience. *Child Development*, 64, 325–347.

Kochanska, G. (1995). Children's temperament, mothers' discipline, and security of attachment: Multiple pathways to emerging internalization. *Child Development*, 66, 597–615.

Kochanska, G. (1997). Multiple pathways to conscience for children with different temperaments: From toddlerhood to age 5. *Developmental Psychology*, 33, 228–240.

Kuhl, P. K., & Meltzoff, A. N. (1982). The bimodal perception of speech in infancy. *Science*, 218, 1138–1141.

Landau, R. (1977). Spontaneous and elicited smiles and vocalizations of infants in four Israeli environments. *Developmental Psychology*, 13, 389–400.

Langlois, J. H., Ritter, J. M., Casey, R. J., & Sawin, D. B. (1995). Infant attractiveness predicts maternal behaviors and attitudes. *Developmental Psychology*, 31, 464–472.

Lazarus, R. S., & Folkman, S. (1984). *Stress, appraisal, and coping*. New York: Springer.

Lee, C. L., & Bates, J. E. (1985). Mother-child interaction at age two years and perceived difficult temperament. *Child Development*, 56, 1314–1325.

Lerner, J. V. (1993). The influence of child temperamental characteristics on parent behaviors. In T. Luster & L. Okagaki (Eds.), *Parenting: An ecological perspective* (pp. 101–120). Hillsdale, NJ: Erlbaum.

Lester, B. M., Hoffman, J., & Brazelton, T. B. (1985). The rhythmic structure of mother-infant interaction in term and preterm infants. *Child Development*, 56, 15–27.

Lewis, M. (1969). Infants' responses to facial stimuli during the first year of life. *Developmental Psychology*, 1, 75–86.

Lewis, M., & Rosenblum, L. A. (Eds.) (1974). *The effect of the infant on its caregiver*. New York: Wiley.

Maccoby, E. E. (1998). *The two sexes*. Cambridge, MA: Harvard University Press.

Mash, E. J., & Johnston, C. (1983). Parental perceptions of child behavior problems, parenting self-esteem, and mothers' reported stress in younger and older hyperactive and normal children. *Journal of Consulting and Clinical Psychology*, 51, 86–99.

Masten, A. S. (1989). Resilience in development: Implications of the study of successful adaptation for developmental psychopathology. In D. Cicchetti (Ed.), *The emergence of a discipline: Rochester Symposium on Developmental Psychopathology* (Vol. 1, pp. 261–294). Hillsdale, NJ: Erlbaum.

Murray, A. D. (1979). Infant crying as an elicitor of parental behavior: An examination of two models. *Psychological Bulletin*, 86, 191–215.

Piaget, J. (1970). Piaget's theory. In P. H. Mussen (Ed.). *Carmichel's Manual of child psychology* (vol. 1) pp. 7.3–732. New York: Wiley.

Plomin, R. (1990). *Nature and nurture: An introduction to human behavioral genetics.* Belmont, CA: Brooks/Cole.

Plomin, R., & Daniels, D. (1987). Why are children in the same family so different from one another? *Behavioral and Brain Sciences*, 10, 1–16.

Plomin, R., DeFries, J. C., & Fulker, D. W. (1988). *Nature and nurture during infancy and early childhood.* New York: Cambridge University Press.

Plomin, R., Loehlin, J. C., & DeFries, J. C. (1985). Genetic and environmental components of "environmental" influences. *Developmental Psychology*, 21, 391–402.

Pomerleau, A., Bolduc, D., Malcuit, G., & Cossette, L. (1990). Pink or blue: Environmental gender stereotypes in the first two years of life. *Sex Roles,* 22, 359–367.

Rheingold, H. L., & Cook, K. V. (1975). The contents of boys' and girls' rooms as an index of parents' behavior. *Child Development*, 46, 445–463.

Rothbart, M. K, & Bates, J. E. (1998). Temperament. In W. Damon (Ed.), *Handbook of child psychology* (pp. 105–176). New York: Wiley.

Rovee-Collier, C. (1987). Learning and memory in infancy. In J. D. Osofsky (Ed.), *Handbook of infant development* (2nd ed., pp. 98–148). New York: Wiley.

Rowe, D. C., & Plomin, R. (1981). The importance of nonshared (E_1) environmental influences in behavioral development. *Developmental Psychology*, 17, 517–531.

Rubin, J. Z., Provenzano, F. J., & Luria, Z. (1974). The eye of the beholder: Parents' views on sex of newborns. *American Journal of Orthopsychiatry*, 44, 47–55.

Sameroff, A., & Chandler, M. (1975). Reproductive risk and the continuum of caretaking casualty. In F. Horowitz (Ed.), *Review of child development research* (Vol. 4, pp. 303–331). Chicago: University of Chicago Press.

Scarr, S. (1988). How genotypes and environments combine: Development and individual differences. In N. Bolger, A. Caspi, G. Downey, & M. Moorehouse (Eds.), *Persons in context: Developmental processes* (pp. 217–244). Cambridge, England: Cambridge University Press.

Scarr, S., & McCartney, K. (1983). How people make their own environments: A theory of genotype-environment effects. *Child Development*, 54, 424–435.

Scherer, K. R. (1984). Emotion as a multicomponent process: A model and some cross-cultural data. *Review of Personality and Social Psychology*, 5, 37–63.

Sears, R. R., Maccoby, E. E., & Levin, H. (1957). *Patterns of child rearing.* Evanston, IL: Row, Peterson.

Seifer, R., Schiller, M., Sameroff, A. J., Resnick, S., & Riordan, K. (1996). Attachment, maternal sensitivity, and temperament during the first year of life. *Developmental Psychology*, 32, 3–11.

Stern, M., & Hildebrandt, K. A. (1984). Prematurity stereotype: Effects of labeling on adults' perceptions of infants. *Developmental Psychology*, 20, 360–362.

Stern, M., & Hildebrandt, K. A. (1986). Prematurity stereotyping: Effects on mother-infant interaction. *Child Development*, 57, 308–315.

Stern, M., & Karraker, K. H. (1988). Prematurity stereotyping by mothers of premature infants. *Journal of Pediatric Psychology*, 13, 253–262.

Stern, M., & Karraker, K. H. (1989). Sex stereotyping of infants: A review of gender labeling studies. *Sex Roles*, 20, 501–522.

Stern, M., & Karraker, K. H. (1990). The prematurity stereotype: Empirical evidence and implications for practice. *Infant Mental Health Journal*, 11, 3–11.

Teti, D. M., & Gelfand, D. M. (1991). Behavioral competence among mothers of infants in the first year: The mediational role of maternal self-efficacy. *Child Development*, 62, 918–929.

Thomas, A., & Chess, S. (1977). *Temperament and development*. New York: Brunner/Mazel.

Thomas, A., Chess, S., Birch, H. G., Hertzig, M. E., & Korn, S. (1963). *Behavioral individuality in early childhood*. New York: New York University Press.

van den Boom, D. C., & Hoeksma, J. B. (1994). The effect of infant irritability on mother-infant interaction: A growth-curve analysis. *Developmental Psychology*, 30, 581–590.

Vogel, D., & Karraker, K. (1991). Effects of developmentally-delayed labeling on adults' perceptions of toddlers. *Child Study Journal*, 21, 251–261.

Wachs, T. D. (1992). *The nature of nurture*. Newbury Park, CA: Sage Publications.

Werner, E., & Smith, R. (1982). *Vulnerable but invincible*. New York: McGraw-Hill.

WIDENING THE LENS
Viewing Fathers in Infants' Lives

Lori Roggman, Lisa Boyce,
& Jerry Cook

8

◆ ◆ ◆ ◆

Infants live with adults who take care of them. These adults may or may not include their fathers. One infant may live with a mother and father. Another may live with only a mother or only a father, or with a parent and grandparent, or with a parent and the parent's romantic partner who is not biologically related to the infant. The presence of fathers and their involvement with their infants varies widely. These variations affect infants' lives in ways we are only beginning to understand.

How should researchers look at fathers and infants in the future? One perspective is offered by examining a trajectory of past research and then looking forward toward where we might be going. We can look at lessons we have learned about fathers in the past. As we began to consider the influence of fathers on infants, our theories began to understand fathers as being an important part of the early environment for infant development (Lamb, 1997). Theories about infant development from earlier in the twentieth century focused almost exclusively on mothers. Fathers were assumed to be in the background and to influence older children, but their influence on infants was ignored. As fathers began to be included in theory and research, they were viewed as providing an additional contribution to the care and stimulation of infants, supplementing that provided by mothers. Early studies on fathers therefore focused on similar behaviors by fathers and mothers. However, the relevant father behaviors, the important factors influencing those behaviors, and the ways infants respond to those behaviors may in fact be very different from those for mothers.

Another perspective is offered by sidestepping our trajectory of past research and looking beyond the limitations of our thinking about fathers. Fathers have been viewed as secondary caregivers, additional parents who are part of back-up systems if primary caregivers, usually mothers, are not available. Fathers have also been viewed as providers, having indirect effects on infant development through their support of their infants' mothers. A father may provide financial and emotional support for a mother who may then provide more responsive care for her infant. However, some fathers may be unavailable, absent, or anonymous. If no father is involved with the infant or no father supports the infant's mother, who will provide that involvement and support? If the involvement can be provided by other caregivers (extended family, child care providers), and if the support of the mother can be provided by other resources in her life (family, friends, community services), then can the father be replaced? If he can be replaced, is there nothing he contributes that is unique?

Viewing fathers as offering merely another source of parenting has limited our understanding of them. If we broaden our view of fathers, we may see something unique they offer for infant development. Sometimes we have glimpsed their unique contribution by comparing them directly with mothers and seeing how they are different. For example, research on fathers and infants has found consistently that fathers play more with their infants and play more physically with their infants than mothers do (Lindsay, Mize, & Pettit, 1997; Parke, 1981; Roopnarine & Mounts, 1998). Nevertheless we have developed few theoretical models that distinguish fathering from parenting. The next generation of research on fathers and infants is likely to offer more theoretical models and research strategies that apply specifically to fathers and are not simply adapted from those that apply to mothers. This chapter will examine our assumptions about fathers (both obvious and not so obvious), explore a broader perspective of fathering, and discuss the whys and hows of future research on fathers and infants.

EXAMINING OUR ASSUMPTIONS

The future of research on fathers of infants will require that we expand our vision of fathers and fatherhood by examining our assumptions about fathers. To develop our ideas about fathers, we need to examine our assumptions about what fathers are as well as our assumptions about what they are not. Some of these assumptions may seem simplistic or self-evident, but it is the nature of assumptions that they are sometimes inadequately explored. Some of these assumptions are so embedded in our notions about fatherhood that they are rarely explicitly made. These assumptions are not erroneous, in the sense of myths or exaggerations, but they often contain unexamined implications. By examining the implications of these assumptions, we may expand our vision of fathers and fathering.

ASSUMPTIONS ABOUT WHAT FATHERS ARE

Fathers Are Men

This seemingly-obvious assumption is usually true. However, the validity and importance of this assumption depends on our theoretical view and our research questions. A recent study looked at the relationship between mothers and their partners who were involved in their children's lives, but partners in the study included both men and women (Chan, Raboy, & Patterson, 1998). In this context of studying mothers and their partners, then, the assumption that the secondary parent is always a man would not be valid. If we are only interested in secondary parents, their gender may not be important. But if we assume that fathers are men, then we should consider a father not simply as an alternative parent, but as an alternative parent of a specific gender. Gender differences may help explain how fathers and mothers make different contributions to infant development. Certain characteristics of men, whether biologically or socially influenced, are inherent in our ideas about fathers. Some of these characteristics may be as simple and biological as their greater size and strength, which allow them to pick up growing toddlers more easily than mothers can. Other characteristics may be as complex and social as their orientation toward work and family, which may present different kinds of conflicts for fathers than for mothers. Research indicating that fathers play more physically (Lindsay, et al., 1997; Roopnarine & Mounts, 1998) and that father behavior differs in other ways from mother behavior (Leaper, Anderson, & Sanders, 1998; Lewis, 1997) may be better understood by examining factors associated with gender differences.

Another implication of the assumption that fathers are men is that at least one aspect of fathering is biological. Biologically, fathering is necessary for reproduction, but some fathers are no longer present in the life of the infant by the time the infant is born. Even the assumption of biological fathering is becoming more questionable as alternative fertility treatments are developed that offer parenthood to mothers without the traditional method of biological fathering. In the previously noted study of mothers and their male or female partners, all of the children were conceived from sperm donors (Chan, et al., 1998). These biological fathers offered no further influence on the infant or the infant's mother beyond their genetic contribution. In this study, then, the biological "fathers" were not present and the secondary parents could not be assumed to be male. If we are interested in secondary parents or mothers' partners, their gender may not be important, but if we are interested in biological fathers, gender obviously is important.

Fathers Are Romantic Partners of Mothers

This assumption applies to fathers who are married to or living with their infants' mothers in romantic relationships, but some fathers are not romantic partners of mothers. Studies of fathers include those who are living with their infants and married to the infants' mothers, biological fathers who are not living with their infants and are divorced or were never married to their infants' mothers, and social fathers or "father figures" who are involved with infants and may or may not be romantically involved with mothers. Social fathers may be relatives, such as uncles or brothers, who are likely to have a long-term relationship—albeit non-romantic—with the mother. Other social fathers may be friends or boyfriends whose future relationships with the mother and infant are more uncertain. Some researchers have studied the effects of fathers by comparing "intact" families to divorced families. This strategy assumes only two categories of fathers, present and absent, and neglects a wide range of possibilities for fathers.

Whether a father is romantically involved with an infant's mother may make a difference in the life of the infant. Fathers and father figures who are romantic partners of mothers are likely to combine a caregiving role with the infant and a sexual relationship with the mother. For the mother, a romantic or sexual relationship may offer a particular quality of emotional support. For the infant, observing an affectionate relationship between the parents or between the mother and a father-figure may offer other benefits, such as learning about emotional expression (Cummings, Zahn-Waxler, & Radke-Yarrow, 1984).

If fathers offer something unique to infant development, it may lie in the nature of relationships between fathers and mothers. Nevertheless, an infant may benefit from interactions with a man regardless of what kind of relationship the man has with the infant's mother. Furthermore, if the essential contribution of fathers occurs indirectly through their relationships with mothers, then perhaps more than one kind of relationship can be a pathway for this indirect contribution to infant development. Examinations of both direct and indirect influences of fathers on infants must take into account the various relationships that may exist between fathers and mothers (Cummings & O'Reilly, 1997).

Fathers Are Parents

Researchers making this assumption recognize that fathers are distinct from men who are not parents. Simply being a parent, by any definition, may not be as simple for fathers as it is for mothers. Whether a father is single, married, or divorced is likely to affect his role as a parent of his infant, perhaps more strongly than it would affect a mother's role.

Assuming a father is a parent implies some further assumptions. To be a biological parent, a father must have been involved in a sexual relationship with a woman, even if only briefly. To know of his parenthood, he must have been aware of that woman's pregnancy. To experience parenthood, he must have remained available or involved after the infant's birth to see how the infant behaves and how it grows and changes. To remain a parent of an infant, he must increase the range and number of tasks for which he is responsible, whether as part of a direct or indirect contribution to caring for the infant. Remaining involved and increasing his responsibilities may affect his life in ways that, in turn, affect his interactions with his infant.

Not all fathers are invited to parenthood. Some fathers are not informed of the pregnancy by the mother. Consequently, mothers are "gatekeepers" who control information about pregnancy and paternity and thereby control fathers' access to fatherhood. When a baby is born, maternity is certain and painfully obvious, but paternity may be uncertain even when it seems obvious. Women may benefit greatly from the support of a loved mate during pregnancy, but if an expectant mother does not choose to allow her sexual partner to be involved as a father, she may leave and take the fetus with her. Some mothers may refuse to divulge the father's name to their infants, particularly teenage mothers (Berry, Miller, & Heaton, 1998). Even if the father is named, he may not remain involved in parenthood if his relationship with the mother ends. In a large research study of low-income families, 35% of mothers claimed there was no father involved in their two-year-olds' lives (Mathematica Policy Research, 1999). In many of these cases, a father is not involved because the mother does not want him to be.

In contrast, some fathers are not only invited to parenthood, they are the sole parent. The number of single fathers in the United States is growing, doubling in number over each of the past two decades, and currently exceeding two million men (Meyer & Garasky, 1993; U.S. Bureau of the Census, 1993). Men now consist of one-sixth of the nation's twelve million single parents, although single mothers still outnumber single fathers in the United States by five to one (U.S. Bureau of the Census, 1998). Only a small percentage of single fathers have children still in infancy, but those fathers offer an opportunity for researchers to sort out the effects of gender and caregiving responsibilities on fathers' behavior with infants.

Fathers Are Breadwinners

This assumption is consistent with society's expectation that fathers provide financial resources and will continue to provide those resources throughout their infant's childhood and into young adulthood. The provision of financial and physical resources may be so important to some fathers, and take up so much of their time, that they are not available for other aspects of fathering. Some fathers, however, do not provide financial resources. Sometimes fathers who do not provide money provide other kinds of resources, other kinds of support, or direct care for their infant. In families in which only the mother is employed, the mother may be the breadwinner and the father may be the primary caregiver of an infant.

Other fathers may provide neither financial nor other kinds of help. Fathers who are not involved in caring for an infant and have little contact with them are less likely to provide financial support. Indeed, when fathers live in the same state with their children and have more contact with them, they are more likely to pay child support (Arditti & Keith, 1993; Lerman & Sorensen, 1996). Nevertheless, the commitment, responsibility, and involvement displayed by fathers may not always be correlated; that is, some fathers may respond to feelings of commitment and responsibility by providing financial resources, but may not be involved in other ways. Some fathers may provide financial resources only as required by law, unrelated to any feelings of commitment, responsibility, or involvement.

Perhaps the most widely accepted assumption about the role of fathers is that they are breadwinners. This aspect of fathering is the most clearly-defined and consistent aspect of cultural definitions of the role of fathers. Other aspects of fathers' roles in family life and of their relationships with their infants are not as clearly defined.

Fathers Are Helpmates

It is often assumed that if a father lives with his infant and the infant's mother, he will provide assistance with household tasks. By performing a portion of household tasks, a father lightens a mother's workload so she is able to spend more time caring for her infant. This is an indirect benefit fathers may offer infants. When a father or other helpmate is not available, the mother's time for infant care may be more limited, and the infant may suffer. When a mother is employed outside the home, there are likely to be even more constraints on her time for household tasks. Fathers of working mothers are more likely to help with household tasks, including providing care for infants and children, but research shows that fathers are not likely to spend as much time on household and caregiving tasks as mothers do even when they work the same number of hours (Pleck, 1985). Thus, variations in the amount of help available from fathers may have particularly strong indirect effects on infants whose mothers are employed.

Fathers Are Caregivers

Researchers often assume that fathers are secondary caregivers. Fathers help mothers and, at the same time, affect their infants' lives by providing some of the physical caregiving that infants require. There is evidence that fathers have increased their involvement in the physical care of infants in recent decades and more frequently take on roles as primary caregivers than previously (Lamb, 1987; Pleck, 1997) but, the traditional caregiving role has belonged to mothers who still provide most of the physical care for infants in the U.S. (Lamb, 1987; McBride & Mills, 1993; Tulananda, Young, & Roopnarine, 1994). Fathers vary widely in how much care they provide. There are, of course, some fathers who provide no physical care whatsoever for their infants, and some who provide all the physical care their infants require. However, efforts to document the extent of caregiving by fathers have shown that most fathers provide some caregiving but very few provide more than mothers do (Bailey, 1994; Hossain & Roopnarine 1995; Lamb, 1987; Pleck, 1985).

The effects of fathers' caregiving behaviors may be direct or indirect. Caregiving offers opportunities for responsive interactions with infants that contribute directly to their social development. Caregiving also offers fathers opportunities to support mothers and reduce mothers' parenting stress, which may, in turn, have positive indirect effects on mothers' interactions with their infants (Jarvis & Creasy, 1991). Nevertheless, not all caregiving provided to infants, whether by fathers or by other caregivers, is responsive to the infant and supportive of other caregivers. Furthermore, caregiving is not the only context for this responsiveness and support; fathers who do not help with the physical care of their infants, for whatever reason, may still find other ways to be responsive to infants and supportive of mothers.

The unique experiences a father provides to his infant, as a source of physical care separate from the mother, may offer not just something more to the infant but something different. Furthermore, a father's involvement in caregiving may buffer the effects of an unresponsive or depressed mother or enhance the effects of a responsive mother (Feldman, Greenbaum, Mayes, & Erlich, 1997; Field, 1998).

Fathers Are Playmates

Our assumptions about fathers often portray them as the "good-time" parent, the one who plays and makes babies laugh. In a typical infant's world, father is a playmate who jiggles, tickles, and plays "rough and tumble" games (Lamb, 1977, 1987). Although fathers may not provide as much caregiving for infants as mothers do, they may provide more fun because they spend more time playing than caregiving (MacDonald & Parke, 1986). Unlike caregiving, where both mothers and fathers respond in similar ways, fathers play with infants in different ways than mothers do (Parke, 1981). Indeed, it may be that fathers' play offers a unique contribution to infant development. Compared to mothers' play, fathers' play is less conventional, more idiosyncratic, more physical, more unusual, and less predictable (Dickson, Walker, & Fogel, 1997; Lamb, 1981; MacDonald & Parke, 1986). Perhaps because of these characteristics, a father is often the infant's preferred playmate (Clarke-Stewart, 1978).

As in their caregiving, fathers may vary greatly in the amount and style of play with their infants. Some fathers may be wonderful playmates but have very little time available for playing with their infants. Some fathers may play more physically than others. Some fathers may be bossier in their play than others. Some fathers may ignore their infants, assuming they will play with them more when the infant becomes a child who is "old enough" to play. Variations in the quantity and quality of fathers' play with infants may have implications for infant development that are as important as the implications of variations in mothers' caregiving.

Like research on caregiving, most research on parent-infant play has focused on mothers (e.g., Damast, Tamis-LeMonda, & Bornstein, 1996; Gustafson, Green, & West, 1979). But fathers play differently than mothers do. From the infant's point of view, playing with father includes physical stimulation and events that are unexpected and unpredictable. Perhaps these differences offer something valuable and unique for infants. For example, father-child play is associated with increased child social competence (Pettit, Brown, Mize, & Lindsey, 1998) and emotional regulation (Roberts, 1998). By including fathers in our study of parent-infant interaction, particularly play interactions, we may be able to identify a wider range of play styles that have specific influences on infant development. For example, physical play that involves a lot of movement may provide experiences that enhance motor development. Fathers are more likely than mothers to provide physical play, but it may be just as valuable for the infant whether it is the mother or the father who provides it. If certain types of play foster certain types of development, it may not matter whether that type of play is provided by a father or by a mother.

ASSUMPTIONS ABOUT WHAT FATHERS ARE NOT

Fathers Are Not All the Same

It is assumed that there is variation in fathering. Indeed, fathering behavior may vary more than mothering behavior. Fathering may range from extensive day-to-day interactions with infants to minimal and infrequent contact. Variations in fathers' behavior are likely to be affected by factors from multiple levels: characteristics of their infants, behaviors by the infants' mothers, pressures from society, and messages from their culture. Variations in fathering may also be affected by characteristics of the fathers themselves. Whether a father is rich or poor, a teenager or a middle-ager, whether he dropped out of high school or finished medical school, all affect how he is likely to interact with his infant. For example, paternal involvement is highest in white-collar and professional fathers (Gerson, 1993) and fathers with more occupational prestige play with their infants more than fathers with less occupational prestige (Grossman, Pollack, & Golding, 1988). If these factors are not examined carefully in studies, it may be impossible to generalize from the fathers in the study to other fathers who may differ in age, income, and education, as well as in their culture, their social environment, their relationships with their infants' mothers, and the characteristics of their infants.

One reason for these variations is the diverse contexts of fatherhood. Mothers most often live with their infants in the same household, and many fathers do too. However, many fathers find themselves in other situations. Some fathers may live elsewhere and only visit their infants. A biological father who is no longer married or in a romantic relationship with his infant's mother may be only a visitor to his infant's home and may live elsewhere. A boyfriend to an infant's mother may also be a visitor who behaves as a father figure to the infant. A father may remain involved with both the mother and his infant and remain nearby in the same neighborhood, but not live in the same household. A father may be involved only from a distance, providing financial support but little else for his infant. All of these situations contribute to a different context for fatherhood, a different array of influences on fathers, and different ecologies for infant development.

Variations among fathers may not mean the same thing as variations among mothers. That is, variations in fathers' behaviors toward their infants may not necessarily have the same kinds of effects on infant development as variations in mothers' behaviors would. The specific behaviors of fathers that influence infant development may be different than the specific behaviors of mothers that influence infant development. Finally, fathering may influence different domains of infant development than mothering does. For example, lack of nurturing by mothers may have a greater effect on security, but lack of attention by fathers may have a greater effect on autonomy or other aspects of development. By studying variations in particular father behaviors in relation to infant development in distinct domains, researchers may identify more specific effects of fathers on infant development.

Fathers Are Not Mothers

Researchers have assumed that fathers are not mothers. Therefore, to understand fathers, researchers have explored the ways that fathers are different from mothers. Despite some similarities in caregiving behaviors, many parenting behaviors are likely to differ between mothers and fathers. From early on, research on fathers has shown that fathers interact with infants using a different style than mothers do: Fathers are more physical and more playful (Lamb, 1977; Parke, 1981). Furthermore, fathers may vary more in their behaviors than mothers and may be more affected by cultural and social factors. Compared to mothers, fathers are, of course, not as affected by the physical changes and challenges of pregnancy, birth, and breastfeeding; fathers experience little change in hormones, health, or caloric requirements in relation to fatherhood.

It is obvious that fathers are not mothers. Understanding how these differences affect infants is important. But it is also important to expand from simple comparisons of mothers and fathers to research designs that include measures of a wider range of behavior than we have typically measured in mothers. Models with more ecological and dynamic perspectives would address some of these concerns about how we measure various aspects of fathering, what other things we measure, and what patterns of relations with infant development we may explore.

A BROADER PERSPECTIVE

A Social Perspective

Margaret Mead wrote in 1949 that "Human fatherhood is a social invention" compared to motherhood which has "biological roots" (p. 183). She later wrote that "the child's tie to its father is a social one" compared to the mother's "deeply biological one" (Mead & Heyman, 1965, p. 45). This anthropological perspective is paralleled by the psychological one used in developmental research. Our theory and research on mothers and infants is based on two strong assumptions: that the mother-infant interaction has a biological basis and that the mother-infant relationship is central to early development. Father-infant research, in contrast, does not have such strong assumptions as a foundation.

The father-infant relationship has, of course, a biological basis in the simplest sense of a genetic contribution at conception. In addition, recent research has indicated some genetic underpinnings for father behavior, albeit less than for mother behavior (Mackey & Day, 1995; Perusse, Neale, Heath, & Eaves, 1994). Nevertheless, the interactions between fathers and infants do not appear to have as strong of a biological basis as the interactions between mothers and infants. Compared to mothers, there are not as many common patterns across cultures (let alone across primates or mammals) in how fathers interact with their infants. Also, the value placed on father-infant relationships does not appear to be as consistent across cultures or as pervasive within cultures as is the value placed on mother-infant relationships.

A Dynamic Perspective

The father-infant relationship appears to be much more variable and therefore more malleable both across cultures and within cultures. Whereas mothering may be more biologically compelled, fathering may be more socially impelled. As a result, fathering may be more disrupted during periods of social upheaval or transition (Mead, 1949). This may influence the development of their children negatively, but it is possible that changes in fathering in response to social changes may also have positive effects on children. It is possible that the father-infant relationship offers a more dynamic response than the mother-infant relationship to changing environmental and social conditions. Specifying these conditions and understanding them may be the main direction that research is needed on the role of fathers in infant development.

As part of studying social and cultural influences on fathers, researchers will need to identify risk factors that explain why some fathers end up ignoring, abandoning, or abusing their infants. Researchers will also need to examine the resilience of some fathers who have all the risk factors but end up supporting, taking care of, and staying involved with their infants. These exceptions, and the stories behind them, will illuminate a broader view of fathers. If our theories only include one kind of father, one model of fathering, those close to the mean and the regression line, we may miss the variance that is the point of how fathering may adapt to social changes. If fathers are indeed more sensitive to changes in the social environment, then fatherhood and fathering may offer a more flexible species adaptation than motherhood and mothering. In considering the ways that fatherhood is unique, as well as the ways that it varies, theoretical models of fathers are likely to be influenced by this idea of adaptive fathering in the coming decades.

A Re-Defined Perspective

The next generation of father-infant researchers are likely to broaden their perspective on fathers by re-defining fathers, fatherhood, and fathering. The term *fathers* is generally used to refer to who fathers are, how they are identified, and how they are related to their infants, but our definitions need to be broad enough to capture many different types of fathers and not omit any of the people who, from the infant's point of view, provide fathering. *Fathering* refers to the particular processes and behaviors by which fathers parent infants and children, but our definitions need to take into account the possibility that these behaviors may vary widely. Also, definitions of fathering should allow for the fact that some of these behaviors may be related to parent gender and some may be unrelated to gender. *Fatherhood* refers to a life situation that provides the experience in a man's life of being a father. But again researchers need to recognize that a wide range of experiences as a father may have an influence on a man, from near or far, from direct and indirect contact with their infants, from occasional play to full-time caregiving. *Adaptive fathering* refers to changes in fathers' behaviors in response to influences from their society and culture, from their infants' mothers, and from their infants themselves. An increased understanding of these influences on fathering in the context of ecological models of infant development will expand our research models for studying fathers and infants in the future.

UNDERSTANDING INFLUENCES ON FATHERING

Understanding potential influences on fathering will help expand our models of the roles of fathers in infant development. An ecological perspective (Bronfenbrenner, 1986) provides a model of infant development that emphasizes the multiple contexts in which infants grow and develop. This model suggests that infant development occurs in the context of the infant's relationships with caregivers, that the relationships between caregivers affect the infant's relationships with them, and that these relationships function in a dynamic way within larger social and cultural contexts. From this perspective, influences on fathers can be explored at several levels moving from the inner circle of father-infant interactions, out to the larger family context including the mother, and then out to social and cultural influences. At each level, examining the possible influences on fathers may illuminate the ways that fathers adapt to their infants, to their infants' mothers, to their society, and to their culture.

Fathers Are Influenced by Infants

Research on fathers should assume that fathering may be influenced by individual characteristics of their infants. Because fathers vary more widely in their responses to infants, whether in caregiving or play, they may be more affected than mothers by a variety of individual characteristics of infants. One characteristic that fathers respond to is infant *gender*. Fathers' tendency toward more physical play is even more pronounced with boys than with girls (Clarke-Stewart, 1978), and in general fathers tend to spend more time with infant sons than daughters (Parke & Sawin, 1980). Thus, it is likely that early interactions with fathers may influence the beginnings of sex-typed behavior.

Fathers may be sensitive to other infant characteristics as well. In fact, fathers are affected differently than mothers by various aspects of infant *temperament*, engaging less with infants who become more negative, whereas mothers engage more with infants who become more negative (Belsky, Fish, & Isabella, 1991). A particularly fussy or active baby may affect a mother and a father differently, and their different parenting responses may then shape different aspects of infant behavior. However, the type of adult response and how it affects a particular type of infant behavior may be more important to understand than the gender of the adult and infant. By studying both mothers and fathers, we may see a wide range of patterns in how infant characteristics affect parent-infant interactions which, in turn, influence infant development.

Fathers Are Influenced by Mothers

Research on fathers should include the potential influence from mothers to fathers. That influence may be direct or indirect, positive or negative.

Mothers are often *gatekeepers* for fathers' access to their children. Mothers may ask for help, they may encourage fathers to be involved with their infants, they may teach fathers what to do with infants, they may criticize fathers' parenting, or they may exclude fathers from parenting. The amount and quality of fathers' caregiving may depend on what is already available from mothers. Fathers' participation in physical caregiving for their infants tends to increase when mothers are employed (Pleck, 1985), yet their play time may actually decrease. When working mothers spend more evening time playing with their infants, there are fewer opportunities for father-infant play (Pedersen, Anderson, & Cain, 1980).

There may be *dynamic interactions* among characteristics and behaviors of fathers, mothers, and infants that result in complex outcomes. Responsive care from a father may be enhanced when mothers provide good models of responsiveness, but fathers may also increase the amount and quality of care if they perceive a lack in the care provided by mothers or a particular need for extra care for the infant. Compared to a father of an easy infant with a responsive mother, a father of a difficult infant with a depressed mother may be called upon to contribute more to the care of the infant. If a father is a responsive caregiver, and his infant forms a secure attachment with him, that attachment is likely to provide a buffer against the effects of an infant's insecure attachment with a mother (Akande, 1994). Anxious attachment relationships between mothers and infants may require fathers to be more involved in caregiving to ameliorate poor infant outcomes.

Fathers Are Influenced by Society

Research on fathers should take into account the influence that society and social change have on fathers. Family employment patterns, work environments, and informal social supports as well as public policy aimed at increasing fathers' involvement and financial support all may affect men's fathering.

One powerful societal influence is the dramatic increase in *maternal employment* in recent decades. This social change has had both direct and indirect influences on how much fathers interact with their infants and the kinds of things they do with them. Work schedules influence father participation in caregiving in complex ways for many dual earner families. Fathers who expand their traditional playmate role to include contributing to household and child care tasks not only increase their involvement with their infants but also provide more opportunities for mothers to engage in unhurried interactions with their infants (Parke, 1996). Thus, increased father involvement in response to maternal employment affects both father-infant and mother-infant relationships.

In addition to maternal employment, a *father's employment* may also influence his fathering. Fathers who spend long hours at work have less time to spend with their children. Younger fathers may have less time to spend with their children than older fathers as they may spend more time at work trying to establish themselves in their career (Parke, 1996). Younger fathers who make less money may take on extra jobs to cover the expense of a young family. Also, fathers who are less established in their profession and those who work jobs that do not provide benefits often do not have the luxury of vacation or sick leave, which would otherwise provide additional opportunities to spend time with their infants.

Other social influences on fathers may come from *other parents* with whom they interact at work or in other contexts. Working fathers have opportunities to interact with other parents in their workplace who may provide informal parenting support. Extended kin, fellow church members, friends, and neighbors may also provide social support to fathers. Fathers who feel supported by family and neighbors are more likely to be involved with nurturing their children than those who feel less supported (Ahmeduzzaman & Roopnarine, 1992).

Public funding and *public policy* both represent societal influences on fathers. Early intervention programs, as required by funding agencies, increasingly address fathers and fathers' involvement in infants' lives by providing both formal and informal social support for fathers. Child support laws compel fathers to be involved in their infants' lives, albeit indirectly, even if they have chosen not to be involved or were initially excluded from their infants' lives. In addition to increasing the family income, child support has positive cognitive and behavioral benefits for children, especially for those children whose fathers willingly pay child support rather than being forced to pay by court orders (Argys, Peters, Brooks-Gunn, & Smith, 1996). More research is needed to investigate effective ways to encourage fathers' financial support and involvement and to evaluate the impact of that support and involvement in infants' lives.

Fathers Are Influenced by Culture

Research on fathers should assume that fathering has been influenced by *cultural changes* in how fathers and fatherhood are perceived. During the last three decades of the twentieth century when mothers increased their employment rates, attitudes about fathers began to shift toward greater expectations of involvement in childrearing. These changes are evident in the views of the public, the media, ideological and political leaders, economists, scientists, lawyers, doctors, and even fathers themselves (Shapiro, Diamond, & Greenberg, 1995). Furthermore, these changes are reflected in the "discovery" of fathers in child development research as more researchers study fathers, consider the role of fathers in their theories of child development, and emphasize the importance of fathers to infants and children (Lamb, 1997) .

The behavior of fathers is influenced by *cultural differences*. Fathers' roles, expected involvement with their children, and responsibilities vary across cultures and ethnic groups (Mortazavi & Karimi, 1992). Studies of fathers in diverse cultures show diversity of fathers' roles depending on the type of society in which they live (Hewlett, 1992). Fathers' behaviors may vary more across cultures than mothers' behaviors do. A recent Society for Research on Child Development Policy Report on fathers states that "cultural values and religious traditions serve to define masculinity and the role of men and fathers in the society" (Engle & Breaux, 1998, p. 12). Changes across the twentieth century in the United States in the theories and research about fathers and in the attitudes and behaviors of fathers suggest that fathers may be more sensitive than mothers to the influence of cultural messages about fathering. Nevertheless, for many fathers, the cultural messages they receive have more impact on their thoughts than on their behaviors (Levant, 1990; Rustia & Abbott, 1993).

CHALLENGES AND CHANGES IN RESEARCH ON FATHERS

Why Study Fathers of Infants?

There are several reasons to focus our nation's research resources on the study of fathers. For those interested in the factors influencing early development in human life, fathers represent an influential factor that has been discovered and rediscovered in recent decades. For those interested in family economics, fathers represent a major source of resources that may have implications for the effects of divorce and welfare reform on infants' lives. For those interested in risk factors in infant's lives, fathers represent risks for abuse, abandonment, and resultant negative outcomes for infants and children. For those interested in resilience, fathers may offer emotional support and care that ameliorate the effects of negative factors in infants' lives. For those interested in social policy, the study of fathers represent a source of information—rather than political rhetoric—to inform our policies about families and children. Finally, for those interested in the outcomes of social change, particularly the effects on family relationships, fathers may reveal a dynamic response to the challenges of a changing world in the adaptive nature of fathering.

Changing Our Views of Fathers

Despite these important reasons for increasing our research on fathers, researchers who study fathers face challenges from social changes in the ways in which fathers are viewed. Research literature (Blankenhorn, 1996; Deutsch, Lussier, & Servis, 1993) and the media present a mixed view of fathers. Evidence that fathers are increasingly likely to provide caregiving for their infants co-exists with evidence that fathers are increasingly likely to abandon their infants and fail to provide for them. A perusal of any local bookstore or newspaper will show classes and books aimed at helping fathers be fathers, resources unavailable a couple of decades ago, but are fathers any more prepared to become parents than they were in the past? Changes in society emphasizes fathers' importance in infants' lives, but are fathers actually more involved with infants than they were in the past? Changes in legal codes at federal and state levels enforce child support orders, but are fathers any more likely to provide financial support than they were in the past? Answers to these questions will shape our views of fathers and will reveal changes, variations, and inconsistencies in who fathers are, what they are like, and what they are doing. Furthermore, changes in our views of fathers will influence our future research on fathers in relation to the early development of their children.

Changing Our Research Methods

Researchers studying fathers also face challenges from general method-ological changes in the study of humans and families. These challenges will come from more general *changes in social research methodology*. Current questions about shifts in social science methodology will influence how we study fathers. Like other social scientists, researchers studying fathers are likely to become more skeptical of significance testing with non-random samples and non-experimental designs. Also like other social scientists, future father researchers will value the integration of qualitative and quan-titative data to paint a richer picture of fathers, fathering, and fatherhood. They will use interview techniques that extend objective quantitative ques-tions with more open-ended qualitative questions. They will ask fathers about fathering directly instead of asking mothers and children about them. They will observe directly instead of asking fathers to describe or report their own behavior. They will study a more diverse population of fathers instead of limiting themselves to fathers who are conveniently avail-able to fill out questionnaires.

Further challenges to father researchers stem from the need to develop *specific methods appropriate for studying fathers* in particular rather than parents in general. Instead of adapting methods developed for mothers, father researchers need to ask new research questions, design new meas-ures, and develop new behavioral coding schemes just for fathers. Researchers studying the influence of fathers on infant development will need to write questions for interviews and questionnaires that take into account the wide range of ways fathers play their roles. For example, fathers in an ongoing study of infants living in poverty were asked about "the ways in which you have had to adjust your life" since having a child. This question was designed to invite fathers to expand on their Likert-style responses to a set of standardized questions about parenting stress. Responses to these questions varied widely from descriptions of responsi-bility such as "giving up bad habits" and "budgeting" to identification of stresses of "staying up nights to take care of the baby" and "having him be sick and not knowing how to make him better" to indications of enjoyment because "he's more fun than stressful" and "school and work are the stressful things, I play with the kids to relax" (Tamis-LeMonda, Roggman, Bradley, & Summers, 1999).

Observers coding behaviors of fathers interacting with infants reported that coding was much more difficult than expected, not only because fathers are different from mothers, but also because the same behavioral definitions used for observing mothers do not always fit the behavior observed in fathers (Tamis-LeMonda et al., 1999). In our observations of fathers' interactions with infants, fathers are more likely than mothers to do the unexpected, to be more physical, to do less talking and less teaching, to repeat what the child likes, and also to vary more widely in their responsiveness to the child and use of toys in play. Furthermore, behavior by a father may affect the infant differently than the same behavior by a mother. For example, restrictive or directive behavior that disrupts the infant's play with a mother may elicit the infant's laughter when it comes from the father. Thus, the meaning of fathers' behavior may depend on the width of the lens used to view them and require an examination of infant responses to father behavior.

Changing Our Interpretation of Data

Future researchers studying fathers will be challenged to understand which differences between the responses of mothers and fathers represent errors and which they represent real differences in the perspectives of each parent. For example, mothers and fathers may answer quite differently when asked to report about what fathers do with their infants. In many cases fathers say they are more involved than mothers say they are, but in other cases mothers say that fathers are more involved than the fathers themselves say they are. In our recent study of a low-income sample of fathers, correlations were around zero between mothers' reports and fathers' reports of father involvement with infants (Roggman, Benson, & Boyce, 1999). Fathers may also provide different data than mothers when asked to report on characteristics of their child such as temperament or behavior problems. The differences between what mothers say and what fathers say may be merely a reflection of fathers' (or mothers') exaggerations of reality, but regardless of their disagreement with mothers, what fathers say about themselves and their infants may offer valuable insight into how fathers experience fathering and how they view their infants. Father research must move beyond comparisons to mothers and look at the patterns of relations among attitudes and behavior for fathers in their own right.

PRACTICAL PROBLEMS WITH FATHER RESEARCH

Access

Researchers studying fathers will also be challenged by several practical problems. One source of practical problems is mothers. Just as mothers are sometimes gatekeepers for fathers' access to their children, so too are mothers often gatekeepers for researchers to have access to fathers. Particularly for research with high risk samples, such as teenage fathers or low-income fathers, mothers may control information about fathers' names and contact information. Mothers, in some cases, also control information about fathers' behavior when they are asked to report about father involvement with infants. If there are alternative ways of contacting the father, the value of data collected directly from fathers suggests that contacting them independently of contacts with mothers is worthwhile.

Availability

One major obstacle for collecting information from fathers is that fathers may have limited time available. Because fathers of infants are more likely than mothers of infants to work and to work longer hours, they may have little time to participate in research. One reason why fathers work long hours is that having a new baby can be a powerful motivator for establishing financial security. This intense and new awareness of responsibility is evidenced in first-time expectant fathers (Shapiro, 1987) and is reported by fathers with infants in our own research (Tamis-LeMonda et al., 1999). Fathers may be working long hours to compensate for a decrease in maternal employment and income. Also, a father may assume that he does not need to interact much with his infant until the infant grows up enough to play. If fathers work more hours than before their infants were born and have little time or inclination to be with their young infants, it may be difficult to schedule fathers for research observations of their interactions with their infants. Also, fathers who do not spend much time with their infants may be less able than mothers to answer questions about their infants' behavior.

Another practical problem in studying fathers is that they may not be available to participate in research during the day. If they work at a daytime job, then their only time available for a research interview or observation would be during evenings and weekends. However, a busy father may not want to sacrifice time during his evenings or weekends for research. The times that are best to schedule fathers for research may also be a problem for researchers who want that time to spend with their own families. Perhaps this is one reason there are more studies on mothers than studies on fathers.

Sensitivity

Another problem with researching fathers is they may be particularly sensitive to the discomfort of being the focus of research. Several fathers in our research commented that they do not like "being under the microscope." A father may feel uncomfortable being observed interacting with his infant if he usually has little contact with his infant. The infant too may show wariness or discomfort if there have been limited interactions with the father. If most infant care is done by the mother, a father may be less experienced and less comfortable than he will be later in his child's life. Even if a father spends a substantial amount of time with his infant, discomfort that he feels about being observed may lead to a problem interpreting the data from videotapes of his interactions with his infant. People generally try to put their "best face forward" when they know they are being videotaped, but this may not hold true for some fathers. A father's desire to show his best self can be negated if he wants to show his displeasure at being videotaped, is tired after a long day of work, or is camera-shy and self-conscious of his parenting skills. If experiencing any of these factors, a father may appear disinterested, unresponsive and inattentive to his infant. In other words, a father's lack of positive response to his infant may be a reaction to being researched and videotaped rather than representative of his ongoing relationship with his infant.

Fathers may also have negative responses to survey questions, interpreting them as implied criticism. For example, common research themes revolve around whether fathers provide financial support and how involved they are with their infants. In our research (Roggman et al., 1999; Tamis-LeMonda et al., 1999), many interview questions ask about father involvement, and fathers occasionally voice the concern that they will be perceived as bad fathers because they spend little time with their infants even though they spend a great deal of time working to provide for their children. If providing for physical needs is the type of child caregiving the father's culture emphasizes most, and his life revolves around meeting this expectation, a limited definition of an "involved father" may exclude him. Questions that reflect a limited definition of father involvement may not only alienate some fathers, but may also omit some important aspects of fathers' contributions to infants' lives. Whether fathers' concerns about participating in research stem from the wording of survey questions, their feelings of inadequacy, their concerns about privacy, or simply the novelty of father research, data collectors and researchers must be quick to identify and resolve these concerns to retain fathers in research studies.

Establishing Trust

In trying to resolve these concerns, researchers are usually aware that they must first establish a relationship of trust. Trust is particularly important for fathers who are concerned about the confidentiality of their responses regarding child support and income. For fathers who are uninvolved with their infants or delinquent in their child support payments, establishing trust is likely to be more challenging than with fathers who are more involved or not delinquent in their child support payments. While trust is often built through informal conversation and self-disclosure, it may also be enhanced by mutual respect and consideration. Consideration by researchers sometimes means getting the data quickly and not "wasting" a father's time. The more efficiently a researcher can complete the procedures, and the more consideration a researcher shows for a father's time, the more likely the father will be willing to participate again.

It is not clear whether fathers' feelings of trust or respect are in any way related to the gender of the researcher. While male researchers may offer a sense of shared experiences with fathers it may be easier for some fathers to confide in female researchers. Fathers often live in a world of men (co-workers, friends, close relatives) and may be wary of female researchers. Infants, however, typically live in a world of women (mothers and their friends and close relatives, child care workers) and may be wary of male researchers. Therefore, there may be both advantages and disadvantages to data collectors of either gender.

Recognizing the Impact of Research

Another practical problem in researching fathers is that simply by asking questions and making observations, researchers may provide an intervention that creates bias in their data. Fathers' participation in research may actually change their attitudes and behavior. Although questions regarding the amount and type of direct interaction with his child may promote a father's feelings of inadequacy, the interviews may also have a positive effect. For example, after listening to questions about playing games or building with blocks with his child, a father may be motivated to increase that particular kind of involvement. By asking fathers to participate in our infancy research and then by asking them about everything they do with their infants, we may implicitly teach fathers about their importance in infant development and about the particular behaviors we expect will have positive effects on their infants.

FUTURE DIRECTIONS FOR STUDYING FATHERS OF INFANTS

New Theories and Methods

To understand the role of fathers in infant development, a broader perspective of fatherhood and fathering will be needed in the future, both in terms of theory and methods. Our research on fathers will be informed by father theory, not just mother/parent theory. This will involve collecting data directly from fathers (not just mothers' reports) and will involve observing fathers' behavior (not just asking them what they do). There will need to be more in-depth studies of fathers in a variety of specific cultural, religious, ethnic, economic, and social groups. Researchers will analyze father data between groups, within groups, and as part of large groups with both fathers and mothers to explore patterns in variations. As in the past, researchers will analyze fathers in comparison to mothers, but they will also analyze father data separately to detect patterns that are unique to fathers, and analyze mother and father data together to identify patterns in behavior unrelated to the sex of the parent.

Complex Contextual Models of Fathering

By taking a broader perspective, research on fathers is likely to become more complex as researchers consider multiple characteristics of fathers and multiple environmental factors that influence them. Characteristics such as their age and socioeconomic status may influence fathering. Social factors may influence fathers, such as their relationships with their infants' mothers or their work lives. The influences of social factors are unlikely to be simple and direct, but rather are likely to involve complex interactions. And all of these factors will be moderated by the cultural context of fatherhood. Finally, research on fathers will become more complex as researchers attend to the impact of social changes on fathers of infants.

Non-Political Research

Research on fathers will be more productive if it is not influenced by political agendas. In the future, research on fathers should avoid influences, sometimes evident in the past, from feminists, anti-feminists, welfare reformers, social liberals, or religious conservatives. Research on fathers should not be designed to support a conservative or liberal political agenda on single parenting or as a feminist or anti-feminist position on men's and women's roles. And research on fathers should not be restricted to researchers who are men or fathers any more than research on mothers should be restricted to women or mothers.

Research as Intervention

Finally, researchers studying fathers should accept that their research is an intervention. Simply by contacting fathers to study them, we let them know of their value and importance. And informing fathers of their value and importance may encourage their involvement and responsibility. Researchers may benefit from explicitly examining the impact of research participation on fathers. When doing research on fathers and developing theories about fatherhood and fathering, researchers make value statements that fathers are important in the lives of infants and that fathers' affect infants' lives.

CONCLUSION

In summary, there are several key issues regarding research on the role of fathers in infant development. Researchers working in this area are encouraged to:

- Examine the assumptions underlying the theories and methods used to study fathers of infants.

- Develop a broader theoretical perspective for understanding the adaptive nature of fathering as a dynamic process in response to context.

- Clarify the definitions of father, fathering, and fatherhood.

- Increase the diversity of populations of fathers studied.

- Develop specific research methods for studying fathers in particular rather than parents in general.

- Recognize research as intervention, including the possibility that fathers' participation may change their behavior.

Changes in theory suggest that future scholars studying the role of fathers in infants' lives will be guided by complex ecological models where context is not only noticed and appreciated but looked at in terms of the life experiences of the father and the dynamic influences in his private life, home life, work life, and social life. Theories about fathers will increasingly consider the complexities of father-child interaction with a dynamic systems view that points out synchrony and mutuality with puzzle-piece complementarity and adaptation under stress. Infancy researchers have begun to study fathers as an important influence in infants' lives, in their roles as one of an infant's significant caregivers, in their unique roles as fathers, and in their roles as partners of mothers. In doing so, researchers' perceptions of fathers have changed from viewing fathers as just another adult around the home to viewing fathers as influencing infant development in multiple ways. As researchers examine their assumptions about fathers and face the challenges to studying fathers, new views and new questions will arise that will guide how we will look at fathers and infants in the future.

REFERENCES

Ahmeduzzaman, M., & Roopnarine, J. L. (1992). Sociodemographic factors, functioning style, social support, and fathers' involvement with preschoolers in African American families. *Journal of Marriage and the Family, 54,* 699–707.

Akande, A. (1994). What meaning and effects does fatherhood have in child development? *Early Child Development and Care,* 101, 51–58.

Arditti, J. A. , & Keith, T. Z. (1993). Visitation frequency, child support payment, and the father-child relationship post divorce. *Journal of Marriage and the Family, 55,* 699–712.

Argys, L. M., Peters, H. E., Brooks-Gunn, J., & Smith, J. R. (1996, October). *Contributions of absent fathers to child well-being: The impact of child support dollars and father-child contact.* NIMH Conference on Father Involvement, Bethesda, MD.

Bailey, W. T. (1994). A longitudinal study of fathers' involvement with young children: Infancy to age 5 years. *Journal of Genetic Psychology, 155,* 331–339.

Belsky, J., Fish, M., & Isabella, R. (1991). Continuity and discontinuity in infant negative and positive emotionality: Family antecedents and attachment consequences. *Developmental Psychology, 27,* 421–431.

Berry, E. H., Miller, B. C., & Heaton, T. (1998, August). *An analysis of partner's age differences in childbearing: Is it teenagers or is it really ruralness?* Annual Meetings of the Rural Sociological Society, Portland, OR.

Blankenhorn, D. (1996). *Fatherless America: Confronting our most urgent social problem.* New York: Harper-Perennial.

Bronfenbrenner, U. (1986). Ecology of the family a context for human development: Research perspectives. *Developmental Psychology, 22,* 723–742.

Chan, R. W., Raboy, B., & Patterson, C. J. (1998). Psychosocial adjustment among children conceived via donor insemination by lesbian and heterosexual mothers. *Child Development, 69,* 443–457.

Clarke-Stewart, A. (1978). And daddy makes three: The father's impact on mother and young child. *Child Development, 49,* 466–478.

Cummings, E. M., & O'Reilly, A. M. (1997). Fathers in family context: Effects of marital quality on child adjustment. In M. E. Lamb (Ed.), *The role of the father in child development* (pp. 49–65). New York: Wiley.

Cummings, E. M., Zahn-Waxler, C., & Radke-Yarrow, M. (1984). Developmental changes in children's reactions to anger in the home. *Journal of Child Psychology and Psychiatry, 25,* 63–75.

Damast, A. M., Tamis-LeMonda, C. S., & Bornstein, M. H. (1996). Mother-child play: Sequential interactions and the relation between maternal beliefs and behaviors. *Child Development, 67,* 1752–1766.

Deutsch, F. M., Lussier, J. B., Servis, L. J. (1993). Husbands at home: Predictors of paternal participation in childcare and housework. *Journal of Personality and Social Psychology, 65,* 1154–1166.

Dickson, K. L., Walker, H., & Fogel, A. (1997). The relationship between smile type and play type during parent-infant play. *Developmental Psychology, 33,* 925–933.

Engle, P. L., & Breaux, C. (1998). Fathers' involvement with children: Perspectives from developing countries. *Social Policy Report*, 12, 1–23.

Feldman, R., Greenbaum, C. W., Mayes, L. C., & Erlich, S. H. (1997). Change in mother-infant interactive behavior: Relation to change in the mother, the infant, and the social context. *Infant Behavior and Development*, 20, 151–163.

Field, T. (1998). Maternal depression effects on infants and early intervention. *Preventative Medicine*, 27, 200–203.

Gerson, K. (1993). *No man's land: Men's changing commitments to family and work*. New York: Basic Books.

Grossman, F. K., Pollack, W. S., & Golding, E. (1988). Fathers and children: Predicting the quality and quantity of fathering. *Developmental Psychology*, 24, 82–91.

Gustafson, G. E., Green, J. A., & West, M. J. (1979). The infant's changing role in mother-infant games: The growth of social skills. *Infant Behavior and Development*, 2, 301–308.

Hewlett, B. S. (1992). *Father-child relations: Cultural and biosocial contexts*. New York: Adline De Gruyter.

Hossain, Z., & Roopnarine, J. L. (1995). African-American fathers' involvement with infants: Relationship to their functioning style, support, education, and income. *Infant Behavior and Development*, 17, 175–184.

Jarvis, P. A., & Creasy, G. L. (1991). Parental stress, coping, and attachment in families with an 18 month-old infant. *Infant Behavior and Development*, 14, 383–395.

Lamb, M. E. (1977). Father-infant and mother-infant interaction in the first year of life. *Child Development*, 48, 167–181.

Lamb, M. E. (1981). The development of father-infant relationships. In M. E. Lamb (Ed.), *Nontraditional families: Parenting and child development* (pp. xx–xx). Hillsdale, NJ: Erlbaum.

Lamb, M. E. (1987). *The father's role: Cross-cultural perspectives*. Hillsdale, NJ: Erlbaum.

Lamb, M. E. (1997). Fathers and child development: An introductory overview and guide. In M. E. Lamb (Ed.), *The role of the father in child development* (pp. 121–142). New York: John Wiley & Sons.

Leaper, C., Anderson, K. J., & Sanders, P. (1998). Moderators of gender effects on parents' talk to their children: A meta-analysis. *Developmental Psychology*, 34, 3–27.

Lerman, R., & Sorensen, E. (1996, October). *Father involvement with their non-marital children: Patterns, determinants, and effects on their earnings, Preliminary findings* (unpublished manuscript). Washington, D. C.: The Urban Institute.

Levant, R. F. (1990). Coping with the new father role. In D. Moore & F. Leafgren (Eds.), *Problem solving strategies and interventions for men in conflict* (pp. 81–94). Alexandria, VA: American Association for Counseling and Development.

Lewis, C. (1997). Fathers and preschoolers. In M. E. Lamb (Ed.), *The role of the father in child development* (pp. 121–142). New York: John Wiley & Sons.

Lindsay, E. W., Mize, J., & Pettit, G. S. (1997). Differential play patterns of mothers and fathers of sons and daughters: Implications for children's gender role development. *Sex Roles, 37,* 643–661.

MacDonald, K., & Parke, R. D. (1986). Parent-child physical play: The effect of sex and age of children and parents. *Sex Roles, 15,* 699–703.

Mackey, W. C., & Day, R. D. (1995). A test of the man-child bond: The predictive potency of the teeter-totter effect. *Genetic, Social, and General Psychology Monographs, 121,* 425–444.

Mathematical Policy Research. (1999, May). *Site by site analysis—Final dispositions; 24-month—Fathers.* Meeting of the Early Head Start Research Consortium, Washington, DC.

McBride, B. A., & Mills, G. (1993). A comparison of mother and father involvement with their preschool age children. *Early Childhood Research Quarterly, 8,* 457–477.

Mead, M. (1949). *Male and female: A study of the sexes in a changing world.* New York: Morrow.

Mead, M., & Heyman, K. (1965). *Family.* New York: Macmillan.

Meyer, D. R., & Garasky, S. (1993). Custodial fathers: Myths, realities, and child support policy. *Journal of Marriage and the Family, 55,* 73–89.

Mortazavi, S., & Karimi, E. (1992). Cultural dimensions of paternalistic behavior: A cross- cultural research in five countries. In S. Iwawaki & Y. Kashima (Eds.), *Innovations in cross-cultural psychology* (pp. 147–151). Amsterdam: Swets & Zeitlinger.

Parke, R. (1981). *Fathers.* Cambridge, MA: Harvard University Press.

Parke, R. D. (1996). *Fatherhood.* Cambridge, MA: Harvard University Press.

Parke, R. D., & Sawin, D. B. (1980). The family in early infancy: Social interactional and attitudinal analyses. In F. A. Pedersen (Ed.), *The father-infant relationship* (pp. 44–70). New York: Praeger.

Pedersen, F. A., Anderson, B. J., & Cain, R. L. (1980). Parent-infant and husband-wife interactions observed at age five months. In F. A. Pedersen (Ed.), *The father-infant relationship* (pp. 71–86). New York: Praeger.

Perusse, D., Neale, M. C., Heath, A. C., & Eaves, L. J. (1994). Human parental behavior: Evidence for genetic influence and potential implication for gene-culture transmission. *Behavior Genetics, 24,* 327–335.

Pettit, G. S., Brown, E. G., Mize, J., & Lindsey, E. (1998). Mothers' and fathers' socializing behaviors in three contexts: Links with children's peer competence. *Merrill Palmer Quarterly, 44,* 173–193.

Pleck, J. H. (1985). *Working wives/working husbands.* Beverly Hills, CA: Sage.

Pleck, J. H. (1997). Paternal involvement: Levels, sources, and consequences. In M. E. Lamb (Ed.), *The role of the father in child development* (pp. 66–103). New York: John Wiley & Sons.

Roberts, P. (1998). Fathers' time. In E. N. Junn & C. J. Boyatzis (Eds.), *Child Growth & Development, Annual Editions, 98/99* (pp. 146–152). Guilford, CT: Dushkin.

Roggman, L. A., Benson, B., & Boyce, L. K. (1999). Fathers with infants: Knowledge and involvement in relation to psychosocial functioning and religion. *Infant Mental Health Journal*, 20, 257–277.

Roopnarine, J. L., & Mounts, N. S. (1998). Mother-child and father-child play. *Early Child Development and Care*, 20, 157–169.

Rustia, J. G., & Abbott, D. (1993). Father involvement in infant care: Two longitudinal studies. *International Journal of Nursing Studies*, 30, 467–476.

Shapiro, J. J. , Diamond, M. J., & Greenberg, M. (1995). *Becoming a father: Contemporary, social, developmental, and clinical perspectives*. NY: Springer.

Shapiro, J. L. (1987). The expectant father. *Psychology Today*, 21, 36–39.

Tamis-LeMonda, C., Roggman, L., Bradley, R., Summers, J. A. (1999, April). *Definitions of father involvement: A multidimensional conceptualization*. Society for Research in Child Development, Albuquerque, NM.

Tulananda, O., Young, D. M., & Roopnarine, J. L. (1994). Thai and American fathers' involvement with preschool-age children. *Early Child Development and Care*, 97, 123–133.

U.S. Bureau of the Census. (1993). *Statistical abstract of the United States, 113th edition*. Washington, DC: US Department of Commerce.

U.S. Bureau of the Census. (1998, March). *Household and Family Characteristics*. Washington, DC: US Department of Commerce. Available: *www.census.gov/Press-Release/cb98-228.html*.

ORIGINS OF ADDICTIVE BEHAVIOR
Structuring Pathways to Alcoholism during Infancy and Early Childhood

Hiram E. Fitzgerald
Robert A. Zucker
Eun Young Mun
Leon I. Puttler
& Maria M. Wong

9.
••••

Alcoholism is the most common form of substance abuse in the United States (Grant et al., 1991) with high rates of co-active psychopathology (37%) and other drug use/abuse (47.3%) (Reiger et al., 1990). Furthermore, the rearing environments of children of alcoholics (COAs) are replete with risk factors known to adversely affect the development of young children (Sameroff, 2000). COAs as young as three years old show signs of behavioral problems (Jansen, Fitzgerald, Ham, & Zucker, 1995), and have depressed levels of cognitive functioning (Poon, Ellis, Fitzgerald & Zucker, 2000) and cognitive achievement (Piejak et al., under review) when they are in first and second grade. These indicators of risk are also thought to be the early antecedents of a subtype of alcoholism that is characterized by earlier onset, more severe expression, denser family history, and higher levels of paternal antisocial personality. However, not all offspring of alcoholics become alcoholics themselves, although there is evidence that COAs are at substantially higher risk for alcoholism and various forms of developmental dysregulation than are children without a family history of alcoholism (Cotton, 1979).

Approximately seven million children under the age of eighteen are reared in homes in which one or more parents have a lifetime diagnosis of alcohol abuse or alcohol dependence (herein after referred to as alcoholism; Russell, Henderson & Blume, 1985). Of the seven million children under eighteen who are exposed to alcoholic parents, approximately 680,000 are less than two years of age, and 1,555,000 are between the ages of two and five years old (SAMHSA, 1998). Many of these children are exposed prenatally to alcohol (Carmichael Olson, Morse, & Huffine, 1998; Larkby & Day, 1997), and nearly a quarter million infants experienced polydrug exposure prenatally, exacerbating their risk for later developmental difficulties (LaGasse & Lester, 2000; Lester, LaGasse & Bigsby, 1998). Prenatal exposure to alcohol does not always lead to full-blown fetal alcohol syn-

223

drome (FAS). Less than about 6% of the children born to women who drink heavily during pregnancy display the classic signs of FAS (Abel, 1995; Braun, 1996). There is no clear answer for why only relatively few women who drink alcohol during pregnancy give birth to children with alcohol-related birth defects or FAS. One hypothesis is that specific sociobehavioral risk factors such as low socioeconomic status (SES) may provide the context for increased vulnerability (Abel & Hannigan, 1995). A related hypothesis is that the effects of prenatal alcohol exposure are influenced by multiple interacting causal variables that include such eco-logical variables as SES, but also intra-organismic and familial variables as well. Animal studies have shown that even moderate maternal drinking (defined as one to three drinks per day) can cause molecular changes in the fetal brain with subsequent impaired learning and memory functioning as an adult (Braun, 1996). These findings are supported in human studies as well. Six year old children who were prenatally exposed to moderate levels of alcohol were smaller in weight, height, head circumference, and palpe-bral fissure width (Day, Richardson, Geva, & Robles, 1994). In addition, there was a dose-response relationship between prenatal alcohol intake and each of the dependent measures.

It is clear that the etiology of alcoholism[1] involves a wide range of bio-logical, psychological, sociological and ecological factors. These factors are embedded within developmental pathways which are influenced by both feedback and feedforward processes (Ford & Lerner, 1992). Despite estab-lished research traditions investigating the effects of prenatal and postnatal exposure to alcohol, there has been little historical commerce between them (Carmichael Olson, O'Connor & Fitzgerald, 2001; Fitzgerald, Puttler, Mun & Zucker, 2000). Similarly, there has been surprisingly little commerce in human research among the literatures on genetic vulnerabili-ty, prenatal exposure to alcohol, and ecological and psychological charac-teristics of rearing environment provided by alcoholic parents. Recent lon-gitudinal studies (Zucker & Fitzgerald, 1991; Zucker et al., 2000) docu-ment the heterogeneity of alcoholisms, while simultaneously describing strong connections between parental alcoholism and problem behaviors in children that are evident as early as age three (Fitzgerald et al., 1993; Zucker, Fitzgerald & Moses, 1995).

Many years ago, the distinguished psychologist Anne Anastasi (1958) challenged researchers to address issues related to how heredity and envi-ronment interact to influence behavior development, while simultaneously taking into account prenatal, early experiential, and cultural influences. Anastasi anticipated contemporary transactional, systemic approaches to biobehavioral organization (Ford & Lerner, 1992; Fitzgerald, Zucker & Yang, 1995; Sameroff, 1995) when she noted that "At each step in the causal chain, there is fresh opportunity for interaction with other heredi-tary factors as well as with environmental factors. And since each interaction in turn determines the direction of subsequent interactions, there is an ever-widening network of possible outcomes" (1958, p. 199). In this chapter we examine issues related to prenatal and postnatal exposure to alcohol in the context of etiologic pathways for neurobiological, behavioral, cognitive, and affective consequences of early exposure to parental alcohol abuse or alcohol dependence. Although lack of space limits the depth of the material that can be presented, our overview reflects concepts of risk aggregation and systemic organization with respect to the precursive events of infancy that seem to be likely contributors to pathways leading to alcohol abuse or dependence later in the life course (Fitzgerald, Zucker, & Yang, 1995; Zucker, 1987, 1991).

GENETIC TRANSMISSION OF SUSCEPTIBILITY TO ALCOHOLISM

There are alcohol-specific risk factors and non alcohol-specific risk factors for offspring of alcoholics. Alcohol-specific risk factors include genetic transmission of susceptibility to alcoholism, prenatal exposure to alcohol, positive alcohol expectancies, and early availability of alcohol at home. Non-alcohol specific risk factors include low socioeconomic status, low parental education, poor parenting, and aggression among family members. Although it is not yet clear how these factors interact to culminate in alcoholism for offspring of alcoholics, it is evident that there are many developmental pathways to this endpoint. In addition, given that children without positive family histories for alcoholism and without alcoholic parents can also become alcohol abusive or dependent, there are obviously even more pathways than we consider here. The pathways of interest in this chapter are those descriptive of the children at highest risk for alcoholism and co-active developmental dysregulation, and those most likely to reflect the reciprocal influences of genetics, the quality of the prenatal environment, and the early post-natal experiences in relation to being reared in an alcoholic family.

Evidence for the heritability of alcoholism is strong for both men and women (Heath, 1995; M. Hesselbrock, 1995; V. Hasselbrock, 1995; McGue, 1997). The literature suggests that there is familial resemblance in manifestations of alcoholism among twins and siblings, and across generations. And in some studies, it is estimated that 40–60% of the variance in the liability for the development of alcoholism can be counted by genetic effects (see Begleiter & Porjesz, 1999). However, as Begleiter and Porjesz point out, the quantitative evaluation of genetic liability from studies of familial resemblance is limited in the sense that we have not identified all genes and their carriers susceptible to alcoholism and that we do not know how genetic susceptibility is transmitted across generations. Furthermore, psychiatric diagnostic classifications have uncertain spurious heterogeneity as well as homogeneity, resulting in both false-positives and false-negatives (Begleiter & Porjesz, 1999). Furthermore, as McGue (1997) poignantly reminds us, although evidence points clearly to the heritability of alcoholism to some extent, it does not point to the genetic determination of its expression.

Prime contenders for biological mechanisms involved in the etiology of alcoholism include synaptic dysfunction in neurotransmitter activity (dopamine, gaba, norepinephrine, and serotonin) (Anthenelli & Tabakoff, 1995). Serotonin is of special interest because of its regulatory influence on functions ranging from body rhythms (a component of temperament), aggression, and sexual responsivity. Twitchell et al. (1998) found that there was a relationship between lower whole blood 5-HT content and high total behavior problems (as measured by the Child Behavior Checklist; Achenbach, 1991) in COAs and non-COAs. However, there was no relationship between father's alcoholism status and child's 5-HT level. In a subsequent study, Twitchell, Hanna, Cook, Fitzgerald and Zucker (2000) hypothesized that puberty moderates the relationship between whole blood 5-HT and both behavioral disinhibition and negative affect in COAs and non-COAs. The relationship was evident for pubescent children, but not for pre-pubescent children. Subsequent analyses suggest that genetic regulation of 5-HTTLPR may influence the behavioral disinhibition (undercontrol) and negative affect that is so characteristic of COAs (Twitchell et al., in press). Finally, a study involving substance abusing adolescent women found a negative relationship between platelet MAO activity and difficult temperament as measured by the Dimensions of Temperament-Revised (DOTS-R) (Mezzich et al., 1994). What these findings suggest is that genetic influences on alcoholism may involve the regulation of neurotransmitter activity but that the expression of the genotype may very well be triggered or mediated by many other factors, including transitional biological events such as puberty and/or intraorganismic characteristics such as temperament.

In search of a psychobiological marker for alcoholism, Newlin and Thompson (1990) proposed a differentiator model, hypothesizing that sons of alcoholics exhibit acute sensitization as blood alcohol level rises and acute tolerance as blood alcohol level falls, compared with sons of nonalcoholics. Therefore, sons of alcoholics find alcohol more reinforcing because they accentuate the pleasurable, excitatory aspects of initial intoxication but attenuate the feelings of anxiety and depression as blood alcohol levels drop. Begleiter & Porjesz (1999) recently extended the differentiator model and suggested that what is inherited in the predisposition to alcoholism is a general state of central nervous system (CNS) disinhibition/hyperexcitability. The CNS disinhibition/hyperexcitability state can be tapped by a decreased P3 component of the Event-Related Brain Potential (ERP), a characteristic not only of abstinent alcoholics and offspring of alcoholics but also of individuals with substance abuse, antisocial personality disorder, and attention deficit hyperactivity disorder (ADHD). Their hypothesis is that the initial state of CNS disinhibition/hyperexcitability can result in a number of externalizing disorders among COAs. And for these children, the exposure to alcohol provides an initially powerful and immediate normalizing effect, which can be more rewarding for them than for non-COAs. In addition, since this relief is transient, it requires larger and larger amounts of alcohol and contributes to the development of tolerance and dependence.

There are two important points to be made in relation to CNS disinhibition/hyperexcitability. The first point is that the CNS disinhibition/hyperexcitability hypothesis does not rule out the possibility that alcoholism results from prenatal exposure to alcohol and other drugs rather than from the genetic inheritance of susceptibility to alcoholism. For example, research shows that there is a similarity between ADHD children and alcohol exposed children in terms of brain regions, with the greatest reduction occurring in the callosal area (Riley et al., 1995). In addition, hyperactivity and attentional deficits that are core problems for ADHD children are often present in children with FAS or histories of prenatal alcohol exposure (Connor & Streissguth, 1996; Nanson & Hiscock, 1990). Considering the evidence of a decreased P3 component of the Event-Related Brain Potential (ERP) among subjects with substance abuse, antisocial personality, and ADHD (Begleiter & Porjesz, 1999), it is possible that there may be common mechanisms for these problems.

The second point about the CNS disinhibition/hyperexcitability hypothesis is that there is considerable individual variability among COAs. Not all COAs become alcoholics and not all children exposed to alcohol experience negative long-term effects. For example, studies frequently report growth deficits among alcohol exposed children from low income families, but do not find comparable deficits among children from middle to high income families. This suggests that SES moderates the effects of alcohol exposure (Day et al., 1994). Socioeconomic status and heavy alcohol consumption are also associated with smoking, poor nutrition, poor health, increased stress, and use of other drugs (see Abel, 1995). Thus, non-alcohol specific risk factors clearly play a major role in the genotypic expression of genetic susceptibility to alcoholism.

The CNS disinhibition/hyperexcitability hypothesis converges nicely with Moffitt's (1993) proposal that the neuropsychological characteristics indicated by temperament are strongly connected to life-course-persistent antisocial behavior. Several investigators argue that difficult temperament in infancy is an early indicator of a high risk pathway to alcoholism (Tarter, 1988; Tarter, Alterman, & Edwards, 1985; Tarter & Vanyukov, 1994). Moffitt suggests that neuropsychological variation in infants can be traced to the disruption in the ontogenesis of the fetal brain. Individual differences in neuropsychological functions reflect differentiation of the nervous system that structures at least one pathway where difficult temperament precedes the appearance of behavioral problems and biobehavioral dysregulation in general. Moffitt asserts that multiple causal factors help to structure this pathway, including both genetic and environmental risk factors such as pre- and post-natal exposure to alcohol, poor nutrition, and low SES. Others have noted that despite heightened exposure to parental divorce and parental conflict (Loukas, Piejak, Bingham, Fitzgerald & Zucker, in press), the level of child behavior problems at the five-to-seven year shift (Ladd, 1996) is most strongly predicted by the level of child behavior problems during the preschool period (Loukas, Fitzgerald, Zucker & von Eye, in press). Thus, difficult temperament during infancy and high externalizing behavior problems during the preschool period seem to reflect two components of an early-forming pathway of risk for developmental psychopathology, including substance abuse. That this pathway seems to organize more easily in male COAs with antisocial alcoholic fathers is a reflection of the dynamic relationships among genetic, familial, and experiential forces in development (Zucker, Ellis, Fitzgerald, & Bingham, 1996).

The means by which genetic predisposition, temperament, prenatal exposure, and/or being reared in an alcoholic family trigger organizational processes remain to be determined. However, evidence suggests that being reared in an alcoholic environment in which one or both parents is alcoholic with co-active psychopathology (e.g., antisocial personality disorder or depression) potentiates risk for biobehavioral dysregulation (Edwards, Leonard & das Eiden, in press; Ellis, Zucker & Fitzgerald, 1997; Fitzgerald, Puttler, et al., 2000; Mun, Fitzgerald, Puttler, Zucker, & von Eye, in press; Wong, Zucker, Puttler, & Fitzgerald, 1999; Zucker et al., 2000). The child's temperamental disposition also contributes to the type of behavior problems and other developmental difficulties the child displays (Fox, Schmidt, Calkins, Rubin, & Coplan, 1996). For example, in the study by Fox et al., shy children with atypical frontal asymmetry were more likely to have internalizing behavior problems, whereas highly sociable children were more likely to have externalizing problems. The heterogeneous nature of alcoholism suggests that gene-environment transactions are likely to be best understood when research is guided by approaches such as Windle's (1997) dynamic diathesis-stress model or Zucker's (1987) risk aggregation probabilistic model, each of which posits systemic approaches to alcoholism etiology.

PRENATAL EXPOSURE TO ALCOHOL

Although prenatal exposure to alcohol does not always lead to negative outcomes for the fetus, it can cause a range of problems involving damage to the fetal brain and central nervous system (Carmichael Olson, 1994; Larkby & Day, 1997; Streissguth, 1997). The fetus is at high risk for the teratogenic effects of alcohol during the first trimester when the rate of morphological differentiation is high. There has been ample animal and human research demonstrating that alcohol is a teratogen. Alcohol consumed by a mother crosses the placenta and circulates in the bloodstream of the developing child. The last trimester of pregnancy is also a period of high vulnerability because brain growth and organization occur at a high rate. Animal research suggests that alcohol exposure during the last trimester of pregnancy may interfere with brain biochemistry, blocking the action of glutamate and resulting in a reduction in the neurons of the forebrain.

The teratogenic effects of prenatal alcohol exposure were first identified only thirty years ago (Lemoine, Harousseau, Bortegru & Menuet, 1968). Shortly thereafter, investigators defined the most severe impact of prenatal exposure as fetal alcohol syndrome, consisting of growth retardation (weight, height, low birth weight), dysmorphic characteristics (craniofacial features), CNS abnormalities (microcephaly), and behavior dysregulation (attention deficit, learning problems) (Jones & Smith, 1973; Jones, Smith, Ulleland & Streissguth, 1973). Occurring at a rate of 6 per 1,000 live births (Institute of Medicine, 1996), FAS is the largest environmental teratogen identified to date.

For quite a few years, investigators have also described fetal alcohol effects (FAE). FAE refers to presumed consequences of prenatal alcohol exposure that fall short of an FAS outcome. However, attributions about the effects of low to moderate levels of drinking on the fetus and on subsequent postnatal outcomes are difficult to link causally to maternal alcohol consumption. The term "alcohol related neurodevelopmental disorder" (ARND) was proposed by the Institute of Medicine (1996) to encompass all prenatal exposure outcomes, excluding those with FAS morphological features, in an effort to encourage investigators to broaden their conceptual models to incorporate multiple indicators of negative influences on the developing organism, including the development of the brain and nervous system.

At birth, the human brain weighs about 350 grams and all of its major segments (lobes) are differentiated. The frontal and temporal lobes are less well developed than the occipital and parietal lobes, reflecting their slower rate of development. By the third postnatal month brain convolutions have increased, as have the lengths of the frontal and temporal lobes. From the sixth to the ninth postnatal month, the color of the cerebral cortex changes from pinkish gray to gray, and by one year of age the gray matter of the brain is clearly distinguishable from the white matter. Sometime during the latter part of the second year of life, the comparative proportions of the lobes are essentially those of the mature brain. Thus, from the third trimester of pregnancy to the end of the second year of life, the brain undergoes its period of most rapid growth and differentiation. It is a time when brain cells migrate, axons grow, synapses connect, and experience-organism interactions modulate the expression of the genotype (Shonkoff & Phillips, 2000). It is a time when the fetus is especially vulnerable to behavioral and structural teratogens (Vorhees & Mollnow, 1987).

Although many teratogenic effects are expressed prenatally within temporal periods when specific structural features are rapidly organizing (referred to as critical or sensitive periods), less is known about the impact of prolonged exposure to potentially stressful environmental events. Interestingly enough, Field, Shanberg, Kuhn, Pelaez-Nogueras and Scafidi (under review) found that depressed mothers with high levels of norepinephrine and cortisol had newborn infants with similarly elevated levels as well as excessive irritability. Although high levels of cortisol are associated with pregnancy and peak during parturition (Jolivet, Blanchier, Gautray, & Dehm, 1974), stress apparently exacerbates these tonic levels in both depressed mothers and their newborns. Although transitions from depressed to non-depressed states over the course of the first three postnatal years apparently reduce such effects, Field and her colleagues also reported that depressed mothers and their infants were more likely than non-depressed mothers and their infants to have right frontal EEG activity (Field, Fox, Pickens, & Nawrocki, 1995). Moreover, depressed mothers and their preschool age children evidenced right frontal EEG activity and elevated cortisol levels (Field, Yando, Lang, Pickens, Martinez, & Bendell, under review). Kagan, Reznick and Snidman (1987) provided evidence that behaviorally inhibited children had higher levels of cortisol than uninhibited children regardless of whether tonic or phasic salivary cortisol samples were analyzed. Cortisol levels were also elevated in infants who were separated from their mothers in the Strange Situation task, especially those infants who scored high on measures of negative affect and distress. Whether pregnant women living with alcoholic men, particularly antisocial alcoholic men, experience increased levels of tonic stress remains to be determined, but to the extent that they do it is possible that the fetus may be exposed to high tonic levels of cortisol, with corresponding negative influences on such brain structures as the hippocampus.

During the past twenty years, neuroscientists have made startling discoveries about the extent to which the structural and functional organization of the brain is affected by experience (Greenough, 1991). Through such techniques as brain imaging, it is now established that much of the wiring of the brain and nervous system occurs as a direct consequence of the organism's interactions with its environment. Although the genotype may set the theoretical boundaries for expression of a characteristic, where an individual fits within these boundaries is very much dependent on experience (Gottlieb, 1991). We already noted that maternal depression has been linked to increased cortisol production. In non-human organisms, high levels of cortisol are associated with the destruction of neurons as well as with reductions in the synaptic connections that create the neural pathways which are essential for adaptive functioning, including such functions as learning, memory, and emotion regulation. Exposure to chronic stress therefore may have a direct negative impact on brain development, particularly on the hippocampus, a structure that is involved in memory for facts and relationships among events (Nelson, 1995). The point is that neuroscience has documented the importance of experience in facilitating or interfering with the structural and functional organization of the brain and nervous system. The question is, to what extent does prenatal and postnatal exposure to alcohol influence the organization of the brain and nervous system? Evidence for prenatal effects is more sharply circumscribed than is evidence for postnatal effects. Nevertheless, results from several longitudinal studies suggest that problems such as difficult temperament, hyperactivity, learning disability, conduct disorder, and depression are best conceptualized as neurobehavioral in order to capture the rich interplay between neurogenesis and experience in synaptogenesis and brain organization (Greenough, 1991).

Regardless of how complete our knowledge of the teratogenic effects of alcohol on the fetus is, failure to include systematic study of the effects of the postnatal rearing environment and contextual influences will result in a failure to understand how prenatal alcohol exposure affects children over the life course (Toth, Connor, Barr, Sampson, & Streissguth, 2000). For example, the rate of FAS varies with social class independently of the amount of alcohol consumed (Bingol et al., 1987), which suggests that co-occurring risk factors aggregate in low socioeconomic classes. To the extent that aggregated risk factors moderate the fetus' biological vulnerability, the teratogenic effects of alcohol may be either exacerbated or ameliorated. The mother's and child's genetic susceptibility to alcohol effects is another factor that may increase or decrease the risk for fetal damage as a result of prenatal exposure (Carmichael Olson, 1994). Research also shows that the effects of dosage, timing, and pattern of use vary depending upon the type of outcome being studied (Larkby & Day, 1997; Streissguth, 1997). For example, binge drinking produces high blood alcohol levels, which may push the teratogenic effect of alcohol over the threshold with resulting damage to the fetus.

REARING ENVIRONMENT: POSTNATAL EXPOSURE TO ALCOHOL

In our discussion of the effects of experience on child development we will draw heavily on work from the Michigan State University-University of Michigan Longitudinal Study (MSU-UM Study). This study has been intensively tracking the life course of three hundred community-recruited families for fourteen of a designed twenty-year study. Families were recruited into the study on the basis of father's alcoholism; maternal characteristics were not a basis for recruitment (Zucker et al., 2000). Data are collected from all family members every three years, beginning when the male target child is aged between three and six years old (Fitzgerald et al., 2000; Fitzgerald, Davies & Zucker, in press; Fitzgerald, Zucker, & Yang, 1995; Zucker & Fitzgerald, 1991; Zucker, Fitzgerald & Moses, 1995; Zucker et al., 2000).

After initial recruitment, alcoholic men were reclassified on the basis of the presence or absence of a sustained history of antisocial behavior over their lifetime; those with a pattern of alcoholism in adulthood in combination with a lifetime history of antisocial behavior were categorized as antisocial alcoholics (AALS) and those without this sustained history were categorized as non-antisocial alcoholics (NAALS) (Zucker, 1987; Zucker, Ellis, & Fitzgerald, 1994). This classification strategy proved highly effective (Table 9.1). For example, AALs are more likely to have had a history of childhood behavior problems, illegal behavior, arrests, chronic lying, relationship disturbances, failed relationships, depression, family violence, neuroticism, poor achievement and cognitive functioning, and low socioeconomic status (Fitzgerald, et al., 1995; Fitzgerald et al., 1993; Ichiyama, Zucker, Fitzgerald, & Bingham, 1996; Muller, Fitzgerald, Sullivan, & Zucker, 1994; Zucker, et al., 1994; Zucker, Ellis, Fitzgerald, & Bingham, 1996; Zucker, Kincaid, Fitzgerald, & Bingham, 1995).

Table 9.1 Composite Indicators of Risky Rearing Environments Provided by Alcoholic Parents and Risky Behaviors Characteristic of Sons of Alcoholics Ages 3 to 5 Years

Children's Risky Rearing Environments	Children's Risky Behavior
Parental history of regulatory dysfunction	Self-regulatory dysfunction
Parental history of psychopathology	Difficult temperament
Antisocial personality disorder	Attachment disorders
Depression	Externalizing problem behavior
Parental poor value structure	Parent–child relationships disturbance
Parental aggression	Schemas for alcohol use and alcohol-linked behavior
Parental cognitive deficiency	Poor value structure
Family low socioeconomic status	Cognitive deficiency
Risk-aggregated community	High risk peer network

Adapted with permission from: H. E. Fitzgerald, L. I. Puttler, E.-Y. Mun, & R. A. Zucker (2000). Prenatal and postnatal exposure to parental alcohol use and abuse. In J. D. Osofsky & H. E. Fitzgerald (Eds.), *WAIMH handbook of infant mental health: Vol. 4.* Infant mental health in groups at high risk (p. 141).

Male COAs have significantly greater externalizing problems (aggression, delinquent behavior, and attention problems) and internalizing problems (depressive and social problems) than do male non-COAs. The externalizing behavior differences are of particular interest because they represent proxy indicators for later alcohol problems. Moreover, these findings are also consistent with a study of behavioral differences in three year olds that predicted adult alcoholism diagnosis (Caspi, Moffitt, Newman, & Silva, 1996). COAs also have lower IQ scores and are more impulsive (Fitzgerald et al., 1993; Poon et al., 2000).

Typing children on the basis of their father's antisocial symptomatology is an effective way to discriminate differences within the COA population. Offspring of antisocial alcoholic fathers have the highest levels of externalizing and internalizing behavior, the highest levels of impulsivity, the highest levels of difficult temperament, and the lowest IQs when contrasted with children of alcoholics or those of community controls (Zucker et al., 2000). In some areas, COAs from non-antisocial but alcoholic families do not significantly differ from normal controls. These differences challenge the traditional literature by suggesting that risk may be bound to specific parental subtypes rather than representing a broad-span vulnerability index (Ellis, et al., 1997).

Subtyping on the basis of father's comorbid antisocial symptomatology is also a strong marker for individual differences in parental risk, and an effective indicator of family level risk aggregation as well. Thus, alcoholic men not only have more other psychopathology, a poorer social adaptation (lower SES), and a denser family history of alcoholism, but they also are downwardly socially mobile from their own parents, they live in families with higher levels of family violence, and there are higher rates of separation and divorce. They also tend to marry women who have similar life histories (Ellis et al, 1997; Fitzgerald et al., 2000; Zucker et al., 1996).

Although it is not possible to isolate contributions of genetic, biological, and psychological effects on these developmental outcome variables, recent studies from the MSU-UM Longitudinal Study suggest that these multiple risk factors are nested densely and that there is an elevated risk for children with multiple risk factors. For example, family environments that are high in the negative expression of emotions mediate child difficult temperament as well as spousal violence as contributors to child externalizing behavior (Ellis et al., 1997; Jansen et al., 1995; Wong et al., 1999). Differences in externalizing and internalizing behavior during the six to eight year range parallel those observed when children were between three and five years old, although over time the level of risk decreases (that is, the level of total behavior problems decreases). Conversely, children from alcoholic families with other co-occurring parental psychopathology are most likely to sustain level of risk (i.e., sustain a "clinical range" rating of externalizing behavior) (Mun et al., in press; Wong et al., 1999). Furthermore, Mun et al. found that children with parents of multiple psychopathology showed elevated levels of distraction and reactivity as measured by the Dimensions of Temperament Survey (DOTS; Lerner, Palermo, Spiro, & Nesselroade, 1982). In addition, the relationships between child temperament and externalizing and internalizing behavior problems were only significant for preschool age children being reared by parents with multiple indicators of psychopathology. The findings suggest that child temperamental characteristics play different roles in the development of behavior problems depending on the context of other risk factors.

Differences in cognitive functioning between male COAs and non-COAs are also evident in early childhood. Preschool age COAs were three times more likely to fall in the impaired IQ (less than 80) range, and such differences were not attributable to fetal alcohol syndrome (Fitzgerald et al., 1993). Parental IQ predicted children's intellectual functioning, with verbal IQ particularly affected among children of antisocial alcoholics. Differences in academic achievement were evident as early as first and second grades (Poon et al., 2000), with children of antisocial alcoholics scoring lower on the Wide Range Achievement Test-Revised spelling and arithmetic scales, while showing poorer abilities in abstract planning and attention. In addition, impulsivity differences between children from antisocial alcoholic families and the other groups were also present and were suggestive of specific impairments in frontal lobe functioning. It is noteworthy that the effects of paternal alcoholism status still contributed to child's intellectual functioning even after controlling for socioeconomic status, parental education, and parental IQ (Poon et al., 2000).

MOTHERS AND DAUGHTERS

Collectively, the literature suggests that risk factors for alcoholism and co-occurring psychopathology are aggregated in a nesting structure that is composed of genetic, biological, neuropsychological, psychological, and ecological factors. However, the weight of this evidence is based on studies of male COAs and the major linkages are presumed to be from father to son. Considerably less attention has been given to etiologic issues in women and to the mother to child relationships that are important in structuring early pathways of risk (Fitzgerald, Zucker, Puttler, Caplan & Mun, 2000). This is especially true for studies of father-to-daughter and mother-to-daughter relationships. At the least, maternal alcoholism poses serious problems for the development of children not only in terms of FAS or ARND, but also via ineffective parenting throughout infancy and early childhood (Werner, 1986).

Alcoholism is a less prominent psychopathology of female adult life than other mental disorders, and the developmental trajectories of use are different than those of men (Gomberg, 1991; Hill, 1995a,b). Although women are more likely to be abstainers (Dawson, Grant & Chou, 1995), nearly 65 million women currently use alcohol in the United States and of these, about 5% conform to a twelve-month diagnosis of alcoholism (Huang, Cerbone, & Groerer, 1998; Kessler et al., 1994). Adolescent and young adult women experience the highest rates of intoxication, drinking problems and episodic drinking, and more recent epidemiologic data indicate that alcoholism among young adult women is close to a 1:2 ratio compared with men. Women with drinking problems are at greater risk of heart disease, breast cancer, osteoporosis, liver disease, and a shortened life span; and an even greater number of women live in households in which an alcoholic male resides (Gomberg, 1991; Hill, 1995a,b). Thus, alcoholism is a serious health problem for both men and women. Is maternal alcoholism a serious health problem for children?

Adult women alcoholics report family environments characterized by inadequate parenting, neglect, insecure attachments to parents, feelings of being unloved, lack of close relationship to mother, and parental conflict (Drake & Vaillant, 1988). It seems increasingly clear that subtypes of alcoholism in women can be identified. Women alcoholics commonly have poor self-esteem, feelings of inadequacy, and depression. As women tend to base their self-esteem on relationships more than men do, it is not surprising that daughters in alcoholic families report high levels of affective/emotional disturbances such as temper tantrums, phobias, nightmares, nervous problems, and enuresis during childhood, and loneliness, nervousness, boredom, and embarrassment during adolescence (Gomberg, 1991; Kavanach & Hops, 1994). Preliminary results from the MSU-UM Longitudinal Study suggest that there may be another subtype characterized by negative affect (depression) (Puttler, Zucker, Fitzgerald, & Bingham, 1998; Zucker, Fitzgerald, & Moses, 1996). Carmichael Olson, Feldman, Streissguth, Sampson, and Bookstein (1998) found high rates of depression among FAS children who received high prenatal exposures, and Day, Richardson, Goldschmidt, and Cornelius (2000) found higher rates of internalizing behavior among children who received moderate prenatal exposure to alcohol.

The work of O'Connor and her colleagues suggests a link between prenatal exposure and postnatal depressive symptoms, such that moderate drinking during pregnancy was associated with higher levels of negative affect during postnatal mother-infant interactions (O'Connor, Sigman & Brill, 1987; O'Connor, Sigman & Kasari, 1992). A longitudinal follow-up when the children were early school age indicated a strong relationship between prenatal exposure and self-reported depressive symptoms; heavier exposure predicted higher self-reported depressive symptoms. Moreover, the combination of maternal depression and high levels of drinking during pregnancy predicted the highest levels of children's depressive symptoms, and these findings were especially evident for girls. Subsequent studies suggest that the quality of the mother-infant attachment relationship is impaired among mothers with high rates of drinking during pregnancy. In a study involving a high-risk sample (low SES single mothers with high alcohol use prenatally), 80% of infants exposed to moderate to heavy maternal drinking prenatally had insecure attachment relationships. In contrast, one-third of the infants exposed to abstinent to light drinkers had insecure attachments (O'Connor, Kogan & Findlay, 2000a, 2000b). O'Connor hypothesizes a developmental model, beginning with prenatal exposure to alcohol and the expression of negative affect during infancy (difficult temperament), that when combined with maternal depression/negative affect, leads to a insecure mother-infant attachment relationship, and expresses as high depressive symptoms by age five (O'Connor, 1996; O'Connor & Kasari, 2000).

CONSTRUCTING MENTAL MODELS OF RISKY BEHAVIOR

Most learning takes place in the context of person-to-person or person-to-object relationships, and especially during the early years of development, learning usually takes place in the context of infant-caregiver transactions. Learning traditionally refers to changes in behavior that occur as a result of experience. Often, learning is placed in opposition to maturation, which refers to changes in behavior that occur regardless of experience. Actually, neither definition is correct, because learning and maturation are not independent processes. Much of what can be learned depends on the organism's readiness, or preparedness for learning. In turn, learning may alter or restructure the rate of maturational change. For example, it may occur as a result of chronic stress or acute trauma.

One of the key things infants learn is that events are related (Fitzgerald & Brackbill, 1976; Fitzgerald & Porges, 1971). That is, they learn that Event A predicts Event B, or that Event B is contingent on the occurrence of Event A. Event A could be a stimulus event in the environment that reliably predicts Event B, as when mother's comforting voice reliably predicts her appearance. Event A could be a behavior that reliably leads to Event B, as when infant crying reliably predicts being fed. What do infants learn from these and countless other contingent experiences with their social and physical environments? At the least, such contingencies have two key outcomes. First, infants learn about quite specific event-relationships in their experiential world: when I cry, mother does (or does not) come in a predictable fashion. Second, they extrapolate a general or overarching principle from the countless context-specific event-relationships they experience. They either learn that events are predictable (to one degree or another), or that they are not (to one degree or another). It is likely that different parts of the brain are involved in these processes, some pertaining to the specific linkages among events, some that are to a degree abstracted from the ongoing flow of events and relationships. Various theorists have discussed this basic proposition in terms of contingency awareness (Watson, 1967), trust (Erikson, 1950), object relations (Spitz, 1965), schema formation (Piaget, 1952), and attachment security (Ainsworth, Blehar, Waters, & Wall, 1978). Regardless of one's theoretical orientation there is a common element to event-relationships, and that element is action. Action means that the organism and the environment affect one another, that the infant and young child adapt within the context of a caregiving environment that itself is adapting to the child, and that while actions take place, higher order "meanings" are distilled from these experiences.

Expectancies do not merely arise from the dynamic relationships between organism and environment, however, they also serve to regulate such relationships because they operate as decision rules or schemata. Decision rules influence behavior because they provide an economical way to process information, to encode novel events and re-construct familiar events. For example, a young child may classify a novel object as a toy because the object conveys features that are consistent with the child's categorization scheme for toys. However, a novel object may lack the critical features that define the child's toy schema making categorization difficult. Under such circumstances, the child must alter the schema or create a new one in order to encode the new object into memory. Repeated exposure to the object transforms it from novel to familiar and transforms the child's schema, mental representation, or neural network for such objects.

Learning the contingencies between father's drinking and his behavior, and the transformations in event-relationships that are a consequence of father's drinking, involves the same processes that we have discussed thus far. During the early years of life the brain undergoes its most rapid structural and functional organization, the infant and toddler construct their initial mental representations for contingent events, and emergent language and semiotic functions facilitate the construction of memory for events. Thus, the developmental processes that regulate normative developmental pathways are the same processes that regulate deviant ones. The processes are the same, but the outcomes are different because they are contextually embedded in the unique home environments and unique rearing practices to which the child is exposed.

Investigators involved with developmental studies of alcoholism and aggression have independently concluded that children as young as three construct action schemas (mental representations, memory structures, scripts, autobiographical memories) about the important social objects in their environments. Action schemas are organizational structures of memory that influence future behavior by guiding selective attention to salient environmental cues and linking those cues to the individual's behavioral repertoire. For example, children of alcoholics will have mental representations of appropriate behavior related to drinking, relating to others in drinking contexts, and expectations about the consequences of drinking. Action schemas originate in the child's experiential world, but they also reflect constructions that others press into memory as they repeat and embellish stories about remembered events (Harley & Reese, 1999). Issues related to post-traumatic stress disorder and reactive attachment disorder (Zeanah et al., 1999) are consistent with the notion that highly conflictual rearing environments have a powerful affect on the autobiographical events children experience and the reconstructions of those events that take place over time. Children who are exposed only to one parent's point of view, therefore, are more likely to construct memories of events that are based in part on that parent's representation of reality. Left unchecked, such representations of reality may become the child's remembrance (reality) of the event.

Study of alcohol expectancies has, for the most part, been linked to the cognitive or cognitive-behavioral literatures (Lang & Stritzke, 1993). Rarely do cognitive theorists, including those assessing alcohol expectancies, conceptualize schemas as also incorporating motivational, emotional, and social aspects of experience. Conversely, ego psychologists focus on the relationship between the subject and the object with special interest in how the subject develops a sense of independence from the object. Three major organizing events impel the infant to differentiate subject and object, to achieve a sense of self, and to negotiate relationships with social objects (Spitz, 1965). For most caregivers, the infant's social smile triggers a fundamental reorganization of subject-object relationships, the infant's wariness to strangers reflects growing representation of familiar social objects, and the "semantic no" marks the toddler's first abstract negation of the object and assertion of the self ("No, I can do it!"). Spitz was primarily interested in the emotional organizers that regulate relationships between self and others, and that enable the infant to construct mental representations of relationships.

The alcoholism literature provides evidence that children of alcoholics, as young as three years of age construct mental representations or schemas about alcohol that include contextual, motivational, and normative aspects of use (Zucker & Fitzgerald, 1991). For example, in several studies Zucker and his colleagues were able to demonstrate that preschool-age sons of male alcoholics were better able to identify specific alcoholic beverages, and to correctly identify a larger number of alcoholic beverages than were sons of non-alcoholics. The preschool-age sons of alcoholics fathers were more likely to have cognitive schemas that included alcohol consumption as an attribute associated with adult male roles. Moreover, differences in the amount of drinking attributed to male adults was predicted by same gender parent's self-reported consumption level. In other words, these preschool age boys already have constructed a mental model or representation of adult use of alcohol (and other drugs), and have direct experience with changes in event-relationships elicited by parental alcohol consumption (Noll, Zucker, & Greenberg, 1990; Noll, Zucker, Fitzgerald, & Curtis,

1992; Zucker & Fitzgerald, 1991; Zucker et al., 1995; Zucker, et al., 2000).

Thus, when considered in the context of a broader developmental literature, alcohol expectancies of preschool age children are extremely complex organizational structures. Moreover, they are unique to the individual child's experiences, autobiographical structures of mind, or what memory researchers refer to as autobiographical memory (Schneider & Bjorklund, 1998). According to Howe and Courage (1997), autobiographical memory for events develops at the same time that the cognitive self develops. Consistent with Spitz' observation that the "semantic no" emerges in the second year of life, Howe and Courage point out that autobiographical memory for events also begins to form in the second year of life. Both Spitz and Howe note the important role that language plays in consolidating memories for events as well as assisting with the consolidation of a concept of self.

Consider, for example, recent findings from studies of the early years of life that are related to the development for memory of familiar events. An explicit assumption of attachment theory (Karlen, 1996) is that memory for familiar events (mother-infant interactions) is related to the development of a working model of self as well as a working model for relationships (Verschuren, Marcven, & Schoefs, 1996). The weight of this literature suggests that children as young as three years of age already have working models or schemas about familiar events. Autobiographical memories are only partially based on experience, however, because they are constructed from experience and are influenced by exposure to others' constructions of experience, particularly those of parents (Schneider & Bjorklund, 1998). When a mother asks her three-year-old, "Where did we go yesterday?" and coaches her child toward constructing a memory of the event, she is helping the child to construct an autobiographical memory. Mothers who elaborate their stories and challenge their toddler's stories with high rates of memory questions tend to have toddlers with richer autobiographical memories (Harley & Reese, 1999). Toddlers who are developmentally more advanced in self recognition also tended to have richer autobiographical memories of shared events. Conway and Pleydell-Pearce (2000) suggest that networks in the left frontal lobe of the brain mediate development of retrieval models in the right frontal cortex. They propose that "abstract lifetime period knowledge is stored in right frontal sites, knowledge of general events in the temporal lobes, and ESK (event specific knowledge) in occipital-parietal networks" (p. 277). They assert that autobiographical memories and the self memory system evolved to control the degree to which event specific knowledge is activated. Appropriate events trigger event specific knowledge automatically.

Children are able to recall unpleasant events as well as they are able to recall pleasant ones (Merritt, Ornstein & Spiker, 1994). Although issues related to post-traumatic stress disorder or reactive attachment disorder (Hinshar-Fuselier, Boris & Zeanah, 1999; Zeanah et al., 1999) do not appear in the alcoholism literature, they seem entirely consistent with the notion that highly conflictual rearing environments can have a powerful effect on the autobiographic events one experiences and constructs over time. For example, Zeanah and his associates have demonstrated that mothers who experienced high rates of serious spousal violence had disorganized attachment relationships with their toddlers. And while it may be the case that witnessing parental violence may elicit fear in young children about the well-being of a parent (Main & Hesse, 1990), it also provides the child with opportunities to code how fathers/husbands can treat wives (or children) especially during drinking episodes. In short, it provides a context for construction of events and events may provide a background for action at some time in the future (e.g., during adolescence and early adulthood). Conway and Pleydell-Pearce (2000) suggest that event specific knowledge related to traumatic experiences is encoded into long term memory "by default with the goals of the working self active during the trauma." The work of Markowitsch, Thiel, Kessler, von Stockhausen, & Heiss (1997) indicates that traumatic memories often trigger a stress response that increases glucosteroid release, which in turn has a negative effect on the hippocampus and medial temporal lobe networks. Interestingly, shrinkage of the hippocampus has been reported in soldiers with post-traumatic stress disorder. Finally, it should be noted that the hippocampus and related limbic structures of the medial temporal lobe mature relatively early in postnatal life and are involved in the development of explicit memory (Nelson, 1995), a component of memory that seems to reach its near-adult level by the preschool years.

Living in a family with an alcoholic parent, with or without other coactive psychopathology, presents numerous occasions to experience the events of drinking, parenting behavior, and marital relationships. It seems reasonable, therefore, to link the literature on the emergence of children's memory for familiar events, including the affective load carried by these events, with studies of alcohol schemas in preschool age children. This linkage suggests a model of early alcohol schema formation that embeds expectancies into a family structure that includes emotional differentiation, self regulation, interpersonal dynamics, and socialization, as well as motivational forces involving beliefs, wants, and desires. This systems approach to the organization of the preschooler's "schema for alcoholism" suggests that the child's schema is composed of at least the four interdependent components listed in table 9.2.

Table 9.2 Hypothesized components of an organizing schema for alcohol abuse or dependence and alcohol-linked behaviors among preschool-age children of alcoholics

---

Sensory-Perceptual

    Sensory identification of substances

    Perceptual discrimination of substances

Cognitive-Motivational

    Attributions about who are appropriate users

    Expectancies related to outcomes based on use

Emotional

    Self-regulatory, self-control processes

    Interpersonal relationships

Social

    Socialization models

    Peer relationships

    Dominance hierarchies/power

Adapted with permission from: H. E. Fitzgerald, L. I. Puttler, E.Y. Mun, & R. A. Zucker (2000). Prenatal and postnatal exposure to parental alcohol use and abuse. In J. D. Osofsky & H. E. Fitzgerald (Eds.). *WAIMH handbook of infant mental health: Vol. 4.* Infant mental health in groups at high risk *(p.* 150).

CONCLUSION

Human development from conception to age three is a time of extraordinary change. The transformations that take place from the union of two single cells to the active, rambunctious, verbal, three year old are truly amazing. The convergence of organizing processes, structural and functional differentiation of the brain and nervous system, and the social embeddedness of human development provides multiple contexts that can facilitate or impede progress toward healthy development. Parental alcoholism and co-occurring psychopathology—nested within an environment consisting of limited parental education, family resources, and family stability, and embedded in genetic and/or congenital influences—surrounds children of alcoholics in a powerful systemic risk structure. To better understand forces that shape the developmental pathways emerging from this risk structure, considerably more attention must be given to research that 1) bridges prenatal and postnatal exposure to alcohol, including genetic contributions to risk and genetic-experiential organizing forces; 2) focuses on the brain-behavior interface, including the regulatory role of neuro-transmitters; 3) expands studies of the effects of alcohol on women, including a concentrated focus on the mother's contributions to child resilience; and 4) frames questions of etiology in systemic terms, including models that attempt to depict the complexity of developmental processes over the life course.

REFERENCES

Abel, E. L. (1995). An update on incidence of FAS: FAS is not an equal opportunity birth defect. *Neurotoxicology and Teratology*, 17, 437–443.

Abel, E. L., & Hannigan, J. H. (1995). Maternal risk factors in fetal alcohol syndrome: Provocative and permissive influences. *Neurotoxicology and Teratology*, 17, 445–462.

Achenbach, T. M. (1991). *Manual for the Child Behavior Checklist/4-18 and 1991 profile*. Burlington, VT: University of Vermont department of Psychiatry.

Ainsworth, M. D. S., Blehar, M. C., Waters, E., & Wall, S. (1978). *Patterns of attachment: A psychological study of the strange situation*. Hillsdale, NJ: Erlbaum.

Anastasi, A. (1958). Heredity, environment, and the question "How?". *Psychological Review*, 65, 197–208.

Anthenelli, R. M., & Tabakoff, B. (1995). The search for biological markers. *Alcohol Health and Research World*, 19, 176–181.

Babor, T. F., & Dolinsky, Z. S. (1988). Alcoholic typologies: Historical evolution and empirical evaluation of some common classification schemes. In R. M. Rose & J. Barret (Eds.), *Alcoholism: Origins and outcome* (pp. 245–266). New York: Raven Press.

Begleiter, H., & Porjesz, B. (1999). What is inherited in the predisposition toward alcoholism? A proposed model. *Alcoholism: Clinical & Experimental Research*, 23, 1125–1135.

Bingol, N., Schuster, C., Fuchs, M., Iosub, S., et al. (1987). The influence of socioeconomic factors on the occurrence of fetal alcohol syndrome. *Advances in Alcohol and Substance Abuse*, 6, 105–118.

Braun, S. (1996). New experiments underscore warnings on maternal drinking. *Science*, 273, 738–739.

Carmichael Olson, H. (1994). The effects of prenatal alcohol exposure on child development. *Young Children*, 6, 10–25.

Carmichael Olson, H., Feldman, J. J., Streissguth, A. P., Sampson, P. D., & Bookstein, F. L. (1998). Neuropsychological deficits in adolescents with fetal alcohol syndrome: Clinical findings. *Alcoholism: Clinical and Experimental Research*, 22, 1998–2012.

Carmichael Olson, H., Morse, B. A., & Huffine, C. (1998). Development and psychopathology: Fetal alcohol syndrome and related conditions. *Seminars in Clinical Neuropsychiatry*, 3, 262–284.

Carmichael Olson, H., O'Connor, M. J., & Fitzgerald, H. E. (2001). Lessons learned from study of the developmental impact of parental alcohol use. *Infant Mental Health Journal*, 22, 271–290.

Caspi, A., Moffitt, T. E., Newman, D. L., & Silva, P. A. (1996). Behavioral observations at age 3 years predict adult psychiatric disorders. *Archives of General Psychiatry*, 53, 1033–1039.

Chassin, L., Curran, P. J., Hussong, A. M., & Colder, C. R. (1996). The relation of parent alcoholism to adolescent substance use: A longitudinal follow-up study. *Journal of Abnormal Psychology*, 105, 70–80.

Connor, P. D., & Streissguth, A. P. (1996). Effects of prenatal exposure to alcohol across the life span. *Alcohol Health & Research World*, 20, 170–174.

Conway, M. A., & Pleydell-Pearce, C. W. (2000). The construction of autobiographical memories in the self-memory system. *Psychological Review*, 107, 261–288.

Cotton, N. S. (1979). The familial incidence of alcoholism: A review. *Journal of Studies on Alcohol*, 40, 89–116.

Davidson, R. J., & Fox, N. A. (1982). Asymmetrical brain activity discriminates between positive versus negative affect in human infants. *Science*, 218, 1235–1237.

Dawson, D. A., Grant, B. F., & Chou, P. S. (1995). Gender differences in alcohol intake. In W. A. Hunt & S. Zakhari (Eds.), *Stress, gender, and alcohol-seeking behavior* (Research Monograph 29, pp. 3–22). Bethdsda, MD: National Institutes of Health.

Day, N. L., Richardson, G. A., Geva, D., & Robles, N. (1994). Alcohol, marijuana, and tobacco: Effects of prenatal exposure on offspring growth and morphology at age six. *Alcoholism: Clinical and Experimental Research*, 18, 786–794.

Day, N. L., Richardson, G. A., Goldschmidt, L., & Cornelius, M. D. (2000). Effects of prenatal tobacco exposure on preschoolers' behavior. *Developmental and Behavioral Pediatrics*, 21, 180–188.

Drake, D. E, & Vaillant, G. E. (1988). Predicting alcoholism and personality disorder in a 33-year longitudinal study of COAs. *British Journal of Addiction*, 83, 799–807.

Edwards, E. P., Leonard, K. E., & Das Eiden, R. (in press). Temperament and behavioral problems among infants in alcoholic families. *Infant Mental Health Journal*.

Ellis, D. A., Zucker, R. A., & Fitzgerald, H. E. (1997). The role of family influences in development and risk. *Alcohol Health & Research World*, 21, 218–225.

Erikson, E. (1950). *Childhood and society.* New York: Basic Books.

Field, T., Fox, N., Pickens, J., & Nawrocki, T. (1995). Relative right frontal EEG activation in 3- to 6-month old infants of "depressed" mothers. *Developmental Psychology*, 31, 358–363.

Field, T., Schanberg, S., Kuhn, C., Pelaez-Nogueras, M., & Scafidi, F. (Under review). Longitudinal follow-up on infants of depressed mothers.

Field, T., Yando, R., Lang, C., Pickens, J., Martinez, A., & Bendell, D. (under review). Longitudinal follow-up of children of dysphoric mothers.

Fitzgerald, H. E., & Brackbill, Y. (1976). Classical conditioning in infancy: Development and constraints. *Psychological Bulletin*, 83, 353–376.

Fitzgerald, H. E, Davies, W. H., & Zucker, R. A. (1994). Developmental systems theory and substance abuse: A conceptual and methodological framework for analyzing patterns of variation in families. In L. L'Abate (Ed.), *Handbook of developmental family psychology and psychopathology* (pp. 350–372). New York: John Wiley & Sons.

Fitzgerald, H. E., Davis, W. H., & Zucker, R. A. (in press). Growing up in an alcoholic family: Structuring pathways for risk aggregation and theory-driven intervention. In R. MacMahon & R. deV. Peters (Eds.), *30th Banff Conference on Behavior Science, Children of disordered parents*. Thousand Oaks, CA: Sage Publications.

Fitzgerald, H. E., & Porges, S. W. (1971). A decade of infant conditioning and learning research. *Merrill Palmer Quarterly*, 17, 79–117.

Fitzgerald, H. E., Puttler, L. I., Mun, E., & Zucker, R. A. (2000). Prenatal and postnatal exposure to parental alcohol use and abuse. In J. D. Osofsky & H. E. Fitzgerald (Eds.), *WAIMH handbook of infant mental health: Vol 4. Infant mental health in groups at risk* (pp. 123–160). New York: Wiley.

Fitzgerald, H. E., Sullivan, L. A, Ham, H. P., Zucker, R. A., Bruckel, S., & Schneider, A. M. (1993). Predictors of behavioral problems in three-year-old sons of alcoholics: Early evidence for onset of risk. *Child Development*, 64, 110–123.

Fitzgerald, H. E., Zucker, R. A., Puttler, L. I., Caplan, H. M., & Mun, E. (2000). Alcohol abuse/dependence in women and girls: Aetiology, course, and subtype variations. *Alcoscope: International Review of Alcohol Management*, 3, 6–10.

Fitzgerald, H. E., Zucker, R. A., & Yang, H-Y. (1995). Developmental systems theory and alcoholism: Analyzing patterns of variation in high risk families. *Psychology of Addictive Behavior*, 9, 8–22.

Ford, D. H., & Lerner, R. M. (1992). *Developmental systems theory: An integrative approach*. Newbury Park, CA: Sage.

Fox, N. A., Schmidt, L. A., Calkins, S. D., Rubin, K. H., & Coplan, R. J. (1996). The role of frontal activation in the regulation and dysregulation of social behavior during the preschool years. *Development and Psychopathology*, 8, 89–102.

Gomberg, E. S. L. (1991). Women and alcohol: Psychosocial aspects. In D. J. Pittman & H.R. White (Eds.), *Society, culture, and drinking patterns reexamined* (pp. 263–284). New Brunswick, NJ: Rutgers Center of Alcohol Studies.

Gould, E., Reeves, A. J., Graziano, M. S., & Gross, C. G. (1999). Neurogenesis in the neocortex of adult primates. *Science*, 286, 548–552.

Gottlieb, G. (1991). Experiential canalization of behavioral development: Theory. *Developmental Psychology*, 27, 4–13.

Grant, B. F., Harford, T. C., Chou, P., Pickering, R., Dawson, Stinson, & Nobel (1991). Prevalence of DSM-III-R alcohol abuse and dependence: United States, 1988. *Alcohol Health and Research World*, 15, 91–96.

Greenough, W. T. (1991). Experience as a component of normal development: Evolutionary considerations. *Developmental Psychology*, 27, 14–17.

Harley, K., & Reese, E. (1999). Origins of autobiographical memory. *Developmental Psychology*, 35, 1338–1348.

Heath, A. C. (1995). Genetic influences on alcoholism risk: A review of adoption and twin studies. *Alcohol Health and Research World*, 19, 166–171.

Hesselbrock, M. N. (1995). Genetic determinants of alcoholic subtypes. In H. Begleiter & B. Kissin (Eds.), *The genetics of alcoholism* (pp. 40–69). New York: Oxford Press.

Hesselbrock, V. M. (1995). The genetic epidemiology of alcoholism. In H. Begleiter & B. Kissin (Eds.), *The genetics of alcoholism* (pp. 17–39). New York: Oxford Press.

Hill, S. Y. (1995a). Early-onset alcoholism in women: Electrophysiological similarities and differences by gender. In W. H. Hunt & S. Zakhari (Eds.), *Stress, gender, and alcohol-seeking behavior* (Research Monograph No. 29, pp. 61–96). Bethesda, MD: National Institutes of Health.

Hill, S. Y. (1995b). Vulnerability to alcoholism. In M. Galanter (Ed.), *Recent developments in alcoholism: Vol. 12. Women and alcoholism* (pp. 9–28). New York: Plenum.

Hinsar-Fuselier, S., Boris, N. W., & Zeanah, C. H. (1999). Reactive attachment disorder in maltreated twins. *Infant Mental Health Journal, 20,* 52–59.

Howe, M. L., & Courage, M. L. (1997). The emergence and early development of autobiographical memory. *Psychological Review, 104,* 499–523.

Huang, L. X., Cerbone, F. G., & Groerer, J. C. (1998). Children at risk because of substance abuse. In Office of Applied Studies, Substance Abuse and Mental Health Services Administration (Eds.), *Analysis of substance abuse and treatment need issues* (pp. 5–18). Rockville, MD: Author (DHHS Publication Document No. (SMA) 98–3227).

Ichiyama, M. A., Zucker, R. A., Fitzgerald, H. E., & Bingham, C. R. (1996). Articulating subtype differences in self and relational experience among alcoholic men via structural analysis of social behavior. *Journal of Consulting and Clinical Psychology, 64,* 1245–1254.

Ikonomidou, C., Bittigau, P., Ishimaru, M. J., Wozniak, D., Koch, C., Genz, K., Price, M. T., Stefovska, V., Hoerster, F., Tenkova, T., Dikranian, K., & Olney, J. W. (2000). Ethanol-induced apoptotic neurodegeneration and fetal alcohol syndrome. *Science, 287,* 1056–1060.

Institute of Medicine (U.S.), Division of Biobehavioral Sciences and Mental Disorders, Committee to Study Fetal Alcohol Syndrome (1996). [TITLE?]. In K. Stratton, C. Howe, & F. Battaglia (Eds.), *Fetal alcohol syndrome: Diagnosis, epidemiology, prevention, and treatment.* Washington, DC: National Academy Press.

Jansen, R. E., Fitzgerald, H. E., Ham, H. P., & Zucker, R. A. (1995). Pathways into risk: Temperament and behavior problems in three- to five-year-old sons of alcoholics. *Alcoholism: Clinical and Experimental Research, 19,* 501–509.

Jolivet, A., Blanchier, H., Gautray, J. P., & Dehm, N. (1974). Blood cortisol variations during late pregnancy and labor. *American Journal of Obstetrics and Gynecology, 119,* 775–783.

Jones, K. L., & Smith, D. W. (1973). Recognition of the fetal alcohol syndrome in early infancy. *Lancet, 2,* 999–1001.

Jones, K. L., Smith, D. W., Ulleland, C. N., & Streissguth, P. (1973). Pattern of malformations in offspring of chronic alcoholic mothers. *Lancet, 1,* 1267–1271.

Kagan, J., Reznick, J. S., & Snidman, N. (1987). The physiology and psychology of behavioral inhibition in children. *Child Development. 58,* 1459–1473.

Karlen, L-R. (1996). Attachment relationships among children with aggressive behavior problems: The role of disorganized early attachment patterns. *Journal of Consulting and Clinical Psychology, 64*, 64–73.

Kavanach, K., & Hops, H. (1994). Good girls? Bad boys? Gender and development as contexts for diagnosis and treatment. In T. H. Ollendick & R. J. Prinz (Eds.), *Advances in clinical child psychology* (Vol. 16, pp. 45–79). New York: Plenum.

Kessler, R. C., McGonagle, K. A., Zhao, S., Nelson, C. B., et al. (1994). Lifetime and 12-month prevalence of DSM III-R psychiatric disorders in the Unites States: Results from the National Comorbidity Study. *Archives of General Psychiatry, 51*, 8–19.

Ladd, G. W. (1996). Shifting ecologies during the 5 to 7 year period: Predicting children's adjustment during the transition to grade school. In A. J. Sameroff & M. M. Haith (Eds.), *The five to seven year shift: The age of reason and responsibility* (pp. 363–386). Chicago: University of Chicago Press.

LaGasse, L. L., & Lester, B. M. (2000). Prenatal cocaine exposure and child outcome. In H. E. Fitzgerald, B. M. Lester, & B. Zuckerman (Eds.), *Children of addiction: Research, health, and public policy issues* (pp. 29–43). New York: Routledge/Falmer.

Lang, A. R., & Stritzke, W. G. K. (1993). Young children's knowledge, attitudes, and expectations about alcohol. In M. Galanter (Ed.), *Recent developments in alcoholism* (Vol. 11, pp. 73–85). New York: Plenum.

Larkby, C., & Day, N. (1997). The effects of prenatal alcohol exposure. *Alcohol, Health & Research World, 21*, 192–198.

Lemoine, P., Harousseau, H., Bortegru, J. P., & Menuet, J. C. (1968). Les enfants de parents á propos de 127 cas. *Quest Medicine, 25*, 476–482.

Lerner, R. M., Palermo, M., Spiro III, A., & Nesselroade, J. R. (1982). Assessing the dimensions of temperamental individuality across the life span: The Dimensions of Temperament Survey (DOTS). *Child Development, 53*, 149–159.

Lester, B. M., LaGasse, L. L., & Bigsby, R. (1998). Prenatal cocaine exposure and child development: What do we know and what do we do? *Seminars in Speech & Language, 19*, 123–146.

Loukas, A., Fitzgerald, H. E., Zucker, R. A., & von Eye, A. (in press). Parental alcoholism and co–occurring antisocial behavior: Prospective relationships to externalizing behavior problems in their young sons. *Journal of Abnormal Child Psychology.*

Loukas, A., Piejak, L. A., Bingham, C. R., Fitzgerald, H. E., & Zucker, R.A. (In press). Parental distress as a mediator of problem behaviors in sons of alcohol involved families. *Journal of Family Relations.*

Main, M., & Hesse, E. (1990). Parents' unresolved traumatic experiences are related to infant disorganized attachment status: Is frightening or frightened parental behavior the linking mechanism? In M. Greenberg, D. Ciccheti, & E. M. Cummings (Eds.), *Attachment in the preschool years: Theory, research, and intervention* (pp. 161–184). Chicago: University of Chicago Press.

Markowitsch, H. J., Thiel, A., Kessler, J., von Stockhausen, H.-M, & Heiss, W.-D (1997). Ecphorising semi-conscious episodic information via the right temporaropolar cortex: A PET study. *Neurocase*, 3, 445–449.

McGue, M. (1997). A behavioral-genetic perspective on children of alcoholics. *Alcohol Health & Research World*, 21, 210–217.

Merritt, K. A., Ornstein, P. A., & Spicker, B. (1994). Children's memory for a salient medical procedure: Implications for testimony. *Pediatrics*, 94, 17–23.

Mezzich, A. C., Tarter, R. E., Moss, H. B., Yao, J. K., Hsieh, Y., & Kirisci, L. (1994). Platelet monoamine oxidase activity and temperament and personality in adolescent female substance abusers. *Personality and Individual Differences*, 16, 417–424.

Moffitt, T. E. (1993). Adolescence-limited and life-course-persistent antisocial behavior: A developmental taxonomy. *Psychological Review*, 100, 674–701.

Muller, R., Fitzgerald, H. E., Sullivan, L. A., & Zucker, R. A. (1994). Social support and stress factors in child maltreatment among alcoholic families. *Canadian Journal of Behavioral Science*, 26, 438–461.

Mun, E., Fitzgerald, H. E., Puttler, L. I., Zucker, R.A., & von Eye, A. (In press). Temperamental characteristics as predictors of externalizing and internalizing child behavior problems in the contexts of high and low parental psychopathology. *Infant Mental Health Journal*.

Nanson, J. L., & Hiscock, M. (1990). Attention deficits in children exposed to alcohol prenatally. *Alcohol: Clinical and Experimental Research, 14*, 656–661.

Nelson, C. A. (1995). The ontogeny of human memory: A cognitive neuroscience perspective. *Developmental Psychology*, 31, 723–738.

Newlin, D. B., & Thompson, J. B. (1990). Alcohol challenge with sons of alcoholics: A critical review and analysis. *Psychological Bulletin*, 108, 383–402.

Noll, R. B., Zucker, R. A., & Fitzgerald, H. E. (1990). Identification of alcohol by smell among preschoolers: Evidence for early socialization about drugs occurring in the home. *Child Development*, 61, 1520–1527.

Noll, R. B., Zucker, R. A., Fitzgerald, H. E., & Curtis, W. J. (1992). Cognitive and motoric functioning of sons of alcoholic fathers and controls: The early childhood years. *Developmental Psychology*, 28, 665–675.

Noll, R. B., Zucker, R. A., & Greenberg, G. S. (1990). Identification of alcohol by smell among preschoolers: Evidence for early socialization about drugs occurring in the home. *Child Development*, 61, 1520–1527.

O'Connor, M. J. (1996). Attachment behavior of infants prenatally exposed to alcohol: Mother infant interaction. In H. C. Steinhausen & H. L. Spohr (Eds.), *Alcohol, pregnancy, and the developing child* (pp. 183–206). Cambridge MA: Cambridge University Press.

O'Connor, M. J., & Kasari, C. (2000). Prenatal alcohol exposure and depressive features in children. *Alcoholism: Clinical and Experimental Research*, 24, 1084–1092.

O'Connor, M. J., Kogan, N., & Findlay, R. (2000a, June). *Maternal supportive presence and child coping skills as moderators of the effects of prenatal alcohol exposure on child attachment security.* Poster presented at the annual meeting of the Research Society on Alcoholism, Denver, CO.

O'Connor, M. J., Kogan, N., & Findlay, R. (2000b, June). *Mother-child interaction as a mediator between prenatal alcohol exposure and child depressive symptoms.* Poster presented at the annual meeting of the Research Society on Alcoholism, Denver, CO.

O'Connor, M. J., Sigman, M., & Brill, N. (1987). Disorganization of attachment in relation to maternal alcohol consumption. *Journal of Consulting and Clinical Psychology, 55,* 831–836.

O'Connor, M. J., Sigman, M., & Kasari, C. (1992). Disorganization of attachment in relation to maternal alcohol consumption. *Journal of Consulting and Clinical Psychology, 81,* 231–236.

Piaget, J. (1952). *The origins of intelligence.* New York: International Universities Press.

Piejak, L. A., Fitzgerald, H. E., von Eye, A., & Zucker, R. A. (under review) social competence of sons of male antisocial and nonantisocial alcoholics during the early elementary years.

Poon, E., Ellis, D. A., Fitzgerald, H. E., & Zucker, R. A. (2000). Intellectual, cognitive, and academic performances among sons of alcoholics during the early school years: Differences related to subtypes of familial alcoholism. *Alcoholism: Clinical & Experimental Research, 24,* 1020–1027.

Puttler, L. I., Zucker, R.A., & Fitzgerald, H. E. (1997). Outcome differences among female COAs during early and middle childhood years: Subtype variations. *Alcoholism: Clinical & Experimental Research, 21,* 82A (Abstract).

Puttler, L. I., Zucker, R. A., Fitzgerald, H. E., & Bingham, C. R. (1998). Behavioral outcomes among children of alcoholics during the early and middle childhood years: Familial subtype variations. *Alcoholism: Clinical & Experimental Research, 22,* 1962–1972.

Reiger, D. A., Farmer, M. E., Rae, D. S., Locke, B. Z., Keith, S. J., Judd, L., & Goodwin, F. K. (1990). Comorbidity of mental disorders with alcohol and other drug use: Results from the Epidemiologic Catchment Area (ECA) Study. *Journal of the American Medical Association, 19,* 2511–2518.

Riley, E. P., Mattson, S. N., Sowell, E. R., Jernigan, T. L., Sobel, D. F., & Jones, K. L. (1995). Abnormalities of the corpus callosum in children prenatally exposed to alcohol. *Alcoholism: Clinical & Experimental Research, 19,* 1198–1202.

Russell, M., Henderson, C., & Blume, S. (1985). *Children of alcoholics: A review of the literature.* New York: Children of Alcoholics Foundation.

Sameroff, A. J. (1995). General systems theories and developmental psychopathology. In D. Cicchetti & D. J. Cohen (Eds.), *Developmental psychopathology: Vol. 1. Theory and methods* (pp. 659–695). New York: Wiley.

Sameroff, A. (2000). Ecological perspectives on developmental risk. In J. D. Osofsky & H. E. Fitzgerald (Eds.), *Handbook of infant mental health* (Vol. 4, pp. 1–34). New York: Wiley.

SAMHSA (1998). *Preliminary results from the 1997 National Household Survey on Drug Abuse* (DHHS Publication Document No. SMA 98–3251). Rockville, MD.

Schneider W., & Bjorklund D. F. (1998). Memory. In D. Kuhn & R. S. Siegler (Eds.), *Handbook of child psychology: Vol. 2. Cognition, perception, and language* (pp. 467–521). New York: Wiley.

Shonkoff, J. P., & Phillips, D. A. (Eds.) (2000). *From neurons to neighborhoods: The science of early childhood development.* Washington, DC: National Academy Press.

Spitz, R. (1965). *The first year of life.* New York: International Universities Press.

Streissguth, A. (1997). Fetal alcohol syndrome: A guide for families and communities. Baltimore: Brookes.

Tarter, R. E. (1988). Are there inherited behavioral traits that predispose to substance abuse? *Journal of Consulting and Clinical Psychology, 56,* 189–196.

Tarter, R. E., Alterman, A. I., & Edwards, K. L. (1985). Vulnerability to alcoholism in men: A behavior-genetic perspective. *Journal of Studies on Alcoholism, 46,* 329–356.

Tarter, R. E., & Vanyukov, M. (1994). Alcoholism: A developmental disorder. *Journal of Consulting and Clinical Psychology, 62,* 1096–1107.

Toth., S. J., Connor, P. D., Barr, H., Sampson, P. D. & Streissguth, A. P. (2000, July). *Longitudinal mental health outcomes of prenatally alcohol-exposed individuals.* Poster presented at the International Conference on Infant Studies, Brighton, England.

Twitchell, G. R., Hanna, G. L., Cook, E. H., Fitzgerald, H. E., Little, K. Y., & Zucker, R. A. (1998). Overt behavior problems and serotonergic function in middle childhood among male and female offspring of alcoholic fathers. *Alcoholism: Clinical & Experimental Research, 22,* 1340–1348.

Twitchell, G. R., Hanna, G. L., Cook, E. H., Fitzgerald, H. E., & Zucker, R. A. (2000). Serotonergic function, behavioral disinhibition, and negative affect in children of alcoholics: The moderating effects of puberty. *Alcoholism: Clinical & Experimental Research, 24,* 972–979.

Twitchell, G. R., Hanna, G. L., Cook, E. H., Stoltenberg, S., Fitzgerald, H. E., & Zucker, R. A. (in press). *Alcoholism: Clinical and Experimental Research.*

Verschuren, K., Marcven, A., & Schoefs, V. (1996). The internal working model of the self: Attachment and competence in five year olds. *Child Development, 67,* 2493–2511.

Vorhees, C. V., & Mollnow, E. (1987). Behavioral teratogenesis: Long-term influences on behavior from early exposure to environmental agents. In J. D. Osofsky (Ed.), *Handbook of infant development* (pp. 913–971). New York: Wiley.

Watson, J. S. (1967). Memory and "contingency analysis" in infant learning. *Merrill Palmer Quarterly, 13,* 55–76.

Werner, E. E. (1986). Resilient offspring of alcoholics: A longitudinal study from birth to age 18. *Journal of Studies on Alcohol, 47,* 34–40.

Wilsnack, S. C. (1991). Sexuality and women's drinking: Findings from a U.S. National study. *Alcohol Health & Research World, 15,* 147–50.

Windle, M. (1997). Concepts and issues in COA research. *Alcohol Health & Research World, 21,* 185–191.

Wong, M. M., Zucker, R. A., Puttler, L. I., & Fitzgerald, H. E. (1999). Heterogeneity of risk aggregation for alcohol problems between early and middle childhood: Nesting structure variations. *Development and Psychopathology*, 11, 727–744.

Zeanah, C. H., Danis, B., Hirshberg, L., Benoit, D., Miller, D., & Heller, S. S. (1999). Disorganized attachment associated with partner violence: A research note. *Infant Mental Health Journal*, 20, 77–86.

Zucker, R. A. (1987). The four alcoholisms: A developmental account of the etiologic process. In P. C. Rivers (Ed.), *Nebraska symposium on motivation: Alcohol and addictive behaviors* (Vol. 34, pp. 27–83). Lincoln: University of Nebraska Press.

Zucker, R. A. (1991). The concept of risk and the etiology of alcoholism: A probablistic-developmental perspective. In D. J. Pittman & H. R. White (Eds.), *Society, culture and drinking patterns re-examined* (pp. 513–532). New Brunswick, NJ: Rutgers Center of Alcohol Studies.

Zucker, R. A. (1994). Pathways to alcohol problems and alcoholism: A developmental account of the evidence for multiple alcoholisms and for contextual contributions to risk. In R. A. Zucker, G. M. Boyd, & J. Howard (Eds.), *The development of alcohol problems: Exploring the biopsychosocial matrix of risk* (NIAAA Research Monograph 26, pp. 225–289). Rockville, MD: Department of Health and Human Services.

Zucker, R. A., Chermack, S. T., & Curran, G. M. (1999). Alcoholism: A lifespan perspective on etiology and course. In M. Lewis & A. J. Sameroff (Eds), *Handbook of developmental psychopathology* (2nd ed., pp. xx–xx). New York: Plenum Press.

Zucker, R. A., Ellis, D. A., Bingham, C. R., & Fitzgerald, H. E. (1996). The development of alcoholic subtypes: Risk variation among alcoholic families during the early childhood years. *Alcohol Health and Research World*, 20, 46–55.

Zucker, R. A., Ellis, D. A., & Fitzgerald, H. E. (1994). Developmental evidence for at least two alcoholisms: I. Biopsychosocial variation among pathways into symptomatic difficulty. In T. F. Babor & V. M. Hesselbrock (Eds.), Types of alcoholics: Evidence from clinical, experimental, and genetic research. Annals of the New York Academy of Sciences, 708, 134–146.

Zucker, R. A., Ellis, D. A., Fitzgerald, H. E., & Bingham, C. R. (1996). Other evidence for at least two alcoholism: II. Life course variation in antisociality and heterogeneity of alcoholic outcome. *Development and Psychopathology*, 8, 831–848.

Zucker, R. A., Ellis, D. A., Fitzgerald, H. E., Bingham, C. R., & Sanford, K. P. (1996). Other evidence that for at least two alcoholisms, II. Life course variation in antisociality and heterogeneity of alcohol outcome. *Development and Psychopathology*, 8. 831–848.

Zucker, R. A., & Fitzgerald, H. E. (1991). Early developmental factors and risk for alcohol problems. *Alcohol Health & Research World*, 15, 18–24.

Zucker, R. A., Fitzgerald, H. E., & Moses, H. (1995). Emergence of alcohol problems and the several alcoholisms: A developmental perspective on etiologic theory and life course trajectory. In D Cicchetti & D. J. Cohen (Eds.), *Developmental psychopathology: Vol. 2. Risk, disorder, and adaptation* (pp. 677–711). New York: Wiley.

Zucker, R. A., Fitzgerald, H. E., Refior, S. K., Puttler, L. I., Pallas, D., & Ellis, D. A. (2000). The clinical and social ecology of childhood for children of alcoholics: Description of a study of implications for a differentiated social policy. In H. E. Fitzgerald, B. M. Lester, & B. Zuckerman (Eds.), *Children of addiction: Research, health, and public policy issues* (pp. 109–142). New York: RoutledgeFalmer.

Zucker, R. A., Kincaid, S. B., Fitzgerald, H. E., & Bingham, C. R. (1995). Alcohol schema acquisition in preschoolers: Differences between children of alcoholics and children of nonalcoholics. *Alcoholism: Clinical and Experimental Research*, 19, 1011–1017.

AUTHORS' NOTE

During preparation of this chapter the authors were supported in part by NIAAA Grant 1RO1 AA 12217 to RAZ and HEF. Correspondence about this chapter can be directed to Hiram E. Fitzgerald, Ph.D. at the MSU-UM Longitudinal Study.

NOTE

1. Adapted with permission from: H. E. Fitzgerald, L. I. Puttler, E.-Y. Mun, & R. A. Zucker (2000). Prenatal and postnatal exposure to parental alcohol use and abuse. In J. D. Osofsky & H. E. Fitzgerald (Eds.). *WAIMH handbook of infant mental health: Vol. 4.* Infant mental health in groups at high risk (p. 150).

THE EFFECTS OF EXPOSURE TO VIOLENCE ON INFANTS
Current Perspectives and Directions for the Future

Joy D. Osofsky

10

$\blacklozenge\blacklozenge\blacklozenge\blacklozenge$

Violence in our society affects even the youngest children far too often, sometimes even occurring in their own homes where they expect and deserve to be protected. Even so, many people have difficulty thinking about infants and toddlers being affected as victims and or even as witnesses to violence. We would like to think that infants and toddlers are so young that they do not understand or are unaffected by the violence that they see, hear, or feel. The situation may be further complicated by the fact that infants and young children who are exposed to violence have no voice and have to depend on adults to take care of them and to speak for them. While young children are sometimes victimized by violence, there is also a risk if they are exposed to too much violence, that they lose the ability to empathize with the victims. In fact, infants and toddlers, even when they do not understand the experience of violence, do remember it. Therefore, it is important that we pay attention to their feelings and behaviors. Caregivers have a responsibility to help infants and young children comprehend the meaning of violence, especially since they do not have language to help them organize their experience and express their feelings. While we cannot prevent infants and toddlers from being exposed to violence either in violent neighborhoods or in their homes, we can certainly help protect them, nurture them, keep their hopes alive, and care for them. In this chapter, I will discuss what is known about the effects of exposure to violence on young children and then discuss prevention, intervention, and treatment strategies for infants and toddlers who have been exposed to violence.

THE EFFECTS OF VIOLENCE EXPOSURE ON YOUNG CHILDREN

Some definitions for discussing the effects of violence exposure on children are in order. Violence is defined as the use of physical force so as to damage or injure. Trauma is an event out of the normal range of normal experience. Children are affected by violence exposure at all ages, however, less is known about the consequences of exposure at younger ages, especially about the long term effects of such exposure. Many people erroneously assume that very young children are not affected at all, believing that they are too young to know or to remember what has happened. However, even in the earliest phases of infant and toddler development, clear associations have been found between exposure to violence and emotional and behavior problems. Infants and toddlers who witness violence show increased irritability, immature behavior, sleep disturbances, emotional distress, fears of being alone, and regression in toileting and language (Bell, 1995; Drell, Siegel, & Gaensbauer, 1993; Jaffe, Hurley, & Wolfe, 1990; Osofsky & Fenichel, 1996; Pynoos, 1993; Zeanah & Scheeringa, 1996). Exposure to trauma interferes with their normal development of trust and later exploratory behaviors (Osofsky & Fenichel, 1994). Consistent reports have even noted the presence of symptoms in these young children very similar to post-traumatic stress disorder in adults, including repeated re-experiencing of the traumatic event, avoidance, numbing of responsiveness, and increased arousal (Drell et al., 1993; Osofsky, Cohen, & Drell, 1995; Osofsky & Fenichel, 1994). In addition to the trauma that young children may experience, it is also important to consider that their parents or care-givers may be numbed, frightened, and depressed when they are exposed to trauma. For the children, it is especially difficult when they cannot depend on the trust and security that comes from caregivers who are emotionally available; consequently, children at any age may withdraw and show disorganized behaviors.

Older school-age children often experience increases in anxiety and sleep disturbances with exposure to violence (Pynoos, 1993). They often have difficulty paying attention and concentrating since they frequently experience intrusive thoughts. They are likely to understand more about the intentionality of the violence than younger children and worry about what they could have done to prevent or stop it (Drell et al., 1993; Pynoos, 1993). In extreme cases, they may exhibit symptoms of post-traumatic stress disorder. Both school age children and preschoolers exposed to violence are less likely to explore and play freely, showing less motivation to master their environment. In our clinical work with children and their families who have been traumatized, it is not unusual for parents to be unaware of their children's difficulty with concentration and school problems that frequently follow trauma from violence exposure. Some studies (Bell, 1995; Bell & Jenkins, 1991) have reported that school-aged children who witness domestic violence often show a greater frequency of externalizing (aggressive, delinquent) and internalizing (withdrawn, anxious) behavior problems in comparison to children from nonviolent families. Overall functioning, attitudes, social competence, and school performance are often affected negatively.

Much more is known about and symptoms recognized in adolescents who have experienced violence exposure throughout their lives. They are more likely to show high levels of aggression and acting out, accompanied by anxiety, behavior problems, school problems, truancy, and revenge seeking. Although some adolescents who witness violence may be able to overcome the experience, many others suffer considerable scars. Some report giving up hope, expecting that they may not live through adolescence or early adulthood. Such chronically traumatized youth often appear deadened to feelings and pain, with resultant constrictions in emotional development. Alternatively, they may attach themselves to peer groups and gangs as substitute family, incorporating and accepting violence as a way of dealing with disputes or frustration (Bell & Jenkins, 1991; Parsons, 1994; Pynoos, 1993; Prothrow-Stith, 1991).

UNDERSTANDING THE IMPACT OF VIOLENCE EXPOSURE ON INFANTS AND TODDLERS

The impact on a child of exposure to community and domestic violence depends on many factors, including the age of the child, frequency and type of violence exposure, characteristics of the neighborhood (including degree of community resources), amount and quality of support provided by caregivers and other significant adults, experience of previous trauma, proximity to the violent event, and familiarity with the victim or perpetrator (Pynoos, 1993). How much a child perceives or remembers a violent experience affects the presence or absence of symptoms and the circumstances under which they are likely to occur (Drell et al., 1993).

Adolescent problems related to violence exposure have been most visible, both in the research and clinical literature and in the media. Less well known are the problems that are frequently seen in younger children who may be exposed to violence as witnesses or victims. A common assumption is that young children are too young to know or to remember what has happened and so witnessing violence has little impact on them. In fact, this assumption is far from the reality. Young children are impacted greatly even by hearing their parents or caregivers fighting through closed doors. Research on understanding the effects of witnessing violence on children has been sorely neglected. Even in infancy and toddlerhood, in the most extreme situations, we have seen symptom patterns in children of posttraumatic stress disorder that are very similar to those seen in war veterans who have been traumatized by violence.

Although very young children may be partially protected from exposure to a traumatic incident because they do not fully appreciate the potential danger (Drell, et al, 1993; Pynoos, 1993), it is crucial to pay attention to their reactions to violence. Even the youngest of children are likely to show emotional distress, immature behavior, somatic complaints, and regressions in toileting and language (Bell, 1995; Drell et al, 1993; Jaffe, Hurley,

& Wolfe, 1990; Margolin, 1995; Osofsky, 1995; Osofsky & Fenichel, 1994; Pynoos, 1993; Scheeringa, Zeanah, Drell, & Larrieu, 1995; Zeanah & Scheeringa, 1997). As previously mentioned, the presence of symptoms very similar to post-traumatic stress disorder in adults have been noted, in the most extreme cases, including repeated reexperiencing of the traumatic event, avoidance, numbing of responsiveness, and increased arousal (Drell, et al, 1993; Osofsky et al., 1995; Osofsky & Fenichel, 1994; Scheeringa et al., 1995).

With exposure to violence at an early age, the child's view of him or herself, the world, and people in it will be impacted significantly. Because the child is so young, the rapid and complex changes that are part of normal development in the earliest years of life influence the infant's or toddler's perceptions, understanding, and experience of violence. The very young child's capacity for perceiving and remembering the experience of violence will affect the symptoms that result from exposure. If the victim or perpetrator is very close to the child, he or she may wonder whether relationships are trustworthy and dependable. If the child is exposed to violence repeatedly, the effects are likely to be more significant and/or severe as the child grows older. He or she will come to expect violence in everyday life, to be unaware of other ways to respond, and, over time, may become immune and unfeeling about such exposure.

It must be remembered that infants have very few ways of expressing their feelings and distress since they do not have language. Yet the exposure to violence has special meaning for very young children. Thus, with violence exposure, frequent responses include difficulty sleeping, clingy behavior, withdrawal, aggression, crying and irritability, eating problems, anxiety, and fearfulness. Regression in both toileting and language is common. For toddlers, it is often possible to help them use words, play, or drawings to express their feelings; however, the symptoms described above for infants are also commonly seen. Recent clinical data regarding interventions and treatment of young children who witness or are victims of violence indicate that early interventions can be quite effective in alleviating symptoms and that the symptom manifestations may be intensified if a child does not receive treatment shortly after experiencing the trauma.

THE IMPACT OF VIOLENCE EXPOSURE ON PARENTS AND THE RELATIONSHIP

For some parents and children, the stress associated with violence exposure and coping with violence as an everyday event affect both mother's ability to parent and children's capacity to form healthy attachment relationships (Osofsky & Fenichel, 1994). Since early relationships form the basis for all later relationship experiences, such difficult early interactions may be problematic for the child's later development. Poverty, job and family instability, and violence in the environment add immeasurably to the inherent difficulties. Although systematic research has not yet been conducted concerning the effects of violence exposure on parenting and the caregiving environment, we know from anecdotal reports that parents who live with violence frequently describe a sense of helplessness and frustration about their inability to protect their children and keep them safe, even in their own neighborhoods (Garbarino, Dubrow, Kostelny, & Pardo, 1992; Lorion & Saltzman, 1993; National Commission on Children, 1991; Osofsky & Fenichel, 1994; Osofsky, Wewers, Hann, & Fick, 1993; Richters & Martinez, 1993). While some parents are able to maintain their strength, creatively finding ways to cope with violent environments, the constant barrage of violence may lead other parents to communicate helplessness and hopelessness to their children.

Protecting children and facilitating their development is a family's most basic function. Regardless of their composition, families are uniquely structured to provide the attention, nurturing, and safety that children need to grow and develop. An important psychological aspect of parenting an infant or toddler is being able to provide a "holding environment" (Winnicott, 1965) in which a parent can both protect a child and allow and encourage appropriate independence. Parents who are aware that they may not be able to protect their children from violence are likely to feel frustrated and helpless. In addition, when parents witness violence or are themselves victims of violence, they are likely to have difficulty being emotionally available, sensitive, and responsive to their children. In trying to help children and parents who have been traumatized by violence exposure, we often will support the parents as they cope with their own trauma in order to help enable them to deal with their children's needs. When parents live in constant fear, their children often lack the sense of basic trust and security that is the foundation of healthy emotional development (Osofsky et al., 1995).

Another burden, rather than support, for parents may result from the traditional societal protectors of children, including schools, community centers, and churches, also being overwhelmed and unable to assure safe environments. Two recent surveys were done to identify issues of trust and safety among a group of African American parents and children living in an inner city environment with a high rate of violence according to police homicide statistics. Thirty-five percent of the parents reported that they did not feel their children were safe walking to school and 54% did not feel they were safe playing in their neighborhood. Only 17% of parents felt that the children were very safe doing these activities. However, the majority (62%) felt that the children were very safe at home and 30% felt they were very safe at school (Fick, Osofsky, & Lewis, 1997). These data are consistent with the responses of their elementary school children, ages eight through twelve, from the same neighborhoods, who reported that they felt much safer at home and in school than walking to school or playing in their neighborhood. In clinical work with traumatized young children and their families, one of the first issues that must be dealt with before any treatment can begin is whether the child and the family feel safe. There are two problems, however, in dealing with chronic community violence: 1) the continued physical reality of the violent environment; and 2) the continued posttraumatic reality for the young child and caregivers.

Exposure to violence may interfere with normal developmental transitions for both parents and children. On the one hand, violence exposure may divert the child from his or her normal developmental trajectory. On the other hand, violence exposure that occurs to their child in the neighborhood may influence parents to become overprotective, rarely allowing their children out of their sight. Yet, encouragement of autonomy is important for development and comes with trust in the safety of the environment (Erikson, 1950). For families living with violence, children's growing independence and normal exploration may be anything but safe and, therefore, not allowed. Parents who are exposed to chronic violence may also become depressed and unable to provide for their young children's needs. Even with heroic efforts, if a parent is sad and anxious, it will be more difficult to respond positively to the smiles and lively facial expressions of a young child. Depressed parents may be more irritable and may talk less often and with less intensity. All of these factors, although understandable, may influence young children to be less responsive and to feel that they may have done something "bad" to contribute to this state of affairs. Thus, supports outside of the family are very important for parents and children exposed to violence.

SUPPORTING STRENGTHS IN YOUNG CHILDREN EXPOSED TO VIOLENCE

An important, but little understood, area concerns the issue of invulnerability or resilience. Which children will experience fewer negative effects in response to exposure to community violence? Results from many studies of resilient infants, young children and youth consistently identify a small number of crucial protective factors for development (Masten, 1997; Masten, Best, & Garmezy, 1990; Rutter, 1993; Werner & Smith, 1982). The most important protective resource is a strong relationship with a competent, caring, positive adult, most often a parent. The most important personal quality is average or above average intellectual development with good attention and interpersonal skills. While catastrophic stressors such as premature birth, war, trauma, and loss can threaten the integrity of a child's ability to think and solve problems, good parenting by either a parent or other significant adult that supports both cognitive ability and positive development of relationships will proceed positively even with adversity. For children living in high violence areas, having a protected place in the neighborhood provides a "safe haven" from violence exposure. Additional protective factors include positive role models, feelings of self esteem and self efficacy, attractiveness to others in both personality and appearance, individual talents, religious affiliations, socioeconomic advantages, opportunities for good schooling and employment, and the opportunity to seek out people and environments that are positive for development. It is crucial to recognize that adult behavior, especially "good enough" parenting, plays a central role in a child's risks, resources, opportunities, and, therefore, his/her resilience.

With the increased emphasis on resilience in recent years, a factor that may improve conditions directly affecting a child's coping ability is effective parenting. Werner (1984) has carried out a landmark study on resilience, describing this phenomenon as the ability to recover from or adjust easily to misfortune or sustained life stress. Resilience is often used to describe the following outcomes in children (Werner, 1994): 1) good outcomes despite risk status; 2) sustained competence under stress; 3) recovery from trauma. Many studies, including those of Werner (1984) and Masten (1997), define a resilient child as one who is more likely to have an adaptable, easy temperament and be more intelligent. A resilient child is also more likely to have a supportive person, often a parent or caregiver, in his or her environment—a person with whom the child has a trusting relationship.

Werner (1984) found in her longitudinal study that resilient children who adapted successfully to adult life had the following protective factors: 1) an adaptable temperament that allowed them to elicit positive responses from caring adults; 2) skills and values that allowed for an assessment of the child's abilities in order to develop realistic educational and vocational goals; 3) parents or caregivers who reflected competence and fostered self-esteem in their children or other supportive adults who fostered trust. Further, resilient children sought out environments that reinforced and rewarded their competencies and helped them successfully handle life's transitions.

Much can be learned from Werner's remarkable longitudinal study. Regarding concerns about adaptive parenting, it is important to note that in her study of 698 babies born on the Hawaiian island of Kauai, resilient youth (about a third of the group) had developed a positive self-concept and an internal locus of control at the time of high school graduation. They displayed a more nurturant, responsible, and achievement oriented attitude toward life than did their high-risk peers who had developed problems in their teens. These boys and girls had grown up in families where they had not experienced prolonged separations from their primary caregivers during the first year of life. All had the chance to establish a close bond with at least one caregiver from whom they received much positive attention when they were infants. Some of this nurturance came from substitute parents, such as grandparents or older siblings, or other members of their extended family. Both parents and substitute parents served as important role models for identification for the children.

A second major body of research and study of resilience has been done as part of Project Competence, a careful longitudinal study directed by Masten and colleagues (in press) following the pioneering work in this area by Garmezy and Rutter (1983). This study includes competent children growing up with little adversity, resilient children growing up with high levels of adversity, and maladaptive children who have not been able to successfully overcome adversity. Again, they have found that the role of a good enough parent is crucial for positive outcomes in these children. Successful children, whether low or high risk, have a history of more resources than maladaptive children. Important factors for good outcomes appear to be better intellectual skills and good parenting.

Resilience in children and youth is not created in a vacuum, even with good enough parenting. Promoting positive development depends on creating healthy systems for youth in addition to healthy individuals. Thus, parents need support from the broader society and environment for parenting, educating, and socializing their children. Further, a very recent study by Masten and colleagues (in press) suggests that future understanding of the impact of factors such as parenting on developmental outcomes could benefit from disaggregating global resources such as "parenting quality" into meaningful components such as dimensions of structure, warmth, and expectations that may relate to conduct, achievement and social functioning with peers under different conditions. For example, Baldwin, Baldwin, & Cole (1990) found that the "structure" dimension of parenting, though not warmth, differed for parents of component children depending on whether they lived in dangerous or safer neighborhoods. In fact, our studies have shown that stricter parenting may be especially protective in unsafe environments (see also Osofsky, 1997).

The development of both resilience and protective factors begins in infancy and longitudinal studies have pointed consistently to factors in very young children that contribute to such strengths. Werner & Smith (1982) reported that 10% of their Asian and Polynesian cohort who had experienced four or more risk factors including perinatal complications, parental psychopathology, family instability, and chronic poverty before the age of two years old developed into competent, confident, caring adults. These resilient young children were described by their caretakers as active, affectionate, cuddly, easy infants with few problematic early behaviors. Similar observations on resilient infants were part of the Coping Project carried out many years ago at the Menninger Foundation (Murphy & Moriarity, 1987). Clinical assessments of 32 Caucasian infants revealed an active, easy-going nature and few feeding and sleep problems. These babies were also notably responsive to people and objects in their environment. Resilient babies are often characterized by responsiveness and warmth as well as an ability to seek out and relate to others in their environment. In our studies of infants of teenage mothers who did better as they developed, we observed similar positive behaviors (Osofsky, 1996).

Rutter (1993) has clarified the issue of resilience further as it relates to parenting. He cites evidence from behavioral genetics indicating that, in many circumstances, nonshared environmental influences tend to have a greater effect than shared ones. Thus, features that impact equally on all children in a family may be less important than those that impact differentially so that one child may be affected more than others. Therefore, it is not uncommon to see a family that is relatively organized, but where one child in the family is scapegoated—or favored—over others. How does a child manage to be resilient under such circumstances? He/she may distance him or herself from what is going on (for example, in some families, quarrels and fights occur and one child may be drawn into the disagreement or dispute and others remain uninvolved). In a home with parental mental illness, a less vulnerable child may manage to find emotional support outside of the home. Children, even very young children, can do a great deal to influence what happens to them. Studies done by Rutter (1990, 1993) indicate that protective effects may result from people actively planning how they deal with what happens to them, thus feeling that they have more control of their lives. Younger children may protect themselves by withdrawing and finding support outside of the family. Older children may be able to actively plan in ways that are helpful to them and make them feel less vulnerable.

A COMMUNITY-BASED VIOLENCE INTERVENTION PROGRAM (VIP)

In 1992, we initiated the Violence Intervention Program for Children and Families (VIP) in New Orleans (Osofsky, 1997) as a direct response to the crisis of rising violence in New Orleans (paralleling that in the United States as a whole) and the fact that ever increasing numbers of children were being exposed to violence as victims or witnesses. Establishing the program was challenging, as the city of New Orleans at that time experienced high levels of violence, there were continual changes in the police force, and much community organizing was met with realistic skepticism about the potential effectiveness of establishing a community-based effort involving outside agencies. My team of social workers and psychologists sat at the table for many months with resident council leaders, police, community agency representatives and mental health professionals, first establishing a level of trust and then deciding what type of program would be most helpful for the infants, children, and families. What has evolved over time is a level of trust and confidence that has permitted the program to grow, gaining an understanding from the police, residents, community schools, and parents that we are available to help, provide education, and offer services. At all times, our goals have been to help build strength within the groups we work with rather than taking over and to be available to provide advice, guidance, and services. Since the city of New Orleans recruited an excellent police superintendent in 1994 with a strong commitment to community policing, our program has evolved and grown at the same time as he and his officers, supported by the city leaders, have been effective in reducing the level of violence in the city and changing the image of the New Orleans Police Department.

The VIP program uses a systems approach designed to work with the whole community to address the problem of violence among our youth and to develop meaningful prevention and intervention efforts. It is startling that homicide has become the third leading cause of death for children between the ages of five and fourteen. In some areas of our inner cities throughout the United States, neighborhoods have become like war zones with children carrying guns and other weapons to school in order to feel safe. Mothers teach their children to watch television lying below the window sills in order to avoid random bullets.

The project aims to decrease violence through a combination of early intervention, counseling, and services to victims as well as education and prevention forums directed at police, parents, and children. A key component of the program is education of police officers about the effects of violence on children and families to increase their knowledge and sensitivity when dealing with violent incidents. In 1995, 350 police officers received such education with continued follow-up during roll call. In 1997, another massive educational effort was initiated for the entire police force, including homicide, juvenile and child abuse. By 1998, the roll call education program reached over 650 officers. Four different evaluations done to determine the effectiveness of the education for police from 1994 to 1999 indicated increased sensitivity to the needs of the traumatized children as well as increased knowledge about resources for referral. The results showed that many more police officers were responsive to the needs of young children traumatized by violence after the training and that they were likely to find ways to help them.

In an effort to reach traumatized children and families as quickly as possible, a 24-hour hotline was established to provide a resource through which children and families touched by violence could seek immediate referral, counseling, and guidance. It is available to police officers and families to obtain advice or information at the scene of community or domestic violence. The police distribute VIP cards with the hotline number to families so that they can seek help if needed. Over the course of three years, we have noted that approximately 25% of the calls on the hotline come from the police and 75% come from families to whom they have given the number. About 60% of the calls are for referrals of children twelve years old or younger (with some children as young as one to two years of age) and approximately 50% of the calls become referrals for mental health services. The funds that have been raised to support the program allow us to provide mental health services to many children and families who could not otherwise afford such services. Over the past year, over 1,200 children have been provided with a variety of therapeutic services.

In 1995, approximately one hundred children and families were referred to our clinic for consultation, therapy, or parental guidance related to exposure to violence. In 1996, as our program expanded, that number more than doubled with referrals of at least 250 children. The number of traumatized children referred for services continues to grow, with approximately 300 new cases referred each year including many very young children. Over twenty children under the age of four were referred in the six months between July 1999 and December 1999). We are have seen an increase in the number of traumatized children and families referred—not so much because more children are witnessing violence—but because more people know about our program and are recognizing the importance of prevention and early intervention. Children and families receive services in the child clinic at Louisiana State University Health Science Center's Department of Psychiatry in addition to ongoing consultations and services provided in the schools and in the community. If families do not have the financial resources to pay for services, they are provided free because of private grant support for the program, as well as crime victims assistance funding from the Louisiana Commission of Law Enforcement through a block grant from the Department of Justice.

In developing our program as a multidisciplinary effort, we worked to find ways to build relationships between community, police, mental health professionals, schools, and day care centers to address issues of prevention and services for referred children who witness violence and suffer from symptoms related to their exposure such as nightmares, disruptive behavior in school, and, in the most extreme cases, post traumatic stress disorder. We continue to problem-solve with police to develop strategies that might work better for child witnesses when they investigate violent incidents. We work with parents to find ways that they can protect their children, keep them safe, and away from scenes of violence because of the potentially-traumatizing impact on both them and their children. Further, we work to build strengths in communities to help both parents and children.

COPS FOR KIDS

COPS for KIDS is a joint program between the New Orleans Police Foundation (NOPF) and the New Orleans Police Department (NOPD) designed to enhance the effectiveness of community police in preventing juvenile crime in public housing developments. By working with businesses, individuals, and organizations around the city of New Orleans, the NOPF and NOPD provide opportunities for education and positive development for high-risk youth. COPS for KIDS assists the police in controlling illicit drugs in low-income housing by providing positive alternatives for the youth who live in the housing. It also helps create a positive bond between youth in the program, NOPD, and local businesses. Created in 1996, COPS for KIDS began operations in three of the public housing developments with the highest levels of violence and crime. In 1998, a third housing development was added to the program. The motto of the program is to "give each kid a hand up rather than a hand-out." This past summer, VIP joined with COPS for KIDS to help supplement the education program by focusing on self-esteem, anger management, and violence prevention for young children who are exposed to violence and in need of additional intervention and outreach efforts. VIP was also available to provide therapeutic services to children and families who were having behavioral problems. VIP's efforts in building on that of the police in exposing the children to different ways of thinking about themselves and their world represents an important expansion of the program and collaboration with NOPD.

Our project has continued to evolve and grow. Evaluation of the effectiveness of the work has been built into our intervention program from its inception so that we will be able to learn about what works and what does not and determine the changes that are needed to make the program more effective. We have developed materials for use in training and intervention, including a police education manual, a children's safety booklet, a parenting booklet, a quarterly newsletter about activities of the program, and a community resource directory.

DIRECTIONS FOR THE FUTURE

It is no longer possible to assume that infants and toddlers are too young to comprehend and react when they are exposed to violence. Still, more education is needed about the effects of violence exposure on children so that health care, mental health care, and child care professionals recognize the signs and symptoms and know what can be done. In this way, infants and young children will no longer be silent victims.

Yet we still have little comprehension of the long term effects of exposure to violence on young children. Studies have been hampered by several factors: 1) difficulties in carrying out randomized trials with samples that are often at very high psychosocial risk; 2) the absence of reliability and validity for many of the measures frequently used to study violence exposure (at least some of the standardized measures that are available to study outcomes and validate the violence exposure measures have been developed on populations coming from different racial and socioeconomic groups than most children exposed to violence); 3) resisting controlled studies that may or may not produce outcomes beneficial to children; 4) experiences of violence exposure are often difficult to hear, and, therefore it may take time and effort to communicate. Further, there is tendency to hide or distort the facts and to avoid dealing with the issues.

To date, much more is known from a retrospective than prospective research lens about processes that lead to violent behavior. Carefully designed evaluation research studies are needed to understand the causes of violent behavior and to learn more about factors that mitigate against violence in high risk situations. Studies should include prospective longitudinal designs to investigate the long term psychological effects of exposure to violence on children with children of different ages, socioeconomic backgrounds, and ethnic and cultural backgrounds. Evaluation is needed of the cumulative effects of repeated exposure and the differential effects of severity of exposure, especially when the child may be familiar with the victim and/or perpetrator.

Research is needed on factors that support the resilience of children and buffer them against adverse effects of violence exposure. Significant longitudinal research has been done on determinants of resilience and conditions that serve as protective factors (see Egeland, Weinfield, Bosquet, & Cheng, 2000; Masten, et al., in press; Rutter, 1993; Werner & Smith, 1982). However, careful longitudinal studies within primarily high risk inner city populations where much of the violence in the United States occurs have yet to be done.

Broad based epidemiologic studies are needed to determine the differential effects of witnessing violence, being victimized by violence, the severity of the exposure, and the differential effects of being exposed to an acute trauma as compared with chronic ongoing violence. If possible, the epidemiological work should attempt to sort out the differential impact of community versus domestic violence exposure on children. Samples should include children of different ages, socioeconomic backgrounds, and ethnic or cultural backgrounds. The inclusion of information about violence exposure would be useful to include in national surveys. This information would be helpful in relation to the training of professionals who work with children as well as in planning prevention and intervention strategies.

Studies are needed about prevention efforts and the processes that lead to violent behavior. To date, little is known about these processes from a research perspective. It is probable that juvenile court judges and probation officers know more about the causes of violence in youth than researchers and interventionists. Related to understanding the causes of violent behavior, carefully designed evaluation research studies are needed to learn more about factors that mitigate against violence in high risk situations.

Far too little attention is given to an understanding of the lives of children who grow up in environments of chronic violence. In clinical work with children under the age of 5 who have been exposed to violence, concerns have been raised about the children's negotiation of developmental transitions in later life. For example, how will young children exposed to severe early trauma cope when they are confronted with later experiences of death and mortality, when they struggle with sexuality during adolescence, or when they deal with anger and aggression as well as affection toward others? This is an area sorely in need of careful research and clinical follow-up studies. Studies should include prospective longitudinal designs to investigate the long term psychological effects of exposure to violence on children. Studies should also include children of different ages, socioeconomic backgrounds, and ethnic and cultural backgrounds. Evaluation is needed of the cumulative effects of repeated exposure, the differential effects of severity of exposure, proximity to the event, and the child's familiarity with the victim and/or perpetrator.

CONCLUSION

Violence and children's exposure to violence is a complex problem that will require multifaceted solutions. Community-based programs that combine primary prevention efforts through education and raising awareness with interventions at a variety of levels—individual, family, and community—are likely to be most effective. It is easy to become overwhelmed in dealing with young children and families exposed to violence with the stress, disorganization, and dysfunction that can result. It is important to be able to understand and communicate to both the family and intervener what can be done to help and what we may not be able to accomplish. For example, if the caregiver cannot provide basic safety for the child, the chances of full recovery and ability to work effectively for change will be greatly hampered. However, keeping the perspective of dealing with the problem at a systems level, involving community groups, schools, and other supports, and with each individual child and family, allows for a more positive framework that will support the victims, the interveners, and the treaters.

REFERENCES

Baldwin, A. L., Baldwin, C., & Cole, R. E. (1990). Stress-resistance families and stress resistant children. In J. Rolf, A. S. Masten, D. Cicchetti, K. H. Nuechterlein, & S. Weinraub (Eds.), *Risk and protective factors in the development of psychopathology* (pp. 257–280). New York: Cambridge University Press.

Bell, C. C. (1995, January 6). Exposure to violence distresses children and may lead to their becoming violent. *Psychiatric News,* pp. 6–8, 15.

Bell, C. C., & Jenkins, E. J. (1991). Traumatic stress and children. *Journal of Health Care for the Poor and Underserved, 2,* 175–185.

Drell, M., Siegel, C., & Gaensbauer, T. (1993). Post-traumatic stress disorders. In C. Zeanah (Ed.), *Handbook of infant mental health* (pp. 291–304). New York: Guilford Press.

Egeland, B., Weinfield, N. S., Bosquet, M., & Cheng, V. K. (2000). In J. D. Osofsky & H. E. Fitzgerald (Eds.), *WAIMH handbook of infant mental health* (Vol 4, pp. 35–90). New York: Wiley.

Erikson, E. (1950). *Childhood and society.* New York: Norton.

Fick, A. C., Osofsky, J. D., & Lewis, M. L. (1997). Police and parents' perceptions and understanding of violence. In J. D. Osofsky (Ed.), *Children in a violent society* (pp. 261–276). New York: Guilford Press.

Garbarino, J., Dubrow, N., Kostelny, K., & Pardo, C. (1992). *Children in danger: Coping with the consequence of community violence.* San Francisco: Jossey-Bass.

Garmezy, N., & Rutter, M. (Eds.) (1983). *Stress, coping and development.* New York: McGraw-Hill.

Jaffe, P. G., Hurley, D. J., & Wolfe, D. (1990). Children's observations of violence: I. Critical issues in child development and intervention planning. *Canadian Journal of Psychiatry, 35,* 466–470.

Jaffe, P. G., Wolfe, D. A., & Wilson, S. K. (1990). Children of battered women. Newbury Park, CA: Sage.

Lorion, R., & Saltzman, W. (1993). Children's exposure to community violence: Following a path from concern to research to action. In D. Reiss, J. E. Richters, M. Radke-Yarrow, & D. Scharff (Eds.), *Children and violence* (pp. 55–65). New York: Guilford Press.

Margolin, G. (1995, January). *The effects of domestic violence on children.* Paper presented at the Conference on Violence against Children in the Family and Community, Los Angeles.

Masten, A. (1997). Resilience in children at risk. In *Research/Practice: A Publication from the Center for Applied Research and Educational Improvement.* Minneapolis: University of Minnesota, College of Education and Human Development.

Masten, A., Hubbard, J. J., Gest, S. D., Tellegen, A, Garmezy, N., & Ramirez, M. (in press). Competence in the context of adversity: Pathways to resilience and maladaptation from childhood to late adolescence. *Development and Psychopathology,* 1998.

Masten, A. S., Best, K. M., & Garmezy, N. (1990). Resilience and development: Contributions from the study of children who overcome adversity. *Development and Psychopathology*, 2, 425–444.

Murphy, L., & Moriarity, A. (1987). *Vulnerability, coping, and growth from infancy to adolescence.* New Haven, CT: Yale University Press.

National Commission on Children. (1991). *Speaking of kids.* Washington, DC.

Osofsky, J. D. (1995). The effects of exposure to violence on young children. *American Psychologist*, 50, 782–788.

Osofsky, J. D. (1996). Psychosocial risk for adolescent parents and infants: Clinical implications. In J. Noshpitz, S. Greenspan, S. Weider, & J. D. Osofsky (Eds.), *Handbook of child and adolescent psychiatry* (Vol. 1, pp. 177–190). New York: Wiley.

Osofsky, J. D. (1997). *Children in a violent society.* New York, NY: Guilford Press.

Osofsky, J. D., Cohen, G., & Drell, M. (1995). The effects of trauma on young children: A case of two-year-old twins. *International Journal of Psychoanalysis*, 76, 595–607.

Osofsky, J. D., & Fenichel, E. (Eds.). (1994). *Caring for infants and toddlers in violent environments: Hurt, healing, and hope.* Arlington, VA: Zero to Three/National Center for Clinical Infant Programs.

Osofsky, J. D., & Fenichel, E. (Eds.). (1996). *Islands of safety: Assessing and treating young victims of violence.* Washington, DC: Zero to Three/National Center for Clinical Infant Programs.

Osofsky, J. D., Wewers, S., Hann, D. A., & Fick, A. C. (1993). Chronic community violence: What is happening to our children? *Psychiatry*, 56, 36–45.

Parsons, E. R. (1994). Inner city children of trauma: Urban violence traumatic stress response syndrome (U-VTS) and therapists' responses. In J. Wilson & J. Lindy (Eds.), *Countertransference in the treatment of post-traumatic stress disorder* (pp. 151–178). New York: Guilford.

Prothrow-Stith, D. (1991). *Deadly consequences.* New York: Harper Collins.

Pynoos, R. S. (1993). Traumatic stress and developmental psychopathology in children and adolescents. In J. M. Oldham, M. B. Riba, & A. Tasman (Eds.), *American Psychiatric Press review of psychiatry* (Vol. 12). Washington, DC: American Psychiatric Press.

Richters, J. E., & Martinez, P. (1993). The NIMH community violence project: Vol. 1. Children as victims of and witnesses to violence. *Psychiatry*, 56, 7–21.

Rutter, M. (1990). Psychosocial resilience and protective mechanisms. In A. Rolf, A. S. Masten, D. Cicchetti, K. H. Nuechterlien, & S. Weintraub (Eds.), *Risk and protective factors in the development of psychopathology* (pp. 181–214). New York: Cambridge University Press.

Rutter, M. (1993). Resilience: Some conceptual considerations. *Contemporary Pediatrics*, 11, 36–48.

Scheeringa, M. S., Zeanah, C. H., Drell, M. J., & Larrieu, J. L. (1995). Two approaches to the diagnosis of posttraumatic stress disorder in infancy and early childhood. *Journal of the American Academy of Child and Adolescent Psychiatry*, 34, 191–200.

Werner, E. E. (1984). Resilient children. *Young Children, 40,* 68–72

Werner, E. E. (1994). Overcoming the odds. *Developmental and Behavioral Pediatrics,* 15, 131–36.

Werner, E. E., & Smith, R. S. (1982). *Vulnerable but invincible: A study of resilient children.* New York: McGraw-Hill.

Winnicott, D. (1965). *The maturational processes and the facilitating environment.* Madison, CT: International Universities Press.

Zeanah, C. Z., & Scheeringa, M. (1996). Evaluation of posttraumatic symptomatology in infants and young children exposed to violence. In J. D. Osofsky & E. Fenichel (Eds.), *Islands of safety: Assessing and treating young victims of violence.* Washington DC: Zero to Three.

Zeanah, C. H., & Scheeringa, M. S. (1997). The experiences and effects of violence in infancy. In J. Osofsky (Ed.), *Children in a violent society.* New York: Guilford Press.

EARLY CHILDHOOD INTERVENTIONS
Now What?

Jon Korfmacher

11

• • • •

This chapter will examine some issues and controversies in intervention programs for infants, toddlers, and their families.[1] It takes a two-pronged approach, exploring the challenges both in implementing these programs and in adequately studying and evaluating them. As such, it joins a host of reviews that have looked at these programs over the past two decades, and wonders why answers to many of the questions raised in reviews of this kind are so maddeningly elusive.

WHAT ARE EARLY INTERVENTION PROGRAMS?

The term "early childhood interventions" is extraordinarily broad, as programs for young children and their families encompass a large number of professions, foci of development, and methods. Early intervention services may mean: health or nursing services for medically fragile infants; services such as physical therapy, occupational therapy, speech and language therapy, and child development activities for children showing developmental delay; family preservation services for families with current child maltreatment; or infant mental health services for cases where there is an identified problem in the parent-child dyad. It may also mean preventative services to statistically "at-risk" families of young children, risk being defined by a number of variables including income, parent age, birth experience and outcome, first-time parenting, and parent history of mental illness or substance use.

The targeted domains of development may be cognitive, social, emotional, physical, or family, in any combination. Programs serve the parent, the child, the dyad, or the whole family. They have various entry points into the family: working directly with the child, focusing on the parent-child relationship, providing direct instruction to the parent about the child, providing emotional or therapeutic support to the parent that indirectly impacts the child, or working with the entire family as a system.

They may be center-based, home-based, or both. Interveners may be para-professionals, nurses, social workers, child development specialists, early childhood educators, counselors, childcare workers, psychologists, or psychiatrists. Programs may start prenatally or at any time after the child's birth. The number of sessions can range from one to the hundreds, with programs lasting from hours to years. From the risk group, to the focus, to the technique, to the evaluation format, there is a "pervasive idiosyncrasy and diversity" (Halpern, 1984; p. 36) that makes it difficult to identify the field.

Not only does complexity reside among programs, the experience of participants within a program can vary quite radically. Targeting the same specific problems for all families who participate in an intervention is usually not realistic. Because they do not all begin an intervention at the same level of risk or resilience, participants within the same project may have radically different experiences—they have differing levels of participation, different relationships with their service providers, and different areas of intervention focus. And even a single participant has different experiences across the time-span of program involvement. Case studies (e.g., Greenspan et al., 1987) demonstrate the multitude of interventions employed for each family throughout their participation in a program.

THE RECURRENT DILEMMA

Do these programs work? Although making summary statements about a field with such disparate elements is daunting, if not impossible, this has not stopped researchers in the last two decades from trying to answer this question. The general conclusion is that the effects of early childhood interventions are positive, but modest. This conclusion is seen both in meta-analyses, with their small to moderate average effect sizes (e.g., Casto & Mastropieri, 1986), and in discursive reviews of the literature, with demonstrations that some studies show positive results, but that others do not (Gomby, Culross, & Behrman, 1999; Gray & Wandersman, 1980; Halpern, 1984, 1990; Heinicke, Beckwith, & Thompson, 1988; Olds & Kitzman, 1993; Patteson & Barnard, 1990).[2] It is difficult to find individual studies with very large or consistent effect sizes. Studies may show significant change in some outcome areas, but not in others. Some sub-groups of families may show benefit, while others do not. Multi-site studies may show program benefits at one location, but not in others. Initial findings may seem promising, but may ultimately disappear over time.

Modest results are a recurrent conclusion, and yet each time comprehensive reviews are published, there seems to be great consternation as to the results, as well as policy-level debates about the value and need for these programs. This has recently been demonstrated in the reaction to the review by Gomby and colleagues (1999), which is critical of the potential of home visiting programs to influence family and child development—a provocative conclusion given the popularity of home visiting as a means of delivering early childhood services.

It seems fair to say that early intervention works, but not as consistently as hoped, not as strongly as hoped, and not across as many areas of the parent's and child's development as hoped. Answering *why* this is so is more difficult. The obvious places to look for answers are in the programs themselves and in the methods used to evaluate the programs. Where you stand on this issue (that is, which side you prefer to "blame" for the modest results) is likely indicative of whether you are a researcher or a service provider.

Problems with Programs

To look at these programs, one must also look at the context surrounding them. Childhood, especially young childhood, may be romanticized in our culture, but that does not necessarily lead us to value children or to value services for those children who are in need. The painful lack of funding available to infant and toddler child care programs—even in the context of welfare reform, where many parents need to be working outside the home—is an obvious sign of this (Scarr, 1998). Plenty of statistics exist to show that government policies at the federal, state, and local levels do not provide for the needs of our youngest (e.g., Annie E. Casey Foundation, 1999). Support for young children and their families is neither mandated nor available for all families in the United States. This is one primary way that services here are different from those in many European countries, where early childhood programs exist within a system of universal care and services for families (e.g., Kamerman & Kahn, 1993). In this context, intervention programs have their work cut out for them in attempting to fill the need of some of the most vulnerable young children and their families.

But even in the most supportive atmosphere, early childhood intervention programs are simply very hard to implement from the top down. Needs of the community to be served must be congruent with program goals, and the services must be culturally relevant for families. A center-based enriched day program, for example, may not be welcome in a rural area where families are scattered over a large distance, or in a neighborhood where families believe strongly in extended family childcare. Local political factors also exist in any early intervention program, and the program manager must establish community support and make sure project goals match those of other influential people within the community (Rolf, Bevin, Hasazi, Crowther, & Johnson, 1982).

This assumes that the programs themselves have clearly-defined plans of action. However, programs often have difficulty articulating these goals, or their theory of change regarding how they expect their specific interventions to reach these goals. It is not unusual to find programs that use a model of family support (see Kagan & Weissbourd, 1994), hoping to see dramatic gains in child cognitive development, when it is not clear exactly how provision of emotional and/or practical support to the parent translates to child cognitive development. This is not to say that it is impossible to have an indirect influence on child development through supporting a parent. But programs need to clearly define *how* the particular support they provide will assist in this goal.

And even well-articulated program goals can be difficult to attain. Service providers may interpret intervention goals differently and engage in their own form of work. For example, an ethnographic exploration of the Child and Family Resource Program (Nauta & Hewett, 1988) suggested why no treatment effects were found for child development scores. Contrary to initial assumptions, little time was actually spent in the tasks designed to target the infant's development. And front line staff have to negotiate these goals with families. Child abuse prevention programs, for example, rarely advertise themselves as such to families (and rarely do families enter these programs with the explicit goal of not abusing their children). Program staff and families frequently have disparate agendas, and both parties need to find some common ground where they can work together.

As in other intervention fields, early childhood interventions also have their share of very difficult families. Prevention programs serving at-risk groups will have families within their caseload with active child maltreatment or significant mental health issues. One such program found *mean* intake scores on a measure of personality functioning to approach clinical ranges for their sample of low-income, first-time parents (Egeland, Erickson, Butcher, & Ben-Porath, 1991). Many early childhood programs, in fact, pride themselves on being able to reach out to vulnerable, stressed, isolated, and distrustful families, providing a lifeline of support. They do this by being open, empathic, and flexible with the parents, working with them on any issues that will foster a positive working alliance.

This looseness in program models seems to be tolerated fairly well in early interventions. So, even though empirically-driven, manualized interventions are increasingly promoted in prevention research and in psychological therapy research (e.g., Institute of Medicine, 1994; Kendall, 1998), there are fewer advocates for such manualized treatments for early childhood programs (Carter et al., 1996; Ramey & Ramey, 1998). Instead, many program designers have taken to heart the conclusions of an influential review of intervention programs across the lifespan (Schorr, 1988) that the best interventions: offer a broad spectrum of services, are coherent and continuous, are fundamentally flexible, and emphasize personal aspects of the intervention, offering families and individual the services they need when they need it.

As such, these interventions may be seen as more ecologically friendly, adaptable to local community concerns, and better able to address the individual needs of families given the contexts that they live in. But perhaps this flexibility may also exist because the field as a whole does not have a very good idea of the best way to approach preventive interventions with infants and toddlers. So a "kitchen sink" approach, where just about anything can be tried and/or tolerated, is an artifact of our searching for viable intervention approaches.

Problems with Research

Program model looseness can also wreak havoc with careful, empirical research design. Difficulties in accurately capturing a program empirically will contribute to the relatively modest results seen in program evaluations. The flexibility so valued in many programs makes systematic and uniform evaluation of progress across participants difficult. Programs can better quantitatively demonstrate their effectiveness if they target selectively, using narrow age ranges with identifiable problems, maintaining a strong focus on very specific areas of change, using standardized assessment procedures, and using standard treatment administration across all families (Halpern, 1984, 1990).

In other words, more explicit and less spontaneous interventions allow evaluations that can demonstrate results more conclusively. But some, like Schorr (1988), call the search for standardized and specific treatments "our yearning for simplicity" (p. 264) and believe they are not realistic for those at highest risk where intervention is most needed. In these cases, providers must be prepared to try different approaches to see what best works for the family's particular needs and level of functioning. The irony, under this reasoning, is that programs more applicable to the "real world" have more difficulty demonstrating their application. The argument is attractive, but unfortunately also unfalsifiable.

This debate has been developing for some time now. Prevention science has often noted that randomized trials need to be considered the "gold standard" for program efficacy examinations (e.g., Institute of Medicine, 1994; National Institute of Mental Health [NIMH], 1993). The reason for this is fairly straightforward. Randomized trials are the only way to demonstrate that families who participate in an intervention perform differently at outcome than other, similar, families who did not receive the intervention. The assignment to a program or comparison group has to be random at the beginning because this greatly increases the chances that the participants in the program and comparison group will be similar at the beginning of the program. If the comparison group is made up of applicants different from the applicants for the treatment group, then some extraneous variable (motivation to change, family configuration, living environment, history of psychopathology, etc.) could produce the differences between the two groups that would then be incorrectly attributed to the program.

As the above demonstrates, however, randomized trials are conservative, focused on ruling out alternative explanations when program effects are found. That is, they are designed to reduce the number of *false positives*, findings where the evaluator may attribute success to the program where there is not success to be attributed. They do very little for *false negatives*, cases where the evaluator may not detect program effects that actually exist.

For example, it is an unfortunate artifact of their design that in randomized trials, one must include in outcome analyses all families assigned to the treatment group, even those families who (for whatever reason) had little or no contact with the intervention program. The reasoning for this is entirely appropriate: Differential attrition must be guarded against, so that one does not have in the treatment group only those families committed enough to stay with the program, so that the researcher simply compares them to all families in the comparison group, including those families that (unknown to the researcher) would have dropped out of the treatment group if they had been assigned to it. It does, however, set up the odd circumstance that families who had no contact with the program are given the same weight and burden of representing the treatment group as those who participated fully and eagerly in the intervention.

Randomized trials are also conservative in that a program may show significant positive changes in families, but these changes will not be valued if the comparison group also shows positive changes. For example, an "unsuccessful" randomized trial of a large-scale home visiting case management initiative, the Comprehensive Child Development Program (CCDP; St. Pierre & Layzer, 1999; St. Pierre, Layzer, Goodson, & Bernstein, 1997), showed that families with a home visitor were no different after five years from a group of families who received typical community services. Both groups, however, showed improvement over time in child language and achievement scores, maternal employment, welfare use, and depression. Rather than being ineffective it may be that the CCDP was simply not *more* effective in bringing about the measured outcomes than typical community services. A randomized trial, however, does not allow for careful examination of this issue. The lack of differences between the treatment and control group leads by default to the conclusion that the treatment was not useful.

Beyond randomized trials, there are features of empirical research in general that can be difficult for program evaluation. Strict advocates of the scientific method emphasize a need for researchers to keep an objective distance from the program that they study. According to this view, researchers should act unobtrusively around the intervention, measuring children and families, but not relating their impressions of measurements until well after the intervention is concluded. Attempts to provide feedback to programs are seen as "experimenter effects" and threaten the study's internal validity.

Although these concerns of losing objectivity and empirical rigor are valid in some evaluation contexts, there is a cost to this rigor. Empirical research establishes artificial constraints on programs, setting boundaries and limitations that disrupt the natural flow of families into program and services. As such, many empirical methods are not equipped to study contextual factors that impinge upon or promote early childhood programs as they exist in local communities. A randomized trial, for example, will alter the motivation of participants in joining a study/intervention, putting off some families who don't want the uncertainty of assignment but also encouraging others who have no interest in the study but for the financial incentives commonly offered for taking part in the research. And referral sources in the community may not want to send families to programs where there is little chance for receiving services if they do not fit selection criteria or are assigned to the comparison group.

Finally, it should be noted that a "hands-off" approach can also have repercussions on the relationship that develops between researcher and program. Program staff may react negatively to the perceived rigidity of client flow and program operations. For example, they may want to make exceptions to the random assignment for families whom they feel particularly need their services, or whom community referral sources strongly pressure them to take. Staff may also find researchers to be withholding of important outcome data that could affect how they work with clients until it is "too late," after the program families under study have terminated. And since a certain amount of skepticism is part of the culture of empiricism, program staff may also feel that researchers are unsupportive of their efforts and are, in fact, actively seeking negative results.

For their part, researchers have difficulties when program staff make modifications to the ways they deliver services after the trial is already underway, changing their program model in a way that may make sense for their current caseload but that wreaks havoc on assumptions of an operationalizable intervention that is similar for all participants. And they may resent the efforts of program staff to draw them into program operation issues, or to become "cheerleaders" for their program, since this could taint how objectively they are seen by their professional community when reporting outcome results (the "allegiance effect"; see Kendall, 1998).

A COMPROMISE

The solution is a broader conception of program evaluation research. Although program evaluations that are tightly experimentally-based (that is, efficacy trials) by their nature do not allow for an active dialogue between the researcher and the clinician, such trials are but one evaluation tool. In contrast to a prevention science approach, a collaborative community action research approach emphasizes methodologies that may be less empirically rigorous, but ecologically more valid (Weissberg & Greenberg,

1998). The model of continuous improvement analyses, for example, where evaluators feed information back to programs and providers during the course of the intervention in order to promote changes or improvements, is increasingly being promoted. Action research methods (e.g., Lewin, 1946; Whyte, 1984) assume a more dynamic and collaborative relationship between evaluator and program. These alternative assessment approaches should be seriously considered for interventions that are in their own period of growth and development, or that exist in a community or context where a strict efficacy trial is not feasible.

Many of these approaches rely heavily on qualitative methodologies. Qualitative examination of program models is a critical aspect of our attempts to understand complicated interventions. Nauta & Hewitt's (1988) ethnographic study, for example, provides insight regarding the importance of monitoring the goals and objectives of program staff. Case studies (e.g. Greenspan et al., 1987; Bromwich, 1981) illustrate important principles of helping families and give a sense of the challenges involved in doing these programs. Focus groups and in-depth interviews (e.g., Gilkerson & Stott, 1998) provide information from the perspective of the families, allowing participants to tell their story of what the intervention means to them.

Obviously, this chapter does not advocate the elimination of randomized trials in early childhood intervention research, but rather advocates that they be seen as only one evaluation tool. Randomized trials are an important source of information about the value of an intervention, but they by themselves cannot determine that value. Other methods of study also inform public and professional opinion. They are subject to different forms of confounds and bias than randomized trials, but if used rigorously, reasonable conclusions can be drawn about a program's value and effectiveness.

Qualitative research and quantitative research can, and should, co-exist. A recommendation for more qualitative research has, in fact, been made by the NIMH Prevention Research Steering Committee (NIMH, 1993). The committee noted that qualitative methodology helps us "understand the exact nature and variability of impact" and provides "indications for refining theoretical and intervention models as well as leads for subsequent studies" (pg. 46). For example, a randomized trial of a nurse home visiting model for first-time, low-income parents and their infants conducted by David Olds and colleagues in Memphis (Olds, Henderson et al., 1999) added a qualitative component to the research plan. One element involved nurses dictating narratives of selected cases or "critical moments" in the treatment process, which were then transcribed and subjected to a content analysis to allow for summary conclusions (Kitzman, Cole, Yoos, & Olds, 1997). Much was revealed about the complexities in conducting home-visiting programs, such as how home visitors focus attention with multiple caretakers for the child, deal with unsafe neighborhoods, and introduce structured parent guidance into visits. The next replication of the program in Denver used this knowledge to further refine both the intervention protocol and the assessment measures.

Broadening the Question

An expansion of methodologies goes hand in hand with an expansion of the types of research questions that need to be asked about an intervention program. Instead of the typical outcome question "Does the program work?", a more important set of questions to ask is "How did the intervention best work? For whom? Under what circumstances?" This involves more complicated analyses—examining participants, program features, the ecosystem where families and programs operate, and the area where client, program and contextual factors intersect—in order to understand the differential response families show to early childhood programs. This line of inquiry is sometimes noted as the study of process, since it is often focused on the processes by which interventions work (or fail to work) and the meanings that participants place on the program.

One example is the examination of the relationship that develops between the service provider and the family. This helping relationship is frequently noted in the literature theoretically and clinically as a crucial change agent in early childhood programs (e.g., Emde, Korfmacher, & Kubicek, in press; Heinicke & Ponce, 1998; Olds & Kitzman, 1993). Early intervention research has studied the helping relationship to some extent, measuring program engagement (Belsky, 1986), program "taking" (Osofsky, Culp & Ware, 1988), the affective bond the subject forms with the clinician (Greenspan et al., 1987), achievement of treatment goals (Barnard et al., 1988), commitment (Korfmacher, Adam, Ogawa, & Egeland, 1997), and program receptivity (Rauh, Achenbach, Nurcombe, Howell, & Teti, 1988). Most of these studies were able to show a connection between program engagement and program outcomes. These are similar constructs to those in psychotherapy process research, such as client openness, which consistently predict psychotherapeutic outcomes (see Orlinsky, Grawe, & Parks, 1994, and Orlinsky & Howard, 1986).

There is an inherent "messiness" to studies of program process that can be problematic. Although the data support the value of client engagement with service providers, for example, we do not yet understand what are the important aspects of the helping relationship to study, or how best to examine them. The above studies operationalized the helping relationship mostly in terms of contributions by an individual within the relationship rather than as a dyadic process. Features specific to the individual helping relationship also need to be considered. For example, the *match* between therapist and patient is frequently shown to be an important program element in adult psychotherapy (see Beutler, Machado, & Neufeldt, 1994).

This is assumed to be so in early childhood interventions, although it has not been extensively studied (Korfmacher, 1998). An additional distinction that should be made is between the parent and child as program participant. With few exceptions (e.g., Liaw, Meisels, & Brooks-Gunn, 1995), there has been no attempt to measure the child's contribution in the intervention, although there is ample evidence from the child care literature (e.g., Howes & Smith, 1995) that child activities in a center-based setting can be reliably measured and the relationship between staff and child can be assessed.

These relationship issues are even more complicated when one takes into consideration other aspects of program process, such as the specific interventions or program curricula that are attempted with families, the amount and frequency of contacts with families, or the efforts that are made to involve family members besides the primary caregiver and child. There are complex interactions between family need and program use, so that a linear relationship between engagement and positive program outcome is likely too simplistic. For example, higher risk families may need more intervention and thus be visited more (Olds & Korfmacher, 1998), although their outcomes may still end up worse than lower risk families who need and use the intervention less frequently.

Participants respond to interventions in unique ways based upon personal histories and characteristics. For example, a recurrent theme in case studies of infant mental health programs (e.g., Greenspan et al., 1987) is that parent participants with childhood histories of loss, trauma, or neglect are more difficult to engage in a treatment alliance, most likely because their internal working models of self and others will not allow for the development of close, trusting relationships with others (see Erickson, Korfmacher, & Egeland, 1992). Different studies have demonstrated this finding empirically on three separate home visiting programs. In two of these studies, the adult attachment interview (Main, 1991)—a measure of how people organize and understand memories of their caregiver from early childhood—were conducted on participants in home visiting programs. In both studies, results showed that mothers who had more difficulty putting past relationships into an organized and coherent perspective were more difficult to engage in a helping relationship (Korfmacher, Adam et al., 1997; Solchany, Spieker, Barnard, & McKenna, 1999). A third study, using a different self-report measure of childhood history, examined mothers who had to switch over to a new home visitor after their original visitor left (Korfmacher, McCullough, & Olds, 1997). Those mothers with a reported history of rejection from their caregivers seemed particularly affected by this relationship disruption, based on outcomes in parent attitudes and feelings of mastery.

Environmental and cultural factors also influence people's response to services. Qualitative study of the Memphis nurse home visiting program noted previously, for example, suggested that teen mothers often felt that they simply did not have time for home visits, given their desire to socialize with friends and their obligations to their extended family network (Kitzman et al, 1997). Although it may have been surprising at first to have teen moms (many not working or in school) who were too busy for biweekly visits, this was a constraint that the nurse home visitors had to work around. Transportation issues, access to a phone, stability of living arrangements, neighborhood safety—all of these are also variables that influence how families respond to and use both home and center-based services.

These program, personal, historical, and environmental factors are crucial avenues of exploration for early intervention research. They will impact the meaning and value families place on services and will help determine their individual trajectories during and beyond the intervention period. Although these factors can be examined to some extent within the context of controlled clinical trials (see Powell & Grantham-McGregor, 1989, for an example of studying program intensity using a randomized trial), it is clear that the complexity of these issues calls for corresponding complexity and flexibility in research methodology to adequately capture the experience of participants.

FUTURE DIRECTIONS

More intensively studying early childhood interventions and understanding the experience of participants in programs and the meaning that they attach to these services needs to be a serious aspect of early childhood intervention research. Forward-looking chapters should always end with a section on what we should do next, so this chapter concludes with a focus on three major points that will likely increase in importance in early childhood intervention research: 1) Examination of change over time; 2) Understanding the service provider; and 3) Contextual and systems issues in early childhood interventions.

Change over Time

For convenience viewed as static entities, most measures of intervention process have been unchanging across an intervention. Psychotherapy research, however, shows that the treatment alliance changes over the course of therapy, and that early alliance is a better predictor of outcome than later alliance (see Horvath & Luborsky, 1993). Examining how the process and meaning of interventions change over time and how these changes effect outcome requires a means of collecting process data from multiple time periods and sophisticated approaches towards analyzing data. New methods of measuring individual difference in development over time (e.g., Collins & Horn, 1991; Speer & Greenbaum, 1995) provide opportunities for studying change in response to intervention. These techniques have not yet been used to study changes in engagement in the intervention itself, although it seems possible in studies that collect process data at multiple time points. Treatment process could also involve the study of smaller units of time. Some psychotherapy studies, for example, use sequential analyses to examine the reactions of clients to specific therapist actions (see Lambert & Hill, 1994) within sessions.

A focus on the temporal dimension also involves an emphasis on the longitudinal nature of both the programs and evaluations. Although early interventions are usually time-limited, occurring over a discrete age or stage, value has always been placed on these programs as ameliorative— promoting strengths or correcting problems in child and family development now to prevent difficulties in the future. This belief has been reinforced by the study of a few interventions that have been followed over a long period of time, and the positive cumulative benefits that are seen in child maltreatment rates, family welfare dependence, juvenile delinquency and social competence (see Yoshikawa, 1995, and Karoly et al., 1998, for reviews). Longitudinal follow-up, however, is a difficult and expensive proposition. Many programs and program evaluations are not set up for tracking families over the long term, and funders may not want to wait ten to twenty years to see if cumulative effects of an intervention will "pay off" at a later date.

And just because some programs do show long term effects, this does not mean that all will. Some studies show program gains that do not last over time. The Infant Health and Development Program, a well-regarded center- and home-based program for premature infants, saw initial gains in cognitive development disappear by the child's eighth birthday (McCarton, Brooks-Gunn, Wallace, & Bauer, 1997). One obvious difficulty is that if there are no high-quality services for children and families to transition to after a time-limited intervention has run its course, then there is no safety net for those who continue to struggle. In other words, an inoculation model of intervention (Ramey & Ramey, 1998), where services occurring early in life are expected to protect children against the slings and arrows of future misfortune, is likely not a viable model. Instead, we need a better understanding of the different pathways on which families embark as a result of participating in different interventions, and how current and future experiences (including future services or lack of services) influence child and family development.

Studying the Helper

The service provider is one of the least understood aspects of early childhood interventions. There has been little systematic exploration of provider contributions to program outcomes. The lack of interest in studying the provider in early intervention is noteworthy, for it suggests a missing source of program variation. Contributions of the helper to the intervention process are obviously important. Case studies from an infant mental health program, for example, suggest that the ability of the clinician to stay with the mother even when drowning in rejection was the primary motivating factor for the mother to remain engaged in and show benefit from the program (Greenspan et al., 1987).

It is important to understand how helpers with different backgrounds and different characteristics approach treatment with participants (who themselves have different backgrounds and characteristics). For example, there is debate about the benefits of using helpers with or without professional degrees (e.g., Wasik, 1993). David Olds and colleagues explicitly studied this issue in a home visiting trial comparing program outcomes for families visited by nurses or paraprofessionals. In general, although both types of visitors produced effects in maternal life course (employment and subsequent pregnancies) and parent-child interaction measures, outcomes were often stronger for the nurse program (Olds, Robinson et al., 1999). The nurse program also showed effects in some child outcomes, such as language development and emotional regulation, where the paraprofessionals did not.

These findings may be because nurse home visitors completed more visits on average and focused more intensely on crucial pieces of the program protocol, such as physical health concerns and parenting issues (Korfmacher, O'Brien, Hiatt, & Olds, in press). Both sets of visitors, however, were trained in the model originally developed for nurses, with only slight modifications for the paraprofessionals. It is unclear what the outcomes would be if these paraprofessionals were trained in a program model more uniquely suited to their abilities and background.

Professional background and status, however, is only one of many different dimensions in which service providers vary, including previous experience, age, ethnicity, personality, and interaction styles. There are ethical issues to consider as well. If the qualities of the service provider are to be studied in the course of an intervention, it is important for the service provider to give official informed consent to participate in the investigation (see Korfmacher, 1998). But in summary, it is surprising—given how obviously crucial they are to any early intervention program—how little we know about what goes into good interventionists besides having good clinical intuitions, needing to be sensitive to others, and having good "people" skills.

Contexts and Systems

Two of the larger contextual issues surrounding early childhood interventions are: whether they should be universal or targeted, and how programs should fit into a larger system of services for children and families. Treatment-oriented early childhood programs (such as infant mental health, family preservation, early intervention programs for children with disabilities) are targeted toward particular populations manifesting difficulties in family functioning or the child's development. Many preventive models, however, are universal. That is, within a geographic area they aim to assist all families with infants or young children. For example, Healthy Families America, a nationwide network of home visiting programs, advocates universal (voluntary) home visiting for all first-time parents (Prevent Child Abuse America, 1999). This is not a universal opinion, however. Based upon his research, David Olds has advocated for targeting services to more vulnerable families (Olds & Kitzman, 1993; Olds, Henderson et al., 1999), although his nurse home visiting model is the only one that has consistently shown sub-group effects with higher-risk families.

An advantage of universal programs is that they may reduce the stigma that can be associated with targeted early childhood programs, where caregivers may feel that they are being labeled as "bad parents" who are being scrutinized by authorities (Krugman, 1993). Most likely, however, a universal approach would need to offer different levels or intensities of services for families depending on their needs. Some families may need a much more intensive intervention, while other low-risk families would need considerably fewer visits. But identifying families for services based on risk level is not an easy task. An examination of Healthy Family America's screening process, for example, found that their system did not do a particularly good job of identifying those families those who were at higher risk (Center on Child Abuse Prevention Research, 1996).

Related to this is the possibility of an integrated system of early-childhood programs. As noted earlier, these systems are fractured in the United States, with different fields, agencies, and professionals laying claim to different aspects of child and family development. So integration of services likely will only be accomplished in small, tentative steps. Recent controversy over the value and role of early childhood home visiting programs in the United States has brought this issue to the forefront. The authors of the critical review of home visiting programs pointed out that other services may be more meaningful and helpful to families (Gomby et al., 1999). As more and more low-income families have working parents due to welfare reform in the United States, for example, the availability of enriched or high-quality child care takes on added significance.

But home visiting programs likely have an important role as part of a continuum or package of services offered to families. Some families will respond to a home visiting program, and may, in fact, only respond to such a way of delivering services. And home visiting may be the only viable option for services to families who live in rural environments. Recently, Early Head Start programs have been allowed to offer combinations of center-based and home-visiting services, depending on family needs and preferences. How such service combinations play out is an important area of study.

CONCLUSION

There is a strong need to move from binary questions regarding whether an intervention for parents and young children works or not to a serious exploration of what occurs inside and around an intervention. How a program is implemented and accepted by participants needs to become a regular part of early intervention studies—planned, promoted, and piloted as any other factor under scrutiny. Such explorations can be beneficial to a field that is feeling increased pressure to "fix" problems of at-risk populations before other treatment fields have to deal with them. Such examinations will also be more ecologically valid and will promote more ecologically valid and appropriate services to families. As Trickett (1997) has noted for prevention programs, examinations that ignore these issues promote the idea of interventions as portable technologies, rather than as "complex, contextually negotiated and constrained sets of activities which may have different meanings and consequences for different populations" (p. 199).

Although it would be pleasant to provide simple conclusions and directions as we move into the next century, as the above quote demonstrates, the avenues of exploration promoted here will not simplify the field. We can instead expect more complications and debate. At the same time, however, such explorations will provide much-needed information. There is a danger in becoming hopelessly lost in the many variables, factors, issues, and dimensions that must be considered. Studies of the experience of the intervention need to take greater prominence, moving beyond secondary and post-hoc analyses of existing data sets. If we are to determine who benefits from which services under what conditions, information will only come when researchers make serious a priori commitments to measuring relevant dimensions, justifying their relevance, providing details on the measures, and being open to alternate methods of study.

The enormous variability that exists in the field of early intervention makes these studies crucial to understanding what is happening in these programs. We now have considerable evidence from the last thirty years that asking limited what-works questions can only produce limited conclusions. Although it will not provide the simple recipe of success for all families who participate in these programs, it can provide understanding as to why there is success for some and how there can be success for others.

REFERENCES

Annie E. Casey Foundation (1999). *1999 Kids Count data book: State profiles of child well-being.* Baltimore, MD: Author.

Barnard, K. E., Magyary, D., Sumner, G., Booth, C. L., Mitchell, S. K., & Spieker, S. (1988). Prevention of parenting alterations for women of low social support. *Psychiatry*, 51, 248–253.

Belsky, J. (1986). A tale of two variances: Between and within. *Child Development*, 57, 1301–1305.

Beutler, L. E., Machado, P. P. P., & Neufeldt, S. A. (1994). Therapist variables. In A. E. Bergin & S. I. Garfield (Eds.), *Handbook of psychotherapy and behavior change* (pp. 229–269). New York: John Wiley & Sons.

Bromwich, R. (1981). *Working with parents and infants: An interactional approach.* Baltimore: University Park Press.

Carter, A. S., Robinson, J., Korfmacher, J., Dean, J., Pipp-Siegal, S., & Clark, R. (1996, May). *Validated parent-infant psychotherapy and prevention programs: Are we ready?* Invited discussion at the Tenth Biennial International Conference on Infant Studies, Providence, RI.

Casto, G., & Mastropieri, M. A. (1986). The efficacy of early intervention programs: A meta-analysis. *Exceptional Children*, 52, 417–424.

Center on Child Abuse Prevention Research (1996). *Targeting Prevention services: The use of risk assessment in Hawaii's Healthy Start Program.* Executive summary prepared for the National Center on Child Abuse and Neglect (NCCAN Grant # 90–CA–1511). Chicago, IL: National Committee to Prevent Child Abuse (Now Prevention Child Abuse America).

Collins, L. M., & Horn, J. L. (1991). *Best methods for the analysis of change: Recent advances, unanswered questions, future directions.* Washington, DC: American Psychological Association.

Durlak, J. A., & Wells, A. M. (1997). Primary prevention mental health programs for children and adolescents: A meta-analytic review. *American Journal of Community Health*, 25, 115–152.

Egeland, B., Erickson, M. F., Butcher, J. N., & Ben-Porath, Y. S. (1991). MMPI-2 profiles of women at risk for child abuse. *Journal of Personality Assessment*, 57, 254–263.

Emde, R. N., Korfmacher, J., & Kubicek, L. F. 2000. Towards a theory of early relationship-based intervention. In J. D. Osofsky & E. H. Fitzgerald (Eds.), *World Association for Infant Mental Health handbook of infant mental health.* Vol. 2. Early intervention, evaluation and assessment (pp 1–33). New York: John Wiley & Sons.

Erickson, M. F., Korfmacher, J., & Egeland, B. (1992). Attachments past and present: Implications for therapeutic intervention with mother-infant dyads. *Development and Psychopathology*, 4, 495–507

Gilkerson, L., & Stott, F. (1997). Listening to the voices of families: Learning through caregiving consensus groups. *Zero to Three, 18(2),* 9–16.

Gomby, D. S., Culross, P. L., & Behrman, R. E. (1999). Home visiting: Recent program evaluations—analysis and recommendations. *The Future of Children*, 9(1), 4–26.

Gray, S. W., & Wandersman, L. P. (1980). The methodology of home-based intervention studies: Problems and promising solutions. *Child Development*, 51, 993–1009.

Greenspan, S., Wieder, S. Lieberman, A. F., Nover, R., Robinson, M. & Lourie, R. (Eds.) (1987). *Infants in multirisk families.* Madison, CT: International Universities Press.

Halpern, R. (1984). Lack of effects for home-based early intervention? Some possible explanations. *American Journal of Orthopsychiatry*, 54, 33–52.

Halpern, R. (1990). Community-based early intervention. In S. M. Meisels & J. P. Shonkoff (Eds.), *Handbook of early childhood intervention* (pp. 469–498). Cambridge: Cambridge University Press.

Heinicke, C. M., Beckwith, L., & Thompson, A. (1988). Early intervention in the family system: A framework and review. *Infant Mental Health Journal*, 9, 111–141.

Heinicke, C. M., & Ponce, V. A. (1998). Relation-based early family intervention. In D. Cicchetti & S. L. Toth (Eds.), *Rochester Symposium on Developmental Psychopathology. Vol. IX: Developmental Approaches to Prevention & Intervention* (pp. 153–193). Rochester, NY: University of Rochester Press.

Horvath, A. O., & Luborsky, L. (1993). The role of therapeutic alliance in psychotherapy. *Journal of Consulting and Clinical Psychology*, 61, 561–573.

Howes, C., & Smith, E. W. (1995). Relations among child care quality, teacher behavior, children's play activities, emotional security, and cognitive play activity in child care. *Early Childhood Research Quarterly*, 10, 381–404.

Institute of Medicine (1994). *Reducing risks for mental disorders: frontiers for preventive intervention research.* Washington, DC: National Academy Press.

Kagan, S. L. & Weissbourd, B. (1994). *Putting families first: America's family support movement and the challenge of change.* San Francisco, CA: Jossey-Bass Inc.

Kamerman, S. B., & Kahn, A. J. (1993). Home health visiting in Europe. *The Future of Children*, 3(3), 39–52.

Karoly, L. A., Greenwood, P. W., Everingham, S. S., Hoube, J., Kilburn, M. R., Rydell, C. P., Sanders, M., & Chiesa, J. (1998). *Investing in our children: What we know and don't know about the costs and benefits of early childhood interventions.* Santa Monica, CA: RAND.

Kendall, P. C. (1998). Empirically supported psychological therapies. *Journal of Consulting and Clinical Psychology*, 66, 3–6.

Kitzman, H., Cole, R., Yoos, L., & Olds, D. (1997). Challenges experienced by home visitors: A qualitative study of program implementation. *Journal of Community Psychology*, 25, 95–109.

Korfmacher, J. (1998). Examining the service provider in early intervention. *Zero to Three*, 18(4), 17–22.

Korfmacher, J., Adam, E., Ogawa, J., & Egeland, B. (1997). Adult attachment: Implications for the therapeutic process in a home visitation intervention. *Applied Developmental Science*, 1, 43–52.

Korfmacher, J., McCullough, J., & Olds, D. (1997, April). *Disruption of the help-ing relationship and its effects on outcome in home visitation.* Paper presented at the Biennial Meeting of the Society for Research in Child Development, Washington, DC.

Korfmacher, J., O'Brien, R., Hiatt, S., & Olds, D. (in press). Differences in program implementation between nurses and paraprofessionals in prenatal and infancy home visitation: A randomized trial. *American Journal of Public Health.*

Krugman, R. D. (1993). Universal home visiting: A recommendation from the U.S. Advisory Board on Child Abuse and Neglect. *The Future of Children, 3*(3), 184–191.

Lambert, M. J., & Hill, C. E. (1994). Assessing psychotherapy outcomes and processes. In A. E. Bergin & S. L. Garfield (Eds.), *Handbook of psychothera-py and behavior change* (pp. 72–113). New York: John Wiley & Sons, Inc.

Lewin, K. (1946). Action research and minority problems. *Journal of Social Issues, 2,* 34–36.

Liaw, F., Meisels, S. J., & Brooks-Gunn, J. (1995). The effects of experience of early intervention on low birth weight, premature children: The Infant Health and Development Program. *Early Childhood Research Quarterly, 10,* 405–431.

Main, M. (1991). Metacognitive knowledge, metacognitive monitoring, and singu-lar (coherent) vs. multiple (incoherent) model of attachment: Findings and directions for future research. In C. M. Parkes, J. Stevenson-Hind, et al. (Eds), *Attachment across the life cycle* (pp. 127–159). London, England UK: Tavistock/Routledge.

McCarton, C. M., Brooks-Gunn, J., Wallace, I. F., & Bauer, C. R. (1997). Results at age 8 years of early intervention for low-birth-weight premature infants: The Infant Health and Development Program. *JAMA: Journal of the American Medical Association, 277,* 126–132.

National Institute of Mental Health (1993). The prevention of mental disorders: a national research agenda. Washinton, D.C.: Author.

Nauta, M. J., & Hewett, K. (1988). Studying complexity: The case of the Child and Family Resource Program. In H. B. Weiss & F. H. Jacobs (Eds.), *Evaluating family programs* (pp. 389–406). New York: Aldine de Gruyter.

Olds, D. L., & Kitzman, H. (1993). Review of research on home visiting programs for pregnant women and parents of young children. *The Future of Children, 3*(3), 53–92.

Olds, D. L., Henderson, C. R., Kitzman, H. J., Eckenrode, J. J., Cole, R. E., & Tatelbaum, R. C. (1999). Prenatal and infancy home visitation by nurses: Recent findings. *The Future of Children, 9*(1), 44–65.

Olds, D. L., & Korfmacher, J. (1998). Maternal psychological characteristics as influences on home visitation contact. *Journal of Community Psychology, 26,* 23–36.

Olds, D., Robinson, J., Luckey, D., O'Brien, R., Korfmacher, J., Hiatt, S., Pettitt, L., & Henderson, C. (1999). *Comparison of pregnancy and infancy home visita-tion by nurses versus paraprofessionals: A randomized controlled trial.* Final report to the Colorado Trust on Home Visitation 2000 (Grant #93059).

Orlinsky, D. E., Grawe, K., & Parks, B. K. (1994). Process and outcome in psychotherapy—noch einmal. In A. E. Bergin & S. L. Garfield (Eds.). *Handbook of psychotherapy and behavior change* (pp. 270–376). New York: John Wiley & Sons.

Orlinsky, D. E., & Howard, K. I. (1986). Process and outcome in psychotherapy. In S. L. Garfield & A. E. Bergin (Eds.), *Handbook of psychotherapy and behavior change* (pp. 311–381). New York: John Wiley & Sons.

Osofsky, J. D., Culp, A. M., & Ware, L. M. (1988). Intervention challenges with adolescent mothers and their infants. *Psychiatry*, 51, 236–241.

Patteson, D. M., & Barnard, K. E. (1990). Parenting of low birth weight infants: A review of issues and interventions. *Infant Mental Health Journal*, 11, 37–56.

Powell, C., & Grantham-McGregor, S. (1989). Home visiting of varying frequency and child development. *Pediatrics*, 84, 157–164.

Prevent Child Abuse America (n.d/1999). Messages from our President and Chairperson. [WWWdocument]. Available: *http://www.childabuse.org/1ar97.html*

Ramey, C. T., & Ramey, S. L. (1998). Early intervention and early experience. *American Psychologist*, 53, 109–120.

Rauh, V. A., Achenbach, T. M., Nurcombe, B., Howell, C. T., & Teti, D. M. (1988). Minimizing adverse effects of low birthweight: Four year results of an early intervention program. *Child Development*, 59, 544–553.

Rolf, J. E., Bevin, S., Hasazi, J. E., Crowther, J., & Johnson, J. (1982). Prospective research with vulnerable children and risky art of preventive intervention. *Prevention in Human Services*, 1, 107–122.

Scarr, S. (1998). American child care today. *American Psychologist*, 53, 95–108.

Schorr, L. B. (1988). *Within our reach: Breaking the cycle of disadvantage*. New York: Anchor Press/Doubleday.

Solchany, J., Spieker, S., Barnard, K., & McKenna, M. (1999, April). *Parents in a home-based early Head Start program: A comparison of hard versus easy to engage parents*. Paper presented at the Biennial Meeting of the Society for Research in Child Development, Albuquerque, NM.

Speer, D. C., & Greenbaum, P. E. (1995). Five methods of computing significant individual client change and improvement rates: Support for an individual growth curve approach. *Journal of Consulting and Clinical Psychology*, 63, 1044–1048.

St. Pierre, R. G., & Layzer, J. I. (1999). Using home visits for multiple purposes: The Comprehensive Child Development Program. *The Future of Children*, 9(1), 134–151.

St. Pierre, R. G., Layzer, J. I., Goodson, B. D., & Bernstein, L. S. (1997). *National impact evaluation of the Comprehensive Child Development Program: Final report*. Cambridge, MA: Abt Associates.

Trickett, E. J. (1997). Ecology and primary prevention: Reflections on a meta-analysis. *American Journal of Community Psychology*, 25, 197–205.

Wasik, B. H. (1993). Staffing issues for home visiting programs. *The Future of Children*, 3(3), 140–157.

Weissberg, R. P., & Greenberg, M. T. (1998). Prevention science and collaborative community action research: Combining the best from both perspectives. *Journal of Mental Health*, 7, 479–492.

Whyte, W. F. (1984). *Learning from the field: A guide from experience*. London: Sage.

Yoshikawa, H. (1995). Long-term effects of early childhood programs on social outcomes and delinquency. *The Future of Children*, 5(3), 51–75.

NOTES

1. Portions of this chapter were modified from a previous manuscript co-written by the author (Emde, Korfmacher, & Kubicek, 2000).

2. As exceptions, there are reviews that have more positive assessments of early intervention programs, such as Ramey & Ramey (1998), Yoshikawa (1995), and Durlak & Wells (1997).

RELATIONSHIPS AT RISK
The Policy Environment as a Context for Infant Development

Emily Fenichel

12

····

At the close of the twentieth century in the United States of America, the greatest threat to healthy development that very young children experience may arise from failures in their relationships with adult caregivers. Several decades of research strongly suggest that children need "at least one person who is crazy about them" in order to make full use of their own gifts, explore what the world has to offer, and overcome the vicissitudes that life will throw in their way. Large numbers of babies and toddlers in this country do not form stable, nurturing relationships with their parents. Many very young children experience disruption and loss—sometimes repeatedly—in their relationships with important caregivers during the earliest years of life. Separation and bereavement are hardly new in human history, but during the past half-century transformations in many domains of economic and family life have profoundly altered both the quality and the quantity of children's experiences with adults in their earliest years. We can still only guess what effects these changes are having on the development of particular groups of children or upon whole generations of citizens.

Can social policy—the allocation of public resources—reduce the risk or mitigate the harm that occurs when nurturing relationships between infants and parents fail to form, are disrupted, or disappear? Given our history and current policy environment, is this country even likely to attempt to use social policy to safeguard, strengthen, or repair relationships at risk? These are the questions that this chapter will explore. But first we must take an imaginary journey. Consider it, if you like, the data collection phase of a thought experiment.

A TALE OF FOUR FAMILIES

Let us imagine ourselves in Martha Washington Medical Center, a teaching hospital in a mid-sized city in the United States, on what used to be called the maternity floor but is now referred to as the "birthing center." Years ago the floor had a few private rooms for affluent patients, semi-private rooms for the Blue-Crossed middle classes, and a ward for Medicaid and charity cases who somehow foiled the best efforts of the hospital's admissions office to direct them elsewhere to give birth. Currently, however, the hospital administrator, hungry for third-party payments from whatever source, woos both Medicaid-eligible and privately insured expectant parents with descriptions of the Colonial decor and celebratory champagne offered at the "Birthing Centre at Martha Washington."

Since the newborns and parents in the Martha Washington birthing center are likely to be reasonably representative of the children and families affected by the current and emerging policy environment in this country, let's visit several of them. (We'd better hurry. They'll be discharged by tomorrow.)

The Lavender Room

In the Lavender Room is Jennifer Talbot-Adams, J.D., age 38, and her husband, Henry Adams IV, age 54. Jennifer is wearing an ivory silk gown and peignoir from Nordstrom's that match the dozen roses in the bedside vase. Henry is wearing a suit he inherited from his father a decade ago. Jennifer and Henry's newborn triplets, Helena, Jessica, and Miranda, born at 32 weeks gestation, are in the Neonatal Intensive Care Unit.

Dr. Singh, the neonatologist, says the girls seem perfectly healthy; they just need to gain some weight. When she delivered this good news, Dr. Singh expected to see some expression of joy on the faces of Jennifer and Henry, but, as she noted in the chart, their affect seemed curiously flat. Could this be "cultural"?, the doctor wondered.

In fact, Jennifer feels angrier at the world than she would ever have thought possible. She'd like to sue the in-vitro fertilization clinic—if they hadn't been so eager to get her money, they would have told her to forget trying to get pregnant for a couple of years and then clone Henry. Since he's got two daughters already, both almost as old as Jennifer, the only attraction this current baby project held for him in the first place was the chance that Jennifer would produce Henry V, heir to the Adams Family of Corporations, Serving American Consumers Since 1852. Damn! The other partners in her law firm resent every second that Jennifer has spent on bedrest in the last three months. And Esmeralda, the nanny that Katherine Prendergast promised to pass on to Jennifer as soon as Jason entered first grade, won't be available for six weeks. With triplets, the Adamses probably need two nannies, anyway. Will they be willing to share the suite Jennifer has fixed up in the basement?

Jennifer is exhausted; her incision hurts; she's pale and flabby from the bed rest. And there's something terribly familiar about the dour expression on Henry's face . . . Oh, God—It's exactly the way he looked that night four years ago when he took her to dinner after the deposition and told her how trapped he felt in his marriage.

The Peach Room

In the Peach Room, the levels of noise and expressed emotion are considerably higher. The television is on full blast, and seventeen-year-old Tiffany Jenkins, on the phone with her Early Head Start family advocate, seems to believe that the louder she speaks the more easily she will be able to make this woman understand that if the state is not going to give her a check for Leonardo (just because she was already getting welfare for Chelsea when she got pregnant with Leo), she has no intention of hassling Tony to sign Leo's birth certificate. Tony has already bought the baby a soccer ball, a football, a basketball, a baseball, and a pair of tiny Air Jordans; she knows he'll do as much as he can for his first-born son.

Enter Virginia, the doula, who was with Tiffany throughout labor and delivery and has returned to serve as lactation coach. Tiffany's not sure about breastfeeding. Tony definitely dislikes the idea. But if Madonna can do it—and let's face it, formula costs the earth—maybe she should try it, even if just to make Virginia feel good.

"Leo, are you hungry? Come to mama. Is this right, Virginia? OK, there you go. Oh, my goodness! Oh, my GOODNESS! Virginia, am I supposed to be feeling, like, uh...? Really? So why doesn't anybody tell you? These girls out here would all be breastfeeding! Leonardo, you are something else—I wish I didn't have to be back at K-Mart in twelve weeks!"

The Blue Room

It's standing room only in the Blue Room. Rosemary and Tom Flynn, both 44 years old and grandparents of two, would love to cuddle their sixth baby, Sean, but eight-year-old Grace, seventeen-year-old Kevin, and 24-year-old Pauline's toddler, Mike, won't surrender him. Besides, Debby Shapiro, from the Down Syndrome Congress, has just come in, one of Tom's brothers and two of Rosemary's sisters are trying to say good-bye, and the Flynns can hear Father Murphy's booming voice getting closer as he comes down the hall. Rosemary and Tom are glad they decided to have the amnio. They have been getting ready to care for Sean for five months now, and, with the help of all the people in the room and many others in the parish—people all over town, really—they have been able to give him a wholehearted welcome. The family has been terrific; the Early Intervention home visitor who gave Sean his first Brazelton will come to the Flynn house Tuesday evening to teach everybody how to help the baby establish sleep/wake patterns; and the Congress Parent-to-Parent group has helped the Flynns think really carefully about who would be the best godparents for Sean and what to tell Grace about her baby brother's Down Syndrome.

Cecilia is the only cousin Rosemary hasn't heard from. Rosemary was ten when Ceci had the baby that no one in the family ever saw; she remembers lots of conversations between her mother and her aunts around that time that stopped or changed the subject as soon as she came into the room. Soon, Ceci and her husband moved out of town. Then Ceci got divorced—more hushed conversations. Well, things are a lot different now. Kids with Down Syndrome are going to college. People accept diversity. The government has special programs, and you don't have to be poor to get free services.

It's hard to believe that it was only thirty-some years ago that Ceci's baby was called a "Mongolian idiot" and shipped off to an institution straight from the hospital. This country would never go back to that kind of attitude!

The Rose Room

The mood in the Rose Room is bittersweet. Carmen and Hector Jimenez think that Julia is the most beautiful baby girl they have ever seen. They are enormously relieved that their daughter seems perfectly healthy. Carmen knows that in this country, rich women and poor women with medical cards go to the doctor many times when they are pregnant. But Carmen never saw a doctor before she came to Martha Washington last night when her contractions were five minutes apart. When Julia was conceived, Carmen and Hector were both working, but their jobs had no health benefits. When Hector was laid off, after Mr. Adams sold the mill to a German company that sold it to a Japanese company that went bankrupt, he could only find day work no matter how hard he tried, and Carmen didn't dare quit her waitress job, even though her back ached and her legs swelled up.

What will they do now? Hector's so smart—if he could have gotten that job at the Korean dry cleaner's, he could have started studying air conditioning repair. But the guy doing the hiring—Hector could swear he recognized him from El Salvador, only then the guy had been in uniform. Better forget it. If Carmen goes back to the diner right away, who will take care of Julia? Caring for a baby should be the mother's job. Carmen knows she is a good mother; if she and Hector can ever get some money together, they'll send to the Dominican Republic for Carmen's older daughter, who has been living with her grandmother since she was three.

Wait—All this thinking about home has just given Carmen a wonderful idea! She'll call Esmeralda, who comes from her village and now takes care of rich people's children. Maybe Esmeralda will know a rich lady who will want Carmen to take care of her baby and will let her bring Julia along.

* * * * *

If the spirit of Charles Dickens were to descend upon my hard drive now, he could create one of his three-decker social novels in less than a fortnight by imagining the potentially intertwined lives of Helena, Miranda, Jessica, Leonardo, Sean, Julia, and their parents. Clearly, in Chapter Two of his chronicle, Carmen would get a job helping to care for the Adams triplets. Then what? Would one or more of the triplets end up in an early intervention program with Sean? Would Leonardo and Julia meet in Head Start? Would Henry Adams, enchanted by his three tiny daughters, not only become a model Nurturing Father at home but also persuade his family foundation to set up a mentoring program for Tony and other non-custodial young fathers? Would Rosemary Flynn and Debby Shapiro meet Jennifer Talbot-Adams when she is assigned by her law firm to help Down Syndrome Congress parents with long-term financial planning? Would Hector and Tiffany enroll in a computer repair course sponsored by the International Union of Electrical Workers, of which Tom Flynn is president? Would Hector, or Tiffany, or both, die of gunshot wounds sustained when, leaving class, they are caught in the crossfire of a gang war? Would Carmen, backed financially by Henry's 82-year-old mother, then seek election to the City Council, pledging a campaign to make the city safe and healthy for all of its children?

Dickens would be sure to insert an aptly named minor character into every third or fourth chapter of his story to represent some salient social program or institution. Mary Sonnenschein would appear as the well-meaning but ineffective director of a therapeutic nursery school for children with developmental disabilities. Prudence Hardhart would impose sanctions on non-compliant recipients of Temporary Assistance to Needy Families in accordance with provisions of the Personal Responsibility and Work Opportunity Reconciliation Act (the spirit of Dickens must already reside in the computer of whoever in the U.S. Congress makes up titles for new legislation). Energetic, outgoing Hiram Wright would run a successful job training and placement program. Serena Benvenidos would impart a sense of welcome and calm to a multi-purpose family resource center in a Latino neighborhood. The fiscal decisions of Alan Greedspin and the Federal Reserve Board would affect everybody, but only Henry Adams, Tom Flynn, and the omniscient narrator would understand how. And somewhere in the manuscript would surely appear the sentence: "It was the best of times; it was the worst of times."

THE POLICY ENVIRONMENT—ONE BABY, ONE FAMILY AT A TIME

Why am I invoking a nineteenth-century novelist to serve as muse for an essay on the policy environment as a context for infant development? Perhaps it's nostalgia. At the close of the twentieth century, when I read even the cruelest "Dickensian" scene in a nineteenth-century British novel, I know from my history books that an army of tireless social reformers will soon appear on the English scene, and that the Welfare State is mere decades away. Perhaps it's an appreciation of the novel's celebration of the individual—telling the tale of the quirky, idiosyncratic, unpredictable, and therefore unique unfolding of a life. Does not open-minded, unfaltering attention to the individual represent the best tradition in clinical practice and social service, as well? Perhaps it's a recognition of the power of anecdote (genuine or fabricated) to shape policy—or at least to "frame the policy agenda"—in this century.

My point is that each baby and family in the Martha Washington Birthing Center will exist within a distinct policy environment. The relationships surrounding each of the babies described above will be affected differentially by not only by laws of nature, but also by laws of economics and of man. It has been observed that the complex public policies of the second half of the twentieth century have produced different impacts for different groups (Steuerle, Granlich, Heclo, & Smith Nightingale, 1998). We need also to understand how particular policies—singly, in combination, or, as often happens, at cross-purposes—come to protect or to jeopardize the life chances of individual babies and their families.

As the philosopher Ortega y Gasset has observed, "I am myself and my circumstances." Every baby and every parent is unique. Babies exist and develop in the context of relationships, and every individual exists in a particular environmental context that deeply affects the person's functioning (Lieberman, 1997/1998). Laws of nature have determined the differing outcomes of Jennifer's, Tiffany's, Rosemary's and Carmen's pregnancies. The "invisible hand" of the free market seems poised to give some of these fictional families a back rub while dealing others repeated slaps in the face. Man-made laws have already shaped the circumstances of the Martha Washington babies and will continue to determine their developmental opportunities. When we look at infant development in the context of the policy environment, we must remember that the allocation of public resources with respect to children and families involves much more than funding direct-service programs. In particular, children's relationships with caring adults may be protected or jeopardized as much—or even more—as by health, education, or social welfare legislation.

Imagining the possible lives of the fictional newborns in the Martha Washington Birthing Center may help us understand the policy environment as a context for infant development. More specifically, we wish to understand how allocation of public resources may promote, protect, or repair the relationships with caring adults that are essential to children's healthy growth. Examining the work of several writers from a range of disciplines who have thought creatively about human development, social forces, political processes, and the interaction of all of these, is particularly useful in exploring three aspects of the larger issue: 1) how past policies contribute to individual differences at birth; 2) how features of the current policy environment may affect children's prospects for security and opportunity in the future; and 3) what alterations in policy content and in the policymaking process itself might make a positive difference in the developmental course of some, or all, of these babies and their real-life counterparts.

BEGINNING WITH BRONFENBRENNER

Over the past three decades, Urie Bronfenbrenner has refined and expanded his thinking about the context in which development unfolds many times over. Bronfenbrenner's most recent formulation of his bioecological model of development (Bronfenbrenner & Morris, 1998) includes the dynamic, interactive relationships among four principal components. The components are *process, person, environmental context*, and *time*. In the process-person-context-time (PPCT) model, unlike in his earliest and still widely cited formulation of the ecological, "nested structures" model (1979), Bronfenbrenner emphasizes the construct of *proximal processes*. These are enduring forms of interaction in the immediate environment, such as feeding or comforting a baby or playing with a young child. A long-standing proposition derived from the bioecological model reads:

> In order to develop—intellectually, emotionally, socially, and morally—a child requires, for all of them, the same thing: participation in progressively more complex reciprocal activity, on a regular basis over extended periods of time with one or more other persons with whom the child develops a strong, mutual, irrational attachment, and who are committed to that child's development, preferably for life. (Bronfenbrenner, 1989, p. 5).

Bronfenbrenner suggests further that:

> . . . the establishment and maintenance of patterns of progressively more complex interaction and emotional attachment between caregiver and child depend in substantial degree on the availability and active involvement of another adult who assists, encourages, spells off, gives status to, and expresses admiration and affection for the person caring for and engaging in joint activity with the child. (Bronfenbrenner, 1989, p. 11)

Making more explicit the distinctive properties of a proximal process, Bronfenbrenner argues that, to be developmentally effective, activities must continue long enough to become increasingly complex. In other words, activities must take place on a fairly regular basis, over an extended period of time. "In the case of young children, a weekend of doing things with Mom or Dad does not do the job, nor do activities that are often interrupted" (Bronfenbrenner & Morris, 1998, p. 996).

In Bronfenbrenner's model, individual development is affected by historical time as well as by the moment-by-moment, day-by-day time in which proximal processes occur. Bronfenbrenner notes the impact of what he calls macrotime—"changing expectations and events in the larger society, both within and across generations, as they affect and are affected by processes and outcomes of human development over the life course" (Bronfenbrenner & Morris, 1998, p. 995). At the close of the century, surveying numerous indicators of children's current well-being and prospects for healthy development in the United States, Bronfenbrenner is far from optimistic about the degree to which the larger environment fosters, rather than interfering with, the development of proximal processes. He sees growing chaos in the lives of families, which interrupts and undermines the formation and stability of relationships and activities that are essential for psychological growth. Moreover, in his view many of the conditions leading to this chaos are the often unforeseen products of policy decisions made both in the private and in the public sector (Bronfenbrenner & Morris, 1998, p. 1022).

SAMEROFF, RUNYAN, AND THEIR COLLEAGUES

A second view of the policy environment as a context for infant development focuses on the impact of multiple interacting risk and protective factors. Some 25 years ago, Sameroff and Chandler suggested that we can best understand the range of developmental outcomes if we recognize that "the child and his caretaking environment tend to mutually alter each other" (Sameroff & Chandler, 1975, p. 237). The child is, in this transactional model of development, "in a perpetual state of active reorganization ... (The) *constants* in development are not some set of traits but rather the processes by which these traits are maintained in the transactions between organism and environment (Sameroff & Chandler, 1975,p. 235, emphasis in the original).

While Sameroff and Chandler wrote in 1975 that "the human organism appears to have been programmed by the course of evolution to produce normal developmental outcomes under all but the most adverse of circumstances" (Sameroff & Chandler, 1975, p. 235), a dozen years later Sameroff and his colleagues looked more closely at processes that contribute to compromised intellectual and social-emotional competence in young children. Seeking to reduce global measures such as "socioeconomic status" to component social and behavioral variables, these investigators considered the multiple pressures of environmental context in terms of: 1) amount of stress from the environment; 2) the family's resources for coping with that stress; 3) the number of children that must share those resources; and 4) the parents' flexibility in understanding and dealing with their children. Studying the impact of ten such risk factors on the development of a group of children from the prenatal period through early childhood living in a socially heterogeneous set of family circumstances, Sameroff and his colleagues found that on accumulation of risk variables, but no single variable, compromised children's intellectual and social-emotional competence at age four. The effects of multiple risk held true within socioeconomic status groups as well as for the population at large (Sameroff, Seifer, Barocas, Zax, & Greenspan, 1987).

More recently, in what they termed a reciprocal study, Desmond Runyan and his colleagues sought to discover whether the cumulative effect of multiple protective factors in the caregiving environment of high-risk preschool children might be associated with positive developmental and behavioral outcomes. They drew on the work of James Coleman, who in 1988 introduced the concept of "social capital"—that is, "features in the social organization, such as social networks, expectations, and trust, that facilitate coordination and cooperation for mutual benefit" (Runyan et al., 1998, p. 12). Runyan and his colleagues hypothesized that the benefits accrued from social connectedness in communities and within families affect the development and well-being of children. They created an index of social capital by assigning one point for the presence of each of the following indicators: 1) the presence of two parents in the home; 2) social support for the primary maternal caregiver; 3) the presence of no more than two children in the home; 4) the presence of people in the neighborhood who help each other out, watch out for each other's children, and can be counted on; and 5) regular church involvement. Child well-being was operationalized as obtaining developmental and behavioral scores well within normal limits upon standard measures including the Battelle Developmental Inventory Screening test and the Child Behavior Checklist.

Runyan and his colleagues studied data from the Longitudinal Studies of Child Abuse and Neglect (LONGSCAN) on 667 children from Baltimore, North Carolina, San Diego, and Seattle who were between the ages of two to five years at the time of the baseline interview. They found that while only 13% of the children in this high-risk sample were classified as doing well, the social capital index was indeed strongly associated with child well-being, more so than any single indicator. The authors observed that "just as Sameroff's study showed that multiple risk factors must be present before a negative impact in child development can be detected, the results of (their) study show that the likelihood of doing well increases when multiple protective factors are present" (Runyan et al., 1998, p. 16).

Interestingly, the multiple protective factors that seemed most closely linked to child well-being (operationalized as scores well within normal limits on standard developmental measures) have to do with relationships. Runyan and his colleagues note that social capital is a relatively new theoretical construct, which has been defined differently by different investigators. Using a Social Capital Index they had created from variables that others had used or that seemed "theoretically pertinent," they found that the indicators that best discriminated between levels of child functioning were: 1) mother's regular attendance at church; 2) mother's perception of access to social support; and 3) mother's perception of the support available from her neighbors. The indicators which suggested that a child might receive a greater allocation of resources within the family—the presence of two parents and fewer siblings—seemed less powerful in this study. Although Runyan and his colleagues suggest that characteristics of their sample may account for this pattern and, in general, recognize that the best constellation of criteria to measure social capital has yet to be determined, it is interesting to speculate about the apparent power of mothers' perceptions of support to influence child development positively. Does this speak to the importance of the quality—not merely the quantity—of a mother's relationships as a factor in child outcome? One also wonders what could be learned from more a more nuanced exploration of children's social and emotional developmental outcomes within a social capital framework. Beyond the issue of developmental scores in the normal range, are the children of "support-rich" mothers more likely than others to be securely attached to their parents and able to form positive attachments to other responsive caregivers in the community? Are they likely to be trustworthy, helpful citizens of their child care centers or school classrooms, building their community's social capital even as young children?

What are the policy implications of Sameroff and Runyan's analyses? In 1987, Sameroff and his colleagues concluded:

> (I)f one views the larger context of environmental influences on the child, there is a large difference between the total number of variables that have an impact on the child's competence and those that are available to be changed by (psychologic) intervention. As professionals we are limited to our own domains of expertise. However, as advocates for a healthier society, we must recognize the breadth of the problems and the multiplicity of social forces that affect our children. (Sameroff et al, 1987, p. 349)

In 1998, Runyan and his colleagues suggested that it is time to "focus attention on the ways in which public policy and service interventions promote or jeopardize the formation of social capital" (Runyan et al., 1998, p. 18). Perhaps it is also time to explore the ways in which social forces, public policy, and service interventions promote or jeopardize the key relationships that, in turn, mediate the impact of the environment on the lives of very young children. The analyses of Robert Hill and Sheila Kamerman and Alfred Kahn could serve as excellent guides to such an exploration.

SOCIAL FORCES AND SOCIAL POLICIES: HILL, KAMERMAN, AND KAHN

In *The Strengths of African American Families: Twenty-five Years Later*, Hill (1997) distinguishes between societal *forces* and social *policies*. Among the social forces he identifies are demographic trends, industrialization, immigration, racism, and sexism. Social policies include urban renewal, affirmative action, fiscal policies, and welfare policies—a range of examples that illustrates the advantage of a general definition of policy as resource allocation.

As we entertain the notion that every baby and family inhabits a distinct policy environment, Hill's analysis of disparate effects of societal forces or policies on different groups is helpful. He uses the term "structural discrimination" to describe "the disparate adverse effects on racial and ethnic groups of societal forces or policies, even if those actions may not have been intended to be discriminatory" (1988, quoted in Hill, 1997, p. 26).

An example of structural discrimination is the federal law that defines one gram of crack cocaine as equal to 100 grams of powder cocaine, and imposes a mandatory sentence of ten years for possessing fifty grams of the former and one year for the latter. Although the law applies to everyone in the United States, its implementation has resulted in disproportionately large numbers of African Americans in prison—including the fathers as well as growing numbers of mothers of infants and toddlers. The impact on these children's chances to experience continuity in their caregiving relationships can be devastating, even if it is an "unintended consequence" of a policy decision.

Hill views the transformation of federal categorical grants to block grants during the 1970s and 1980s (the process characterized by Steuerle as complex public policies producing different impacts for different groups) as another example of structural discrimination. According to Hill, block granting contributed significantly to the shift in government resources from blacks and low-income groups to middle-income groups and communities (Hill, 1997, p. 40). In order to support or enhance the functioning of African American families, he argues, public policies must incorporate an analysis of the potential and actual impact of social policies on families from various ethnic and class backgrounds. According to Hill, effective policies must also oppose racism and target resources to groups and communities based on social and economic need (Hill, 1997, p. 180).

While Hill focused primarily on the impact of societal forces and social policies on African American families, Sheila Kamerman and Alfred Kahn analyze the phenomenon of family change in general, the developmental needs of infants and toddlers in particular, and policies in the U.S. and abroad that affect children and families. Their 1995 volume, *Starting Right*, sets out a three-pronged policy agenda, including: 1) an income strategy to assure children the essentials; 2) health, child care, and family support services; and 3) assurances of adequate parental time for the care of young children (Kamerman & Kahn, 1995). This third "prong" speaks directly to Bronfenbrenner's emphasis on the importance of time as a necessary condition of the developmental effectiveness of a relationship, as well as to an historical era in which it is no longer safe to assume that parents and young children will have adequate time together unless this public good is supported by specific social policies.

Unfortunately, Kamerman and Kahn see little prospect of accomplishing this agenda. In their 1997 analysis of family change and family policies in the United States, they observe that "the United States has no explicit national, comprehensive family or child policy, nor has there been any such policy or cluster of policies in the past" (Kamerman & Kahn, 1997, p 308). Rather, they describe a tradition in this country that has included an "emphasis on individualism, the separation of Church and State, family privacy, a strict work ethic, a limited role for government generally and for the federal government in particular, a stress on the private sector in economic and social policy, an openness to immigration, a history of slavery followed by continuing racism, and ambivalence in recent years regarding women's roles" (p. 410).

More specifically, Kamerman and Kahn point to large holes in the social infrastructure—no national health insurance or health service, no family or child allowance, no maternity or parenting insurance, no housing allowance, no universal early care and education; categorical policies targeted at specific population or "problem" groups; "inconsistent, often inadequate and even conflicting responses" to women's changed behavior in the workplace and in the home; and "non-interference with most families and social control of those with problems as the primary family policy objective rather than sustaining and buttressing families as in countries with explicit, universal family policy" (p. 410).

They conclude that, although the pace of family change in the United States has accelerated rapidly since the 1960s, "it appears doubtful that the near future will see family policy responses in the United States more in line with progressive European welfare state traditions" (Kamerman and Kahn, 1997, p. 411).

MODELS FOR CHANGE: STEUERLE AND LAKOFF

C. Eugene Steuerle and his colleagues would probably agree with Kamerman and Kahn that policies responsive to the needs of contemporary families in the U.S. are unlikely to emerge from the policy environment as it now exists. Consequently, they call for massive changes in the policy environment itself. In *The Government We Deserve: Responsive Democracy and Changing Expectations* (1998), Steuerle and his colleagues examine economic and family transformations in the U.S., government finances, and the kinds of political processes available in our society for reaching policy choices about what should be done—and how to do it.

Steuerle and his co-authors identify changing risks for children. These include children's economic poverty, which is increasing, especially relative to older generations, and the shrinking percentage of time that children spend with parents due to increasing rates of divorce, out-of-wedlock birth, and the absence of fathers (Steuerle et al, 1998, p. 49). They call for "investment in emotional and educational learning through quality contact with adults in the earliest years" and supporting families "by revising current government tax and expenditure policies, such as those that penalize secondary workers in two-income couples and marriage between low-income individuals" (Steuerle et al., 1998, pp. 6–8). These authors note that federal social insurance policies designed decades ago to protect the public against the risks of old age, sickness and unemployment (for example, Social Security, Medicare, and unemployment insurance) fail to match the risks faced by individuals and families today. Moreover, legislatively mandated automatic growth in the social insurance commitments made in the past drastically limits the discretionary funds available to policymakers to design a more flexible, adaptable social insurance framework. In other words, if Congress were to recognize the existence of a "relationship risk" that threatens the healthy development of children, it would be hard put to find resources and funding streams to support policies designed to promote and protect stable, caring relationships for children.

Of course, the policy environment consists of more than the Congress, or even of government itself. Steuerle and his colleagues describe the current policy environment as "hyper-democracy—a policy environment that is . . . democratically open both to contending voices and to ruthless manipulation" (Steuerle et al., 1998, pp. 98). They observe that such "policy problems" as welfare, education, budgets, and health care are used as metaphors to cover deeper cultural worries about issues "that no government official or public policy can fix" and call for "a new democratic citizenship (that will) involve citizens, one at a time, trying to do the right thing for the population as a whole, supported by improved media communication, deliberative and thoughtful public dialogue, and responsible civic education" (Steuerle et al, 1998, pp. 6–8).

A similar point is made by cognitive linguist George Lakoff, who argues that political policies are derived from what he calls "family-based moralities," which are largely constructed from unconscious conceptual metaphors (Lakoff, 1996). Because understanding political positions requires understanding how they fit family-based moralities, conservative and liberal political positions are impossible to compare on an issue-by-issue basis. "There are no neutral concepts and no neutral language for expressing political positions within a moral context" (Lakoff, 1996, p. 385). Using the tools of cognitive linguistics to examine "issues of worldview, that is . . . everyday conceptualization, reasoning, and language" (Lakoff, 1996, p. 3), Lakoff suggests that people who espouse a "strict father" morality (the morality of reward and punishment) tend to be conservative, while people whose worldview includes a "nurturant parent" morality (morality as empathy, nurturance, and interdependence) tend to be politically liberal. Based on his reading of attachment and socialization research, Lakoff concludes that the nurturant parent model is superior as a method of childrearing. He argues, however, that "the challenge in contemporary America is to create a nurturant society when a significant portion of that society has been raised either by authoritarian or neglectful parents" and as a consequence does not share the nuturant parent worldview (Lakoff, 1996, p. 378).

These and other astute observers seem to suggest that we must change the U.S. policy environment itself in order to create and sustain social policies that will protect the relationships that nurture young children. If it is true that every individual in the United States exists within a distinct policy environment, it is also true that every person is uniquely situated to affect policy. Some people have money; some have eloquence or media savvy; some can play the risky game of identity politics. Most of us can vote for elected officials, and more and more of us are offered the opportunity—for better or worse—to vote in referenda on life-altering policies like bilingual education, affirmative action, and the right to assisted suicide. Fewer and fewer of us, however, exercise our political power.

RELATIONSHIPS AT RISK: THE POLICY ENVIRONMENT AS A CONTEXT FOR THE DEVELOPMENT OF INFANTS AND ADULTS

Turning once again to the four families of the Martha Washington Birthing Center, we can identify ways in which their circumstances and opportunities, as individuals and as partners in relationships, have been shaped by political, economic, social, scientific, cultural, and intellectual trends in history. The imagined scenarios offer illustrations of Bronfenbrenner's process-person-context-time model, Sameroff and Runyan's conceptions of the interaction of multiple risks and multiple protective factors, Hill's and Kamerman and Kahn's analyses of societal forces and social policies, and Steuerle's and Lakoff's assessments of cultural and psychological factors that both shape the policy environment and mediate its impact on different groups of children and families. The scenarios also offer clues to the ways in which these parents and children might help to bring about historical change, including changes in the policy environment that will affect their development and that of future generations.

In the Adams, Jenkins, and Jimenez families, societal forces—divorce, out-of-wedlock adolescent parenthood, and immigration—have disrupted or aborted parent-child relationships in the past and may affect the newborns as well. Expectations—whether internally generated or imposed from outside—that mothers of infants will work outside the home will powerfully affect almost all the Martha Washington newborns, from a very early age. The public and private-sector policy decisions that have already made so much of a difference in the circumstances and life chances of these babies include choices about, at a minimum:

- the level of support available for research on reproductive technologies

- health insurance coverage of amniocentesis and in-vitro fertilization

- federal and state eligibility requirements for Aid to Families with Dependent Children (AFDC) and, since 1996, Temporary Assistance to Needy Families (TANF)

- the target population, philosophy, design, and funding of services for infants and young children with disabilities, low-income families with infants and toddlers, and adolescent parents

• what constitutes legal immigration and the penalties for illegal immigration

• the taxation or exemption from taxation of religious institutions, nonprofit organizations, the wages of low-income parents, and capital gains.

This list is intentionally small and scattered, meant simply to indicate the obvious, as well as the not-so-obvious, arenas in which social policy—the allocation of public resources—may support or undermine the stability, sensitivity, and responsiveness of a young child's relationships with caregiving adults.

The Martha Washington Birthing Center scenarios illustrate the impact of policy *change*, whether gradual or abrupt. Forty years ago, institutionalizing an infant with Down syndrome (Ceci's baby) would have been routine. Today, children with Down syndrome are expected not only to live at home but to participate fully in community life. But with the rapid pace of advances in reproductive technology and the unpredictability of attitudinal change, is it out of the question to imagine that forty years in the future, parents who choose to give birth to a child with Down syndrome will receive no publicly funded subsidies or services for themselves or their child? Would such a policy be so very different from denial of public assistance to a baby conceived and carried to term by a mother while she is receiving welfare benefits for one or more already-born children?

However one evaluates the positive or negative, intended or unintended consequences of actual or imagined policy choices, such thought experiments help one recognize the paths through which the policy environment affects the proximal processes that are at the center of Bronfenbrenner's model of development. Consider the time factor. How many policy choices, public and private, singly and in combination, currently serve to diminish the amount of time very young children in the U.S. are likely to spend in "progressively more complex reciprocal activity, on a regular basis over extended periods of time with one or more other persons with whom the child develops a strong, mutual, irrational attachment"? Parents of infants and toddlers in all socioeconomic brackets complain of a "time crunch" or "time deficit" (Zero to Three, 1997) that prevents them from spending the amount of time with their very young children that they would like, or think their children need. In non-parental care, staff turnover among underpaid infant/toddler child care professionals cuts short the time available for building strong, intimate caregiver-child relationships—even though the child may spend many hours each day in the child care environment.

Suppose that a child's lack of opportunity for "progressively more complex reciprocal activity, on a regular basis over extended periods of time with one or more other persons with whom the child develops a strong, mutual, irrational attachment" were reframed as a "relationship risk"—

one of those risks, like old age, disability, major illness, and unemployment, against which society provides public protection, since the risk is deemed too universal and too serious to leave entirely to individual planning or the marketplace (see Steuerle et al., 1998, p. 82). Might social insurance then pay for parental leave for a year or two at the beginning of life, as well as for twenty years of retirement at the end? Might subsidies be provided for infant/toddler child care in addition to higher education? One could even find a precedent in Supplemental Security Income (SSI), which provides stipends to low-income children who have significant disabilities that their parents can use for special equipment, respite care, family recreation, or other goods and services that will maintain a child in his family—in strong, mutual relationships—who might otherwise require institutional care.

We began this chapter by asking two questions: Can social policy reduce the risk or mitigate the harm that occurs when nurturing relationships between infants and parents fail to form, are disrupted, or disappear? Given our history and current policy environment, is this country likely even to attempt to allocate public resources to safeguard, strengthen, or repair relationships at risk? Exploring the first question, we have found a number of thinkers with persuasive arguments and proposals for public investment in nurturing relationships—within families, and between families and community sources of social support. The answer to the second question seems much more elusive. If social policies are indeed a matter of metaphor, perhaps a literary imagination is called for after all. Assignment: Complete a novel that begins:

It was the best of times; it was the worst of times. It was a time of risk; it was a time of promise.

REFERENCES

Bronfenbrenner, U. (1979). *The ecology of human development: Experiments by nature and design.* Cambridge, MA: Harvard University Press.

Bronfenbrenner, U. (1989). *Who cares for children?* Paris: UNESCO.

Bronfenbrenner, U. (1993). The ecology of cognitive development: Research models and fugitive findings. In R.H. Wozniak & K. Fischer (Eds.), *Scientific environments* (pp. 3–44). Hillsdale, NJ: Erlbaum.

Bronfenbrenner, U., & Morris, P. A. (1998). The ecology of developmental processes. In W. Damon & R. M. Lerner (Eds.), *Handbook of child psychology: Vol. 1. Theoretical models of human development* (pp. xx–xx). New York: John Wiley & Sons, Inc.

Hill, R. B. (1997). *The strengths of African American families: Twenty-five years later.* Washington, DC: R&B Publishers.

Kamerman, S. B., & Kahn, A. J. (1995). *Starting right: How America neglects its youngest children and what we can do about it.* New York: Oxford University Press.

Kamerman, S. B., & Kahn, A. J. (1997). United States. In S, B. Kamerman & A. J. Kahn (Eds.), *Family change and family policies in Great Britain, Canada, New Zealand, and the United States* (pp. 307–421). Oxford: Clarendon Press.

Lakoff, G. (1996). *Moral politics: What conservatives know that liberals don't.* Chicago and London: The University of Chicago Press.

Lieberman, A. F. (1997/1998). An infant mental health perspective. *Zero to Three*, 18, 3, 3–5.

Runyan, D. K., Huner, W. M., Socolar, R. R. S., Amaya-Jackson, L., English, D., Landsverk, J., Dubowitz, H., Browne, D. H., Bangdiwala, S. I., & Matthew, R. M. (1998). Children who prosper in unfavorable environments: The relationship to social capital. *Pediatrics*, 101, 1, 12–18.

Sameroff, A. J., & Chandler, M. (1975). Reproductive risk and the continuum of caretaking casualty. In F. Horowitz, M. Hetherington, S. Scarr-Salapetk, et al. (Eds.), *Review of child development research* (Vol. 4, pp. 187–244). Chicago: University of Chicago Press.

Sameroff, A. J., Seifer, R., Barocas, R., Zax, M., & Greenspan, S. (1987). Intelligence quotient scores of 4-year-old children: Social-environmental risk factors. *Pediatrics*, 70, 3, 343–348.

Steuerle, C. E., Gramlich, E. M., Heclo, H., & Smith Nightingale, D. (1998). *The government we deserve: Responsive democracy and changing expectations.* Washington, DC: The Urban Institute Press.

Zero to Three. (1997, April). *Zero to Three national survey among parents of zero-to-three-year olds.* Washington, DC: Author.

Contributors

Laura Bates, Ph.D.
Michigan State University

Lisa Boyce, Ph.D.
Utah State University

Domini R. Castellino, Ph.D.
Duke University

Priscilla Coleman, M.A.
West Virginia University

John Colombo, Ph.D.
University of Kansas

Jerry Cook, M.A.
Utah State University

Martha Farrell Erikson, Ph.D.
University of Minnesota

Emily Fenichel, M.S.W.
Zero to Three: National Center for
Infants, Toddlers and Families

Hiram E. Fitzgerald, Ph.D.
Michigan State University

Katherine Hildebrandt Karraker, Ph.D.
West Virginia University

Jon Korfmacher, Ph.D.
Erikson Institute

Jacqueline V. Lerner, Ph.D.
Boston College

Tom Luster, Ph.D.
Michigan State University

Eun Young Mun, M.A.
Michigan State University

Joy D. Osofsky, Ph.D.
Louisiana State University

Leon I. Puttler, Ph.D.
University of Michigan

Joanne Roberts, M.A.
New York University

Lori Roggman, Ph.D.
Utah State University

Terrill F. Saxon, Ph.D.
Baylor University

Amy R. Susman-Stillman, Ph.D.
University of Minnesota

Mark Swanson, M.D.
University of Arkansas

Catherine S. Tamis-LeMonda, Ph.D.
New York University

Maria M. Wong, Ph.D.
University of Michigan

Robert A. Zucker, Ph.D.
University of Michigan

Author & Subject Indices

Author Index